Yale Western Americana, 27

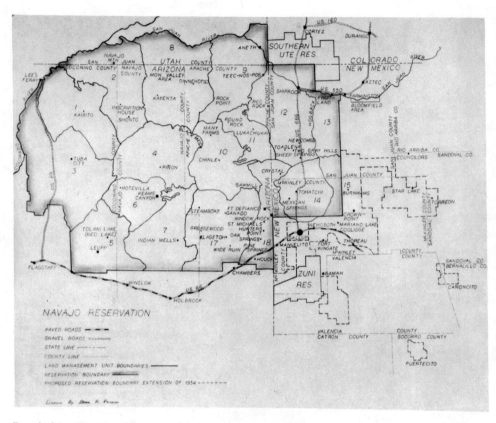

*Frontispiece:* The Navajos were the most numerous surviving Indian people and their reservation was the largest in the United States. Several attempts were made during the New Deal to expand reservation boundaries further into New Mexico.

# THE NAVAJOS
# AND THE NEW DEAL

Donald L. Parman

New Haven and London   Yale University Press

1976

Published with assistance from the foundation
established in memory of Amasa Stone Mather
of the Class of 1907, Yale College.

Designed by John O.C. McCrillis
and set in Baskerville type.
Printed in the United States of America by
The Murray Printing Co., Forge Village, Mass.

Published in Great Britain, Europe, and Africa by
Yale University Press, Ltd., London.
Distributed in Latin America by Kaiman & Polon,
Inc., New York City;
in Australasia by Book & Film
Services, Artarmon, N.S.W., Australasia;
in Japan by John Weatherhill, Inc., Tokyo.

To Nadyne

# Contents

# Illustrations

Figures 1–7 follow p. 144 in the text.
All photographs were taken by Milton Snow of the Indian Service.

# Preface

In this study of Navajo affairs during the New Deal era, I have tried to keep two basic goals in mind. My first goal has been to tell the story of the tribe's experience as objectively as possible. Because of the controversial nature of the federal programs and the criticisms they aroused, the facts of the situation have become intermingled with an inordinate amount of innuendo, gossip, rumor, and fantasy. I have tried to penetrate through this mass of misinformation by tapping a wide variety of original sources and by reconstructing what I believe is a fairly accurate account of the Navajos' experiences during the New Deal.

My second objective has been to assess the philosophy of Indian affairs that Commissioner John Collier attempted to implement after he assumed office in 1933. The central theme of Collier's policies was an uncompromising rejection of past efforts to assimilate Indians into white society. As commissioner, Collier sought to carry out a philosophy of cultural pluralism which both tolerated and encouraged Indians to be Indians. Unfortunately little scholarly research has been done on New Deal Indian affairs. Collier's own writings provide an outline of his goals and attempts to realize these objectives, but his autobiography and other books are partisan and defensive. More detached studies on Indian affairs have not yet been completed which would provide a detailed and mature consideration needed for the subject. Treatments of Indian topics in the 1930s have either been very limited in scope, or, in the case of tribal histories, so cursory that the authors pass over the New Deal with a few generalizations lauding Collier's reform ideals. I have tried to reveal more precisely how New Deal Indian policy operated on the Navajo reservation, as opposed to the theories and programs conceived in the Washington office.

The Navajos seem to me to be ideal for the purpose of a "field" evaluation of New Deal Indian policy. They were (and are) the largest single tribe in the United States, their land had never been allotted and still remained under tribal ownership, and their institutions were basically intact in 1933. Collier appears to have used the Navajo reservation as a sort of staging ground for his administration, as shown in the early introduction of conservation programs and livestock reduction, as well as later attempts to implement tribal self-government, to preserve the Navajos' religious and cultural heritage, and to provide a bicultural education.

The Navajo experience also demonstrates how tribal factions and white interests responded to Collier's programs. As was true of other tribes, Navajos had loosely defined factions of "traditionalists" and "progressives." The reactions of these two groups, the shifting of Navajo leaders from support of to opposition to the government, and the responses of whites are the most complex but fascinating aspects of this study.

My obligations to people who aided my research are many. David Brugge of the National Park Service, who formerly served at Hubbell's Trading Post, Ganado, Arizona, and is now stationed in Albuquerque, New Mexico, offered innumerable acts of kindness during my two visits to the Southwest and answered many letters requesting information. I received similar cooperation from Robert Kvasnicka of the National Archives, Robert Jordan and Joseph Huld of the Los Angeles Federal Records Center, Myra Ellen Jenkins of the New Mexico State Records Center and Archives, Judith Schiff of the Yale University Library, Fathers Emanuel and John of St. Michaels Mission, and Gerald Ogden, former graduate student at the University of New Mexico and presently employed by the Department of Agriculture. In addition, I owe a considerable debt to the interviewees listed in the bibliography. I corresponded with several of these individuals after our first conversations, especially Mr. and Mrs. Rudolph Zweifel and Moris Burge.

Donald J. Berthrong, head of the History Department at Purdue University, read a draft of the present study, made many helpful comments, and gave me much encouragement during the research and writing stages. I greatly appreciate the assistance of Dennis Parks and his capable staff at the second floor reference desk at Purdue Library who repeatedly showed a truly amazing ability to find background materials on obscure topics. Christine Anderson, former graduate assistant in the History Department, checked footnotes, helped compile the bibliography, and proofread the early drafts. My wife, Nadyne, typed the first draft and Joyce Good and the secretaries

in the History Department completed the later versions. My youngest son, Steven, drew the map which appears in this volume.

Finally, grants from Purdue University's Summer Faculty XL
Program, the American Philosophical Society, and the National
Endowment for the Humanities provided released time from teach-
ing and greatly hastened the completion of the study.

# THE NAVAJOS
# AND THE NEW DEAL

# 1

## By Way of Background

The New Deal launched a variety of major programs on the Navajo reservation to alleviate poverty, disease, and other afflictions affecting the tribe in the 1930s. The Navajos' reaction to the federal efforts was mixed because much of what was attempted violated some of their most important customs and patterns of life. But before the story of the Navajos' experience with the New Deal can be discussed in a meaningful way, a brief review of the tribe's history and social and political institutions, as well as their relationships with successive waves of Spaniards, Mexicans, and Americans who claimed the region in which Navajos lived, is necessary.

The Navajos are truly a composite of many outside influences. They belong to the Athapascan language family, which is represented by numerous Indian groups stretching from the southwestern United States to California, the Pacific Northwest, Canada, and Alaska. Athapascans appear to have been latecomers in the many Indian migrations across the Bering Straits during the ice age. Exactly how and when the Navajos arrived in the Southwest is unclear, but it was probably around A.D. 1300. Equally uncertain are the circumstances of their separation from the neighboring Apaches, another Athapascan tribe.

First coming to the Southwest as small bands of hunters, the Navajos settled east of the present reservation, in the area of southern Colorado and north central New Mexico, and began a long process of cultural adaptation and borrowing from nearby Indians which still persists. Through trading and fighting, the Navajos soon formed contacts with the Pueblos along the Rio Grande. Captured Pueblo women, for example, introduced farming, weaving, and new religious ceremonies to the Navajos.

When the Spanish moved into New Mexico in the seventeenth

century, raids against the intruders and trade ties during periods of peace brought additional changes. The Spanish introduction of sheep, goats, and horses created their present pastoral economy. Refugees from the various Pueblo revolts of the seventeenth century fled to the Navajos and further strengthened the cultural bond between the two peoples. Although the Navajos never accepted the Pueblos' mode of living in fixed villages with a formal government, they did adopt many other Pueblo traits. By the early nineteenth century the borrowings from the Pueblos and Spanish had transformed the Navajos from hunters into farmers, herders, and marauders.[1] Much of the same pattern of contact and borrowing characterized Navajo existence during later periods when the Mexicans and Americans gained control of the Southwest. Their long habitation in a single region led the tribe to develop a culture which blended many influences without ever abandoning the core of their own heritage.

Tribal unity among the Navajos was based on common cultural traits rather than political authority exerted by a set of chiefs or a council. Their language and religion formed important means of cohesion, but the heart of Navajo unity was the family and related customs.

The organization of the Navajo family was matrilineal as was true of many other Indian tribes. Children traced their descent through their mother and not their father. A marriage usually demanded that the new husband leave his own family and reside with his wife's people. He became something of a drudge who found that his father-in-law and other elders in his wife's family assigned him the onerous tasks. A wife could terminate the marriage by merely sending her husband back to his own people. If the marriage produced several children and the husband prospered, he gained a certain amount of independence by moving his family away from the immediate vicinity of the wife's family. They would, however, still live within hailing distance of her parents. An additional symbol of the successful husband's prestige would be his marriage to a second wife who, to avoid personal friction, was normally a sister of his first wife.

These patterns of marriage resulted in an extended family consisting of an older Navajo mother, her husband, and their unmarried

1. Edward H. Spicer, *Cycles of Conquest, The Impact of Spain, Mexico, and the United States on the Indians of the Southwest, 1533–1960* (Tucson, 1962), pp. 210–13.

children together with her married daughters and their families. Such an extended family operated as a unit and members were expected to care for and accept responsibility for each other. Failure to look after one's relatives ranked as a very serious offence. Because of frequent divorces and high death rates, the responsibility for rearing children frequently fell to relatives. It was (and still is) not uncommon for grandparents or aunts and uncles to rear such children as their own offspring.

The term "outfit" describes a larger but more fluid social unit than the extended family. A situation often developed in which two or more extended families with strong kinship ties lived in the same general locale and maintained close ties. Members frequently visited back and forth and cooperated in the care of livestock, farming, or paying the costs of religious ceremonials. The most respected elder served as a spokesman for the outfit and represented it in such problems as disputes between members within the group or with outsiders. The cooperation among families in an outfit was not obligatory and depended largely on the personal force of the outfit's leader.

The Navajo clan was a broader social institution than the outfit, but it was still highly important. Navajo tradition identifies four clans but by the twentieth century there were some seventy-five divided into nine major groups. Many of the clan names derive from places where they originated. Others, however, were borrowed from neighboring tribes. A child automatically became a member of his mother's clan, but he also had a close relationship to the clan of his father.

The effect of the clan was similar to kinship ties in the extended family. Even though members' biological relationships had no real meaning, two people of the same clan or of closely related clans could not marry, for such a union was considered incestuous. Clan members also identified with each other very closely, using the terms "brother" and "sister" in greeting and offering courtesies to each other even at a first meeting. Such amenities permitted a Navajo to travel far away from his own extended family and still be fairly certain of encountering someone from the clan of his mother or father who would treat him as a relative. The potential usefulness of the clans as a source of unity among the Navajos was, however, largely negated by the intense rivalries and jealousies they provoked. In much the same fashion that angry whites revile each other's ancestry, Navajos in a dispute use derogatory remarks about each other's clans.[2]

Whether the Navajos ever had a political unity in terms that whites understand is unclear. Perhaps when the tribe was small and lived in a limited area, some form of overall authority existed. According to Spanish reports in the 1600s, Navajos had war chiefs and peace chiefs, but these impressions may represent nothing more than what the Spanish thought they saw in temporary factions of Navajos desiring to continue or stop hostilities with the whites. Likewise, the political importance of the Naach'id, a tribal ceremonial, as a unifying device is not entirely certain. Anthropologists agree that the Naach'id had a religious significance as a mass curative ceremony, but they disagree on whether tribal political and military decisions were regularly made at such gatherings. In any case, the last Naach'id was held in 1859 and the Navajos attending the ceremony rejected a recent peace treaty negotiated with the United States. The death of many leaders in subsequent fighting with the Americans severely disrupted whatever political solidarity the Navajos possessed earlier.[3]

After their military subjugation, the Navajo institution which came closest to formal government was the headman system, a network of local leaders chosen by the Indians. The selection of a headman traditionally was made by an assembly attended by all adults and the person chosen had to receive the nearly unanimous consent of the entire community. Prolonged discussions usually occurred before a choice was made.

Once named, a headman needed outstanding ability to be effective. He required wisdom and oratorical skills to conduct assemblies of his people, to address ceremonial crowds, and to negotiate with outsiders. The headman especially needed shrewdness in dealing with white officials. As an intermediary, he had to try to interpret the demands of the lightskinned aliens to his own people and, more importantly, to be able to resist their demands. Much of his time would be taken up with his followers' personal problems—settling

2. Clyde Kluckhohn and Dorothea Leighton, *The Navaho* (Garden City, New York, 1962), pp. 100–14.

3. David Brugge, "Early Navajo Political Structure," *Navajo Tourist Guide* (1966), pp. 22–23.

disputes, persuading people to be faithful to their mates, and reminding the strong to look after helpless relatives.[4]

The headman's multitude of duties had to be accomplished without enforcement powers or coercion. All his persuasion, shrewdness,
and brow-beating were useless against a follower who refused to
cooperate. A capable headman attracted many followers, exerted
wide influence, and enjoyed prestige. But if he neglected his duties,
seriously erred, or misjudged followers' sentiments, his power slipped
and his supporters would switch loyalties to another leader. Repeatedly whites from the Spanish period onward failed to recognize
the indefinite nature of Navajo political authority. Peace treaties
signed with an important headman, whom the whites mistakenly
thought was a tribal leader, were hopelessly ineffective. The headman
had no control over Navajos outside his own area and they continued
to raid without restraint. His own young warriors were likely to keep
up hostilities, using the perfectly logical excuse that they had not
agreed to peace. Even more tragic were situations in which whites
forced a local leader into a decision that he knew his supporters
opposed. Inevitably such dictated agreements not only meant dis-
obedience among the headman's followers but served to discredit him.
Thus, Navajos saw government as a highly fluid, transitory, and
flexible mechanism.[5]

At first the Navajos experienced little change after the arrival of
Americans in the Southwest during the Mexican War, but within
two decades the tribe faced a trauma which exceeded anything in
their past. Initially, the Americans merely became another target
for the tribe's enthusiastic marauding. American military expedi-
tions usually found Navajo leaders cooperative, but the raids renewed before the white units returned eastward. By 1862, Washington's patience for the Navajos' seeming duplicity came to an end.
General James H. Carleton was ordered to punish their transgressions
by launching a full-scale military expedition. The campaign which
followed witnessed no climactic battles, but it brought decisive
results. Colonel Kit Carson of the New Mexico Volunteers, with a
force of 600–700 men, moved into the Navajo area in the summer of
1863 to destroy the tribe's food sources. Carson's troops, aided by

4. Kluckhohn and Leighton, *The Navaho*, pp. 117–22.
5. Ruth Underhill, *Here Come the Navaho* (Lawrence, Kansas, 1953), pp. 130–43.

auxiliaries from other tribes, penetrated into the heart of the Navajo country and applied a "scorched earth" policy to livestock, grain, and orchards. Within six months frightened and starving Navajos crowded into Carson's headquarters to surrender. How many evaded capture is unknown, but the figure was probably high. Some fled to remote areas in the west and north, while others found refuge with the Jemez Pueblos. Caravans of capitives made the "Long Walk" from their homeland to Fort Sumner or Bosque Redondo in eastern New Mexico. By the winter of 1864, 8,570 Navajos were in their new home.[6]

Once located at Fort Sumner, the Navajos underwent an even more traumatic experience. For four years the federal government lavished funds in a futile attempt to teach the Navajos how to farm on irrigated land. If the once proud marauders were not disheartened by this indignity, crop failures brought on by drought and grasshoppers and raids by other Indians finished breaking their morale. The Navajos' pleas that the heat of the Pecos Valley made them sick resulted in part from their intense desire to return to their beloved homeland. Finally in 1868 federal officials were persuaded to return the tribe to western New Mexico. A treaty signed the same year specified the terms of their release.[7]

The impact of the "Long Walk" and the Fort Sumner experience deeply affected subsequent Navajo attitudes toward Americans. Older tribesmen interviewed in the late 1930s and 1940s still vividly remembered the events. They frequently referred to Fort Sumner for clarifying time relationships in recounting their lives and their more-or-less stereotyped comments and descriptions about the suffering at Fort Sumner indicated that the experience had a searing emotional impact. Certainly Navajos thought of the sojourn to eastern New Mexico in terms of a horrible uprooting from a familiar lifestyle. Such fears possibly made Navajos, especially their leaders, unusually submissive to federal officials after 1868. When opposition to federal programs during the New Deal became most intense, for example, many older Navajos warned the objectors to quiet down or the army would punish the tribe.

6. For a recent work on Carson's campaign, see Lawrence C. Kelly, ed., *Navajo Roundup* (Boulder, Colorado, 1970).

7. Lynn R. Bailey, *The Long Walk, A History of Navajo Wars, 1846–1868* (Pasadena, 1970).

Only a few renegades continued raiding after the tribe returned to its homeland. The bulk of the Navajos industriously used their government allotment of sheep in 1868 to redevelop their life as herdsmen and farmers. A succession of government agents came to the Fort Defiance Agency after 1868. Some were capable men who found themselves terribly frustrated by the living conditions at the agency, the vastness of their jurisdiction, the lack of funds to conduct their business, and their inability to stop incursions of whites and outside Indians on the Navajos. For the best agents, the scattered nature of the Navajo population and the language barrier made government control over the tribe highly tenuous. Other agents were men of indifferent ability, unwilling to tackle problems. Whether good or bad, the agents operated through the local headmen to effect government policies. This sort of indirect rule discredited many of the native leaders and brought something less than absolute obedience, but it was the best the agents could do.

The appearance of white traders among the Navajos after 1868 brought more significant changes. Although the tribe for centuries had traded with other Indians and the Spanish and Mexicans on a casual basis, the American merchants operated from fixed trading posts. Navajos brought their wool, lambs, rugs, and jewelry to the posts to barter for yard goods, sugar, coffee, tools, and other basic necessities of the white world. The trading post, like the whites' country store, additionally became a social center where Indians congregated to exchange news and gossip.

Because of the seasonal nature of wool and lamb sales, the trader also became a pawnbroker. The often-criticized credit system permitted Navajos without barter goods to use their jewelry and other valuables as security for purchases. The pawn was redeemed when the Indians later sold their wool or lambs. The potential for conflict between customer and merchant by such methods was virtually unlimited. The language barrier and the inability to understand crude white accounting systems often led Indians to conclude that transactions were unfair even when the trader was honest—and not all were. In addition, traders were usually rugged and independent individuals who sometimes dealt gruffly with the sensitive Indians. These factors, coupled with the Navajos' aversion to the wealthy, sometimes produced intense resentment against traders, although many were well liked and trusted by their clients.

Beside altering the Navajos' material culture, the trader acted as a vehicle for change in many intangible ways. If trusted, he would be asked by Navajos for personal advice or to settle family disputes. Traders often served as an important link between the government and the Navajos by explaining new policies and how the Indians could best meet them. The more enterprising traders frequently represented their customers by approaching Indian Service officials to win their support for such projects as irrigation systems, roads, or wells. Traders even became arbiters of style and quality in weaving and silverwork by keeping examples of rugs and jewelry at the posts and demanding that Navajos duplicate them.[8]

Still another important problem which required the Navajos to modify their customs was the shortage of land after 1868. The reservation granted in 1868 was a rectangle of three and one-half million acres in northwest New Mexico and northeast Arizona. Despite the fact that many tribesmen lived off the reservation, squatting on the public domain, the Navajos needed more land for their herds within a surprisingly short time. By 1883, Agent D. M. Reardon reported that the tribe had "too many sheep" and he pleaded for funds to develop new water sources so pastures remote from existing springs could be grazed. In words prophetic of New Deal reports, Reardon pointed out the low quality of Navajo sheep, complaining that the fleeces yielded only one pound of wool and the lambs were badly undersized. "The number of sheep could be reduced fully one-half (I believe two-thirds)," if the Navajos would improve the breeding and management of their herds. Reardon was also appalled by the huge numbers of "useless horses" owned by Navajos and felt that they should be sold and replaced by cattle, but he warned that the Navajos would have to undergo "radical changes in their modes of thought" before they would relinquish their surplus equestrian stock. The outspoken agent also described severe erosion problems on the reservation, stating that channels thirty to forty feet in width had recently been carved into the soil after heavy rains fell upon the overgrazed land.[9]

8. Ruth Underhill, *The Navajos* (Norman, Oklahoma, 1956), pp. 144–95; Frank McNitt, *The Indian Traders* (Norman, Oklahoma, 1962). For a study of more recent trading, see William Y. Adams, *Shonto: A Study of the Role of the Trader in a Modern Navaho Community* (Washington, 1963).

9. D. M. Reardon to the Commissioner of Indian Affairs, 14 August 1883, Fort Defiance Letterbook, 21 June 1883 to 2 October 1883, Window Rock Area Headquarters.

To meet the Navajos' growing need for more grazing land, the federal government expanded the reservation by executive orders several times after 1882. The treaty reservation of 3.5 million acres grew to over 14 million acres by 1930. The annexations were mostly in Arizona to the south and the west of the original reservation. Unfortunately, the enlargements were made after the need had already arisen and the Navajos had moved onto the land. Even worse the government did nothing to improve livestock breeding and management. As a result, the Navajos' need for land was never fully met.[10]

Unfortunately, the expansions did not encompass an area east and south of the reservation which became known as the "checkerboard." Here a complex situation developed because land ownership was divided among New Mexico, Arizona, federal public domain, the Santa Fe Railroad, and private individuals. Navajos, not understanding the boundaries of the reservation, had run livestock in the checkerboard since their return from Fort Sumner but were pushed aside by white ranchers who penetrated the area in the late nineteenth century. Endless squabbles over trespass and use of water holes resulted. During the early twentieth century, friendly traders and Indian Service officials frequently intervened on the Navajos' behalf by applying for 160-acre allotments on the public domain. Much as in the case of homestead legislation for whites, the Indian allottees were required to occupy their land for five years before they received final title. Unfortunately, obtaining allotments for the Navajo was an inadequate solution, for no one could exist on such small holdings, and many Navajos failed to retain the papers necessary to patent their claims. The checkerboard remained an unsolved problem which aroused even greater controversies during the New Deal.

The expansions of the reservation by the turn of the century had created a jurisdiction much too large for a single agent to handle from Fort Defiance and, in line with the trend during the Progressive period to decentralize administration, the Indian Bureau broke the reservation into six superintendencies. The Southern Navajo district, with headquarters at Fort Defiance, covered the southeastern part of the reservation. The Northern Navajo area took in the northeast section of the reservation with a headquarters located at Shiprock. Tuba City became the administrative center for the Western Navajo

10. Underhill, *The Navajos*, p. 149.

superintendency. Leupp was established to care for Navajos living in an annexation in the southwest corner of the reservation. Two of the superintendencies presented peculiarities. The superintendent at Keams Canyon administered the Navajos who lived within the Hopi treaty reservation and also the Hopis themselves. The Eastern Navajo superintendency was established at Crownpoint, outside the reservation proper, to provide services for Navajos living in the New Mexico checkerboard.[11]

Dividing the reservation into six jurisdictions brought the Navajos into somewhat closer contact with federal officials and increased the tempo of government activities. The men sent to command the new jurisdictions generally reflected the government's current efforts to hire a new type of superintendent—a person of ability, honesty, and drive instead of the often corrupt and usually mediocre political appointee of the past. The effects of stronger leadership resulted in the funding of irrigation projects, the start of rudimentary agricultural extension services, improved medical care, establishment of tribal courts, and water development for livestock. Special efforts were made to place more Navajo children in boarding schools.

Yet the increased government services did not drastically alter Navajo life. The new superintendents still found that they could exert authority only through the local headmen. The uneducated or "camp Navajo" rarely came into contact with officialdom except when Indian police came to capture terrified children for schools, to arrest someone accused of a crime, or to break up a polygamous marriage. Although Navajo superintendents were more honest than the old political appointees, they were perhaps more arbitrary. Similar to many progressive reformers of the period, the superintendents were convinced that their values should be adopted by all. Hence, they expended much of their time and moral indignation on discouraging elements of Navajo culture at variance with white mores. This, in turn, created several rebellions and near rebellions on the reservation. The use of federal troops to put down the disturbances revived memories of Bosque Redondo and reenforced tribal fears of the army.[12]

Also at the turn of the century, the Navajos entered into their first

11. Ibid., pp. 220–23.
12. Robert L. Wilken, *Anselm Weber, O.F.M., Missionary to the Navaho* (Milwaukee, 1955), *passim*.

permanent relations with Christian missionaries. In 1897 the Episcopalians started a small hospital at Fort Defiance and a year later the Franciscans founded St. Michaels Mission a few miles to the south. Soon afterward the Methodists located at Shiprock, the Baptists at Two Grey Hills, the Christian Reformed Church at Rehoboth, and the Presbyterians at Ganado. New outstations were established periodically and existing facilities were expanded. Even though few Navajos became converts, the missionaries soon rivaled the traders in influence. Navajos were attracted by the medical services of the missions which were usually better than those the crude government hospitals offered. Of much greater importance were the schools operated by missions. These maintained higher academic standards than government schools and graduates were usually well versed in conventional subject matter and especially excelled in reading and speaking English. A surprisingly high percentage of mission school graduates became tribal leaders and minor government employees.

Missionaries also became an important factor in shaping government policies and programs before the New Deal. In part, their interest in reservation affairs was related to their own vested interests such as winning official permission to open a new mission or being allowed to provide religious instruction for children in government schools. Opinionated and energetic, missionaries often took a very active role in broader reservation questions. If something offended them, they did not hesitate to protest to a congressman or the Indian Bureau. Mission groups also worked behind the scenes through Navajo converts who were important tribal leaders. Many of the issues that missionaries raised were related to denominational rivalry, especially between Protestants and Catholics. Such disputes were invariably bitter and had a devisive effect on the tribe, at least among Christian Navajos.

In searching for some way to reduce the gap between the government and individual Navajos, Superintendent John Hunter began to organize chapters of Leupp Navajos in the early 1920s. When he was promoted to the Southern Navajo district a few years later, he carried the new program there, too. Other superintendents soon formed similar organizations in the 1920s. By 1933 over 100 chapters had been formed, although not all areas of the reservation participated in the program.

The chapter functioned in making local decisions, settling disputes, and organizing self-help projects. Each chapter was headed by a president, vice president, secretary, and treasurer who were elected by a majority vote. Meetings were held monthly and each chapter sent a representative to a central council. Typical projects undertaken by the organizations were putting up chapter houses, working on irrigation ditches, or building roads. The government supplied the materials and the chapter members donated the labor.

Whether the chapters really changed the old headman system seems most unlikely. Most observers felt that majority rule procedures were followed only to please the superintendents; the real decisions were still made by the traditional Navajo method of discussing a question until all consented. In large part, the popularity of the chapter movement was doubtlessly based on the government subsidies for projects. These permitted the pragmatic Navajos to complete needed tasks and, at the same time, to enjoy the companionship of others. Approximately half of the chapters died out during the New Deal when government subsidies and encouragement of the program ended.[13]

As the chapter movement was quietly getting under way, the discovery of oil at Hogback on the Northern Navajo jurisdiction in 1922 touched off a controversy. The new discovery raised some important legal questions about the Navajos' rights to the royalties. That portion of the reservation included in the Treaty of 1868 posed no problem, as all parties agreed that the tribe had full claim to oil revenues on treaty land. Although the Hogback well was on treaty land, debate arose about future leases in areas added to the reservation by executive orders since 1868. Most western politicians insisted that oil royalties from executive order lands must be distributed equally to the federal government, to the states, and to the reclamation fund as directed by the General Leasing Act of 1920. In the midst of the dispute, Secretary of Interior Albert G. Fall issued an administrative order that executive order lands would be considered the same as those in the public domain. His action meant that the Navajos would receive no revenues from any leases on portions of the reservation added since 1868. A wave of criticism of the Fall order

13. Richard Van Valkenburgh, "The Government of the Navajos," *Arizona Quarterly* 1 (Winter 1945): 72–73.

was voiced by opponents who believed that Indians should receive oil revenues from all reservation lands.[14]

Leading the attack was a young white named John Collier whose interest in Indian problems was of very recent origin. A native of Georgia, educated at Columbia University and the Collège de France, Collier had pursued a career in social work in New York, Georgia, and California. He was fascinated by the possibility of cooperative community action and planning for recent immigrants. In 1920 he visited the Taos Pueblo in New Mexico during their impressive Christmas rituals. The Pueblos represented all the things that Collier had sought to develop in his previous career as a social worker—a group of people living and making decisions communally.

A year later Collier returned to New Mexico to organize the Pueblo groups into an intertribal council to fight against Secretary Fall's Bursum Bill. This legislative proposal threatened to cancel Pueblo land claims first recognized by the Spanish and reconfirmed in 1848 when Mexico ceded the Southwest to the United States. Collier also objected to Fall's recent discouragement of native ceremonies. Deeply impressed by the spirituality of Indian life, the young reformer viewed Fall's restrictions as an illegal denial of religious freedom. To carry out the fight against Fall, Collier led a delegation of Pueblo elders, dressed in native costumes and carrying gold canes which traditionally symbolized authority, to eastern cities to raise funds and to lobby in Washington. The publicity which he aroused with his colorful delegation and the sympathetic response of congressional leaders quickly made Collier a prominent spokesman for the Indians.

Collier increased his influence when he became executive secretary of the newly organized American Indian Defense Association. In subsequent years, he edited the organization's publication, *American Indian Life*, wrote articles on Indian problems for various national journals, and testified frequently at congressional hearings. Through Senator William H. King of Utah, Collier in 1927 secured a comprehensive investigation of Indian conditions by a subcommittee of the Senate Indian Affairs Committee. The subcommittee's hearings, conducted between sessions of Congress, lasted into the New

14. Lawrence C. Kelly, *The Navajo Indians and Federal Indian Policy, 1900–1935* (Tucson, 1968), pp. 48–58.

Deal period and Collier participated in its work on many reservations. Thus, Collier, from his entry into Indian affairs in 1921 until his appointment as commissioner in 1933, maintained a militant crusade in behalf of the American Indian.

Although Collier's interest in Navajo oil rights was secondary to his battles in behalf of the Pueblos, he nevertheless toured the reservation during 1922 to study the problem and met with white officials and missionaries. "The Navajos," Collier wrote soon afterward, "are the Indian tribe within the United States who have kept the prehistorical culture system most nearly unchanged and unweakened." Collier was especially concerned that Navajo oil royalties be used wisely and in a way which would not destroy the tribe's indigenous civilization. He wanted the money to be spent to improve their schools, health facilities, and in land development.[15]

When Fall was ousted in 1923 for his involvement in the Teapot Dome scandal, his successor, Herbert Work, retracted the administrative order denying oil revenues to Indians and kept the question in limbo. A long and complex legislative battle ensued in which Collier's group demanded that Indians receive full payment from all oil. Finally in 1927, in what Lawrence Kelly calls "the most important single piece of general Indian legislation in the 1920's," Congress approved a measure which guaranteed all oil royalties to the Indians on executive order lands.[16] Ironically, the issue had lost its immediate importance for the Navajos. No oil had been discovered outside the treaty reservation and national overproduction led the Indian Bureau by the late 1920s to discourage additional explorations.

In the meantime, the Indian Bureau decided that the Navajo administration needed revision because of the problems presented by oil leasing. An official conversant with legal technicalities was needed to supervise leasing for the entire reservation. In mid-1922, Herbert J. Hagerman of New Mexico, a former territorial governor and rancher, was named "Special Commissioner to Negotiate with Indians." The appointment was coupled with a decision that the Navajos should have a formal tribal council to represent the entire reservation on leasing. The reason for establishing a council stemmed from the Treaty of 1868 because Article X required that any future cessions of land must have the consent of three-fourths of the adult

15. John Collier, manuscript for article, Reichard papers, MNA.
16. Kelly, *The Navajo Indians*, p. 100.

male population.[17] The size of the reservation and its population made an assembly of all Navajo men impossible. Hence, regulations issued in January 1922 created a tribal council to represent the tribe and laid out a set of bylaws. Each of the six jurisdictions were to elect one delegate and one alternate to serve on the council for four-year terms. The regulations further specified that the special commissioner must be present at all council meetings and that members could be removed by the Secretary of the Interior upon just cause.

After being briefed on his duties in Washington, Hagerman returned to New Mexico in early 1923 to take up his new post. A meeting with the Navajo superintendents produced several revisions in the original directive organizing the tribal council. Most of the alterations dealt with minor procedural matters, but one important change eliminated the equal representation of delegates and alternates from the six superintendencies. Instead, twelve delegates and twelve alternates made up the council and the number from each jurisdiction was proportional to its population. The new regulations also deleted the clause that council members could be removed by the Secretary of Interior.

Even before the council held its first meeting at Toadlena in July 1923, Hagerman learned that serious factionalism had already developed between the Southern Navajo leader Chee Dodge and the Northern Navajo spokesmen. The division seems to have started with a personal clash between Dodge and the superintendent at Shiprock. Indians from the latter area claimed that Dodge had deceived them when he interpreted at the meetings of the local council and oil companies in 1920 and that he had tried to dominate their decisions on leases. A rumor soon arose that one oil firm had bribed Dodge.[18]

Chee Dodge, the object of this controversy, was a colorful and fascinating personality who came as close to being a tribal spokesman as any Navajo leader in the 1920s. Born around 1860 and orphaned three years later, Chee was cared for during the Navajos' exile in Fort Sumner by an aunt. When the tribe returned to Fort Defiance, his aunt married a white trader named Perry H. Williams. Dodge received a few months of formal schooling at Fort Defiance, but his

17. For a sketch of Hagerman, see ibid., p. 62. A copy of the treaty can be found in Charles J. Kappler, ed., *Indian Affairs, Laws and Treaties*, II (Washington, 1904), pp. 1015–20.

18. Kelly, *The Navajo Indians*, pp. 63–70.

knowledge of English and skill in interpreting came mostly from his association with his foster uncle and other whites at the military post. He became an official government interpreter about 1880 and retained the position for many years. During the same decade he worked for Dr. Washington Matthews, an army physician at Fort Wingate and amateur anthropologist who first published works on Navajo ceremonials and legends.

Dodge's interpreting soon brought him additional prominence. Manuelito, a former war chief, was the most noted leader of the Navajos after 1868 and served as a "Head Chief" for the entire tribe in its dealings with the Fort Defiance agents. When alcoholism and age weakened Manuelito, Dodge was named to replace him around 1884. Dodge subsequently became the intermediary called upon to negotiate with the Navajos, to interpret, and to advise officials. He developed strong ties with other tribal leaders, affiliations that were reinforced by his marriages to headmen's daughters and by his contacts with local delegations concerning tribal affairs.

By the turn of the century the Navajo patriarch had become involved in various business ventures—trading posts, money-lending to Navajos and whites, and large-scale ranching. His knack for making money made him a wealthy person, the eventual owner of a mansion near Crystal, and a possessor of Buick touring cars. The automobiles became Dodge's hallmark. They were always equipped with white sidewall tires and with spares mounted on the front fenders inside chrome covers. A son acted as Dodge's chauffeur and sped him to meetings. The middle-aged Dodge was a curious admixture of the traditional Navajo leader and an irascible, shrewd businessman-rancher fully able to hold his own in the white man's competitive world.[19]

Although Chee's prestige won him the chairmanship of the first tribal council, his troubles with the faction from the Northern Navajo did not end, instead they worsened progressively during the next few years. Chee's main opponent from the Shiprock area was J. C. Morgan, an educated Navajo and a graduate of Hampton Institute. When named to the council in 1923, Morgan was a teacher in the Indian Service. Two years later he was employed as a translator and

19. Anselm Weber, "Chee Dodge," *The Indian Sentinel* (April 1918): 33–36; Richard Van Valkenburgh, biographic sketch of Henry Chee Dodge, Van Valkenburgh papers, AHS.

assistant to Reverend L. P. Brink, a missionary of the Christian Reformed Church at Farmington, New Mexico.

Many factors accounted for Morgan's conflict with Dodge. Morgan represented the increasing number of returned students from boarding schools who formed a faction known as the "progressives." Bitterly resentful of the influence of Dodge and the "traditionalists," the progressives felt that the older leaders were ill equipped for leadership and too easily dominated by federal officials. The younger Navajos also complained that Dodge's group was not interested in securing measures which would bring the Navajos into the main stream of American life. Indoctrinated at boarding school with the belief that Indians must assimilate into white society, Morgan's faction carried this ideal back to the reservation. They felt that Dodge's group excluded them from jobs and roles of leadership for which their education qualified them. The latter complaint undoubtedly had validity, for Indian Service officials found that returned students not only lacked rapport with most tribesmen, but that they were apt to raise embarrassing questions about reservation policies.[20]

Coupled with these differences were sharp disagreements between Dodge and Morgan over their religious affiliations. Dodge was a Catholic and close to the Franciscan fathers at St. Michaels Mission. He maintained an apartment at the mission for several years, the priests assisted him with his business interests and correspondence, and he sent his four children to Catholic schools. However, he was an enthusiastic tippler and the parties at his mansion were rumored to be genuine tests of the guests' ability to consume food and drink.

Morgan, in contrast, was a moralistic fundamentalist. Obviously referring to Dodge, Morgan frequently demanded in council speeches that tribal leaders serve as moral examples. While a teacher at Shiprock, Morgan had bitterly resisted Catholic efforts to offer religious instruction at the school. Later as a missionary, he regularly warned Navajos not to become Catholic converts, claiming that they would be shipped overseas to fight in the Pope's wars.[21]

Dodge's personal reaction to Morgan and the returned students

20. For a sketch of Morgan, see the writer's article, "J. C. Morgan: Navajo Apostle of Assimilation," *Prologue: Journal of the National Archives* 4 (Summer 1972): 83–89.
21. Father Marcellus to Haile 25 November 1924, Haile papers, UAL; Trockur Interview.

did little to lessen the antagonisms between the two factions. The proud Dodge had little patience with the noisy agitation of the educated Navajos. They were, in the patriarch's eyes, loud-mouthed upstarts who should remain quietly in the background and follow the traditional Navajo practice of deferring to their elders.

Many of the council's deliberations after 1923 would be shaped by the factionalism which arose between the powerful Dodge and his outspoken critic from Farmington. A notable example of this rivalry was a dispute in 1925 and 1926 over the use of Navajo oil royalties to pay for building a bridge across the Colorado River in the highly remote northwest corner of the reservation at Lee's Ferry, Utah. For several years Congress had adopted the practice of providing reimbursable funds for projects on Indian reservations. Such grants stipulated that the Indians must use tribal funds to pay back the government. In reality, reimbursable loans were seldom repaid, and they were usually nothing more than a technique for winning the approval of projects that Congress would not finance through gratuitous funds. In authorizing the Lee's Ferry Bridge, Congress granted $100,000 in reimbursable funds, to be matched by an equal amount by Arizona, and the Navajos must eventually pay back their share from tribal funds.

The controversy over the Lee's Ferry Bridge had repercussions in both Washington and the council itself. John Collier charged that saddling the Navajos with a $100,000 reimbursable loan was an open raid by whites on the new oil royalties. When defenders of the bridge argued that it would benefit the tribe by opening up the reservation to tourists and giving Navajos access to the outside world, Collier retorted that few Navajos lived in the remote area and in no way would a new bridge help the tribe. Instead, the pressure for a new bridge came from the National Park Service which wanted to link the north and south rims of the Grand Canyon National Park and from the Fred Harvey restaurant chain which held hotel and food concessions at the Grand Canyon. While Collier failed to prevent Congress from appropriating money for the projects in 1926, his attacks underscored the idea that federal actions aided whites more than Indians.

The dispute over the Lee's Ferry Bridge also symbolized an important change in the mood of the Navajo council. At the meeting in 1925 some delegates were unwilling to approve all the measures the

Indian Service officials submitted. Morgan proposed that the government consult with the council before it appropriated reimbursable funds in the future. Although the council never acted on Morgan's resolution, the days of a permissive council approving whatever Hagerman or the superintendents wanted were drawing to a close.[22]

Dodge apparently had misgivings about the Lee's Ferry Bridge, but typically he raised no objection. He later recalled the "great pressure that was brought to bear on me to oppose the Lee's Ferry Bridge; at that time I felt the Government was doing what it thought best for the Indians as well as the white people and for that reason I was prepared to stand with our Government. I fully agreed with its arrangements, and now the bridge is going up and everybody seems entirely satisfied."[23]

Dodge's response to the controversy was a typical example of the way in which he dealt with federal officials. Chee's first response to a serious question would be to delay in hope of either evading the problem or else finding out how Navajo sentiment ran, quieting possible criticism, and working behind the scenes with officials. Dodge would rarely speak out publicly against the government. When pressed into taking a stand he disliked, Dodge might state his misgivings forcefully to officials in private, but he would still eventually relent to the goodness and wisdom of Washington.

A far more important tribal dispute in the same period involved the feasibility of spending oil royalty funds to buy nonreservation lands for poorer Navajos. The growing Navajo population and overgrazing had prompted several attempts at legislation to expand the reservation in previous years, but the congressional delegations of Arizona and New Mexico defeated each bill. The failures led to the expenditure of tribal funds to lease lands outside the reservation. This was expensive and offered no permanent solution to the problem. Dodge proposed that additional land be bought in New Mexico with fifty percent of the oil royalties from a period of several years. Morgan opposed Dodge's plan at the 1927 council, asking instead that oil royalties be used to benefit returned students and for water development on the reservation itself. He partially carried his point when the council agreed to utilize only twenty-five percent of the oil

22. Kelly, *The Navajo Indians*, pp. 81–86.
23. Dodge to Scott Leavitt, 23 January 1928, St. Michaels Mission.

revenues for new land.[24] Embittered by his defeat, Dodge requested
that the tribal council be disbanded. The Northern Navajo delegates,
he complained, had caused so much trouble that he felt it could not
function properly.[25]

The seriousness of the land and overgrazing problem was fully
revealed in 1930 by a range survey of the reservation directed by
William H. Zeh, an Indian Service forester.[26] Zeh estimated that
2,360,000 acres of the 14,360,000-acre reservation were barren and
incapable of supporting livestock. He calculated the total number of
Navajo sheep and goats at 1,300,000 head or a figure which allowed
nine to ten acres per head for grazing. With the depleted state of the
range, twenty to thirty acres per head were needed if the land was to
recover its capacity. This meant Navajos possessed at least twice the
amount of livestock which the range should be carrying. Zeh warned
also that he had not included in his figures an estimated 37,000 cattle
and 80,000 horses that also grazed on the reservation.

Zeh endorsed efforts to obtain additional land outside the reservation, but he thought that no final solution could be found by that
means. The only real answer for the overgrazing problem was a
drastic change in range management on the reservation itself. He
suggested that short-term measures were needed to control rodents,
eliminate surplus horses, and develop more wells and springs. The
latter need was especially urgent because Navajo livestock destroyed
much vegetation, not through grazing, but by trampling grass in
getting to and from the widely separated sources of water. But a long
term solution depended on a thorough program of education in
livestock management for young and old Navajos. Such training
should emphasize the sale of surplus horses, goats, and older sheep.
Navajos also needed to upgrade the bloodlines of their remaining
sheep, so they produced heavier fleeces and larger fall lambs. Zeh
warned that these corrective measures would be extremely difficult to
realize because Navajo livestock management practices were in-
trenched by generations of habit.

Zeh's chilling report also noted that the depression had already
badly disrupted the Navajos' economy and contributed to even more

24. Kelly, *The Navajo Indians*, pp. 115–21.

25. Dodge to Commissioner Burke, 14 February 1928, St. Michaels Mission.

26. William H. Zeh, "General Report Covering the Grazing Situation on the Navajo
Reservation," SCS Records, UNML.

overgrazing. Wool prices had dropped to seventeen cents per pound in 1930 and the Navajos' fall lambs that year had brought only four to four and one-half cents per pound. Zeh reported that some areas had marketed up to eighty percent of their lamb crop, but other regions had been unable to sell any. The unsold stock were retained in the Indians' herds and contributed to even more overgrazing. Dividing the total income from sheep and goats by the Navajo population, Zeh calculated that the average Navajo received an annual income of sixty dollars.

Unfortunately, the winter of 1931–32 brought even deeper distress to the Navajos. Huge snow falls occurred in midwinter and the temperature dropped to as low as $-20°$. With the grass thickly blanketed, the Navajos could do little to care for their livestock except to shake the snow off bushes so the animals could eat the twigs and small limbs. Around Ganado, rains fell on top of the snow, forming an unusually thick crust of ice.

The suffering that the Navajos endured during the bitter winter aroused the sympathy of white traders long inured to seeing destitution. George Hubbell, operating a post at Piñon, wrote in January 1932: "I feel sorry for these people. The government [sent] up about 80 bags of flour which lasted one day and now every day from 10 to 30 come in wanting rations, nearly all of them afoot, men, women, and children; many of them stay all night and of course I have to feed them. . . . It is indeed piteful, and then they have to go back home without any food, lagging $\#$ 10 shoes, underware and a shirt.

The last truck from the Cannon [Keams Canyon?] brought shoes, underware and blankets and 6 cc of baking powder no flour or sugar. My goodness, of course I keep out of the mess but I see everything and cannot help but wonder what is to be done."[27]

Even the most sympathetic traders could do little to counter the Navajos' plight. The posts continued to accept the Indians' pawn. When that was exhausted, the Navajos began to spend the dimes and quarters that they normally used as buttons. Low wool prices compelled many Navajo women to increase rug weaving, but traders could not find outlets in an already sluggish market. In truth, the

27. George Hubbell to Lorenzo Hubbell, Jr., 31 January 1932, Hubbell Trading Post.

traders themselves often faced bankruptcy. Their prosperity was directly linked with the Navajos' sales of wool, lambs, and rugs; both struggled to survive a financial depression and the crushing winter.[28]

When spring arrived in 1932, hundreds of thousands of dead livestock littered the Navajo range. Desperate to salvage what they could, the Indians pulled the wool from sheep carcasses and carried the foul stuff in burlap bags to trading posts. The traders had to discount the price they paid for the wool, but the Navajos sold it anyway. By summer the stench of dead wool surrounded every trading post on the reservation, a smelly reminder of the tragic winter losses. A tough people who had proven themselves able to adapt to change and hardship, the Navajos found themselves plagued by natural and economic forces that they could not cope with or understand. Dimly aware that whites, too, were under duress, Navajos repeatedly asked traders if their Uncle Sam had gone broke.

A year later the tribe discovered that their favorite uncle not only would pour funds into the reservation to relieve distress but that New Dealers suddenly wanted them to preserve their heritage and to have a greater voice in reservation affairs. In terms of achieving these goals, the Navajos seemed ideal. Isolation from the rest of American society, ability to change without abandoning the essence of their culture, and the existence of a tribal council indicated that the Navajos, seemingly at least, needed little help in meeting Washington's aspirations. Indeed, the Navajos' situation appeared so promising that the New Dealers enthusiastically turned the reservation into a giant pilot project where ideas could be tested before being tried on other tribes.

28. Young Interview.

# 2

## The New Deal Comes to the Navajos

Franklin Roosevelt's election as President in 1932 created speculation about the possible changes in Indian affairs after his inauguration. During the Hoover administration Indian Commissioner
Charles J. Rhoads and Assistant Commissioner J. Henry Scattergood
had instituted limited reforms in education and health. John Collier,
however, felt that Indian affairs still needed a thorough revision and
he advocated that the Rhoads-Scattergood team be ousted. Con-
jecture also arose about the post of Secretary of the Interior, an
appointment which had primary importance to Indian policy.
Residents of New Mexico and Arizona were particularly concerned
because of their large Indian population and because the Department
of Interior's decisions affected such important vested interests as lumber, ranching, mining, oil, natural gas, and irrigated farming.

Despite their interest, few successfully predicted Roosevelt's final
choice for the Secretary of the Interior. Traditionally, the head of
the Interior Department had been a westerner who sympathized
with the region's peculiar problems and needs. Roosevelt was rebuffed, however, by several western leaders whom he asked to become
his Secretary of the Interior. His selection of Harold L. Ickes, a resident of Chicago without much political background in the West,
surprised many political observers. Ickes possessed no national reputation and, at Collier's urgings, he had sought unenthusiastically
an appointment as Commissioner of Indian Affairs. Ickes soon decided to abandon this quest and try for Secretary of Interior. As he
later expressed his feelings, "It would be no more painful or fatal to
be hung for a secretary than for a commissioner."

Ickes' trip to Washington seeking support for the post brought
only discouragement, but in mid-February he was invited to meet
Roosevelt in New York. He stopped by Washington a second time to

solicit political help and again he received the strong impression that his quest was hopeless. After being introduced to Roosevelt in New York, the president-elect stunned Ickes by declaring that he was to become Secretary of Interior. A similar selection, Ickes said, "wouldn't happen again in a millennium."[1]

Ickes and his wife, both long active in Progressivism and other reform movements, had developed considerable interest in Navajo affairs before 1933. Mrs. Ickes, a state legislator in Illinois, previously had traveled to the Southwest for her health. She stayed at a hostelry named Casa del Navajo, located east of the reservation at Coolidge, New Mexico. Owner B. I. Staples was then trying to improve the quality of Navajo rugs and silverwork and to promote their sale. Annually he visited the East with a party of Navajos to lecture on the tribe and to publicize its crafts. After his own visit at Casa del Navajo, Ickes himself became interested in Staples' work and in 1931 helped draw up a charter for the United Indian Traders Association. The organization originally sought to abolish imitation Indian jewelry and soon became a voice for most Navajo traders.

The Ickes' visits to the Southwest soon involved them in Navajo affairs and Indian reform. They helped found the Gallup Intertribal Ceremonial and both worked intermittantly for Collier's American Indian Defense Association. In 1933 Mrs. Ickes published *Mesa Land*, a popular and sound book on tribes of the Southwest. Shortly before the New Deal, the Ickes bought a hogan-style summer cottage near Coolidge.[2]

The appointment of John Collier as Commissioner of Indian Affairs was only slightly less startling than that of Ickes. Collier claimed that he had no interest in the post other than seeing that a person of enlightened views was appointed. Indeed, Collier hoped to retire as a lobbyist and devote himself to studies of Indian-white relations.[3] His desire to secure a reform-minded commissioner was not shared by the prestigious Indian Rights Association of Philadelphia which advocated the continuation of the Rhoads-Scattergood administration. Another prominent candidate was Edgar B. Merritt, a former assistant commissioner who had been demoted to a minor

1. Harold L. Ickes, *Autobiography of a Curmudgeon* (New York, 1943), pp. 265, 270.

2. *Gallup Independent*, 31 March 1933, p. 5. For information on Staples, see Frank McNitt, *The Navajo Traders* (Norman, Oklahoma, 1962), pp. 236–38.

3. John Collier, *From Every Zenith* (Denver, 1963), p. 169.

post in the Indian Bureau by Rhoads and Scattergood. Merritt's most important asset was the backing of his brother-in-law, Senate Majority Leader Joseph T. Robinson of Arkansas. The prospect of Merritt's appointment incensed Collier who felt that the former assistant commissioner symbolized all the past shortcomings of the Indian Bureau—white raids on tribal funds, insufficient rations for school children, repression of leadership, and political favoritism.

Among the various candidates,[4] Collier was the best known among the Indians. His militant reform efforts and appearances at many investigations of Indian reservations had brought him into contact with many tribal leaders, Indian Service workers, and westerners. The reactions to Collier were often hostile. Many older Indian Service employees regarded him as an eastern crank and idealist. Dissatisfied Indians, however, usually believed that Collier deserved the post because of his past efforts in their behalf.

Among the Navajos, Collier had more support than any other single candidate, but he was far from a unanimous choice. In January 1933 four chapters of the Southern Navajo endorsed Collier,[5] probably reflecting the influence of Roman Hubbell, a member of the famous trading family and long-time friend of Collier. A few days later the executive committee of the Returned Students Association met at Gallup to confer on endorsing a new commissioner. The organization had been formed a year earlier by J. C. Morgan to battle against Chee Dodge and the traditionalists and to elevate educated Navajos to tribal leadership. Howard Gorman, a Navajo mission worker at Ganado, served as president and Morgan as secretary. The Returned Students had organized twelve local chapters with a membership of some 300 younger Navajos by the time of the Gallup meeting.

The group's stormy deliberations over endorsing a new commissioner were an accurate forecast of future tribal politics. The executive committee agreed on the need for a nonpolitical selection and

4. *Gallup Independent*, 2 February 1933, p. 2. Minor candidates included Lewis Meriam, a scholar who in 1927–28 headed an important and comprehensive study of Indian affairs popularly known as the Meriam Commission; Nathan Margold, a New York attorney and associate of Collier; Reuben Perry, a long-time Indian Service worker and presently head of the Albuquerque Indian School; Walter V. Woehlke, former editor of *Sunset Magazine* where many of Collier's articles appeared; and Cato Sells, a former commissioner.

5. Ibid., 23 January 1933, p. 1.

more continuity in Indian policy. The possibility of endorsing Collier, however, roused Morgan's anger. He submitted a resolution
charging that the reformer wanted to keep Indians "in the blanket"
by encouraging native dances and traditions instead of educating
his people in a modern way of life. The Morgan statement recommended that the commissioner be an educator interested in Indian
progress. John Curley of Ganado, whose local chapter had endorsed
Collier, took up the reformer's cause during the discussion. Curley
maintained that Collier alone had defended the Indians' land and
water rights. Finally the group decided to strike all reference to Collier in any resolution sent to president-elect Roosevelt. Confusion
then developed over who should be endorsed. A resolution supporting
Henry Roe Cloud, a Winnebago and superintendent of the Haskell
Institute, was prepared as a compromise. Evidently the discussion
became too heated for Morgan, who seized the resolution and, as
seems typical in Navajo group controversies, "withdrew" from the
meeting. As a result no one was endorsed.[6]

Ickes' selection as Secretary of Interior enhanced Collier's chances
immensely, but a stalemate developed between the reformer, who
had the backing of Ickes, and Merritt, who had the support of the
powerful Senator Robinson. In April President Roosevelt resolved
the issue by inviting Ickes and Robinson to his office. Roosevelt said
that he had received many protest letters against Merritt. When
asked for his reaction, Ickes bluntly replied that Merritt was unqualified for the job. Roosevelt then told Robinson, "Well, Joe, you see
what I am up against. Every highbrow organization in the country
is opposed to Merritt, and Secretary Ickes, under whom he would
have to work, doesn't want him."[7]

To his many critics in the Indian Bureau, Collier's appointment
had dreaded implications. Such people found "themselves in the
position of a fellow who suddenly learns that his most hated enemy
has become president of his company."[8] As events soon proved, the
old guard's apprehensions were justified. Many Indian Bureau
officeholders in the Washington office and in the field were demoted

6. Ibid., 4 February 1933, p. 1; 6 February 1933, p. 1. For a discussion of "withdrawal"
in Navajo politics, see Aubry W. William, Jr., *Navajo Political Process* (Washington, 1970),
p. 56.

7. Harold L. Ickes, *The Secret Diary of Harold Ickes*, I (New York, 1953), p. 19.

8. *Gallup Independent*, 25 April 1933, p. 1.

and transferred to insignificant and remote posts as Collier freely reshuffled personnel.

Observers, both in and out of the Indian Service, viewed Collier's selection with some question. Previous reforms had usually floundered because of field workers' indifference or antagonism to change. It was doubtful whether Collier could carry out his frequently stated views that Indians should be freed from Bureau control and allowed to assume leadership. Despite such potential obstacles, Collier was uniquely equipped for his post. No previous commissioner had a more comprehensive understanding of Indian affairs and their administration than Collier. The term "new deal" was an apt description of federal Indian policy after Collier took office.

The relationship between Collier, Ickes, and Roosevelt needs clarification to correct false impressions created by New Deal propaganda. Although publicity frequently pictured Roosevelt as vitally interested in Indian affairs, his role was minimal and his statements on the subject were likely ghost-written by Collier. Still, one of the most remarkable features of the New Deal was Roosevelt's willingness to appoint men of unconventional ideas, such as Collier, and to give them a free hand in government. Ickes, however, was strongly involved in Indian reform when he first took office. During the freewheeling early months of the New Deal, he and Collier conferred almost daily on current problems before their regular office hours. Later, the press of other responsibilities and greater administrative formality gradually forced Ickes to remove himself from much involvement. Nevertheless, he still supported Collier by occasional press releases, stinging public statements, and at least one appearance before the Senate Indian Affairs Committee. After 1933, however, the major burden of achieving New Deal Indian policy fell upon Collier.[9]

Collier's association with Indian affairs before 1933 created a highly developed philosophy which the new commissioner sought to implement. The main goal of previous federal policy had been the assimilation of Indians into the life of middle-class white society. In part Collier disliked this approach because of its cruel side effects— the trauma of children being wrenched from their parents and

9. Zimmerman Interview; William Zimmerman, Jr., "The Role of the Bureau of Indian Affairs since 1933," *Annals of the American Academy of Political and Social Science* 311 (May 1957): 31–40.

shipped to distant boarding schools and the wedge driven between educated Indians and the older generation. But the main reason for his opposition was that teaching Indians to live like white men destroyed a wholesome, beneficial, and vital way of life. The death of their native culture was, in Collier's eyes, a tragedy more regrettable than past physical mistreatment of Indians. Collier considered a people and their culture as synonymous and the assimilation of Indians into white life meant, in effect, the end of their existence. He believed very strongly that whatever remained of Indian heritage must be preserved and renewed if at all possible. Cultural revival would not only prove beneficial to the morale of Indians, but their heritage, he believed, offered lessons that whites could well use in ordering their own lives. Collier advocated a cultural pluralism which combined various ways of life with each group tolerating and enriching the others.

Collier's critics repeatedly charged that he wanted to return Indians to the blanket. Such an assessment was overdrawn. Collier fully recognized that contacts between Indians and whites would inevitably produce change. What was needed, he suggested, was a different approach for dealing with such alterations. Instead of federal policy dictating the process, the Indian Bureau should allow the Indians to select those aspects of the dominant culture which would be beneficial to themselves. Federal efforts should center on assisting and easing the impact of transformations; self-rule should typify official programs rather than paternalistic control.

Translated into every day policy, the Collier philosophy of Indian affairs was revolutionary. He demanded that Indians be allowed to reorganize their tribal governments and, through them, to take an active role in the administration of reservation affairs. Children should no longer be separated from their parents in remote boarding schools, but they should attend day schools and return to their families at night, learning to live both among their own people and off the reservation.

When applied to specific problems, Collier's reforms sought to protect Indian land and natural resources and raise their standard of living. He was alarmed that Indian lands had constantly diminished and fallen into white hands, especially after the passage of the Dawes Severalty Act of 1887 which divided most reservations into individually owned allotments of land. Desperately Collier wanted to stop this erosion of real estate and to add new land wherever possible. His goal could be achieved by restoring land to tribal ownership when allottees died or decided to sell their allotments instead of allowing holdings to be purchased by whites. Collier also hoped to use tribal funds and federal grants to secure additional land and to consolidate scattered allotments into larger and more useable units.

Collier was equally sensitive to white exploitation of Indians' land and natural resources. Through leases of land, minerals, and timber to whites, the Indians lost much of the potential wealth needed to raise their low standard of living. Collier maintained that Indians wherever possible must start utilizing their own resources. Once Indians gained control of their land, Collier hoped to develop more irrigation, to initiate tribal enterprises, and to improve Indian farming methods and livestock management. Influenced by the severity of the depression and the Indians' poverty, Collier's aspirations for economic improvement were modest. He never demanded that Indian income reach parity with that of whites. He sought only to elevate Indian income permanently to a subsistence level and to insure that the demoralizing effects of charity could be removed.

If Collier's economic goals were modest, the same was not true of the revision he wanted in the Indian Bureau's general role. Whenever a conflict of interest developed between Indians and whites, the government would no longer act as an arbiter for the two sides. The Indian must now have "his day in court," and the Bureau must act as his defending attorney and not his judge or prosecutor.

Many of Collier's goals were applicable to the Navajos' situation in 1933. From his previous associations with the tribe, the new commissioner knew that Navajo culture and religion were basically unaltered, especially in the more remote portions of the reservation. Emphasis could be placed on preserving an already viable native culture rather than restoring a few remnants which had survived the inroads of assimilation. The Navajos were also ideal for implementing Collier's day-school program. Since less than one-half of the Navajo children were being educated in 1933, new day schools on the reservation could achieve his aspiration of a dualistic training for Indian students. Finally, Collier saw in the Navajos' headman system and council an opportunity to realize his goal of tribal self-government.

Fortunately, the Navajo reservation proper had never been allotted under the Dawes Severalty Act because officials recognized
that desert conditions would not permit farming. Hence Collier's
goals on land consolidation did not fully apply. In the checkerboard
areas to the east and south of the reservation, however, the Navajos'
situation closely resembled allotted reservations and here he hoped
to consolidate the scattered tracts, placing part of the land under
tribal ownership and expanding the reservation to the south and east.
In addition, Navajos both on and off the reservation could use Collier's techniques to better living standards.[10]

The emphasis of the New Deal in 1933 was not, however, on the
application of Collier's philosophy to Indian affairs, but rather on the
frantic organization of relief programs. Even before Collier assumed
office, Congress passed the Emergency Conservation Work Act,
which authorized the program popularly known as the Civilian
Conservation Corps. The legislation called for reforestation of federal,
state, or private lands where projects would contribute to the protection of resources on public property. Reforestation was interpreted
broadly to include soil erosion control, reseeding depleted range
land, development of recreation facilities, and various other projects.
Congress also authorized CCC projects on Indian reservations; they
were considered federal property and, therefore, eligible for conservation work.[11] An unsolicited bonus had suddenly been dropped
into the Bureau's lap which would more than offset recent cuts in
Indian Service appropriations and would allow field officials to
achieve conservation projects that would have taken years to accomplish with regular funds.

The Navajos and other tribes in the Southwest fared exceptionally
well in the separate CCC program established for Indian reservations
in 1933. The plan announced in late April called for an expenditure

10. For descriptions of Collier's ideas, see his *From Every Zenith* (Denver, 1963); Lawrence C. Kelly, *The Navajo Indians and Federal Indian Policy* (Tucson, 1968), pp. 155–58;
Ward Shepard, "Land Problems of an Expanding Indian Population," in Oliver La
Farge, ed., *The Changing Indian* (Norman, Oklahoma, 1942), pp. 72–83; *Annual Report of
the Secretary of the Interior*, 1933 (Washington, 1933); and *Gallup Independent*, 15 May 1933,
pp. 1, 3. Stephen J. Kunitz's article, "The Social Philosophy of John Collier," *Ethnohistory* 18 (Summer 1971); 213–19, suggests that Collier's ideas were derived from the
social philosophy of both the Progressive and New Deal eras. Kunitz also attributes
Collier's interest in Indians to his rejection of the industrial revolution and concomitant
individualism.

11. U. S., *Statutes at Large*, 73, pt. 1, pp. 22–23; *Congressional Record*, 73rd Cong., 1st
sess., 1933, 87, pt. 1, p. 862.

of $5,875,000 with seventy-two camps on thirty-three reservations. New Mexico and Arizona were to receive forty-three of the camps, twenty-five of which were assigned to the Navajos. The program was indeed timely because the Navajos were victims of a drought which one observer said was unprecedented in severity. A local newspaper reported that Navajo livestock was suffering from a shortage of water and that the tribe was headed for a disastrous year unless rains fell soon. Beside the dry weather, low prices and slow markets still persisted, causing most traders to reject credit sales of goods even when secured by pawn.[12]

The prospect of CCC projects boosted the morale of Navajos and whites alike. Nearly every issue of local newspapers carried headlines on the new El Dorado. In early June the superintendents received orders to enroll workers, and whether young or old, progressive or traditionalist, the Navajos came in droves to sign up for jobs. One Navajo, frantically riding horseback to an enrollment station near Chinle, hailed down a group of fellow tribesmen jammed into a truck which was chugging across the reservation. Learning that they were also going to sign up and fearful that he would be too late, the Navajo solemnly gave them his census number and demanded that they enroll him, too. Unlike other tribes, the Navajos had no qualms about the physical examinations and immunizations required of new enrollees. Even the rumor that the Army was running the camps did not deter them. Every available Indian Service and mission doctor was quickly mobilized to administer physical examinations. John Hunter, superintendent of the Southern Navajo, reported that he had almost filled his quota of 1,200 enrollees after only four days, but the work program would not come close to meeting the needs of the Indians.[13]

On June 6, Louis C. Schroeder of New York, an expert on camp management, arrived in Gallup to set up the CCC administration for the entire reservation. Immediately he began to assemble a staff, to confer with the Navajo superintendents, and to plan the project work. Forrest Parker, a trader who had married into the Hubbell family, was named as Schroeder's assistant.[14] A CCC district headquarters was established in Albuquerque. Local superintendents forwarded

12. Roman Hubbell to Collier, 6 May 1933, File 19414, 1933, 344, CCC-ID, NA, RG 75; *Gallup Independent*, 13 April 1933, p. 3, and 8 March 1933, p. 1.
13. John G. Hunter to Thomas Dodge, 10 June 1933, LAFRC, Box 72925.
14. *Gallup Independent*, 7 June 1933, p. 1.

their proposed projects to the district office where foresters and
engineers reviewed them. Collier, in the meantime, encountered
delays in getting CCC funds released to the Indian Bureau even
though he wanted to launch the program quickly to relieve the
Indians' distress and to take advantage of the summer weather.

Confusion existed when officials began planning CCC projects for
the Navajos in June. Numerous people—engineers of various types,
recreation experts, range specialists, foresters, etc.—were hired and
brought in from outside the Southwest. Regular Indian Service
employees and the new arrivals conferred endlessly in Gallup to plan
the projects and camp organization. Even at this early stage, controversies arose. A debate, for example, took place over whether the
government should operate stores at camps for the Indians or allow
traders to sell them supplies. Parker helped the financially pressed
traders to kill the scheme for government commissaries. Another plan
called for the purchase of one hundred large caterpillar tractors,
costing some $400,000, to build truck trails on the reservation. The
proposal also requested additional money to be spent on other heavy
equipment. Bad as reservation roads were, people familiar with the
Navajos' situation knew that the tribe's most desperate need was for
water development to combat the drought.[15] The road building
equipment was reportedly ordered and then cancelled, but part of it
arrived later even though the plan had been dropped in favor of
water development. At best the planning was confused and ill-
developed and many projects were chosen unwisely.

Around July 1 Collier finally received the money to start CCC
field operations. Crews of enrollees worked at a wide range of projects, both in 1933 and in later years. Some used teams of horses and
small scoops commonly called "slips" to build dams across minor
streams or arroyos to catch and store water for livestock during the
infrequent rains. CCC enrollees additionally worked on digging out
springs, drilling new wells, setting up windmills, and installing
storage tanks. Others built truck trails into the heavily timbered
Fort Defiance plateau to provide better access to the tribe's valuable
timber resources and to fight fires. Indian crews, carrying bags of
poisoned grain, crisscrossed Navajo ranges in a huge rodent eradication program.

The CCC jobs were invaluable to many Navajos. Some reportedly

15. Forrest Parker to Lorenzo Hubbell, Jr., 27 June 1933, Hubbell Trading Post.

were so undernourished that they collapsed when first put to work. Camp managers were ordered to supply a special diet of whole wheat bread, brown rice, tomatoes, and dried fruit.[16] The CCC wages were not adequate by white standards, even in a depression, but they were terribly important to the enrollee, especially if he owned no herd of sheep and goats. The thirty dollars per month, plus two dollars per day for those who supplied teams, allowed the long-destitute Indians to buy food and clothing for their families. The result was an economic boom for Navajos and whites. It was, in one trader's words, "a grand and glorious feeling" to see money flowing into the posts again.[17]

However, the new wage economy quickly but permanently altered the old pattern of barter trading. Many Indians could not work on federal programs unless they were extended credit to buy food for their families and clothes and tools needed for their jobs. The traders depended on their customers to bring their monthly checks to the post to repay debts. But the shrewd Indians quickly learned that a federal check could be cashed at another trading post or in an off-reservation town, and thus they could obtain cash without satisfying their creditors.

In part, unpaid debts became a problem because of the Navajos' delight in deceiving traders. The Navajos had a long-standing philosophy of "let the trader beware." Rolling sheep in sand before shearing, watering fleeces, or hiding rocks in the middle of wool sacks were accepted tactics in outsmarting the traders. If caught, the Navajos blandly and good-naturedly smiled at the trader. If successful, their mirth at the trader was open. For the most part the duplicity was a friendly game played by both sides. The trader usually won, but even his rare losses could be recouped the next time the offender sold his wool or lambs. With the introduction of a wage economy, the merchant lost his monopoly over the local Indians. A countertactic was found almost as soon as the problem arose. Within days after the CCC started, Indian enrollees in some areas had to sign forms authorizing their checks to be forwarded directly to the trader who had extended them credit. The Indians obviously were expected to cash their checks and pay off their accounts. To curb possible abuses by traders, John Hunter, superintendent of the Southern

16. Jay B. Nash to Collier, 4 August 1933 in *Indians at Work* 1 (September 1933): 6.
17. Young Interview.

Navajo, instructed post operators not to extend over fifteen dollars
of credit per month to CCC workers and ordered that the remaining
fifteen dollars be given in cash. Overextension of credit by traders,
Hunter warned, would result in giving the checks directly to the enrollees. Precisely what role the government should take in this
matter bothered the sensitive Collier. While he could not condone
failure to repay loans, he did not want Indian Service workers collecting debts for the traders.[18] The problem was part of the more important effect of transforming from a barter to a cash economy which
started in 1933 and has persisted without resolution.

While final arrangements were being completed to launch the CCC
program in late June, a party of officials arrived in Gallup from
Washington to study the conservation problems of the reservation.
The group's little noticed visit became the seed for a sweeping land
management project for the Navajos and eventually led to the
national conservation programs of the Soil Conservation Service.
The reasons for the study of Navajo land started with two unsigned
memos prepared earlier in June. These proposed that an erosion
experiment station be located somewhere on the reservation. One
purpose of the station would be to study new methods of erosion
control, but its major function would be educational. The memos
asked that one hundred CCC enrollees be sent to the station for a one
month course in erosion control. Each group of students would be
drawn from a single chapter or locality and the ten most able people
would be retained in school the following month as cadres for further
study and to help train the next group. The ten would then return to
their home area and supervise local conservation work. If the program operated for two years, the memos continued, the Navajos
would have 2,400 people trained in conservation and "hereafter, the
chapters themselves would take over, as a purely Indian activity, an
intensive program of erosion-control work all over the Navajo Reservation."[19]

Collier's lack of qualified conservation experts in the Indian

18. The form used in the Greasewood area stated: "Until further notice you [CCC
foreman] are requested to deliver my check, covering work done under the Emergency
Conservation Program, to me through ———, Indian Trader." See Joe Yazzie, Greasewood Chapter, 16 July 1933, and John G. Hunter to Trading Posts, 24 July 1933,
Hubbell Trading Post; *Gallup Independent*, 7 July 1933, p. 2.

19. Unsigned memos to John Collier, 7 and 8 June 1933, File 19414, 1933, 344,
CCC-ID, NA, RG 75.

Service, especially during the start of the CCC projects, forced him to appeal to the Department of Agriculture for assistance in starting the erosion experiment station. He quickly won the cooperation of Secretary of Agriculture Henry A. Wallace, who invited Collier to confer with department soil erosion experts. On June 9 Collier and Indian Bureau leaders met with Agriculture officials in the office of H. G. Knight, Chief, Bureau of Chemistry and Soils. Included in the USDA party was H. H. Bennett, then a little known figure in the Bureau of Chemistry and Soils. Within three years, Bennett would become a powerful force in the New Deal farm programs and famous as the "father of the Soil Conservation Service."

The conference gave little evidence of its portentousness. When Collier presented his desire to establish an erosion control station, the USDA leaders raised no objections. The group then decided to send representatives to Gallup on June 26 to study conservation problems and to formulate a plan of action. Bennett was to serve as informal chairman for the survey and the USDA would be represented additionally by field workers currently stationed in the Southwest. Collier's son, Charles, would head a contingent of four or five men from the Indian Service.[20]

Although the survey conducted by Bennett's group was very cursory, it had enormous importance for the future administration of Navajo affairs. Bennett's men were on the reservation for just a week or so and could visit only a few areas in the southeastern region. Most of their statistics obviously came from Zeh's earlier study. Despite this, they convinced Collier that he must swiftly launch a major conservation program and completely restructure the reservation administration to solve the Navajos' long-standing grazing problems.[21]

Bennett's report stressed that the reservation had already been severely damaged by soil erosion. Originally the top soil had been very stable, but years of overgrazing had killed the vegetation and exposed the land to the ravages of water and wind erosion. Much of this damage was of recent origin. Soil around the bases of small trees had washed or blown away, leaving the trunks perched on stilt-like

20. Knight to Wallace, 9 June 1933, File 19414, 1933, 344, CCC-ID, NA, RG 75; *Gallup Independent*, 26 June 1933, p. 1. Charles Collier served as a dollar-a-year assistant to his father the first year or so of the New Deal.

21. Collier to Knight, 10 June 1933, File 19414, 1935, 344, CCC-ID, NA, RG 75.

roots above ground level. In sandy soils, the wind had often scooped out "blow-outs" or holes in the ground, formed dunes, and scoured off the top soil. The most fertile areas, the lowlands, were subject to water runoff from the steep uplands which carved deep arroyos in the flat valleys. The intense overgrazing extended even into the stands of timber where hungry sheep and goats ate young saplings and kept the forests from reproducing themselves. The survey report estimated that about seventy percent of the land had been seriously eroded. Some of it had already passed the point of recovery, but large areas could be restored, at least partially.

The recommendations of the Bennett report partly followed the original conception of an erosion station for experiments and instruction in conservation. The station site recommended was an area at Mexican Springs, some twenty-five miles northwest of Gallup. The varied terrain in this locale duplicated almost any condition on the reservation and was ideal for demonstrating a wide range of corrective techniques. Other proposals outlined a much broader approach toward solving the overgrazing problem than originally envisioned. The report suggested that Congress be asked to authorize a "Navajo Reservation Authority charged with the duty of developing and putting into effect . . . a plan for the preservation and restoration of the Navajo range and livelihood." Designed along the lines of the Tennessee Valley Authority, the conservation agency would be responsible solely to Collier and have the best available personnel, plus independent funding to effect a restoration of the reservation's productivity.[22]

The implications of the Bennett report were highly significant. If implemented, the reservation would no longer be a patchwork of six separate jurisdictions with each superintendent reporting to Washington and acting more or less independently in whatever rehabilitation effort—irrigation, livestock breeding improvement, education,—he cared to emphasize. Instead, the administration would be consolidated under the control of a general superintendent. These were Collier's ideas when he visited the reservation in July to attend his first session of the tribal council at Fort Wingate.

The meeting of the tribal council in 1933 had been preceded by a

22. Report of the Conservation Advisory Committee, 2 July 1933, File 31777, 1935, 344, NA, RG 75.

new election of delegates in which the Returned Students Association had gained strong representation. The group became politically effective and unified soon after the heated meeting to endorse a new commissioner. In late February, Howard Gorman announced a platform which asked for a teacher for every thirty children as promised in the Treaty of 1868, scholarships for students qualified to enter advanced studies, placement services to find jobs for returned students, and a magazine for educated Navajos to keep alive the ideals they learned in schools. Soon afterward Gorman mailed detailed questionnaires to former Navajo students asking their opinions about various methods by which they could upgrade their own situation and improve the conditions for the tribe as a whole. The responses indicated that many educated Navajos felt tanning and leatherwork cooperatives offered the best avenues for economic advancement.[23]

When the election of a new tribal council took place in April, the Returned Students endorsed a slate of their own candidates for both delegates and alternates. Out of the seven candidates supported for the twelve delegate posts, all but one were elected, giving the Returned Students control of half of the voting seats on the council.[24] On June 1, the new council elected as chairman Thomas Dodge, who was Chee's son and an attorney in Santa Fe. The younger Dodge's election may seem unusual because of the animosity between his father and Morgan. Thomas Dodge and Morgan, however, were fairly close friends in 1933, and the new chairman frequently consulted with Morgan after taking office. Even later when Morgan vigorously attacked the government and Dodge supported it, they retained their earlier friendship.[25]

Collier surely sensed the irony of his first appearance before the Fort Wingate council on July 7. As a reformer he had been vilified and called a troublemaker and once even kicked off the reservation; now he was being hailed as a dedicated defender of an abused minority. Indian Service workers who had bitterly resented Collier's earlier attacks were suddenly forced to take orders from him. Traders and

23. *Gallup Independent*, 24 February 1933, p. 4, and 28 February 1933, p. 1; Gorman Interview.

24. *Gallup Independent*, 29 April 1933, p. 1.

25. Thomas Dodge to writer, 25 November 1972.

local whites who had feared that his administration would be a disaster were ecstatic about the federal funds he pumped into the moribund reservation economy.

One thing which had not changed was Collier's appearance. A Gallup reporter noted that the commissioner arrived in town disheveled and badly needing a shave.[26] Utterly without concern for grooming, Collier always appeared rumpled. He invariably dressed in baggy and wrinkled suits that looked like oversized rejects from a used-clothing sale. He smoked incessantly. Usually he puffed away on cigarettes, but when he became worried periodically about that habit, he switched to a battered corncob pipe which he constantly fondled and relighted. In truth he was something of an ascetic who devoted his sizable talents and energies toward realizing his program of Indian reform.

The Fort Wingate council met in a gala atmosphere complete with band concert and Indian dances. An estimated 1,200 Navajos traveled to the session on foot, by horseback, and in cars and trucks. They overcrowded the school auditorium and a public address system was installed for those left outside. A score or more of major Indian Service and CCC officials attended from reservations of the Southwest or the Washington office.

Chee Dodge and Dashne Clah Cheschillige, former chairmen of the council, attended and participated in the discussions. Dashne had headed the council prior to Thomas Dodge's election and he would occasionally figure in tribal affairs during the early years of the New Deal. A native of the Shiprock area, the forty-one-year-old Dashne possessed an easy command of English and a reputation as a vigorous orator. He was among the first Navajo students to be educated. After attending a boarding school at Fort Lewis, Colorado, Dashne became a star student at Shiprock in the early twentieth century. Because of his obvious skills in interpreting and agriculture, he stayed on at Shiprock for several years as an agency employee. He later became one of the few Navajos who succeeded in business for himself, first as a trader and later as a filling station operator. During the mid-1930s the thickset leader would virtually retire from tribal politics, probably because he had a large family to support but also because Morgan's increasing power left little room for competitors. Dashne, however, would reemerge as a significant leader in the final years of the New Deal.

26. *Gallup Independent,* 5 July 1933, p. 1.

The Fort Wingate meeting had the trappings of an important session, but it achieved few tangible results. Thomas Dodge gave Collier a very complimentary and eloquent introduction, calling him the "Plumed Knight of the Indian Cause." Collier's address reviewed the Navajos' overgrazing, land shortages, and overpopulation and asked that the council members meet the problems with the fullest talents possible. He reaffirmed his belief in Indian self-rule, promising repeatedly that the government no longer wished to direct reservation activities but would act only as a servant to whatever programs the tribe wanted.[27] During the discussions which followed, Collier outlined various other facets of his plans for the Navajos. Day schools, he emphasized, probably would be built throughout the reservation by Public Works Administration funds to educate the Navajo children not presently in school. The new schools would also provide community centers with classes for parents, shops to repair wagons and tools, and medical facilities. Collier made no mention of closing the existing boarding schools, but he clearly intended to deemphasize them. When quizzed on lumber and oil contracts which had been revised before the New Deal without the council's permission, Collier promised to investigate the matter carefully and report back on whether the contracts could be voided and renegotiated.

The factionalism of past council sessions reappeared several times during the Fort Wingate deliberations. Dashne Clah Cheschillege recently had protested Dodge becoming chairman because the young lawyer lived in Santa Fe and, in Dashne's opinion, could not carry out his duties properly. Dodge met the criticism by promising to return to the reservation. J. C. Morgan voiced his resentment against the oil royalties being spent outside the Northern Navajo jurisdiction and complained that his area could use tribal revenues for an irrigation project along the San Juan River. In discussing Collier's proposed new day schools and base hospital, the council was still divided by internal jealousies as each group of delegates sought to obtain maximum funding and facilities for their own jurisdiction.

The council also exhibited considerable animosity toward government employees. Marcus Kanuho from Leupp attacked extension personnel who dealt with range management, farming, and the

27. "Minutes of the Eleventh Annual Session of the Navajo Tribal Council Held at Fort Wingate, New Mexico, July 7 and 8, 1933," Department of Interior Library, Washington, pp. 1–5.

dipping program. Other delegates supported Kanuho's complaint that agency personnel did nothing and did not teach the Navajos proper methods of farming or livestock management. A resolution to dismiss the workers passed without objection.

Young Dodge and Collier agreed beforehand that the council needed restructuring to make it more representative of Indians from all regions of the reservation. The chairman appointed a committee and asked them to examine such possibilities as doubling the size of the council by making alternates regular delegates and electing the chairman and vice chairman by a popular vote of the entire tribe. Dodge asked the committee members to report their recommendations at the next council.

Collier's most important goal during the council was to win permission to establish the erosion experiment station. During the first day, he called on H. H. Bennett to summarize the findings of his recent investigation. Bennett emphasized that the reservation badly needed the benefit of experiments and education which a station could achieve. Observing that the area around Mexican Springs was an ideal location for the project, Collier promised that any site must be approved by both the tribal council and local Indians. Alfred G. Sandoval of the Southern Navajo attacked the council's hesitant reaction. "It seems to be the nature of the Navajo . . . ," Sandoval complained, "that he is always suspicious. No matter if a man is trying to save him, he is always suspicious that he is going to kill him."[28] Dodge appointed a committee to draft a resolution expressing the council's sentiments and the next day the delegates approved the Mexican Springs location. CCC crews started fencing off the large area as soon as the residents gave their consent to the project.

When the tribal council reassembled at Tuba City for a special meeting on October 30,[29] Collier augmented his vague and general statements at Fort Wingate with specific and comprehensive plans. The meeting was of pivotal importance, for Collier's proposals included the main ingredients of the government's program during the next decade. The commissioner opened his presentation by declaring that he had always believed Navajos needed to consolidate

28. Ibid., p. 22.

29. "Minutes of the Navajo Tribal Council Held at Tuba City, Arizona, October 30–31 and November 1, 1933," Department of Interior Library, Washington. See especially pp. 17–19, 34–47, 61–62 for materials on Collier's proposals and the council's reactions.

tribal administrative procedures. One headquarters under the direction of a single superintendent, he explained, would permit policy-making for the entire reservation instead of the confused situation of six separate jurisdictions. He maintained that the present headquarters were too remote from most Navajos and the old centers should be replaced by twenty-five subagencies scattered throughout the reservation.

In presenting these suggestions Collier skillfully tied the reorganization to other aspects of his program. Each subagency would not only handle local administrative matters, but it would also serve as a day school and community center. Some seventy new day schools would be built, but those at the subagencies would be more elaborate and contain medical facilities for a doctor and nurse. In addition to education and health, the subagencies would direct local conservation projects. Collier met possible objections by suggesting that reorganization could proceed slowly so as not to disrupt existing services. Present government personnel would not leave the reservation but be retained and brought closer to the Navajos in the subagencies. The tribe, he promised, would receive better services without increasing the cost to the government.

Although reorganization was important, Collier's plans for a conservation program were much more significant and struck at the center of the Navajos' basic economic and social values. Collier must have anticipated this, for he broached the subject very carefully. He opened by reviewing the various funds he had secured for the Navajos. A grant of $940,000 had been approved for irrigation projects and he claimed that this would add 15,000 acres of tillage or five acres of subsistence farm land for 3,000 Navajo families. The commissioner next cited a grant of $1,250,000 from the CCC and the WPA to establish erosion experiment stations throughout the reservation. He mentioned the day school construction and, in passing, the likelihood of a road program in the near future.

After this background, Collier finally presented his central point that the Navajos must reduce their livestock holdings during the next four or five years. Unless a reduction was effected, the rest of his program would be futile. What good, he asked, could day schools achieve if the land deteriorated to the point where it no longer supported the Navajos? Collier estimated the reduction should be at least 200,000 sheep and 200,000 goats. The latter would never be allowed to regain their current numbers even after conservation projects had restored range productivity. The persuasive commissioner promised, however, that wage work would offset the Navajos' loss of income from their livestock by at least threefold. Collier explained that the government already had statutory authority to enforce grazing regulations, but he preferred to act through the tribe itself. In closing, he emphasized his faith in the council's wisdom: "We believe that the condition is so extreme and so well known to you that you would make the adjustment and sacrifice even if the government were not prepared to compensate you as it is."

Collier then called upon A. C. Cooley, director of extension in the Bureau, to project the effect of herd reduction upon the tribe's future income. Cooley used a chart to present his ideas with a blue line representing the number of sheep and goats, a red line representing the income from livestock, and a yellow line representing wages derived from federal projects. The chart indicated that tribal income would actually increase during the next four years even though reductions would be made annually through 1935. Cooley's clenching argument was that the Navajos' income after 1937 would be equal to that of the present even though their herds would number 500,000 head less and wage work on conservation projects would be stopped. Cooley explained that improved grazing conditions and better livestock breeding and management would boost the income from each sheep. The average weight per fleece was three pounds at present and this would increase to an estimated five pounds by 1937. The value of fall lambs would rise some sixty-five percent by the later date.

Despite the impressive presentations, the Navajo delegates were not overawed. Jim Shirley, an alternate from the Southern Navajo, pointedly asked when the Indians would get to talk. It was the second day of the council and no one had spoken yet except officials. The councilmen's questions about herd reduction were equally blunt. How will people not on government jobs survive without their livestock? Why should the tribe reduce sheep and goats when bad winters periodically decimated their herds anyway? Why work for wages when the traders soon got all the money? One delegate, referring to Cooley's chart, asked why all three lines—red, blue, and yellow—could not rise simultaneously. Clearly, the prospect of a herd reduction touched nerve endings.

Henry Taliman, a young educated Navajo from Oak Springs, raised the strongest objections against reduction. He pointed out that sheep allowed the Navajos to survive under the most adverse conditions. His people were stockmen, and except for those living near agencies, they did not understand or favor wage labor. The Navajos, Taliman stated, had been through a series of bad years and their range would recover itself when the drought ended. The young Navajo criticized Collier for tying herd reduction into the rest of his program. Reduction should be kept separate and time given to the Navajos to work out the problem locally.

However the dissenting opinions quickly vanished under Collier's pressures. The entire council met in executive session that evening with only Collier and a few top officials present. No minutes were kept, but Collier evidently overcame the opposition to herd reduction, for Taliman completely reversed his position the next day. Instead of leading the attack on Collier, he now offered a resolution which item by item endorsed the commissioner's program. Little attention was given to an agreement that Collier apparently made with the council during the closed session. The bargain, mentioned only briefly and indirectly, was that Collier would secure legislation to expand the reservation in Arizona and New Mexico and the tribe in return would accept the conservation program and herd reduction.[30]

After Taliman presented his resolution the final day, herd reduction provoked little discussion, but a heated debate resulted over the provision for consolidating the reservation administration. Not surprisingly, J. C. Morgan and other Northern Navajo delegates objected. Morgan, a formidable debater, complained that the council needed more time to consider the matter and to confer with their local constituents before approving such a drastic change. Otherwise, he had no strong personal feelings on consolidation and could accept the remainder of Collier's program without qualms. Robert Martin, Morgan's lieutenant, openly expressed the strong separatist sentiments typical of Northern Navajos. "We want to be left out of this consolidation plan entirely," Martin emphasized.

30. The closest reference to this matter was Collier's comment regarding reorganizing Navajo administration: "Nobody back in Washington is waiting on your action concerning administrative consolidation but from the standpoint of appropriations . . . and being able to pass your land or boundary bill, a great deal depends on your acting unanimously on the other part of the resolution [i.e., conservation]." Ibid., p. 71.

"We are able to set up our own government. . . . We can work out our own problems so we want to be left alone over in New Mexico." Morgan's subsequent attempt to delete the consolidation item from the resolution failed and the entire package passed by a two-thirds majority.

During the council's deliberations, Collier announced that he had received a telegram from Washington authorizing the first purchase of livestock. The Federal Emergency Relief Administration had agreed to buy from 50,000 to 100,000 Navajo sheep. Collier immediately conferred with his advisors on prices to be paid to the Indians and they decided on two to three dollars per head for wethers (castrated male sheep) and one to one and one-half dollars per head for ewes, supposedly the same amount traders would have paid. No goats were to be purchased. Chee Dodge expressed misgivings about the price for ewes to the council. He predicted accurately that the low price would not persuade Navajos to sell their productive breeding stock but only their culls. The net result would be the retention of the better animals and little change in the number of lambs produced.[31]

The Tuba City council foreshadowed the strengths and weaknesses of the New Deal self-government policies. While Collier did not autocratically force the council to accept his program, his strong tactics produced the same result. In contrast to the council members, who had no inkling of the proposals nor time to prepare arguments, Collier was highly persuasive in presenting his case and his subordinates were able to support him with charts, facts, and figures. Additional leverage was derived from relief work which supplied jobs to several council members. Finally, there always seemed to be the implied threat that existing benefits would not be continued or new ones added unless the council consented to an unwanted action such as herd reduction. Although Collier sincerely believed in Indian self-rule, the pressures that he and later officials exerted often compromised this ideal.

If the Navajo council leaders had been accustomed to the rough and tumble tactics, sharp bargains, and compromises of white parliamentary deliberations, they might have been able to resist Collier at Tuba City and later councils. But the deference they felt

31. Ibid. See especially pp. 62–63, 72, 76, 93 for other matters debated during this session.

for the government largely negated the possibility. Also, the Navajo
custom of painstakingly arguing a question through to complete
agreement was never permitted in the short council sessions. Repeatedly delegates remarked they wanted more time to think over
proposals, but officials retorted that they were due back in Washington and required decisions now or program funds would be lost. The
result of such a situation placed the council in a political crossfire
between federal officials' demands and their own followers' wishes.

The comments of George Bancroft, a delegate from Tuba City, are
especially revealing about the dilemma typically faced by council
members. When the debate over consolidation of the reservation
became most heated at the Tuba City meeting, Bancroft pleaded:

> I am at a loss. I do not know what to do about this [consolida-
> tion issue]. I do not know whether I am for it or against it be-
> cause of the reason it is so sudden. I have not talked about it
> with my people and because there is an audience of Tuba City
> people here, I want to get an expression from them as to what to
> do. At the time they elected me to be the delegate for this
> particular jurisdiction, one of the promises I made my people
> was that if anything came up in connection with their welfare I
> would notify them and act according to their permission. Now
> I want to ask the people how they feel about it. This is so sudden.
> I do not know, maybe you [people from Tuba City] are in favor
> of the men who are against this resolution or maybe you are for
> these others who are in favor of it. It is getting warm in here
> anyway so we should go outside for a little while.[32]

Fortunately for Bancroft, the council did recess for fifteen minutes to
allow him to consult with his followers, but most delegates obviously
had no such opportunity.

Other actions of the council at Tuba City were far less important
than the conservation program and the reorganization of administration. Collier reported that the lumber contract with Lutcher and
Moore of Orange, Texas, was no longer binding and the council
terminated the agreement. Collier warned, however, that the oil
contracts were still in force. The council then withdrew the power of
attorney given to the Secretary of Interior in 1923, insuring that the
council would approve all future bids on oil contracts.[33] The delegates

32. Ibid., p. 62.
33. Ibid., p. 33.

debated at length the need to regulate traders' practices but the resolutions adopted were surprisingly tentative. The council closed with several of the Indians expressing their gratitude to Collier. Friendly closings, despite bitter deliberations, were a regular part of council meetings. Along with unanimous consent, Navajo political behavior demanded that all participants should end a meeting in a spirit of harmony.

The stock reduction agreed to by the Tuba City council started as soon as Collier received funds for the project. On November 16 final arrangements were made between the Department of Interior and the Federal Emergency Relief Administration for a grant of $200,000 to the Indian Bureau for the purchase of 100,000 Navajo sheep. The Indian Service was to transport the sheep to railroad shipping points, send them to packing companies for processing, and then distribute the canned meat to needy Indians.[34] Collier immediately issued orders to the Navajo superintendents listing the quotas for each jurisdiction and directing them to initiate the sale and transportation of sheep from the reservation to shipping points. The numbers purchased were based on the livestock holdings of each jurisdiction. Accordingly, the Southern Navajo district was directed to sell 32,000 sheep, the Northern Navajo 20,000, the Eastern Navajo 15,000, the Western Navajo 15,000, the Hopi 10,000, and the Leupp 8,000.

The actual purchase of the sheep was in the charge of Frank B. Lenzie of the Washington office, while Indian Service workers and CCC enrollees collected the sheep and drove them to the shipping points. The chapter leaders of the Southern Navajo and Eastern Navajo were called together and assigned quotas for their respective areas. They, in turn, returned home and told each family how many sheep to sell.[35] In the other jurisdictions where chapters were scattered or nonexistent, the sales were apparently conducted by headmen and local traders. Whatever the means, the program was completed without delay. *The Gallup Independent* reported on December 7 that loading pens in the city were jammed with sheep and the bulk of the 40,000 animals shipped from there would be sent to packing plants within a few days.[36]

34. S. M. Dodd, Jr. to Indian Office, 16 November 1933, Fechner File, CCC-ID, NA, RG 75.

35. *Gallup Independent*, 18 November 1936, p. 1, and 22 November 1933, p. 1.

36. Ibid., 7 December 1933, p. 1.

The fanatic hostility that Navajos later displayed against livestock reductions did not occur in 1933. The Indians realized that the regular fall market had failed and they viewed the government purchase as a replacement for normal sales. Even so, the methods used for the sheep purchases were faulty and provided an added Basis for later resentments. In his memo to the superintendents outlining the program, the commissioner ordered that no poor quality sheep be purchased and that "every effort should be made to purchase stock from the Indians owning large herds rather than from the small owners."[37] In practice neither admonition was followed. Because of the large herders' pressures, all owners sold approximately the same percentage of their sheep and poor quality animals were accepted. The reduction by straight percentages, instead of on a graduated scale, permitted the commercial sheepmen to cull their herds of nonproductive animals. As Chee Dodge had warned, a numerical reduction was achieved but little diminution in productive capacity.

Like the Indians, local whites initially approved Collier's program in 1933, especially since the new commissioner was able to meet that most important criterion of political success, the securing of large sums from government coffers. The delivery in June of $30,000 worth of new Chevrolet trucks at Gallup for the CCC program, for example, aroused an enthusiastic response in the local paper.[38] The coming weeks showed that the trucks were only the beginning as Collier announced plans for day schools, hospitals, roads, irrigation, and a new tribal headquarters. But white approval began to diminish soon afterward. The reversal was largely the result of local white hostility toward the easterners who established the CCC program. Many newcomers were experts in recreation and summer camp management from eastern universities who had no experience with the Southwest, Navajos, or the reservation. Their efforts to teach the Indians "the play spirit," their obsession over camp sanitation, and their relative indifference to material accomplishments in project work created much ridicule among hard-bitten Southwesterners.[39]

Unfortunately, the local white reaction impeded acceptance of Collier's plans. Residents near the reservation assumed that supervisory jobs should be distributed among themselves and not to

37. Collier to S. F. Stacker, n.d., Indians-Navajo file, AHS.
38. *Gallup Independent*, 23 June 1933, p. 6.
39. Young Interview.

educated outsiders. The fact that the more lucrative appointments were made in Washington and not through local patronage upset both the job seekers and Democratic politicos in Arizona and New Mexico. Moreover, many regional whites strongly believed that only someone born in the area, who had grown up around Navajos, could understand them and knew how to deal with them. Local whites took delight in the inexperience and alleged mistakes of the easterners. It was not until the "so-called specialists" left the reservation in the late summer, according to a newspaper story, that local whites rescued the CCC program from collapse in the Eastern Navajo area and effective project work started.[40]

Local antagonisms toward New Deal programs on the reservation did not end when the first wave of easterners returned home in the fall. Resentments over patronage continued, although perhaps in diminished form. New difficulties constantly appeared as various New Deal plans got underway. Competition between the border towns to win the location of the new tribal headquarters and the base hospital, traders' problems with extending credit to Navajo wage earners, and resistance to extension of the reservation, were all to create new controversies and opposition toward Collier and the government.

For the Navajos, however, the first months of the New Deal brought many bounties. CCC jobs allowed thousands to offset the ill-effects of the depression, pay back debts at trading posts, and prepare for the long winter months when the emergency work slowed. Despite the hesitant attitude of Morgan's faction, most tribal leaders were impressed by Collier's appearances at council sessions and his many plans for the tribe's betterment. For such supporters, the Navajos had a commissioner who not only sympathized with their needs, but who also encouraged them to achieve self-rule. During its first stage the New Deal appeared to be a giant give-away. Few Navajos fully realized that the program approved at Tuba City demanded major sacrifices.

40. *Gallup Independent*, 10 October 1933, p. 1.

# 3

## The Second Herd Reduction and the
## Wheeler-Howard Referendum

Good-bye, Little Goat, good-bye
Don't cry, Little Goat, don't cry,
Though you go away, you will not stay,
You'll return in cans by and by.

"The Return," Tribal Council, Keams Canyon, July 12, 1934

"What good is just money? You earn it, have it, spend it,
or save it, but it doesn't grow or hatch or increase."

Navajo speaker, Shiprock, May 20, 1935

Having won initial approval of his overall program at the Tuba
City Council, Collier sought to implement particular aspects in the
following years. One of the commissioner's most important goals in
1934 was to win the Navajo council's endorsement of the Wheeler-
Howard bill, the most significant and innovative change in Indian
legislation since the Dawes Act of 1887. Collier clearly hoped to
use the new measure to destroy past policies and to achieve his
philosophy of Indian affairs. The most noteworthy provisions of the
original bill, at least for the Navajos, were the procedures by which
Indians could create their own local governments. To do so, a tribe
had to ratify the legislation through a tribal referendum, write a
constitution, obtain approval of it by the Secretary of Interior, and
ratify it by a second referendum. Once chartered, the new tribal
government would exercise powers much like local municipalities.
Tribal councils could pass their own ordinances and establish local
courts to try misdemeanors. More importantly, the tribal councils
would carry out many functions currently handled by the Indian
Service. Tribal governments could remove federal employees for
cause, inspect the annual budgets prepared by superintendents, and
exercise a veto over the spending of tribal funds.

The original Wheeler-Howard bill also contained several provisions for upgrading economic conditions on reservations. It, in effect, repealed the Dawes Act by prohibiting the further allotment of reservation lands and the sale of private Indian holdings to whites. Through purchases, exchanges, and consolidations, the measure attempted to increase the size of Indian lands and to block the checkerboard tracts off into larger and more usable holdings. Using the chartering procedures, tribal governments or groups could obtain money from a revolving fund to start such enterprises as sawmills, canneries, and livestock associations. To promote native leadership and increase the number of Indians employed on reservations, the Wheeler-Howard bill would provide scholarships for students who desired more than a high school education.

The legislative procedures for enacting the Wheeler-Howard bill were unusual. After being drafted during the winter of 1933–34, the bill was introduced in Congress and discussed by committees in both the House and the Senate. Afterward, it was explained to regional congresses of Indians throughout the West. In the closing weeks of the 1934 session, the congressional committees revised the provisions drastically, particularly weakening Collier's plans for land policy and the degree of control exerted by tribal councils.

Collier, however, explained the Wheeler-Howard bill to the Navajos even before the congressional committees finished their initial hearings. Appearing before the council at Fort Defiance on March 12 and 13, 1934, Collier apparently wanted to test the delegates' reactions and win a preliminary endorsement. He found that the complicated legislation, which ran forty-eight pages, challenged his powers of summary. Nevertheless, he opened his explanation by stressing that the Wheeler-Howard bill in no way threatened Navajo rights under the Treaty of 1868. Collier went on to emphasize that the Navajos need never worry about having their reservation allotted, for the bill repealed the Dawes Act of 1887. He next enumerated the benefits provided by the bill, such as the revolving fund of $10,000,000 for tribal enterprises and the program for scholarships. Collier and Felix Cohen, a lawyer in the Department of Interior who had helped draft the Wheeler-Howard bill, both outlined the self-government features of the legislation.

The discussion of the Wheeler-Howard bill among the council members was surprisingly short. The only note of dissension was J. C.

Morgan's comment that the Navajos wanted more time to study the legislation. Collier replied that haste was necessary if the bill were to be passed in the current session of Congress. He thought the revolving fund and scholarships should require no additional study as Navajos ought to understand and endorse such matters automatically. The only difficult aspect was self-government, but Collier maintained that "Navajos can reach a conclusion in less time than it took us to write the bill." Despite these admonitions and what was probably some heavy pressuring behind closed doors, the council decided to defer any decision on the Wheeler-Howard bill until its next meeting the following month.

Aside from the discussion of the legislation, important controversy resulted from Collier's request that the council approve a second herd reduction. The commissioner cited several factors which necessitated a new sale of livestock, but his main arguments were that the Indian Bureau could not insure passage of pending New Mexico and Arizona boundary bills or obtain more conservation funds unless the council agreed to another reduction.

As outlined to the council, the plan for the second herd reduction emphasized selling more goats than sheep. During the coming year, Collier wanted the tribe to dispose of 150,000 head of adult stock out of which at least 100,000 head must be goats. All remaining male goats must be castrated and the government would provide improved billies to develop milk goats for family use. The plan also called for the sale of all wethers each fall, with the Navajos keeping only enough female lambs to maintain existing breeding stock. In effect, at least eighty percent of the sheep and goat crop must be sold annually. Officials promised that this reduction would be the last if the Navajos maintained the recommended grazing load in the future.

From an ecological point of view, the proposal for a second reduction was very sound. Goats depleted ranges because their close grazing killed vegetation. They also grazed very rapidly, eating a small amount and then rushing to another spot. When mixed with sheep, goats tended to crop off the best forage from the less aggressive sheep and keep the herd moving too rapidly. Mixed herds as a result trampled more grass than necessary. Goats were also objectionable because they provided only meat to their owners and were not usually marketable. Sheep, however, provided meat for home consumption plus wool and fall lambs for sale.

Collier warned that Congress would not fund the reduction and that the Navajos must assume that burden themselves. He offered three alternatives for financing the new sales. First, the tribe might request a reimbursable loan of $225,000 from Congress to be paid back from future oil royalties. Second, they might tax all sheep and goats at seven and one-half cents per head at dipping time. Third, the council might place a wage tax of ten percent on Navajos working on relief programs. Collier requested that the delegates discuss the three alternatives among their constituents and make a decision at the next council.

In discussing the proposed herd reduction in the council, neither Collier nor the delegates fully realized how intense the hostility to the new sale would be. Collier, in fact, merely repeated his earlier defense that the government would provide more than enough wage work to offset the loss of income from livestock. "So," Collier explained, "we don't feel that it is asking you to do anything very hard to ask you to reduce your stock . . . when you are being compensated two or three times as much as you give up year by year."

The delegates' reactions to the second herd reduction demonstrated either full support or objections only to its particulars. Chee Dodge defended the conservation measure even more than Collier. He reminded the council that employment opportunities by New Deal agencies had saved many returned students from becoming loafers. The only resistance to reduction, Chee predicted, would be among the large herders. These people should be forced to pay a feed tax on every animal they grazed above a minimum number. Navajos had caused overgrazing themselves and they had, in Dodge's words, "no kick coming."

J. C. Morgan asked if small herds could be exempted from the reduction. The council quickly agreed that herds of under 100 sheep and goats should not be affected but that small owners should sell and replace goats with sheep. Becenti Bega, a delegate from the Eastern Navajo, objected to reduction outside the reservation because his constituents were not allowed to work on CCC projects. This issue was not resolved.

Only Fred Nelson, a Navajo from the Hopi area, raised strong objections to the herd reduction. Nelson admitted that the tribe had not fully met the first reduction quotas, but he questioned whether the government had fulfilled its part of the bargain. Where were all the conservation projects that Collier had promised, Nelson asked, and when would the government add more land to the reservation? Nelson also believed it unfair for the Navajos to pay for the new livestock sales. "For the white people," Nelson demanded, "the good old dollar is where they get their substance of life and the Navajos get their substance of life from the goats and the sheep, so it would not be fair to the Navajo to give up their goats and not the white people part of their dollars." Despite Nelson's objections, the council approved the second livestock reduction without a dissenting vote.[1]

Less than a month later, the council reconvened at Crownpoint to discuss the Wheeler-Howard bill again. Because of the pressures of guiding the legislation through Congress, Collier did not appear but sent James M. Stewart, director of the Land Division in the Washington office, as his representative. After a few preliminaries, Stewart—at the insistence of the delegates—began to read the Wheeler-Howard bill section by section, pausing after each to explain and answer questions. With the delegates seated on hard benches, the presentation was not conducive to winning the support of the council which raised numerous irrelevant or semantical questions. After a day and a half of desultory proceedings, Becenti Bega declared that the Wheeler-Howard bill was too difficult to understand and that he only wanted to talk about the goat reduction for the Eastern Navajo.

With this, the reading stopped and a general discussion of the bill began, resulting in a furious clash between the Morgan and Chee Dodge factions. Morgan started with a cutting attack on the legislation, asserting that uneducated Navajos could never understand it. Unless given professional leaders, the tribe would be like a ship "without a pilot." Morgan insisted that Navajos had never asked for the bill and it would cause only confusion and pain in the future. He pictured the Wheeler-Howard bill as treating Navajos as foreigners and, reading from the Constitution, he charged that the legislation would take away rights granted by that document. Collier, he complained, was trying to isolate Indians from the rest of the country.

1. See "Minutes of the Navajo Tribal Council held at Fort Defiance, Arizona, March 12 and 13, 1934," St. Michaels Mission, pp. 1–51, for the council's discussion on these matters. A nephew of Manuelito, Bega was an older headman with wide influence in the Eastern Navajo area and a close cooperator with S. F. Stacker, the superintendent at Crownpoint. Bega was somewhat discredited because of his support for the government in the referendum on the Wheeler-Howard Act in 1935. He died in April 1936. See *Santa Fe New Mexican*, 20 April 1936, p. 4.

Morgan saved his most biting comments to scorn the Navajo elders present. Such men, Morgan cried, "understand nothing about civilization; can't understand one word of what we are saying this afternoon. What about them? Can we lead them?"

Morgan's speech brought an angry rebuttal from Chee Dodge. Dodge, who venerated tradition and believed in compliance with government wishes, told the delegates that the offer of self-rule should be accepted as the latest in a series of beneficent government gifts dating back to the Treaty of 1868. Dashne Clah Cheschillige, the other former chairman, also endorsed the Wheeler-Howard legislation, stating that it would provide real power for the tribe and protect its natural resources. In a direct attack on Morgan's views, Henry Taliman emphasized that self-rule could only benefit the tribe and he denied that it would mean a return to the blanket.

The tense debate ended with seven delegates endorsing the Wheeler-Howard bill and the five Morgan delegates abstaining. The government's victory had serious consequences. Quite clearly, the long-standing feud between the traditionalists and returned students had spilled into the New Deal era. More importantly, the government had been unable to obtain the unanimous consent that Navajo decision-making demanded. Morgan and his followers now felt no restraint against future opposition to the Wheeler-Howard Act and Collier's handling of Indian affairs.

Despite the emotional outburst, the battle over the reform legislation was secondary in importance to the impending herd reduction agreed to in principle at Fort Defiance. Again resorting to a closed session, the council discussed herd reduction and decided to request a reimbursible loan of $225,000 from Congress to pay for the goat sale. The following day delegates and audience listened intently as a range expert reviewed the grazing situation. The 1933 dipping records had revealed 1,152,000 head of sheep and goats on the reservation. The first reduction had removed approximately 90,000 head. This plus sales to the CCC, schools, and traders, plus home consumption had dropped tribal holdings to an estimated 786,000 head. The Navajos stirred uneasily when the official predicted that the lamb and kid crop of 1934 would bring this figure back up to 1,036,000 head. Even more unsettling was the information that the reservation had a grazing capacity of approximately 600,000 sheep and goats. From this must be subtracted 50,000 horses and cattle which were the equivalent of 200,000 sheep, leaving room for only 400,000 actual sheep and goats. Even after listening to the situation, Navajo delegates afterward seemed only dimly aware of the serious-ness of bringing livestock levels into conformity with range capacity.

A third important issue considered by the Crownpoint meeting was the creation of a Navajo mounted patrol. The need for a new force to supplement the small number of Indian policemen at the six agencies grew out of the great increase of bootlegging at the start of the New Deal as whites revived a time-honored means of relieving Navajos of their wages. Although the eighteenth amend-ment was repealed, federal laws still prohibited sales of liquor to all Indians either on or off reservations. Illegal sales were most common in and around Gallup, New Mexico, a traditional weekend center of Navajo trade and vice. Gallup bootleggers either contacted their customers in back alleys or dispensed the firewater at CCC camps and at ceremonials on the reservation. Chairman Thomas Dodge had provided the main criticism of the problem. Dodge not only wanted additional law enforcement against bootlegging on the reservation, but he threatened a boycott of Gallup itself for its failure to act against illegal liquor sales, prostitution, and gambling within the city. The vice problems in Gallup were always serious, but they peaked during the Intertribal Ceremonial held annually in the late summer, when thousands of Navajos and other Indians attended the large tourist attraction.

The council had discussed these problems in 1933 and Collier had promised to investigate the possibility of funding a mounted patrol from emergency monies. So Stewart announced at Crownpoint that the Indian Office had received permission from the CCC to finance a force of thirty men.[2] Members of the mounted patrol were to be carried on the CCC payroll and were to receive $42 per month plus a small supplement for horse hire. A captain and two lieutenants would receive slightly higher pay.

The attempt to thwart bootlegging started optimistically. On April 23, 1934, the patrol recruits reported to Fort Defiance for a week of training under Louis C. Mueller, director of law enforcement in the Indian Service. Only five patrolmen could speak English, so an interpreter translated Mueller's instruction into Navajo. Later

2. "Minutes of the Navajo Tribal Council Held at Crownpoint, New Mexico," 9–11 April 1934, LAFRC, Box 72907, pp. 1–48, 60a–63.

the mounted patrol was placed under Forrest Parker, who had had charge of the CCC since 1933.[3] After several initial successes, problems developed with the mounted patrol. One lieutenant was discharged for being drunk on duty, and Thomas Dodge and Parker completely reorganized the force in late 1934.[4] It existed for another year only to be incorporated into a new tribal police unit in 1936.

By the adjournment of the Crownpoint council, government activities among the Navajos were greater than in 1933, especially in reshaping reservation administration. The new central headquarters, which had been presented and accepted during the October 1933 council session, began to take shape in 1934. Considerable rivalry developed between the towns along the southern border of the reservation to gain the site of the tribal headquarters. Holbrook, Winslow, Chambers, and Gallup vied with each other in a classical campaign of letter writing, pressure politics, and small town boosterism. The stakes involved were high. Any of the border towns blessed with the new agency could expect a huge increase in trade from government workers and Indian visitors, greater wholesale and retail sales to reservation inhabitants, and increased freighting opportunities. Based on their letters, the competing towns seemed unaware that Collier might locate the headquarters on the reservation.[5]

After inspecting several prospective sites with a committee of Indians, Collier located the tribal headquarters at Window Rock. It was five or six miles south of Fort Defiance, the historic center of Navajo administration, and twenty-five miles northwest of Gallup. The location was highly scenic with huge reddish sandstone formations surrounding the area. A few hundred yards north of the future sites of the council house and the main administrative building stood the impressive and high natural stone bridge which gave the headquarters its name. What factors beside a beautiful setting prompted the location are unclear. Very likely Collier sought to please the Dodges by locating near their home territory. He may also have anticipated the passage of the New Mexico boundary bill which would have extended the reservation eastward and placed Window Rock close to the center of the Navajo population.

3. *Santa Fe New Mexican*, 23 April 1934, p. 6, and 19 May 1934, p. 3.

4. *Gallup Independent*, 21 December 1934, p. 1.

5. See Lloyd C. Henning to Isabella Greenway, 15 June 1934 and other correspondence of same period in Isabella Greenway papers, AHS.

Whatever the reasons, the Window Rock location aroused white criticism for several months. Residents of the other border towns complained that Gallup would obtain most of the trade from the new headquarters. Morgan's group and white missionaries believed that the proximity to Gallup exposed many Navajos to that city's vice activities, especially in 1934 and 1935 while Window Rock was being built.

To William H. Zeh, the veteran Indian Service forester, fell the unenviable task of consolidating the old six jurisdictions into a central headquarters. Named as "Acting Administrator" on May 24, 1934, Zeh did not relinquish his previous post at Albuquerque as director of forestry for the Southwestern Indian reservations but assumed control over Navajo affairs on a part-time basis from offices in Gallup. His first task was to coordinate several programs—CCC, roads, irrigation, building and day school construction, forestry, and soil erosion—which were already largely operating on a reservation-wide basis. Collier ordered the six superintendents to forward all correspondence dealing with these programs through Zeh instead of directly to the Washington office. The orders outlining Zeh's duties stated: "It will be your place to see that these separate plans of various services are consistent with the general single all-Navajo program."[6] The commissioner also placed Zeh in control of new health and education programs.

Soon after his appointment, Zeh met with the superintendents, Soil Erosion Service officials, CCC leaders, and several Indians at Mexican Springs. His statement that the meeting "was to clear up some misunderstandings and to create a more desirable spirit between units," very likely meant that regular Indian Service workers and SES personnel were involved in one of their many disagreements.[7] Zeh's next action was to move all major officials in charge of emergency programs into Gallup. Somewhat later in 1934 the superintendents were also transferred to that city.

Maintaining their hostility, by mid-July 1934 the Morgan faction in the tribal council was opposing Collier openly. Even before the session of Keams Canyon, some council members were threatening

6. Collier to Zeh, and Collier to all Navajo Superintendents. . ., 23 May 1934, Office File of Commissioner John Collier, NA, RG 75.

7. Zeh to Collier, 13 June 1934, Central Classified Files, File 30153, 1934, 800, NA, RG 75.

a revolt against the impending stock reduction.[8] The real explosion at the council meeting came when Morgan and Collier clashed over the new day school program. The commissioner informed the council that recent fund cuts in operating expenses for education had jeopardized the day schools planned for the reservation. To avoid this, he suggested that the boarding schools at Tohatchi and Chinle be converted into day schools. Although only two of ten boarding schools would be affected, most delegates objected to the commissioner's proposal. They viewed the boarding schools as an affirmed success, while the day school program remained unproven.

Morgan particularly interpreted the closing of the boarding schools as a major threat. A product of the boarding system himself and intensely proud of being a graduate of Hampton Institute, Morgan supported a formal and disciplined education which removed students from their homes and schooled them like white students. Addressing the commissioner directly, he charged that "when you speak about closing the boarding schools, you are simply slapping the boys and girls in the face because that is where they get their start. If it was not for the boarding schools, we would not have been here today." Morgan continued by condemning the day school program because it meant returning the children home to the filth, ignorance, and disease of the parents' hogans each night. He told of visiting one day school personally and hearing the teacher tell the children to do what they pleased during the last half hour of the day. "They began to sing and holler and pretty soon they had a Yae-be-chai and Squaw Dance going on." The idea of pagan chants in schools was horrifying and counter to everything the zealous Morgan sought in education.

Collier's response to the Morgan outburst avoided recriminations, but the attack clearly irritated him. The commissioner replied that boarding schools presently educated only a small portion of Indian children and also failed to prepare Indian youngsters to assume life in white society. Collier estimated that nine out of ten graduates "returned to the home life in the old way." Morgan's assertions about Navajo homes being hazardous to health were true, Collier admitted, but he maintained that "we intend to develop the day schools in such a way that they will help meet that problem in a way that boarding schools never can do." Despite his defense, the council delegates' support for boarding schools forced Collier to compro-

8. *Albuquerque Journal*, 13 July 1934, p. 7.

mise.[9] He announced later that the school at Chinle would become a combination day and boarding school but Tohatchi would be entirely a day school.[10]

The threatened revolt over the impending reduction of goats never occurred. Perhaps the delegates were relieved by Collier's announcement that no reimbursible loan would be necessary because he had secured funds from the Drought Relief Program. His new proposal for the much-discussed reduction called for the purchase of 150,000 goats and up to 50,000 sheep. Officials had prepared a contract for the council which specified that the goat sale was binding on the tribe, while disposing of the sheep was voluntary. Otherwise, the terms for the reduction remained the same as previously agreed to.

The delegates responded to the new plan with many of the same objections heard at earlier councils. Becenti Bega, the Eastern Navajo delegate, reminded Collier that he had promised to secure boundary legislation in New Mexico and Arizona, but only a bill for the latter had passed.[11] Would it not be possible, Bega inquired, for the Navajos to sell just half their quota of goats and put the other half of the federal grant in savings for some future project? Without going into the intricacies of federal budgeting, Collier quashed Bega's proposal by asserting categorically that the New Mexico boundary bill would pass in the next session of Congress. After prolonged discussion, the council unanimously approved the goat reduction once again.[12]

The council session at Keams Canyon increased Collier's difficulties with Morgan and his faction. Earlier Morgan had been evasive, but the confrontation at Keams Canyon had been very direct and hostile. The differences which separated Collier and Morgan, as before, were related to each's conception of the handling of Indian affairs. However, Morgan's objections won little sympathy from the mass of Navajos. Most tribesmen, it seems clear, reacted to Collier and his programs on totally materialistic grounds. They cared little about the abstract question of assimilation versus cultural pluralism. Instead, they worried about whether Collier would allow them to

9. "Minutes of the Meeting of the Navajo Tribal Council," Keams Canyon, Arizona 10–12 July 1934, LAFRC, Box 72907, pp. 27–40.

10. The changes Collier proposed for Tohatchi and Chinle were temporary, if effected at all, and both schools remained basically boarding institutions. Thompson Interview.

11. Congress, in the session just concluded, had passed the Arizona boundary bill, but the counterpart for New Mexico had been trapped in the House.

12. "Council Minutes," 10–12 July 1934, pp. 66–86.

keep their sheep and goats, whether they could obtain relief jobs, and whether their children would be fed, clothed, and housed nine months of the year in government boarding schools. Morgan needed to use tribal disgruntlement over these issues before he could effectively arouse the Navajos against Collier.

The government provided powerful support for Morgan's cause by its conduct during the second herd reduction in the late summer of 1934. Indeed, no single event of the troubled New Deal era so deeply and completely antagonized the tribe against Collier as the second livestock sale. The entire episode revived old but still vivid memories of Carson's campaign and the horrors of Bosque Redondo. Like these earlier traumas, the second herd reduction bred a fear and anguish which lasted for decades. Indeed, the New Deal still conjures up a tangled image to Navajos of goats being shot and wastefully allowed to rot, of government workers taking away stock from already destitute families, and of tribesmen starving because their herds were too small to provide sustenance during the harsh winters. Older Navajos for years afterward recalled mournfully how Collier wrecked the livestock industry and spoke of him as a devil who cruelly took away their livelihood. The Navajos' intense resentments may have invariably mingled elements of exaggeration and distortion with what really happened but, nevertheless, their fears and hatreds were no less real and powerful.

The actual reduction program in 1934 differed little from that of the previous year. Collier experienced delays in getting the funds released after the council's approval in July, but he notified local administrators to begin the purchases in mid-September when he received a grant of $250,000. His orders to field workers stipulated that the Navajo herders must be paid one dollar per head for their goats and two dollars for sheep.[13] Quotas for each type of livestock were assigned to the six agencies.[14] The government designated sales

13. Collier to Keith Southard, 20 September 1934, LAFRC, Box 33551.
14. A. C. Cooley, "The Navajo Sheep and Goat Purchases," *Indians at Work* 2 (1 October 1934): 13. This article breaks down the quotas as follows:

|                   | Goats  | Sheep  |
| ----------------- | ------ | ------ |
| Northern Navajo   | 32,000 | 10,000 |
| Eastern Navajo    | 27,000 | 7,000  |
| Southern Navajo   | 51,000 | 15,000 |
| Western Navajo    | 20,000 | 8,000  |
| Hopi              | 13,000 | 6,500  |
| Leupp             | 6,000  | 3,500  |

points throughout the reservation and field men started the purchases later in September. Actual sales came close to achieving the quotas assigned to each agency as the government purchased approximately 50,000 sheep and 148,300 goats.[15]

Conditions on the reservation, however, were far less conducive for the reduction in 1934 than in the previous year. Wage work and the first livestock sale had somewhat revived the Navajo economy and destitution no longer helped offset potential resistance. The large herd owners again resisted a graduated reduction and demanded that everyone give up an equal share of livestock. Despite government assurances that herds of under 100 would not be affected, most officials in carrying out the purchases did not interfere with wealthy Navajos' pressures on small owners but allowed the Indians to decide the matter among themselves so long as they met the quotas assigned. Once again the small owners' deference caused them to cave in to the persuasions of the wealthy. If the small herder retained enough animals to support his family or if he had a government job, the loss of the livestock was more of a psychological blow than a material loss. But some Indians sold sheep and goats that were needed to feed themselves and reduction struck at their only livelihood.

The question of whether the government used force in the second reduction remains controversial to this day. Officials emphatically maintained that the sales were always "legitimate," both before and after 1934, because the tribal council approved each reduction program. They argued also that reduction was always voluntary, at least in the sense that no force was ever used by field workers in the actual collection of livestock.[16] Such a contention seems questionable. Contrary to Collier's orders, some officials very likely did use force, or something close to it, to secure the livestock. This seems particularly true among the Eastern Navajos where government personnel viewed reduction as the price that the Indians must pay for obtaining the New Mexico boundary bill.[17]

Even if coercion was not used, government field workers tended to

15. "A Comparison of Government Reduction on the Eastern Jurisdiction with the Reservation. . .," n.d., Indians-Navajo file, AHS.

16. Fryer Interview, 1970.

17. Richard Van Valkenburgh, "Report of Survey Made of Destitute Navajo Indians outside Proposed New Mexico Boundary Extension," Van Valkenburgh papers, AHS; Phelps-Stokes Fund, *The Navajo Indian Problem* (New York, 1939), p. 9.

conduct the reduction in a brusque manner. Assigned to meet a
quota and busy with the work of counting and penning livestock at
the sales points, the harried officials took little time to justify the
reduction to each herd owner. When a Navajo objected to selling,
the government workers found it much easier to say, "you have to
reduce because John Collier says you have to."[18] This saved not only
a long and futile argument, but it neatly transferred the responsibility onto Collier. Such statements may very well be an important
reason why the commissioner's name became almost a swear word
among the Navajos.

Even the weather played a role in making the second herd reduction a traumatic event. The entire Southwest in 1934 was caught
in one of the worst droughts in history. Newspapers throughout the
summer reported that lack of rainfall and record high temperatures
had burned up the ranges and forced white ranchers to sell their
stock to the government.[19] Because of the dust bowl conditions, many
of the Navajo sheep and goats were too weak to make the long drives
to the shipping points. Recognizing this, government workers
allowed Navajos at the sales stations to butcher many animals before driving the remainder to market.

Undoubtedly many of the sheep and goats died during the drives,
but the Navajos were totally incensed by the wanton mass killing of
goats by the government. Despite the many reports of these, the only
incident of a slaughter of goats which the writer has been able to
document with certainty occurred at Jones Canyon. Carl Beck, a
government stockman, purchased a herd of sheep and goats at
Navajo Mountain in the extreme northwestern edge of the reservation. Beck then herded the animals south over one of the most scenic
but rugged parts of the reservation. When he reached the Inscription
House trading post, twenty-five miles from Navajo Mountain, Beck
decided that the animals would never survive the additional drive of
forty-five miles on to Tuba City where trucks waited to haul them to
a railroad station. Beck took the herd to nearby Jones Canyon and
ordered them shot.[20] The Jones Canyon incident, and possibly a

18. Wagner Interview.

19. *Santa Fe New Mexican*, 7 August 1934, p. 6, and 22 August 1934, p. 5; *Gallup Independent*, 3 August 1934, p. 1.

20. Fryer Interview, 1970. Navajos whom I questioned about the mass slaughters were
sure that several killings occurred but were vague as to time and place, often confusing the
goat slaughters with horses shot in an earlier campaign to eliminate dourine.

few other mass slaughters, did not typify the second reduction or those which came later, but the Navajos, nevertheless, firmly believed that they did.

The massive antagonism toward the second herd reduction was based on the complex and profound attachment Navajos held for their sheep and goats. Glimmers of their thinking were apparent from the older council members' repeated remarks equating their attachment for livestock to whites' lust for money, but Collier, despite his sympathy for Navajo culture, did not fully comprehend how deeply the tribe felt about the subject. Equally remarkable, he never commissioned a study on the subject, although he subsidized several investigations of other cultural topics. A careful analysis of Navajo attitudes toward their animals would not have produced an instant solution, but it might have averted some of the problems, and it certainly would have guided New Deal efforts at livestock regulation and range management along somewhat different lines. Unfortunately, only in recent years have anthropologists clarified the important relationships between livestock and the Navajos' central social and religious concepts.

Despite their suspicion of persons who have acquired wealth too quickly, Navajos largely determine social status by the amount of stock a family owns. Thus Chee Dodge was venerated only in part because of his past experience and ability to deal with federal officials. He and other prominent leaders were additionally respected because they possessed horses, sheep, jewelry, and blankets. In fact, the Navajos' economic concepts came amazingly close to approximating the puritan work ethic of whites. James F. Downs, an anthropologist, found in his interviews that "families will tell with pride how their immediate ancestors began life with only a few sheep but increased the herd through perseverance, the proper exercise of ritual power, and right living."[21] With refreshing directness and honesty that many whites might well emulate, the Navajos integrated their hopes for prosperity into their religion. The man who entered the sweat lodge for personal purification also used this religious activity to sing for the increase of his herds and even success in a future horse race.

In addition to these attitudes, Navajos have traditionally in-

21. James F. Downs, *Animal Husbandry in Navajo Society and Culture* (Berkeley, 1964), pp. 92–99.

tegrated their livestock into their family life. Prior to New Deal livestock regulations, Navajo parents customarily set aside part of the increase of their herds for their children as patrimony when they married. With all members sharing ownership, the herd became a focal point for the entire extended family. Each day the flock was driven out of the pen near the hogan and herded by youngsters under the careful supervision of adults. Even the grand matron of the family might herd, either trudging behind the sheep and goats with a staff and rattling a tin can filled with pebbles, or, in a more regal manner, astride a horse. Lambing, shearing, castrating, and moving the herd to new pastures united the family, and members normally absent because of outside work or marriage appeared to help on such occasions. Women of the family emerged from their hogans in the early evenings, even in bad weather, and congregated around the stock pen to gossip, joke, and laugh in a "time of relaxation and gratification," as they awaited the return of the herd.[22]

The fact that the second sales program concentrated on goats which had little or no market value did not lessen the Navajos' objections. Even though traders seldom purchased goats, small herders liked the ignoble animals for that very reason. If a family became too indebted at the local trading post, the operator might confiscate their sheep, but he would be unlikely to take away their goats. A mixed herd therefore served the dual function of providing a marketable commodity during periods of prosperity and a guaranteed meat supply during hard times.

Perhaps no other cultural disparity so widely divided whites from Navajos as the subject of livestock. Whites express affection for domesticated animals through a sentimental kindness, but Navajos frequently vent pent up emotions by mistreating their livestock and pets, even beating them to death in a blind rage. Yet Navajos value their livestock in a way that few whites can understand. When Anglo-American ranchers agitated to sell their cattle and sheep to the federal drought relief programs in 1934, they no doubt regretted the loss, but their main concern was to avoid the social stigma of bankruptcy and to retain possession of their land.[23] Operating without individual ownership of land and having no strong taboo against

22. Ibid., pp. 91–92.
23. Resolution of the New Mexico Wool Growers Association, 24 August 1934, Chavez papers, UA.

financial insolvency, the Navajos still sensed that herd reduction would disrupt the very fabric of their existence, threaten some of their most central social and religious values, and raise questions for the future that federal wages could not answer. To the Indians, the sight of their stock being butchered at the gathering pens during the second reduction and the reports of wanton slaughters of goats, whether true or not, was a sickening experience. They would adamantly oppose all future reductions with an intensity which often approached violent rebellion.

Even though the second herd reduction provided strong support for Morgan's campaign against Collier, he was slow to grasp the opportunity. Instead, his attack against the government in 1934 and 1935 centered on the day school program and the Wheeler-Howard Act. The latter measure, having been passed by Congress in June 1934, still had to be approved by a tribal referendum before the Navajos would come under its provisions. The controversy over the Wheeler-Howard Act was a nagging affair which kept both red and white inhabitants of the reservation aroused for many months.

Resentment of white traders and their strong influence over Navajo opinion was critical for the tribe's acceptance or rejection of the Wheeler-Howard referendum. Continually irked by the government's failure to assist in debt collection, the traders shared the Navajos' fears that herd reduction would devastate the reservation economy, resulting in sharply reduced sales at the trading posts. The traders' greatest concern with the bill, however, involved the issue of Indian self-rule. From the first discussion of the Wheeler-Howard bill, the traders feared that the council might banish them from the reservation or take over the trading posts and operate them as cooperatives selling goods furnished by the government. Such action would not only ruin the traders, but would cripple the large wholesalers in the border towns who supplied the posts with goods and marketed their rugs and jewelry.[24]

Collier moved quickly to quiet the traders' fears. Two weeks after the close of the Fort Defiance Council, James M. Stewart met with members of the United Indian Traders Association to assure them of their continuation on the reservation. Stewart stressed that self-

24. Clarence Iden to Dennis Chavez, 22 March 1934, Chavez papers, UA. Iden was president of Gross, Kelly & Co. of Las Vegas, New Mexico, a wholesale firm which had a branch in Gallup.

government would not immediately take place among the Navajos and repeatedly promised that no tribe would be fully ready to assume its own direction for at least a decade. Reminding the traders that government programs had benefitted them as well as the Navajos, Stewart asked for the white group's support in implementing Collier's plans.[25] His plea failed to overcome the traders' hostility or to enlist their support for the passage of the Wheeler-Howard Act.

At their own meeting later in March, the United Indian Traders Association still expressed alarm that they might be expelled from the reservation. The group wanted the legislation amended to include specific causes for which a post operator could be ousted and to guarantee that the government would not locate cooperatives in their midst.[26] Meeting during the Crownpoint council on April 9, the traders again unanimously opposed the Wheeler-Howard bill.[27]

Despite this vote, the post operators' tenuous position on the reservation allowed few of them to fight openly against the government during the referendum campaign. Licensed by the Indian Service and unable to own the land on which their posts stood, no trader could afford to jeopardize his investment and future earnings by openly opposing Collier's brainchild, but many covertly influenced Navajos to oppose the legislation. Such undercover resistance proved harmful, for the government badly needed the active support of this influential group.

The attitude of the missionaries toward the Wheeler-Howard Act was mixed. The Catholics accepted self-government with few questions. One priest, Father Berard Haile, viewed Collier's general policies as the long-awaited realization of his own dreams for a centralized administration and a revival of tribal unity. A very strong supporter of Chee Dodge and the traditionalists, Haile especially welcomed the creation of a council which would reflect the sentiment of Navajos at large.[28] Presumably other Francisians encouraged Navajo converts to accept the Wheeler-Howard Act, but their number was very small.[29]

25. "Notes on Meeting of Indian Traders at Fort Defiance, March 21, 1934," LAFRC, Box 72941.

26. United Indian Traders Association to Collier, 3 April 1934, Isabella Greenway papers, AHS.

27. P. J. Moran to Greenway, 17 April 1934, Isabella Greenway papers, AHS.

28. Father Berard Haile to Collier, 2 February 1934, Haile papers, UAL.

29. Collier to Haile, 1 May 1934, Haile papers, UAL.

Among the major Protestant denominations, sentiment for the Collier legislation ranged from strong misgivings to open antagonism, with a decided tendency toward the latter. Baptist, Presbyterian, and Christian Reformed Church missionaries serving on the Navajo and Hopi reservations met in March 1934 and denounced the Wheeler-Howard bill. One of their resolutions stated that the "Indian must be saved by a process of Christian assimilation into American life, not by carefully guarded and subsidized segregation."[30]

Of the three denominations, the Christian Reformed Church displayed the strongest opposition to the Wheeler-Howard legislation both before and after its passage. Christian Reformed missionaries became almost paranoid with the fear that self-government might be used to ban them from the reservation. They were also dismayed by the possibility that the despised medicine men might be invited into the new day schools to teach students the religious traditions of their tribe.[31] Reverend L. P. Brink, Morgan's employer at Farmington, in a church magazine requested that members at large write their congressman and "ask that the Wheeler-Howard Bill, which was rushed through in the last moments of the last session, be repealed" and "protest against John Collier being continued in office as Commissioner of Indian Affairs and the whole bunch of radicals that are in cahoots with him."[32]

Once the Wheeler-Howard Act passed, Morgan was highly instrumental in achieving its rejection by a tribal referendum. Although Brink spoke some Navajo, his assistant was the only Protestant missionary with the linguistic and oratorical skills to wage a campaign against the legislation. By late 1934 Morgan had become vehement in his criticisms of Collier and the Wheeler-Howard Act. His repugnance for Navajo traditions at times even exceeded that of the white missionaries. "The traditional stories are bad, in fact some of them are rotten to the core," Morgan wrote in a church publication in late 1934. In the same article, he charged that medicine men were shysters and quacks who thwarted progress among his people.[33]

Morgan zealously applied his ideals about assimilation to his own

30. *Santa Fe New Mexican*, 26 March 1934, p. 1.

31. R. H. Pousma, "Rehoboth Jottings," *The Banner* 69 (27 April 1934): 380; William Goudberg, "Alarm Felt about a Bill Now before Congress," *The Banner* 69 (11 May 1934): 429.

32. L. P. Brink, "By Way of Introduction," *The Banner* 69 (21 December 1934): 1116.

33. J. C. Morgan, "A Voice from an Indian," *The Banner* 69 (21 December 1934): 1117.

life and he took an enormous pride in being a "whitened" and successful Indian. Trained in carpentry at Hampton Institute, Morgan held several jobs before entering the Indian Service in 1914 where he enjoyed a successful career as a shop instructor and band leader at the Crownpoint and San Juan (Shiprock) boarding schools. After becoming Brink's assistant in 1925, he advanced very quickly through his work in preaching, translating religious materials, and teaching Christianity to school children. The church placed him on important mission boards, allowed him to take charge of the mission at Farmington when Brink's frequent illnesses forced him into inactivity, gave him a car and mileage expenses, and paid him a salary commensurate with white missionaries.

Morgan's attire and public behavior bespoke his dedication to assimilation even more strongly than his career. Unlike many educated tribesmen, Morgan never wore Navajo clothing or jewelry, but he always dressed in a well-tailored suit and a white shirt and tie. He invariably carried a briefcase, perhaps to remind onlookers of his importance in tribal and church affairs. Morgan saw to it that his three sons attended white schools at Farmington and he took enormous pride in their successful completion of high school. As Morgan viewed his own life, he had been rescued from the primitive ignorance of Navajo camp life by the government and he had succeeded in life because of education, living among whites, and conversion to Christianity.[34] With the fullest dedication, he was determined to see that other Navajos had the same opportunity by his defeating of Collier and the referendum for the Wheeler-Howard Act.

After passage of the Wheeler-Howard Act in June 1934, Morgan began to expand his political activities beyond the reservation. In late August 1934, he attended the organizational meeting of the American Indian Federation in Gallup. The group drafted a constitution and elected Joseph Bruner, a Creek of Sapulpa, Oklahoma, as president. Bruner, who claimed the spurious title "Principal Chief of the Five Civilized Tribes," had already become a foe of Collier's while the Wheeler-Howard bill was still in Congress. His organization subsequently became a rallying point for the commissioner's most rabid enemies and its propaganda blended super patriotism, fundamentalist Christianity, and Ku Klux Klan attitudes. The

34. See the author's "J. C. Morgan: Navajo Apostle of Assimilation," *Prologue: The Journal of the National Archives*, 4 (Summer 1972): 83–89.

group reportedly developed friendly ties with the German-American Bund and anti-Semitic groups. Scurrilous attacks in the organization's newsletters during the 1930s pictured Collier as a communist whose policies were masterminded by foreigners. Although friendly toward assimilation, the Federation's propaganda sometimes advocated the abolition of the Indian Bureau and the release of Indians from its dictatorial control.[35]

The Gallup convention elected Morgan "First National Vice Chairman" for a two-year term. With what may have been false modesty, Morgan said that he "tried to decline the election because there are hundreds of men and women of the Indian race capable of such [a] position that should be elected, but the pressure was so great that I had to accept." He expansively predicted that the Federation would go down in "the history of the Indians as one of the great events."[36] Although Morgan attended the group's second convention in San Diego in 1935,[37] his involvement afterward lessened for some reason. Possibly he disagreed with the Federation's extreme right-wing stance, but he may have learned that Bruner and some other leaders were peyotists, a subject completely revolting to Morgan.[38]

Morgan's campaign against the Wheeler-Howard Act was an uphill struggle. He later claimed that he had only $142 to wage the battle and that only two other Navajo leaders, Howard Gorman and Robert Martin, assisted him. Despite these handicaps, Morgan's efforts proved very successful. He started his agitation well before the government began its own operations and used his potent oratorical skills at numerous chapter meetings and gatherings around Shiprock and Crownpoint during late 1934 and early 1935. He also penned several articles critical of the legislation in the *Farmington Times Hustler*. His messages were a stronger version of views he had expressed before in the council. Unless Navajos rejected the Wheeler-Howard Act, he warned his audiences, they would find themselves barred from future progress and turned into a side-show attraction

35. The writer has never located a complete file of the news-letters issued by the Federation. Scattered copies can be found in the National Archives and in the Chavez papers.

36. *Farmington Times Hustler*, 7 September 1934, p. 4.

37. Ibid., 26 July 1935, p. 1.

38. Hazel W. Hertzberg, *The Search for an American Indian Identity, Modern Pan-Indian Movements* (Syracuse, 1971), pp. 47, 280, 289.

and human zoo for the delight of easterners, tourists, and anthropologists. He emphatically condemned Navajos who supported the Wheeler-Howard Act, claiming that they had been duped into joining Collier's "monkey show" by accepting favors from the government. The effect of what he considered unconstitutional legislation would be to place the Navajos in a permanent status of inferiority.

Twice Morgan interrupted his campaign against the Wheeler-Howard Act to visit Washington during February 1935. On his first appearance he joined other representatives of the American Indian Federation who met informally in the Senate Office Building with western congressional delegations to complain about New Deal Indian policies. The Federation very likely wanted the Wheeler-Howard Act repealed, but delegates chiefly objected to the Bureau's interpretation that a majority of the eligible voters, rather than a majority of those voting, had to cast ballots against the Wheeler-Howard Act before it was defeated in tribal referenda.[39] Morgan probably used this opportunity to urge the Arizona and New Mexico congressional delegations to plead for the discontinuation of the Navajo central administration and the restoration of the old six agencies. Later that same month he returned to testify before the Senate Indian Affairs Committee on the matter of redefining the criterion for what constituted a majority vote.[40] Congress amended the Wheeler-Howard Act to meet the Federation's complaints and a simple majority of those voting applied when the Navajos later decided on the measure.[41]

The government inaugurated its own campaign in support of the Wheeler-Howard Act in late February at a conference of field workers, missionaries, and traders held at Fort Wingate. Zeh's purpose in calling the group together was to counter "misinformation and misunderstanding" before the vote that was set for March 29 and 30.[42] Translated into more realistic terms, his statement meant that official optimism about the success of the upcoming vote had diminished, for Morgan had already won many Navajos over to his side.

The acting administrator's chief ploy for reversing the trend against the government was to recapture the support of the traders.

39. *Farmington Times Hustler*, 1 February 1935, pp. 1, 4.
40. Ibid., 15 February 1935, p. 1.
41. U. S., *Statutes at Large*, 99, pt. 1: 378.
42. *Gallup Independent*, 26 February 1935, p. 2.

This he tried to achieve by changing the official policy toward debt collection. A new order, released about the time of the Fort Wingate conference, allowed traders to revive procedures resembling those employed when the CCC first started operations in 1933. Project foremen of the various work programs were to issue forms to each Navajo laborer stipulating that his check would be sent to the post where he had credit. The trader could then take seventy-five percent of the check for past debts or new trade and the remainder had to be placed in a savings account maintained by the Indian Service.[43] Whether this policy was ever carried out is doubtful. If it was, there is no evidence that traders en masse suddenly endorsed the Wheeler-Howard Act.

Zeh also tried to win the support of Chee Dodge during the Wheeler-Howard campaign. Despite the old leader's outspoken support for the measure earlier, Dodge's relationship to Collier was always a somewhat fitful affair with periods of disenchantment followed by reconciliations. Unfortunately for the government, Chee had settled into one of his crotchety moods in early 1935. In a confidential memo to Collier, Zeh suggested that the old gentleman was becoming childish and had been offended by some slight by the commissioner at the last council. Chee needed a bit of cajoling, perhaps by a trip to Washington, to bring him out in support of the Wheeler-Howard Act.[44]

During the first stages of the canvass, Dodge's public silence severely handicapped official efforts to counter Morgan's opposition. Even the trip to Washington prescribed by Zeh did not change Chee's position. Indeed the elder statesman in May reputedly threatened to disinherit Thomas Dodge if he continued to support the Wheeler-Howard Act.[45]

Most Navajos were too confused by the campaign and recent events to reach a deliberate and rational decision on the Wheeler-Howard Act. The legislation had been modified many times since Collier first outlined its original provisions to the council in 1934. Even in a simplified final version, government spokesman faced a

43. M. L. Woodward to United Indian Traders Association, 6 March 1935, Isabella Greenway papers, AHS.

44. Zeh to Collier, 26 March 1935, Office File of Commissioner John Collier, NA, RG 75.

45. Sally Lucas Jean to Collier, 8 May 1935, Collier papers, YU.

difficult and complex task in explaining the legislation to the Indians. The Navajos had to reach a conclusion based on oral translations of government officials' speeches. To an illiterate people unaccustomed to decision-making and worried by Morgan's irresponsible charges, the government meetings probably contributed to greater confusion than understanding. In addition, the way of life of the reservation since the start of the New Deal had been shaken by an unending series of charges, promises, and reversals of plans. A community might be granted a day school at one time and then suddenly officials would cancel construction for some reason. Collier had promised that the centralized headquarters would be accompanied by more substantial government services from the subagencies, but the new installations were still incomplete and no district officials had been appointed by 1935. In the meantime, the Navajos had lost their old six agencies and familiar government personnel had been transferred off the reservation or to the Gallup offices.

Even the tribal council, which never possessed grass roots ties with constituents, had seemingly been eliminated. Having met six times in one year, the government seemed to lose interest in calling a session after Keams Canyon in July 1934. Newspaper reports the following December spoke vaguely of council committee meetings and discussions of tribal affairs in Gallup, but it was never clear what actions were taken at the meetings or if the decisions were binding. Apparently Collier and Thomas Dodge felt that council meetings had become too chaotic and a committee structure would be more workable. The council did not meet even in regular session in 1935. The fate of the chapters was little better. Lack of government support for the local organizations caused many to wither with inactivity.[46] Those which remained viable soon became forums where Morgan agitated against the Wheeler-Howard Act.

The trend against a favorable referendum could not be entirely blamed on government officials' failure to act. Following the Fort Wingate conference in February, Zeh and a team of local and Washington officials staged large meetings at Fort Defiance, Shiprock, Crownpoint, Leupp, Keams Canyon, and Tuba City to explain the legislation. Chairman Thomas Dodge and most of the council delegates attended. From all appearances, Zeh adherred to Collier's admonition that no pressure, only explanation, be used at these

46. See Elizabeth Pablo to Window Rock, 12 January 1936, LAFRC, Box 33557.

meetings. Despite Morgan's charges that the government stiffled or bribed opponents, he attended some rallies and may have spoken.[47] At the close of the six big sessions in mid-March, groups of government workers prepared to stage smaller meetings, but Ickes suddenly postponed the voting dates from March 29 and 30 to May 30 and June 1. Zeh told reporters that Southern Navajo leaders had requested the delay because bad weather and impassible roads made it impossible to meet local Indian groups.[48] In reality, the government wanted more time to counter what one official privately admitted was "the present swing away from the Wheeler-Howard Act."[49] Some time later the date of the vote was again reset for mid-June.

As the referendum time drew near, the government mounted an all-out drive to win a majority for the Wheeler-Howard Act. Government spokesmen met Indians at chapter houses and trading posts throughout the Navajo country. Walter Woehlke, Collier's field representative, came from Washington to take charge of the campaign and other top officials appeared to assist. The government's hopes seemed to receive a major boost when Chester E. Faris, newly appointed general superintendent, coaxed Chee Dodge into supporting the Wheeler-Howard Act and the two left immediately on a three-week speaking tour of the reservation.[50]

Chee's support was largely offset by questions aroused by his sudden change of heart and a rumor that the government had bribed him with $50,000. The charge was false and circumstantial evidence indicates that the main reason for Chee's reversal was his son's appointment as an assistant to Faris. Nevertheless, Morgan followers were altogether ready to believe much worse things of anyone who supported the hated Wheeler-Howard Act.[51]

A week before the vote, Collier flew west for a last-minute appeal to the Navajos. The commissioner met with the council informally at Fort Wingate on June 10 and reemphasized that adoption of the Wheeler-Howard Act guaranteed their land would never be allotted. Tempers became heated when Leo Parker, a young educated council

47. *Gallup Independent*, 26 February 1935, p. 2, and 9 March 1935, p. 1.

48. Ibid., 16 March 1935, p. 1.

49. W. V. Woehlke, "Memorandum on Navajo Problems," 27 March 1935, Office File of Commissioner John Collier, NA, RG 75.

50. Woehlke to Collier, 22 May 1935, Collier papers, YU.

51. Matthew K. Sniffen to J. M. Steere, 19 August 1935, Isabella Greenway papers, AHS.

member from Manuelito, bluntly interrupted Faris' speech to the council and demanded that the Indians be allowed to express their views. Parker went on to charge, among other things, that fellow councilman Henry Taliman had told the Navajos they would lose the New Mexican boundary extension and all government jobs unless they voted for the Wheeler-Howard Act. Denials by Collier and delegates' protests against Parker's rudeness failed to stop him from continued heckling.[52] The following day, Howard Gorman denounced Collier as a communist at a meeting of some 1,000 people at Fort Defiance. Collier flared back that Gorman had let his religious beliefs prejudice his thinking.[53] Morgan continued his own rallies against Collier in the Shiprock and the Crownpoint areas. By election day, the excitable Morgan had convinced himself that the government had, through the traders, bribed Navajos with money or goods to vote for the act.[54]

On June 14 and 15, the Navajos left their hogans and traveled to polling stations where they participated in their first general tribal vote. It was also their initial experience with secret paper ballots. An "X" mark with an indelible pencil signified approval of the Wheeler-Howard Act, while an "O" meant rejection. The Navajos' proclivity for graphic description led them immediately to tab the event as the "circle and cross election." The vote of 7,679 for the Wheeler-Howard Act and 8,197 against, a loss by 518 votes, was a narrow but shocking repudiation of Collier's administration. The defeat evidently was also unexpected as the commissioner had confidently stated two days earlier that the government campaign had reversed the trend against the act and he predicted approval by a wide margin.[55]

Even the most cursory examination of the voting patterns indicates that Morgan had been tremendously effective in his meetings during the previous six months. The only areas which strongly supported the government were the Leupp and Keams Canyon districts with favorable votes of 701 to 74 and 1,322 to 63 respectively. The Western Navajo with a vote of 872 to 472 and the Southern Navajo with 3,276 to 2,291 both supported the referendum, but by more slender margins. The Eastern Navajos cast 1,904 votes against to 1,115 for.

52. *Gallup Independent*, 11 June 1935, pp. 1, 4.
53. *Santa Fe New Mexican*, 12 June 1935, p. 1.
54. Morgan to L. T. Eugene Ness, 14 June 1935, Isabella Greenway papers, AHS.
55. *Santa Fe New Mexican*, 12 June 1935, p. 1.

Morgan's own northeast corner of the reservation proved decisive, rejecting the Wheeler-Howard Act by a vote of 2,773 to 536.[56]

The main reason for the government's defeat was not Morgan but the left-over feeling against the second herd reduction. The sight of the diminished herd coming out of the family sheep pen each morning constantly reminded many Navajos during the long campaign that the government had threatened their only meaningful livelihood. Perhaps unavoidably, many Indians came to connect the Wheeler-Howard Act with the herd reduction and John Collier. Morgan did not have to play the complete demagogue for Navajos to associate the legislation and livestock sales. He had merely to allude to herd reduction and his aroused audiences reached the desired conclusion spontaneously. Neither did Morgan or fellow spokesmen bother to explain that reduction and the referendum were not directly related questions.

Collier's usual imperturbability faded as he reacted to the Navajos' rejection of his favored ideals. In an open letter to the tribe soon after the referendum, Collier made little effort to conceal his bitterness and disappointment. He expressed the belief that many Navajos who voted against the Wheeler-Howard Act thought that they were keeping the government from taking their sheep and goats. Although not mentioning Morgan by name, the commissioner's bitter condemnation of those who spread falsehoods pointed clearly toward the native missionary. In reviewing the financial benefits of the Wheeler-Howard Act, Collier noted that Navajos had excluded themselves from $993,950 in grants and loans during the fiscal year of 1935. In addition, the tribe had not gained the protection of its natural resources and immunity to allotment of their land.[57]

The widely distributed letter raised editorial eyebrows among even newspapers normally sympathetic to Collier. The *Albuquerque Journal* termed the message "injudicious," especially the reference to the Navajos' loss of funds. Collier's comment tended to confirm the charge that the government used jobs and money as an inducement to win Indian support.[58] Several editorial writers sensed the irony in Collier's position. An expert propagandist and not always tender

56. A full breakdown of the vote among the polling stations is available at St. Michaels Mission.

57. Collier, "A Message to the Navajo People Through the Superintendent, from the Commissioner," 21 June 1935, File 59055, 36, 344, Navajo Part 3, CCC-ID, NA, RG 75.

58. *Albuquerque Journal*, 28 June 1935, p. 8.

critic of the Indian Bureau during his reform career, the commissioner should not complain now about unfair tactics of his opponents.
Citing that Navajos already had "shown more volition and judgment than many white communities could boast," the *Santa Fe New
Mexican* asked that Collier not punish the tribe, but abide by his
promise that the acceptance of the Wheeler-Howard Act was entirely voluntary.[59]

Unfortunately, the government officials continued the controversy
over the Wheeler-Howard referendum for several months. Roman
Hubbell, the pro-government trader, believed the vote had been an
unfair assessment of tribal opinion and he quite likely inspired a
newspaper story soon after the referendum which reported that
Navajos living in Arizona wanted to be brought under the legislation
because they had approved it.[60] With the tribe still in a turmoil,
government spokesmen should have stifled even the hint of any plan
for dividing therese rvation along state lines. Hubbell's proposal
immediately aroused Morgan. In a statement in the newsletter of the
American Indian Federation, he expressed the fear that Collier
would punish the tribe, declare the election results void, and call a
new referendum.[61]

The controversy took on national overtones when Matthew K.
Sniffen, Secretary of the Indian Rights Association, published a
field report in August 1935 after his annual inspection of western
reservations. Like most members of his organization, Sniffen had
long disagreed with Collier's ideas on Indian affairs and wanted the
moderate assimilation approach of the late 1920s continued during
the New Deal. His visit to the Navajo reservation shortly after the
referendum confirmed Sniffen's worst expectations. Denouncing the
"New Dealers" as a "group of super-educated 'freaks' or sentimen-
talists," Sniffen fully agreed with a dissident's comment that the
reservation was "one h—1 of a mess."[62] The Quaker reputation for
kindly expression suffered additional blows when Sniffen detailed his
objections to Collier's programs. The herd reduction, referendum

59. *Santa Fe New Mexican*, 26 June 1935, p. 4.

60. Roman Hubbell to Collier, 16 June 1935, Collier papers, YU; *Gallup Independent*,
17 June 1935, p. 1.

61. Morgan to Bruner, 19 June 1935, open letter in a news-letter of American Indian
Federation, Chavez papers, UA.

62. Matthew K. Sniffen to J. M. Steere, 19 August 1935, Isabella Greenway papers,
AHS.

campaign, day schools, Window Rock headquarters, and law and order each received withering criticism. Sniffen's report was distributed widely to people interested in Indian affairs and published in *Indian Truth*, the association's journal.

The Sniffen blast stimulated Collier to reply with equal force in several strongly worded open letters in October. Beside accusing Sniffen of factual errors, Collier protested that the Quaker writer had fallen victim to the warped views of Bruner, Morgan, and others in the American Indian Federation. These people, Collier warned, had opposed every government effort to rescue Navajo land from destruction by overgrazing and erosion.[63]

Collier's hopes for a resubmission of the Wheeler-Howard Act suffered a decisive setback when the tribal council finally met in late January 1936 at Fort Defiance. The one day session, called at short notice and attended by Collier, dealt with whether Navajos should petition Congress for a new referendum. According to a local paper, the council divided on the question very sharply with Morgan demanding that any Navajo delegation sent to Washington to discuss a new referendum must include an equal number of supporters and opponents of the Wheeler-Howard Act. Morgan used an attack on herd reductions to good advantage in objecting to another vote. This tactic doubtlessly contributed to the council's decision to table a petition for a second referendum.[64] The delegates' action meant the final deathblow to the Wheeler-Howard Act among the Navajos.

The defeat of the Wheeler-Howard Act was more of a temporary blow to Collier's prestige than a permanent barrier to realizing his policy goals for the tribe. By pressure and fiat he could still largely guide Navajo affairs to suit himself. He could juggle future budgets to see that the tribe received funds to offset any losses of money for such purposes as scholarships, revolving loans, and organization of self-government. The commissioner could also reorganize the Navajo council to make it more representative. Collier's main defense of the legislation had been that it guaranteed the reservation would never be allotted, but this was a bogus argument and allotment could easily be avoided by his own actions.

63. Collier to Steere, 29 October 1935, LAFRC, Box 33572.

64. *Gallup Independent* article quoted in the *Farmington Times Hustler*, 31 January 1936, p. 1. The writer has never been able to locate a copy of the minutes of this council although it appears to have been a formal meeting. Neither has the writer discovered any minutes of the Executive Committee.

In reality, the basic nature of Indian policy had traditionally depended on the forcefulness of the current commissioner, modified somewhat by his major assistants and field leaders. There already existed more than enough legislative authority for any reforms that Collier might want to achieve and the conduct of Navajo affairs after mid-1935 changed little because the tribe rejected the Wheeler-Howard Act. Perhaps most important, the main goals of the Navajo New Deal after 1935 were livestock regulation and land management, issues which had little connection with the provisions of Collier's cherished legislation. In sum, the controversy raised by the long campaign over the Wheeler-Howard Act only further handicapped efforts to administer Navajo affairs after June 1935.

# 4

## Early Land Management Operations and the
## Faris Administration

Land management on the Navajo reservation during the New Deal rivaled the importance of such goals as self-rule and preservation of tribal culture. Certain aspects of the conservation programs, most notably herd reduction, became well known. The sale of livestock, however, was only one part of a larger but less apparent attempt to correct overgrazing and to provide alternative means of livelihood. Indicative of the importance of conservation in Collier's thinking was his willingness in the fall of 1933 to take Navajo administration out of the hands of the Indian Service and place it under the Soil Erosion Service.[1] His later attempts to integrate land management operations into the central tribal headquarters at Window Rock caused a split among the regular Indian Service employees and the conservationists that practically paralyzed all reservation administration by late 1935. Only by a drastic shakeup of top personnel was Collier able to end the feud and restart his conservation plans.

The first major land management project was the establishment of the erosion station at Mexican Springs in the summer of 1933. This operation quickly became and always remained the "showpiece" for all types of practical and experimental activities in conservation on the Navajo reservation. Important visitors of the New Deal era, such as Henry Wallace, M. L. Wilson, and Rexford Tugwell, included Mexican Springs on their itineraries during visits to the Southwest, so they could see the effects of a complete program of range rehabilitation.

H. H. Bennett and Charles Collier selected the site at Mexican

1. Bruno Klinger to D. S. Hubbell, 8 April 1937, "Establishing of Navajo Experiment Station," SCS Records, UNML.

Springs during their survey of the reservation erosion damage in
July 1933. After the council approved the project, young Collier
negotiated with Mexican Springs Indians several times before they
reached a final agreement on July 15. By its terms, the Navajos
permitted the area to be fenced and promised to remove their livestock while the range was being restored. The government agreed in
return to pay fees to the Indians during six months of each year,
presumably so they could rent nearby grazing land for their livestock. During the other half of the year, the government guaranteed
employment on the project to at least one member of each Indian
family. The agreement contained several other provisions, but the
most important was the promise of a new day school.[2]

Supported with an initial grant of $250,000 from CCC funds,
work at Mexican Springs started under an acting director who
supervised fencing the area in mid-1933. Range restoration and
erosion control work were delayed until a staff could be hired the
following spring, when experts in range management, erosion
control, soils, ecology, and other fields commenced a very active
program of conservation projects and experiments. Their efforts in
1934 were climaxed by a large celebration in November when a
new community center was dedicated.[3]

In late 1933 Secretary Ickes had created the Soil Erosion Service
within the Department of Interior under Bennett and other conservationists borrowed from the Department of Agriculture. Blessed
with the powerful Ickes' backing and a grant of $10,000,000 in
PWA funds, the SES immediately became an active force on the
Navajo reservation. This led Collier to think in terms of a "Navajo
Project," or the creation of a network of demonstration areas like
Mexican Springs throughout the reservation where SES technicians
could undertake work and study the tribe's problems.[4] Collier finally
persuaded Hugh G. Calkins, who had earlier rejected the job, to
organize the Navajo Project. A former Chief of Operations in the
Forest Service in New Mexico and Arizona, Calkins was widely
respected in conservation circles for his land management theories.
He was a strong advocate of designing land-use programs along
major watersheds rather than the more piecemeal approach of

2. Ibid.
3. *Gallup Independent*, 6 November 1934, pp. 1, 3.
4. Klinger, "Establishing of Navajo Experiment Station," SCS Records, UNML.

proceeding along arbitrary political boundaries. His concept influenced the creation of conservation districts when the Soil Conservation Service began its national programs later in the New Deal.[5]

By the spring of 1934 Calkins had a small army of SES technicians assembled on the reservation to activate the Navajo Project. During the next year and a half, thirteen demonstration areas were established. They ranged in size from only a few hundred acres to nearly 40,000 acres in the case of the Kayenta Demonstration Area. Their total size, including Mexican Springs, amounted to about 180,000 acres or 1.2 percent of the total reservation area. Although most of the projects focused on livestock husbandry and range restoration, the purpose of others varied. At least one emphasized improved farming methods. One or two demonstration areas were devoted to controlling severe erosion adjacent to highways so that Navajo travelers could see the corrective measures. On some demonstration areas the government assumed all expenses for land use improvements, but on others local Navajos contributed part of the labor free.[6] The important demonstration areas, if publicity is any guide, were those at Mexican Springs, Ganado, and Steamboat. All three concentrated on range rehabilitation and improvement of animal husbandry practices.

The first stage of establishing the demonstration areas differed little from the general procedures employed at Mexican Springs in

---

5. Smith Interview.

6. In 1935, the following demonstration and cooperative areas and their acreages were listed in an SCS report on the Navajo Project. Mexico Springs was not included. See the "Annual Report of the Navajo Project," 1935, SCS Records, UNML.

|  | Acreage |
|---|---|
| Chilchinbito | 14,667 |
| Kayenta | 39,040 |
| Piute Canyon | 500 (agricultural) |
| Moenave | 10,171 |
| Frazer | 5,627 |
| Ganado | 7,825 |
| Steamboat | 30,000 |
| Klag-E-Toh | 4,048 |
| Canyon de Chelly | 1,800 |
| Mariano Lake | 6,810 |
| Cove | 22,400 |
| Highway 666 | 300 |
|  | 143,194 |

1933. E. R. Smith, a forester who served as Assistant Director of the Navajo Project, and co-workers traveled extensively to find areas on the reservation where topography, erosion, and plant cover were representative. Once having reached a prospective site, Smith and his men walked or rode horseback to inspect conditions.

After the selection of an area, Smith met with local headmen or chapter officers to arrange terms. Using an interpreter, several day-long sessions were required to reach agreement on fees, wages, and arrangements for livestock removal. A day school or some similar bonus usually had to be promised before the astute Navajo bargainers accepted the proposal. But these issues were not Smith's major hurdle in convincing local Indians they should permit a demonstration area. His greatest problem was to convince the Navajos that their land, with proper care, additional water development, and improved livestock management, could produce more income than in the past even though fewer animals would be grazed. Smith's problem was a microcosm of the same obstacles that plagued government officials endlessly in the future.

After the agreement, Smith rode horseback with the Indian leaders and personally flagged the fence lines to thwart misunderstandings on boundaries. Next the stock had to be counted and removed as agreed. This frequently caused discontent among Indians who often felt that somehow they had been deceived.[7]

Once demonstration areas were established, a thorough program of range restoration was designed for each. A team of technicians mapped the area, studied soil types, determined the amount of forage available, estimated the amount of livestock the range could graze, and located water sources. After compilation, SES personnel studied the information carefully before drawing up a master plan for rehabilitating the land. The actual field work of the SES resembled the projects being conducted by the CCC, but the operations on the demonstration areas were invariably far more sophisticated. SES engineers favored an intensive use of all sorts of dams, terraces, and water-spreading devices to control erosion completely. Where banks of arroyos and washes had caved away, Navajo crews set out countless willows, tamarisks, cottonwoods, and other shrubs and trees to stabilize the damage. Through reseeding, developing water supplies, and rodent control, SES leaders sought to maximize the grazing

7. Smith Interview.

capacity of the area and to illustrate solutions for the Navajos' problems at large.[8]

One of the major obstacles faced by the technical personnel who established the demonstration sites was an almost complete lack of data needed for their work. SES leaders discovered that no one had ever developed a map of the reservation of sufficient accuracy and detail to design local conservation projects. Parts of the reservation had never been mapped. To draw up project plans, the technicians had to leave their Gallup offices, travel to the demonstration area, and then sketch a map by hand before they returned to plot in the corrective measures.[9]

Similar problems existed about information on the reservation in general. SES workers learned that no exact statistics existed on how many sheep and goats the Navajos had owned in the past. A dipping program started a few years before to eradicate scabies gave reliable figures for the recent period, but no information existed on previous numbers. They also lacked knowledge on the number of horses and cattle Navajos owned, on how much of their livelihood came from livestock as compared to farming and other sources, and on whether overgrazing and erosion were chronic problems or of recent origin. In essence, SES leaders saw the entire reservation as a huge mystery known only through general and hearsay information.

The lack of basic data for planning conservation projects was dismaying to the highly trained scientists and administrators. No one, to their minds, could possibly correct the Navajos' problems without first obtaining accurate evidence and the technicians proceeded to gather information on their own. In 1934 the government commissioned the Fairchild Aerial Survey to make a mosaic photographic map of the entire reservation. The project, which covered 24,500 square miles, was the largest aerial survey conducted up to that time.[10]

The demonstration areas, especially Mexican Springs, became scientific laboratories as they continued to gather a wide range of information after 1934. Workers measured the amounts of rainfall, average daily temperatures, and wind velocities at different heights

8. Hugh G. Calkins, "General Working Plan for the Navajo Project," 1 March 1934, LAFRC, Box 72942.

9. "Annual Report of the Navajo Project," 1935, SCS Records, UNML.

10. "Navajos on the Map," *Indian Truth* 11 (April 1934); 4.

off the ground. Other personnel studied ground temperatures at various levels of the subsoil to calculate evaporation rates. Agronomists and horticulturalists fenced off small experimental plots within demonstration areas and raised hundreds of different varieties of native and exotic (or nonindigenous) grasses, plants, and trees to determine their usefulness in restoring the land. Throughout the New Deal era, workers collected seeds and cuttings for bushes and trees which they planted or set out at nurseries on the reservation. On other experimental plots, soil engineers measured rates of erosion and estimated how quickly natural vegetation recovered when not grazed. This information was then compared to plots where simulated grazing was maintained at moderate or severe levels. Tests were also conducted to see how effective various types of dams, terraces, and water spreaders were in combating erosion.

Photography played an interesting and important part in the work conducted at the demonstration areas. The government established "photographic stations" at numerous sites and a professional photographer visited each station at designated times to take pictures as an experiment progressed. These "before and after" pictures provided a visual record so technicians could study the effectiveness of a given conservation technique and, in the process, the photographs proved extremely useful in wrangling more funds from superiors who drew up budgets in Washington offices.

Although the SES received relatively little notice, the size of its staff and operations rivaled the more widely publicized programs of the CCC, PWA, and WPA. By mid-1935, the Navajo Project had eighty-five regular employees, mostly college-trained whites, who carried out technical, administrative, and clerical functions. In addition, the project hired 705 Navajos as stipulated by the cooperative agreements which established the demonstration areas. This figure did not include an unspecified number of Indians who contributed their labor on some of the work. The project also owned forty-eight heavy trucks, eighty-eight lighter vehicles, and a sizeable number of caterpillar tractors, scrapers, terracers, and other field equipment. At some demonstration areas, Calkins constructed compounds consisting of living quarters and offices for the field staff, garages for the maintenance of vehicles and equipment, and other structures such as livestock sheds and bathhouses.[11] In short, the SES

11. "Annual Report of the Navajo Project," 1935, SCS Records, UNML.

became an elite group whose well-financed activities were one of the most impressive New Deal efforts to solve the Navajos' problems.

Livestock in the demonstration areas was either totally removed or sharply reduced during the two-year rehabilitation phase. By this time, the SES had become the Soil Conservation Service and this organization took over the livestock management. Based on estimates of grazing capacity, SCS officials rigidly limited the number of livestock allowed back on the demonstration areas. Field workers almost universally allowed only sheep or cattle to be replenished and either banned or severely curtailed horses and goats which were less productive.

SCS experts also tried to revise herding practices in the demonstration areas. Instead of allowing each family to drive its own sheep to and from pasture each day, several herds were experimentally combined into a large band cared for by Indian shepherds. The band was rotated among several pastures to place an equal burden on the grass and to give it time to recover between grazings. At night the sheep were bedded down on the range to avoid "scalping" the vegetation around the hogans and watering spots, a condition common with the Navajos' normal herding practices.

Nothing upset the SCS supervisors more than the Navajos' habit of not castrating their bucks and allowing them to run year round with the ewes. The indiscriminate mating and in-breeding were believed to cause the extremely low-quality stock typical of most Navajo herds. Allowing the ewes to be bred early was viewed with equal disdain. It resulted in lambing during cold weather which killed many of the offspring. Castration of male lambs, the introduction of registered bucks, and the establishment of ram pastures to delay mating became standard practices in the management of demonstration herds.

The main purpose of the demonstration areas was, of course, to show the Navajos that range rehabilitation and improved livestock management would allow the Indians to graze fewer livestock and to protect their land with no permanent loss of income. To illustrate the point, SCS workers kept accurate records on the percentage of lambs which survived and their market value at sale time each fall. Equal care was given to recording the weight, quality, and value of fleeces from mature sheep. The data was then compared to information on regular Navajo herds. In 1936 officials at the Ganado Demonstration Area reported that its experimental herd had a ninety-three percent lamb crop and that the lambs reached an average weight of sixty-eight pounds by the time of sale in October. The wool clip of adult sheep averaged 8.17 pounds and the revenue per animal totaled $5.78. In comparison, unimproved sheep had a sixty-one percent lamb crop and the fall lambs, although one to three months older, weighed only forty-five pounds when sold. The average fleece weight of unimproved sheep was five pounds and the return per animal was $3.08. [12] Greater disparities appeared when SCS workers made comparisons in later years. In the sense that most Navajos could not duplicate the extra care and supplemental feeding sheep received in the demonstration areas, the SCS comparisons were somewhat misleading. Nevertheless, considerable validity must be given to the government's contention that a careful conservation of Navajo land and an improvement in livestock breeding and management would permit sustained grazing without a permanent drop in income.

Those in charge of the demonstration areas experienced severe problems in trying to convince most Navajos they should reform their land management and livestock practices. Repeatedly after 1935, SCS project managers staged "demonstration days" and local Navajos, partly enticed by a free barbecue lunch, trooped in to see what was taking place behind the fenced sites. Officials took them on tours of projects to show the dams and other structures designed to prevent erosion and slow water runoff. The visitors saw seedlings thriving along washes and reseeded grass growing where once the terrain had been eroded and barren. Officials also equipped a small truck with movies, charts, models, "before and after" photographs, and posters for the demonstration days and they used its contents to reenforce their teaching on conservation. Even more graphically, officials set up "living" exhibits consisting of improved ewes, bucks, and wethers. The animals, along with their fleeces, were displayed with data on their weight and value compared to the sheep raised outside.

The Navajos who attended such gatherings enjoyed the tours and graphic dislays, especially the movies which were then a novelty, and they appreciated the barbecue, but they found many SCS ideas strange and hard to accept. No Navajo wanted to entrust his family's herd to some outsider. It was even more unthinkable that the sheep

12. "Navajo District Annual Report," 1936–37, SCS Records, UNML.

and goats would not be returned to the family pens each night. Attempts at communal herding failed completely. The Navajos were equally unconvinced about overgrazing. When demonstration workers emphatically noted how grass inside the demonstration areas grew tall and lush compared to the vegetation outside, they found themselves both amused and frustrated by Navajos' retorts that it rained more inside the improved areas.[13]

In large part the Navajos could not accept government admonishments about land conservation and livestock management because they still lived in a prescientific world. In their fatalistic view, the range would come back only when the weather and other natural factors changed for the better. An important contributing cause for their rejection of improved management was the animosity created by the demonstration areas themselves. Each Navajo family had a definite idea of the extent of its range land and the presence of government fences was disturbing. Like most humans Navajos tended to think the grass was greener on the other side, but normal envy turned into hostility when barbed wire made the adage come true. Dissident Indians repeatedly made threats to cut down the government fences when the herd reduction program revived in 1937. The residents within the demonstration areas also frequently complained that the terms agreed to in 1934 were unfair or that the government had violated the original compact. Thus, the demonstration areas became a minor but emotional part of the larger controversy over livestock removal.

As the time for the completion of Window Rock approached in 1935, Collier and other Washington leaders began to consider ways to integrate the work being done in the demonstration areas into the consolidated administration already started by Acting Administrator William H. Zeh. Collier's concern for conservation was only of recent origin and can be attributed to his close contacts with Henry Wallace, M. L. Wilson, H. H. Bennett, and other New Deal figures associated with the national movement to protect natural resources. Reinforcing his interest were Walter Woehlke, Robert Marshall, and Ward Shepard of the Indian Office, who were strong devotees of conservation and also among Collier's closest friends and advisors.[14]

13. Fryer Interview, 1970.
14. Woehlke entered the Indian Service soon after the start of the New Deal and became Collier's main field representative except for one or two periods when he was

An additional reason for Collier's desire to integrate conservation work into the administrative consolidation was his wish to coordinate the activities which had "mushroomed" on the Navajo reservation since the advent of the New Deal. Three general types of federal activity existed in 1935. The Indian Service still handled such traditional responsibilities as education, health, irrigation, management of tribal funds, and law enforcement. The work relief programs, operating largely under CCC and PWA budgets, had been established to provide employment, develop land and water resources, and build the day schools. The SCS operations constituted still a third category of activity with a separate budget. Although Collier was never noted for administrative efficiency, even he must have recognized the amount of waste within this maze of agencies, especially the duplication of the SCS and CCC.

Still another compelling reason for integrating the reservation administration was Collier's need for qualified personnel who could provide the type of data needed to understand the Navajos' land and economic problems before effective solutions could be devised. There were too few Indian Service foresters, irrigation engineers, and other specialists to carry out the sizeable programs that Collier envisioned for the Navajos and other tribes. If he relied on existing staff, the rehabilitation effort among the Navajos would be the same as in the past—sketchy, poorly supervised, and underfinanced. Although Collier was an accomplished executive lobbyist, the Indian Service's budget declined during the first years of the New Deal.[15] With Congress unwilling to expand regular appropriations, Collier's best chance to gain emergency funds and hire technicians was from the Department of Agriculture.

---

employed by other agencies. Robert Marshall and Ward Shepard were both foresters. Marshall directed the Forestry Division of the Indian Service until his death in 1939. Shepard served in the Indian Bureau as Collier's advisor on land policy until he took a leave of absence in 1936 to join the Forestry School at Harvard University. Extensive correspondence between Collier and these three men can be found in the Collier papers, YU.

15. The regular appropriations reached a peak in 1932 with $27,030,046.73. In 1933 the figure declined to $22,140,098.35, in 1934 to $18,966,545.67, and in 1935 to $16,275,185. In addition, the government depended upon money derived from tribal funds to administer reservations. This amounted to ten percent of the gratuitous appropriations during the 1920s. Because of the depression, however, this source dropped from $3,415,046.19 in 1932 to $1,426,915 in 1935. See *Annual Report of the Secretary of Interior, 1934* (Washington, 1934), p. 116.

All of these factors guided Collier's planning for the organization of the Window Rock headquarters. He hoped to achieve a bureaucratic integration of traditional Indian Service functions with those being conducted by the welter of new programs and agencies which the New Deal had created. Ideally, all parts would neatly mesh together so that experts could study the reservation conditions and send on their information to planners at Window Rock, where solutions would be devised for Navajo problems that would be sound and yet acceptable to the Indians. Collier could thus fulfill his goal of using technical and social science expertise to serve Indian needs while implementing self-rule.[16]

Reports from the reservation in early 1935 advised Collier to complete the unified administration quickly or his plans for the tribe would be jeopardized. Zeh at that time warned Collier that the Navajos as a whole had not accepted his major programs to date— stock reduction, conservation, day schools, and the Wheeler-Howard Act. Zeh believed that the situation could still be rescued if Collier would quickly appoint a general superintendent who would provide a sense of stability and direction that had been lacking in tribal affairs since the abandonment of the six agencies.[17]

Two months later Woehlke visited the reservation and concluded that Collier must reassess all past policies. He criticized the first two herd reductions for impoverishing the small owners without harming the large herders who unfairly dominated the tribal council. The livestock sales had created what Woehlke called a "Navajo proletariat" dependent on wages from temporary relief work. He suggested that Collier call the council, together with Chee Dodge and Dashne Clah Cheschillege, and demand they accept a complete and equitable redistribution of land and livestock. The plan should then be amended to the New Mexico boundary bill, which was still pending, to give it the force of law.[18]

The Zeh and Woehlke reports caused Collier to bring top Indian Service workers, SES leaders, and tribal leaders to Washington in

16. For the best statement of Collier's views on the need to merge traditional functions of the Indian Service with technical work see Collier to Bennett, 20 December 1935, File 31777, 1935, 344 NA, RG 75.

17. Zeh to Collier, 26 January 1935, Office File of Commissioner John Collier, NA, RG 75.

18. W. V. Woehlke, "Memorandum on Navajo Problem," 27 March 1935, Office File of Commissioner John Collier, NA, RG 75.

early April 1935. Included in the delegation from the reservation were Zeh, Calkins, Thomas Dodge, Chee Dodge, Dashne Clah Cheschillege, and at least five other Navajo leaders who made up the mysterious Executive Committee.[19] The group from the reservation met daily with the Indian Office staff for nearly two weeks and they discussed "all of the many-sided Navajo problem . . . with extreme freedom," according to Collier. The Navajo leaders were able to reach substantial agreement after "theoretical propositions had faded out and concrete propositions had taken their place."[20]

During the Washington conferences, the general Navajo program was reassessed by officials from the Office of Indian Affairs and the SES. On May 1, 1935, Collier issued a statement entitled "Navajo Policies and Program,"[21] which revised reservation administration. Much of the text merely reiterated previous goals, but the policy statement also contained substantial changes for the coming years.[22]

One new theme was the added importance that conservation was to have in the future. "Navajo Policies and Program" mentioned a social and economic survey in the immediate offing and spoke of additional studies of reservation conditions to provide adequate information. Stock reduction henceforth would be on a sliding scale and a system of "base preferences" which forced larger sales on wealthier herders. The reservation was also to be divided into land management districts based upon watersheds. These districts would be used for administering and organizing stock reduction and con-servation programs. The SES would, in summary, expand its func-tions in the demonstration areas and shift its emphasis to developing a program of conservation for the entire reservation. Each major federal activity on the reservation was discussed—forestry, irrigation,

19. *Gallup Independent*, 2 April 1935, p. 1. The Executive Committee—Henry Taliman of Fort Defiance, Billy Pete of Keams Canyon, George Bancroft of Tuba City, John Perry of Crownpoint, and Nal Nishi of Leupp—was apparently comprised of one del-egate from each of the old six agencies, but the Shiprock representative had evidently refused to serve. These five men visited Senator Carl Hayden's office around April 15, 1935, to request more land in Arizona. Whether Chee and Dashne were regular or ex-officio members of the Executive Committee is not clear. See unsigned memorandum, "Navajo Indians," 15 April 1935, Isabella Greenway papers, AHS.

20. John Collier, "Editorial," *Indians at Work* 2 (1 May 1935): 2.

21. "Navajo Policies and Program," 1 May 1935, Statistics Division-Reports and Other Records, Navajo Agency, NA, RG 75.

22. In this same period the Pueblo administration was consolidated in a manner very similar to the Navajo. See Wallace to Collier, 10 July 1935, File 31777, 1935, 344, NA, RG 75.

water development, farm and home extension, roads, CCC, health, and education—in terms of how it should contribute to the general rehabilitation of the Navajos.

"Navajo Policies and Program" placed responsibility for achievement of the government programs on a general superintendent who would "receive the greatest amount of authority feasible under the law." This official would report directly to Collier rather than through the division heads in the Office of Indian Affairs. The Navajo chief administrator would also have complete authority over the hiring, transfer, and promotion of personnel, the initiation of new policies, and the inspection of all activities on the reservation.[23] The general superintendent, in short, would be a sort of subcommissioner.

Three days before the issuance of "Navajo Policies and Program," President Roosevelt signed legislation which ended the SES and established the Soil Conservation Service as a permanent agency in the Department of Agriculture. Bennett and the personnel whom Ickes had "borrowed" from Agriculture were suddenly transferred back into that department. Calkins, for example, soon left Navajo work and became a district director of the SCS in Albuquerque. Coming after Ickes' campaign to create a "Department of Conservation" and his defeat in a bitter power struggle with Wallace, the shift of the SES to Agriculture potentially could have been disastrous for Collier's hopes of harnessing technical skills and funds needed for Indian reservations. But the transfer really did little to change Collier's plans because of his close association with the Secretary of Agriculture.[24] This rapport even permitted the Commissioner to act as an intermediary between Ickes and Wallace after the transfer of the SES to Agriculture. With Ickes' blessing, Collier soon negotiated a cooperative agreement between the Indian Service and Agriculture which unified SCS work into the Window Rock administration as planned in the April conferences.[25]

23. Collier to Rexford G. Tugwell, 11 May 1935, File 31777, 1935, 344, Central Correspondence Files, NA, RG 75.

24. This conclusion is based on unrecorded statements by E. R. Fryer during our interview in 1970. He recalled that Collier and Wallace were close friends, admired each other, and seemed to share a similar mystical outlook. Fryer first observed their friendship when he was brought to Washington in early 1936 to interview for the superintendency and Collier took him to see Wallace. Fryer's subsequent visits to meetings of Collier and Wallace reaffirmed this first impression.

25. Collier to Rexford G. Tugwell, 11 May 1935, File 31777, 1935, 344, Central Correspondence Files, NA, RG 75.

The revision of the Navajo programs and the interagency compact between the Indian Service and the SCS essentially divided the administration of the reservation into two parts. The land management division had charge of all activities which in any way related to land use, including research surveys, soil erosion control, irrigation, water development, CCC, range management, forestry, roads, and extension. All of these functions now came under the direction of the SCS official who directed the land management division and served as an assistant to the general superintendent. Other activities such as health, education, regulation of traders, and relations with the tribal council were placed in a second division headed by another assistant to the general superintendent. According to the agreement, the general superintendent maintained a limited veto over SCS activities, but serious disputes between the two agencies would be referred to Washington where officials in the Indian Office and Agriculture would resolve them.[26]

Although the cooperative agreement theoretically unified the Navajo administration, several factors hampered its future operations. Perhaps the most important was that the SCS and the Indian Service still maintained separate budgets. Hence, the SCS assistant to the general superintendent and many of his field workers were paid by that agency, but some of the employees under his command were funded by the Indian Service or other agencies. This arrangement obviously created a fertile ground for disputes. Also the cooperative agreement lacked the permanency which the general program badly needed. It fell far short, for example, of the "Navajo Authority" which Bennett had recommended in 1933, or of Woehlke's more recent suggestion that Collier secure statutory backing for a land management plan. The unified program for the Navajo reservation was actually an ad hoc affair chiefly cemented together by the personal friendship of Collier and Wallace.

On May 13, 1935, Collier announced the appointment of Chester E. Faris as the first general superintendent. The choice for the challenging position at first seemed ideal. The new appointee possessed an

26. The administration of the Hopis at this time was placed under a separate superintendent at Keams Canyon who dealt with only members of that tribe. All conservation work on the Hopi reservation, however, had to be cleared through the general superintendent of the Navajos. Collier to A. G. Hutton, 6 July 1935, File 31777, 1935, 344, Central Correspondence Files, NA, RG 75.

unblemished record of thirty years experience in the Indian Service and his selection satisfied all interested groups.[27] A native of Indiana, Faris began in the Indian Service in Wyoming on the Shoshone reservation. He transferred to New Mexico in mid-career and later received a dual appointment as head of the Santa Fe Indian School and superintendent of the Northern Pueblo Agency.[28] Through field inspections he had already gained some familiarity with Navajo affairs and sometime around 1930 he had been asked to take charge of the reservation. He had refused the appointment, pleading that one man could not handle the entire tribe.

Faris's strongest qualification from Collier's standpoint was undoubtedly his genuine affection for Indians and their respect for him. At the Santa Fe Indian School, Faris had always encouraged students to develop their skills in native arts and crafts and he strongly rejected the notion that Indians or their way of life were inferior. He also maintained a strong interest in Indian history. Blessed with a fine head of white hair and a dignified manner, Faris had always been able to deal with Indians easily because they respected him as an elder statesman. He represented the most progressive element of the old-line Indian Service workers and his appointment to the Navajo post was meant as a final reward to a distinguished career.

Collier coupled the appointment of Faris with several other important shifts of personnel. G. A. Trotter, another experienced and widely respected Indian Service leader, was transferred from the superintendency of the Zuni reservation to assist Faris in conventional administrative matters. The assistant in charge of the land management division was F. D. Matthews, who had earlier served as an assistant to Calkins. To handle law enforcement, trading relations, and liaison with the Navajos, Collier named Thomas Dodge as a special assistant to the new general superintendent.

When Faris first appeared on the reservation later in May 1935, he found himself in a virtual cauldron because Morgan's bitter campaign against the Wheeler-Howard referendum had reached its most controversial stage. Wild rumors circulated that new livestock reduc-

27. A strong endorsement of Faris was given by the Indian Rights Association. See "Navajo Program," *Indian Truth* 11 (June 1935): 3.

28. This background material on Faris was derived from a small collection of his personal papers in the Special Collections Department at the University of New Mexico Library.

tions would soon be imposed. Once the election was over, Faris visited Indians throughout the reservation to quiet their fears and win their support, but he found this tactic gave him little respite from Indian complaints. The Navajos repeatedly asked about new reductions, the inactivity of the tribal council, and the whereabouts of the old superintendents. Even as "a man of many gray hairs," Faris could not counter the backlog of Navajo bitterness.

Faris also faced intense pressures to open the new tribal headquarters at Window Rock. The $980,000 building program had been repeatedly delayed by red tape so that construction had not started in earnest until early 1935.[29] In the meantime, criticisms about the vice problems of Navajos visiting the temporary headquarters in Gallup continued. Collier and other leaders increasingly felt that they must extricate the central administration from that city and offer Navajos something tangible to replace the old six agencies. By the time Faris arrived, the new headquarters was being rushed to completion, but work on the buildings and utilities was still incomplete by late July when the first handful of personnel and their families arrived.[30] The tribal headquarters was not fully occupied until 1936.

Even after Window Rock began to function, it continued to be a source of contention. In the absence of the subagencies that Collier had promised in 1933, Navajos had to come from all over the reservation to see officials about their problems. Few Navajos possessed pickups or cars and traveling to the new headquarters by wagon or horseback involved genuine hardships for those who lived in remote areas. As a temporary expedient, school principals and field workers at the old agencies tried to handle local administration. The Indians, however, demanded that they be allowed to discuss their affairs with the superintendent or "number one" man as had been the case under the old six agencies.

Today the Window Rock headquarters, along with the day schools and other buildings of the period, remains as the most identifiable vestige of the New Deal era. The Council House quietly dominates the entire complex at Window Rock. Made of native stone, the circular structure stands some thirty feet high and is roughly seventy feet in diameter. It was obviously intended to harmonize with the tribal culture and the desert landscape and to foster tribal unity. In

29. *Albuquerque Journal*, 1 January 1935, p. 2.
30. *Santa Fe New Mexican*, 29 July 1935, p. 1.

keeping with the hogan design, the main door opens to the east—the source of good fortune in Navajo folklore. Large vegas (or logs) which rest on square pillars built up from the outer wall converge at the center of the Council House to support the roof. Wood panels carved by Gerald Naylor, a Navajo artist, adorn either side of the main entrance. Inside the council chambers, Naylor and his assistants painted a panorama of murals depicting the key events of Navajo history.

The main office building at Window Rock was located across the street directly east of the Council House. Whether Collier and the architects deliberately chose that direction with an underlying symbolic intent is not known but, the Navajos, then or now, would have trouble accepting the idea that much good fortune has ever come out of the government offices. Although the administrative building was large, containing offices for the general superintendent, the council chairman, and numerous officials, the one-story structure was designed along functional lines and neither it, nor the rest of the buildings, can compete esthetically with the taller Council House.

Whatever chance, probably slight to begin with, that Faris had to dispel Navajo hostility was soon ended by a third herd reduction in August 1935. Collier still intended to see that Navajos abided by the council's 1934 agreement to sell eighty percent of the increase of their herds and to castrate all male goats. Neither of the two terms had been met and dipping records in 1934 indicated 938,793 head of sheep and goats on the reservation. Together with horses and cattle, Navajos still owned 1,238,493 sheep units, nearly twice the estimated grazing capacity.[31] With the 1935 lamb and kid crop, the livestock load threatened to become as serious as in 1933.[32]

In addition to this problem, the Navajos had not used relief wages as the government had expected. Officials had hoped that the Indians would save their earnings and sell off marketable livestock through

31. The term sheep unit was used by SCS personnel to calculate the numbers of livestock and proper grazing loads. A sheep or goat counted as one sheep unit while each cow was reckoned as the equivalent of four (sometimes five) sheep units and each horse as five sheep units. By studying the amount of palatable vegetation in any given area, range experts could estimate the amount of sheep units that should be placed on the land.

32. C. E. Faris, "Navajo Stock Removal Program for 1935," 23 August 1935, Indians-Navajo file, AHS; "Annual Report of the Navajo Project," 1935, SCS Records, UNML.

the trading posts to pay for living expenses as they had in the past. Instead, the security-minded tribesmen had kept their animals and used their wages to buy goods at the trading posts.[33]

Amazingly, Collier and his major administrators anticipated no particular difficulties with the third herd reduction. They believed that the commercial market for fall lambs in 1935 would remove the better quality animals. This meant that the government would have to buy only cull sheep and goats. The latter remained special objects of attention as approximately one-half the purchases would be goats. Again Collier found outside funds by securing $400,000 from the Federal Relief Administration to purchase 200,000 animals.[34] Navajos were to be paid $2.00 per head for mature ewes, $1.50 for goats, and $1.00 for female lambs. Unlike previous reductions, government workers were to take no part in the sales or drives to shipping points. Traders were to handle the entire operation by paying Indians the prices officially established and then receiving reimbursement and a commission after the sheep and goats were marketed. In addition, traders were asked to report the number of livestock sold through commercial channels, so the government would know the total number removed from the reservation.[35]

Begun in mid-August 1935, the third herd reduction immediately encountered strong resistance from the Navajos. The United Indian Traders Association soon telegraphed Collier that herders were disposing of only their cull ewes and a few goats. Medium and large owners were retaining at least half of their fall lambs for breeding stock. Since all commercial buying, according to the telegram, would cease by October 10, there was no chance of reducing livestock numbers through the regular fall market.[36] Because of the Indians' opposition, only 16,225 sheep and 14,716 goats were sold in the 1935 reduction, far short of the goal of 200,000. Having spent only $61, 882, Collier shifted the excess funds to Acoma and Laguna to conduct livestock reduction programs there.

The 1935 reduction was the final of the three general and "voluntary" livestock sales undertaken since the start of the New Deal. All three had suffered from a lack of planning and fairness because the temporary funds had to be spent quickly and without a chance to

33. J. G. Hamilton to All Indian Traders, 27 August 1935, LAFRC, Box 18744.
34. John Pohland to Ivan F. Albers, 5 August 1935, LAFRC, Box 72938.
35. Faris, "Stock Removal," 23 August 1935, Indians-Navajo file, AHS.
36. United Indian Traders Association to Collier, n.d., 1935, LAFRC, Box 18744.

justify or explain the sales to Navajo stockmen. Whether or not the problem of tribal antipathy could have been averted by a more deliberate approach is highly debatable, but certainly the first three reductions proved a crippling handicap to future efforts when far more rational and equitable methods were employed to bring live-stock numbers into a balance with grazing resources.

During the same period that Faris assumed administrative re-sponsibility for the Navajos, the SCS began a series of reservation surveys which provided the information that land use planners wanted. Their first field work was designed to collect data on the physical condition of the Navajos' land. The 1935 surveys gathered information in seven catagories—range, soils, forest, fauna, erosion, vegetation, and agriculture. Reconnaisance teams made up of ten or so white experts and a similar number of Indian assistants started the investigations in the spring of 1935 and completed them the follow-ing year. Their surveys not only collected data on existing condi-tions but also suggested remedial measures. Tabulated onto maps and charts, their findings were sent to the tribal headquarters and used to plan land-use programs for each part of the reservation.[37]

A second type of field research, the "human survey," started in the summer of 1935 on an experimental basis. Truly innovative, the survey attempted to combine the methodology of the "hard sciences" with economics, sociology, and anthropology. Teams from various disciplines went from hogan to hogan to interview, through inter-preters, family leaders to learn about the functioning of Navajo institutions, distribution of livestock, concepts about property and land use, credit relations with traders, and data on housing, diet, and clothing.[38] Although the questions resembled the federal census, particularly the emphasis on economics, the categories for the human survey were much more detailed and sophisticated. In 1935 human surveys were tried in only two demonstration areas and one local community. With some revision and refinement in methodology, the investigations continued over the entire reservation for the next few years under the more descriptive title of the "Human Dependency Survey."[39]

Much of the credit for the design of these surveys belonged to

37. "Annual Report of the Navajo Project," 1935, SCS Records, UNML.

38. "Memorandum on Social and Economic Survey," 9 May 1935, LAFRC, Box 72942.

39. "Annual Report of the Navajo Project," 1935, SCS Records, UNML.

Eshref Shevky, a native of Turkey who served as the regional director of research under Calkins. After an early education in science, Shevky briefly attended an agricultural school in England before coming to the United States in 1913. He worked on farms in various parts of the country and studied agriculture at the University of Minnesota. Shevky subsequently authored or coauthored an impressive list of scientific papers and in 1922 he completed his Ph.D. at Stanford University. Despite his scientific career, Shevky maintained a strong interest in the dynamics of social change and how the scientific method might be applied to relieve human problems. He first met Collier in 1922 and the future commissioner soon persuaded him to conduct a survey of health and economic conditions of the Taos Pueblos. The study became a prototype for investigations that he later designed for the Navajos. The Turkish scholar was widely read in anthropology, sociology, economics, education, and colonial administration before he joined the Indian Service in 1935.[40]

The preliminary findings of both the land use and human dependency surveys in 1935 and 1936 confirmed the direst assessments of the Navajos' problems. Out of nearly 15,000,000 acres on the reservation, only 1,239,071 acres were being utilized according to their potential capacity for grazing or farming. Another 1,640,837 acres were designated as barren or waste land. The remaining 12,183,203 acres were classified as over-utilized to some degree, with 5,852,090 acres considered as "very severely over-utilized." To members of the land management division, the fact that approximately eighty percent of the reservation was overgrazed—over thirty percent severely so—meant that the Navajos must either make better use of their resources or receive a permanent federal dole. SCS leaders no longer spoke merely of livestock overpopulation but began to discuss how many of the 50,000 Navajos the reservation could support if every available resource were developed to the maximum. It became clear that more Navajos must utilize more irrigated land and the SCS

40. Shevky vita, 21 June [1935?], Collier papers, YU. Shevky's first name was often listed as Richard. Shevky faced a series of extremely unfair attacks from Joseph Bruner and the American Indian Federation during the mid-1930s, although the attacks had nothing to do with his work on human dependence surveys. The accusations invariably depicted Shevky as an evil and diabolical Turk and were linked with the organization's charges that Collier's administration was un-American and communistic.

even considered the possible relocation of some tribesmen to areas outside the reservation.

The seriousness of the situation led Ickes to issue grazing regulations on November 6, 1935, which established new approaches to land management and livestock controls. Announced by Collier a month later, without any endorsement of the tribal council, the new livestock program called for the creation of grazing districts which would become the basis for future land management administration. When studies of range conditions had determined the grazing capacity of each district, Collier would promulgate this figure in sheep units to the Navajos. The Indians living in each district would then use their chapter organization or a livestock association to formulate a land-use program and reduce livestock numbers to the recommended level. At the same time, the Navajos would redistribute the remaining livestock and grazing rights to insure an equitable share for all. Anticipating resistance, the Ickes regulations empowered Collier to effect a land use program for any district which failed to do so voluntarily.[41]

The new regulations represented a partial but very significant shift in Collier's philosophy of self-rule for the Navajos. He still felt that the tribe should, and possibly would, regulate its own livestock numbers, but he now recognized that arbitrary means might be needed to realize this goal. The commissioner had also altered his original concept of local administrative units for the tribe. In 1933 he had pictured the subagencies as devices for improved health and educational services and community action, but the creation of grazing districts indicated that their main function would be to conduct the conservation program.

The new emphasis on conservation and the power of the SCS brought to a head a factionalism among government employees which had been brewing since the beginning of the New Deal. Only glimpses of the earlier feuds can be detected in the official correspondence, but what had been mostly localized and sub rosa disputes suddenly became general and apparent at Window Rock by late 1935. One faction in the dispute was made up of the older Indian

41. *Albuquerque Journal*, 8 December 1935, pp. 1, 3; Ickes, "Regulations Affecting the Carrying Capacity and Management of the Navajo Range," 6 November 1935, LAFRC, Box 33551.

Service personnel inherited by Collier when he took office. Strong believers in assimilation, the pre-New Deal workers privately disagreed with the commissioner's ideas about cultural pluralism and self-rule for Indians. Having served when the Indian Service received few funds, the old-line employees saw the huge grants for conservation, day schools, Window Rock, and other programs as a shameful waste.[42] In their opinion the government should maintain a status quo policy and carefully spend its money on education, health, and other functions aimed at relieving immediate needs and promoting the Indian's merger into general society.

The old guardsmen were restrained before 1935 by the simple fact that they had no alternative employment. Even so, older field workers passively resisted New Deal programs. Some of the difficulty, for example, in the government's failure to win Navajo support during the Wheeler-Howard referendum allegedly sprang from older Indian Service workers' unwillingness to speak out in its behalf to local Indians.[43]

The special object of the experienced workers' displeasure was the SCS group who became dominant in tribal administration. The SCS men were deemed as young, overeducated, and cocky upstarts out to usurp all power to themselves. Correctly sensing how important sheep and goats were to the tribe, the assimilationist faction automatically condemned SCS efforts at herd reduction. With a sense of nostalgia, older hands reminisced that before the New Deal the tribe always had a dependable supply of sheep and goats to survive the worst winters or droughts, but now they had only temporary government jobs. Unconvinced that the reservation was overgrazed, the old-line workers were especially incensed at SCS teams who wasted time and money in counting blades of grass, making soil tests, measuring ground evaporation rates, and performing other nonsensical tasks. Out of their scorn came the often-repeated assertion that the SCS cared more about the land than it did for the Navajos.

The SCS personnel certainly were not hesitant to reply to the charges. Highly confident in the scientific validity of their work, they

42. For a strongly worded condemnation of New Deal programs by a conservative Indian Service worker, see Albert H. Kneale, *Indian Agent* (Caldwell, Idaho, 1950), *passim*.

43. Alan Hulsizer to Sally Lucas Jean, 15 April 1935, Collier papers, YU.

emphatically denied any lack of interest in Navajo welfare by pointing out that the Indian Service did not employ a single anthropologist
at the start of the New Deal, while the SCS always maintained
various types of social scientists who advised on conservation programs and helped conduct the human dependency surveys. They
also claimed, with some justification, that the SCS people worked
far more closely with Navajos in the field than did Indian Service
personnel, who remained in their offices and saw only those Navajos
who came to them. SCS workers also questioned the quality of
older employees in the lower echelons of the Indian Service. Although
the people at the top staff positions were capable, the bottom positions were a dumping ground for men too unfit and unenergetic to
hold more demanding jobs.[44]

The suspicions and criticisms among the two white groups soon
became enmeshed with the Navajos' own factionalism and disenchantment with government programs. When Collier appeared at
Window Rock for an impromptu meeting of tribal leaders and
federal officials on December 6, 1935, he admitted that many Navajos
now associated the livestock reductions and the conservation program
with the SCS.[45] Even though he accepted full responsibility for past
policies and maintained that he had personally endorsed livestock
removal since 1933, his defense of the SCS indicated how deeply
antagonism toward that agency affected the Indians' thinking.

The official bickering, however, was only one of several factors
causing unrest among the Navajos. The herd reduction in the fall of
1935, rumors of additional livestock removals, and reports of another
vote on the Wheeler-Howard Act circulated the reservation.[46]
Morgan, who had been amazingly silent after his earlier victory over
Collier, showed signs of launching a new campaign against the gov-

44. Smith Interview. The differences between the old guard and SCS workers were
not as clear cut as the arguments I have described might indicate. Most of the employees
of the pre-New Deal saw some merit in parts of the government programs, especially in
the CCC. Even the most tolerant and capable, however, found it difficult to adjust to the
new modes of thought and hurried action demanded by the New Dealers. Also the feud
was complicated by disagreements among those officials appointed after 1933. As will be
discussed in the chapter on education, some of Collier's strongest disciples felt that the
Navajo administration was overly dominated by a concern for conserving the tribe's
physical resources and worried too little about its human needs.

45. Remarks of Commissioner Collier . . . at the Navajo Central Agency, 6 December
1935, LAFRC, Box 33551.

46. Morgan to Faris, 7 January 1936, LAFRC, Box 72947.

ernment to oppose the demonstration areas. Chee Dodge also complained that the SCS had not lived up to the agreements made when
the demonstration areas had been set up. Still another cause for
hostility was the failure of the tribal council to meet. By 1936 eighteen months had lapsed since its last session and even the Executive
Committee now seemed to be nonfunctional. Thomas Dodge warned
Collier that if he called a council meeting, the delegates would pass
a resolution condemning the SCS.[47]

The unrest among the Indians, however, was slight compared to
the dispute that erupted at Window Rock in early 1936. Collier's
hopes that Faris could make the Indian Service and the SCS function in unison at Window Rock had miscarried badly. What specifically caused the elder statesman to come to loggerheads with
Matthews and the land management division remains unclear. Very
likely, he never believed wholeheartedly in the conservation program
or at least the necessity for drastic livestock reduction, and his dispute
with Matthews was a result of the clash between old-line workers and
the SCS. Faris upset the land management division in the fall of
1935 when he distributed a large herd of cattle among the tribe
despite the SCS workers' objections.[48] The immediate reason for the
explosion very likely dealt with Faris's unwillingness to accept the
establishment of new grazing districts and additional herd reductions
as SCS leaders demanded.[49] Whatever the cause, Calkins, Shevky,
and Matthews believed that Collier must replace Faris with someone
more cooperative.[50]

Walter Woehlke and Ward Shepard led the drive to oust the
respected general superintendent. Both men were in the Southwest
in January 1936, helping plan some new land surveys. Highly

47. Woehlke to Collier, 15 January 1936 [sic.], Collier papers, YU. The date is obviously in error and Woehlke meant 1936.

48. The Indian Service acquired 12,000 cattle in the fall of 1935 through purchases
made in 1934 by the Agricultural Adjustment Administration. The federal government
had shipped the herd to northern Mexico to recover their weight, but the high cost of
grazing and feed forced its return to the United States a year later. Collier's acceptance of
the cattle for Indian reservations led to one of numerous clashes between the Indian
Service and livestock interests of Arizona and New Mexico. The white ranchers protested
that the cattle would depress the already low market prices. However, the acquisition
was sound for the Indians. The high quality of the cattle made them excellent for improving the breeding of Indians' nondescript animals. Faris accepted at least 3,000 head
and possibly more. See *Albuquerque Journal* 18 October 1935, p. 1, and 24 October 1935,
p. 12.

49. Faris to Morgan, 10 January 1936, LAFRC, Box 72947.

50. Shepard to Collier, 18 January 1936, Collier papers, YU.

agitated after attending conferences at which Faris rejected SCS proposals, Shepard insisted in one lengthy telegram that Collier should act immediately for the entire Navajo program was disintegrating because of "incurable incompetence" at the top.[51] Woehlke's messages agreed that Faris no longer cooperated with SCS officials, but the field representative seemed unsure of whether the situation was beyond redemption. Woehlke proposed a Machiavellian scheme by which Collier would end the imbroglio with both Faris and the tribal council. By bringing Thomas Dodge, other Navajo leaders, and Faris to Washington, Collier would be able either to resolve the superintendent's conflict with the SCS or remove him, and then dismiss the old council and create a new one free from the control of the large herders.[52]

Collier made his decision to reassign Faris and deal with the council problem far more deliberately than Shepard or Woehlke wanted. He totally refused Woehlke's scheme to block a council resolution adverse to the SCS by "impounding" Dodge and other leaders in Washington. "If the big sheep-owner interest is going to flare out at a meeting," Collier asked, "may it not be just as well to let it flare out?" Admitting the need for personnel changes at Window Rock, the commissioner wanted to visit the area and talk to Faris and other participants in the feud before taking any action.[53]

Evidently, Collier was unsure what course to take. He had no guarantee that a replacement of Faris would solve the mess. Even finding someone with sufficient force and intelligence to gain control over the tangled situation doubtlessly delayed matters. By mid-February Collier decided that Faris must be relieved, but the commissioner was still not sure whom to appoint. Chee Dodge advised Collier and Ickes that only a stern army officer could settle the unrest and rule his tribe in a just manner.[54] Both officials strongly rejected Chee's suggestion. Collier then asked Dr. W. W. Peter, director of medical work on the reservation, to become general superintendent, but he refused. The delays in naming a replacement unfortunately created new rumors, led to even more unrest, and placed Faris under considerable embarrassment.[55]

51. Shepard to Collier, 11 January 1936, Collier papers, YU.
52. Woehlke to Collier, 15 January 1936, Collier papers, YU.
53. Collier to Woehlke, 15 January 1936, Collier papers, YU.
54. Chee Dodge to Collier 13 February 1936, File 9219, 1936, 162, NA, RG 75.
55. Faris to Collier, 27 February 1936, Office File of Commissioner John Collier, NA, RG 75.

Finally on March 29, 1936, Collier announced that E. R. Fryer, director of land-use programs among the Pueblos, would take over Navajo affairs. Faris became one of Collier's field representatives, a prestigious post usually reserved for the more distinguished Indian Service workers in the closing years of their careers.[56] Reassignment came more as a form of relief than an indignity to Faris. He remarked to Fryer when the new superintendent came to Window Rock to take office, "I wish you well; I suppose I'm just too old for this sort of thing; I just had to tell John Collier that I couldn't possibly do it, so that is the reason for my leaving."[57]

The replacement of Faris marked the nadir of federal efforts on the reservation during the New Deal. At the time all of the government's major plans seemed to be stagnating. The number of livestock still remained much higher than even the most optimistic estimates of grazing capacity. The unified administration was still incomplete. The day schools had finally opened in the fall of 1935, but not the subagencies. Collier seemed unable to decide what to do with the tribal council.

Interagency rivalries, criticism of whites, and Navajo resistance to conservation were the most important problems facing Fryer in March 1936. Of the three, only the bickering between the SCS and Indian Service personnel offered any opportunity for an immediate and complete solution. The time-honored techniques of hiring, firing, and transfers of employees, plus strong policy enforcement, could create the unified administration that Collier demanded at Window Rock. There was some chance that the support from missionaries, traders, and Indian reform organizations might be partly restored, but this would require time. Navajo hostility, however, was obviously not susceptible to instant amelioration even by the most subtle cajolery. Given this background, Collier faced the uncomfortable alternative of either abandoning the conservation effort entirely to win back Navajo support or putting the stalemated plans for the grazing districts into operation regardless of tribal sentiment. In naming Fryer, he had decided to push the conservation effort to completion.

56. *Albuquerque Journal*, 30 January 1936, p. 1.
57. Fryer Interview, 1970.

# 5

## The Creation of the Navajo Service

The reassignment of Chester E. Faris and the appointment of E. R. Fryer as general superintendent in March 1936 brought little basic change to the government's policy for administering Navajo affairs during the coming years. Instead Fryer's main tasks involved fulfilling unrealized plans, many of which dated back to 1933. More specifically, he hoped to end the interagency feuding, to complete the administrative consolidation started in 1934, and to devise a land management program which would adjust livestock holdings to grazing capacity. Fryer's chief objective was to begin active leadership and to put the government's house in order.

The new superintendent's background, training, and experience were almost completely antithetic to those of men who normally headed major reservations. Born in Mesa, Arizona, of Mormon pioneer stock, Fryer grew up in the Salt River Valley near the Pima reservation. His associations with local Indian youngsters brought him a fair fluency in Pima. After high school, Fryer attended the University of Washington majoring in fisheries and forestry. He had ranched in the Sierra Ancha Mountains of central Arizona before entering the Forest Service as an assistant ecologist. In late 1933 Fryer first came to the Navajo reservation in the contingent of Soil Erosion Service technicians assembled by Calkins at Mexican Springs. As an SES employee, Fryer worked at Mexican Springs, helped locate the demonstration areas, and supervised conservation projects at Ganado.[1]

The chief reason for Fryer's appointment as superintendent of the Navajos was his success as director of land management operations among the Pueblos in 1935. He negotiated long-term stock reduction

1. Fryer Interview, 1970.

agreements with the Laguna and Acoma Pueblos despite difficulties in getting the leaders' consent and even greater problems in overcoming the large owners' opposition when actual stock removals took place. These successes and his ability to avoid interagency troubles which disrupted Faris's administration led observers to comment that the Pueblo conservation program, despite a later start, was at least a year ahead of that of the Navajo reservation. When the administrative fracas broke out at Window Rock in late 1935, Fryer was first suggested as a likely, although untried, candidate to replace Faris.[2]

To the Navajos, the new superintendent seemed much too young to be holding such an important post. A tall and good-looking man of thirty-five when appointed, Fryer possessed a trim physique and unlined face which disconcerted Navajo headmen when first introduced to him. Quite frequently at outdoor meetings leaders would shake his hand and then solemnly, and without disrespect, lift up his hat to gaze closely at his hair. Fryer's curly blond thatch invariably led the baffled Indians to exclaim to bystanders, "but he doesn't have any gray hairs!"[3] The handicap of a youthful appearance proved to be only temporary. A few years at Window Rock, without question the toughest assignment in the Indian Service at the time, not only made his lack of age of secondary importance, but it brought a sprinkling of gray which answered the Indians' needs.

In the long run, the characteristics which upset the Navajos more than Fryer's appearance were his forceful disposition and his directness in dealing with them.[4] The new superintendent was very much a New Dealer, who ardently believed that land management and herd reduction could solve the Navajos' problems. He also frequently left the office routine at Window Rock to spend a good portion of his time visiting local trouble spots. Such travel involved psychological strain and some physical danger, but he believed that he had to support field workers in person, for their effectivenes could be ruined by any loss of prestige. There was seldom anything oblique or subtle about Fryer's approach during his appearances at even the most hostile meetings. When he discovered, for example, that Navajo interpreters tended to soften his statements, he hired Howard Gorman to trans-

2. Shepard to Collier, 11 January 1936, Collier papers, YU.
3. Fryer Interview, 1970.
4. Trockur Interview.

late. Gorman rendered Fryer's words with the full meaning and impact that he intended.[5] As Morgan and his followers learned from various confrontations, the young superintendent had a short temper and he blazed back at their charges with emotional force. Fryer was a stubborn and forthright battler. Probably no other type of leader could have succeeded in what Collier wanted done and yet withstood the resulting criticism.

Despite the fact that many Navajos disliked Fryer, the new superintendent had been a strong advocate of the tribe since his earlier stay on the reservation. After his return as superintendent, Fryer's affection became even greater. He learned enough Navajo to follow conversations although he never developed a speaking fluency in the difficult language, and he also acquired a fairly full understanding of tribal culture. Perhaps most important, Fryer took on the Navajos' causes as his own. In such matters as overpricing at trading posts, white bootleggers, the vice problem at Gallup, and the New Mexico boundary bill, the young leader defended the tribe's interests with the same fervor that he employed to achieve the policy goals of the government.

Ickes and Collier very obviously wanted a thorough shakeup of the Window Rock administration when they appointed Fryer to achieve the long-delayed reorganization. As late as March 1936 some business was still being handled at the six agencies. One visitor to the reservation at this time reported that some Navajos still conducted affairs at the older local offices rather than using the Window Rock headquarters.[6] Fryer's initial task was to create an administrative machinery which completed the consolidation and ended the rivalry between the Indian Service and the SCS. Out of the agencies' unification came the Navajo Service.

The new organization was designed at a conference of SCS and

5. Gorman's change from a close associate of Morgan to an employee of the Navajo Service grew out of his personal problems. When he left his first wife about the time of Fryer's appointment, Gorman was fired at the Ganado Mission. Fryer soon hired him as an interpreter-assistant and he remained a progovernment leader.

6. Moris Burge, a field worker for the National Association of Indian Affairs, headed by Oliver La Farge, visited the reservation in March 1936 and filed a report containing this impression. See Moris Burge, "Field Report, Navajo Reservation, March, 1936," Statistics Division—Reports and Other Records, Navajo Agency, NA, RG 75. A supporter of government efforts, Burge authored a fuller pamphlet entitled *The Navajo and the Land*, Bulletin 26, National Association on Indian Affairs, Inc., and American Indian Defense Association, Inc., 1937.

Indian Service personnel held at Albuquerque shortly before Fryer's appointment. As in earlier attempts at consolidation, officials tried to integrate the conventional functions of the Indian Service with New Deal emergency programs and SCS operations. The concept for achieving the integration, according to government statements, utilized "converging rather than parallel lines of responsibility."[7] All departments at Window Rock under the new scheme, regardless of their function or budgetary support, reported to Fryer. He, in turn, became responsible to SCS Regional Conservator Calkins for land management affairs and to Collier for other matters.[8] When Collier visited Window Rock to install Fryer in office, the commissioner suggested that the revised organization be named the Navajo Service.

In April 1936, Fryer completed an overhaul of the land management division. W. G. McGinnies, formerly a faculty member of the University of Arizona, became director of land management. Three assistants served under McGinnies. One dealt with the administration of forestry, range management, extension, and related programs. Another managed construction activities such as drilling wells, irrigation development, and road building. The third assistant supervised all planning and surveys.[9] Everything not associated with land management fell under Fryer's direct supervision, including law and order, tribal council relations, education, health, land rentals, transportation, clerical tasks, and disbursments. Supervision of these activities fell to G. A. Trotter, the capable assistant superintendent under Faris. Thomas Dodge also remained as special assistant to Fryer and soon resigned as chairman of the tribal council. Dodge's chief role was to handle liaison with the Navajos which often entailed traveling with Gorman to observe protest meetings.[10]

Soon after these revisions, Fryer consolidated relief and employment matters into one office. Several problems had created the need for the change. New Deal work programs had frequently competed with each other for workers which drove up wages. In other instances, several members of wealthy families had been appointed to federal

7. "Narrative Section, Annual Statistical Report, 1936," Statistics Division—Reports and Other Records, Navajo Agency, NA, RG 75.

8. Ibid. There is little evidence that Calkins fully exerted his power to direct conservation work on the reservation, although he probably retained general control.

9. "Organization of the Land Management Division," n.d., File 4285, 37, 346, CCC-ID, NA, RG 75.

10. Gorman Interview.

jobs, while poorer Navajos often could not find employment. Finally, the government possessed no records on many Navajos who needed relief supplies because of age or other disabilities. By August 1936, the Navajo Service finished an employment census so that the more deserving received jobs. At the same time, Fryer issued orders standardizing wage scales for all emergency work programs.[11]

Fryer accompanied the administrative changes with major personnel shifts. He concentrated on the old-line Indian Service workers whom he believed incapable of adjusting to the Navajo Service.[12] In most cases he followed the established tradition in the Indian Service of transferring unwanted employees to other reservations. Such shifts and outright dismissals raised strong condemnations of Fryer.

Collier's promise to support the shakeup was sorely tested when Fryer, without consulting the commissioner, reassigned Forrest Parker to a CCC post in Phoenix. An in-law of the influential Hubbells and a personal friend of Collier, Parker had directed the CCC and the Mounted Patrol since late 1933. Fryer's appointment of C. H. Powers to head the CCC and Fred Croxen, a former U. S. Border Service worker, to reorganize law enforcement brought a letter from Collier in which he obliquely questioned the wisdom of the Parker transfer. Fryer's terse reply that he had shifted Parker because he doubted the need for him in CCC work and questioned his capacity for police work went unrebutted.[13]

The administrative reordering and personnel reshuffling in 1936 were accompanied by strong efforts to develop an esprit de corps among all government workers on the reservation. Indeed, the hope of making the Navajo Service viable and effective became, as he freely admitted, an obsession with Fryer.[14] His pep talks repeatedly admonished government employees to forget bureaucratic rivalries and to unite behind the government program. He ordered large decals with the words, "Navajo Service," placed on the doors of all government vehicles as a means of giving visibility to the new

11. "Report on Employment," 6 August 1936, and "Memorandum to All Administrative and Supervisory Personnel. . . ," 6 August 1936, Statistics Division—Reports and Other Records, NA, RG 75.

12. Fryer Interview, 1970.

13. Parker to Collier, 13 May 1936, and Fryer to Collier, 28 May 1936, Collier papers, YU.

14. "Proceedings of the First Annual Navajo Service Land Management Conference," 2–6 March 1937, Flagstaff, Arizona, St. Michaels Mission.

organization. The many shifts of officials in the 1936 reorganization were in themselves helpful in achieving a sense of unity, for employees had been so indiscriminately mixed together that they hardly knew whether they worked for the Indian Service or the SCS.

The establishment of land management districts in the summer of 1936 exceeded in importance Fryer's administrative changes. Though first announced in November 1935 when Ickes approved the new grazing regulations, the boundaries of the districts were not completed until May 1936. The achievement of this task was certainly the most significant example of using cultural and land-use data in the administration of Navajo affairs and it had a tremendous import for the future. The technicians laying out the districts had originally planned to use Calkin's concept that land management operations should be based on watersheds and other geographic features. Except where mountains or other terrain barriers existed, however, natural factors played a minor role in the Navajos' relationship to their land. Instead, the primary determinants of land use were small communities made up of outfits or closely related extended families. These Indian groups normally respected each other's range and agricultural land and the government workers, by drawing district lines between their holdings, did little to disrupt the existing patterns of grazing or farming.

This discovery, however, did not provide an adequate rationale for establishing districts to administer land management programs. There were far too many family-oriented communities on the reservation for the government to use them as subagencies. The surveyors found a workable basis by drawing boundaries which coincided with economic patterns formed by the trading posts. Because of poor transportation and other deterrents, Navajo trade tended to gravitate toward the nearest post, creating a local "economic basin." Once this pattern became apparent, the field workers realized they had only to ask Navajos where they customarily traded and the district lines could be easily drawn by enclosing several trading areas. Thus, by combining terrain features, the land holdings of related extended families, and the economic basins, the surveyors outlined eighteen land management districts. In most cases the district headquarters could be located at the most important trading post within a district and frequently the same locations were also the sites of day schools. Although the district boundaries were revised in minor details from time to time, their establishment was one of the unique and lasting contributions of the New Deal.

Two of the new land management districts had peculiarities which made them different from others. The Hopis were placed in District 6, their traditional living and grazing area, but some Navajo families also lived in this area. Before Fryer's appointment, all land management activities among the Hopi had to be approved by Window Rock and he continued to exert this control. A superintendent at Keams Canyon, however, administered all other Hopi affairs. Fryer never felt comfortable trying to represent both tribes' needs and in 1938 he abandoned all authority over the Hopis when Collier completely revised their administration.[15] The government also created District 19 in the New Mexico checkerboard as a temporary administrative arrangement to carry out conservation work until the passage of the New Mexico boundary bill. This "mythical district" was eventually dropped in favor of other arrangements.

Following creation of the boundaries, a new set of human dependency surveys quickly were conducted within the districts. The most important information collected dealt with the grazing capacity of each district and the number and classes of livestock each family owned. Fryer asked government stockmen to be especially careful in counting sheep and goats during the dipping season of 1936. Quite obviously his main interest was to assemble the information needed to renew livestock reduction in 1937.

The training of personnel to supervise the conservation work in the districts started soon after the boundaries were drawn. A class of trainees gathered at Window Rock in June 1936 for an intensive course on the program and plans for the land management districts. Except for education, every major office at Window Rock sent a representative to instruct the class. The subject matter focused on irrigation, forestry, and soil erosion with a special stress on range and livestock management. After their classwork, the candidates were given written tests. Based on the results and their general performance, the top nineteen men were then assigned as supervisors to the land management districts in the summer of 1936. A few others

15. See "Commissioner John Collier's Meeting with the Hopi Indians at Oraibi, Arizona, July 14, 1938," LAFRC, Box 72947.

became assistants at the more important districts. Until the work season of 1937, the supervisors did little except become acquainted with the local Indians and the area.[16]

The district supervisors' previous employments were varied, but most had had practical experience in livestock raising in the Southwest. A few had been stationed on the reservation before 1933, while others had served in the emergency work programs launched since the New Deal. Several were members of trading families. Apparently most had completed only high school. All of the first group were white, but in at least two or three instances educated Navajos later were appointed. In general the quality and diligence of district supervisors varied considerably and Fryer in his more confidential messages to Collier often complained that he needed better men for some districts. A handful of supervisors, however, later advanced to fairly high positions in the Indian Service.

In the spring of 1937 the Navajo Service hired range riders to assist with district administration. Some of the men employed lived at the district headquarters, but others worked from outlying points in the districts. Usually of indifferent educational achievements and insensitive to Navajo culture, a majority of the range riders were former cowboys or small ranchers driven out of the cattle business by the dustbowl and depression. Most were like a job applicant from Texas who described himself as "no movie cowpuncher, [but] I know which end of a cow gets up first."[17] Unlike many white newcomers to the reservation, the cowboys' background protected them against loneliness and isolation.

The district supervisors and range riders played an important role in the day-to-day administration of Navajo affairs after 1936. They were directly involved in forcing livestock reduction upon the tribe and bore the brunt of the Navajos' resistance to further livestock sales and other government programs. While Fryer and Window Rock officials might visit trouble spots at times of crisis, the work of supervising dipping, organizing roundups of cattle and horses for branding and counting, and delivering grazing permits to Navajos fell to supervisors and range riders. The hard physical labor of livestock operations was far less trying to them than the psychological

16. Mr. Zweifel Interview; "District Supervisors School," *The Navajo Service News* 1 (1 July 1936): 10.
17. "First Annual Navajo Service Land Management Conference," 1937.

strain of threats and intimidation which occurred after the renewal of reduction in 1937. To the average Navajo, the district supervisor and range riders were the government and Navajo Service officials always feared that local Indians would release their pent-up hostility against reduction by attacking district personnel. Remarkably only one such assault took place before 1942.

The discontent and tensions suffered by the spouses of district personnel far exceeded that of their husbands. Some wives felt that it was extremely unfair for the government to assign their husbands to such hazards without better police protection. In addition to feeling fear and bitterness, the women often complained about the crude housing provided, their boredom, and restricted contact with other whites. These wives struggled to keep busy with housework, reading, daily trips to the local trading post, and horseback riding, but they found that inventing activities failed to relieve their worries.

One wife of a range rider later wrote a book filled with bitter memories of the petty jealousies and discrimination she had encountered from other government workers. An educated woman, she felt that a rigid caste system prevailed among Navajo Service workers. Teachers, for example, blamed her husband because his participation in stock reduction efforts caused recalcitrant Navajo parents to withhold their children from school. She found herself ostracized by government employees in higher salary brackets even though they lived nearby and suffered from the same isolation.[18]

In several land management districts where irrigation and farming were important, the government appointed farm extension workers to the district staffs. These field workers looked after the maintenance of the irrigation systems, especially the task of cleaning out the canals and laterals each spring. They also arranged loans for the Navajos to buy seed and the tools needed to raise their crops and generally assisted the Indians in any way possible with planting, cultivation, and harvesting.

Without question, the land management districts brought the Navajos into closer contact with government workers than at any previous time. A capable district supervisor and his assistants met with local Navajos frequently to explain government policies, to plan programs, and to answer questions. The supervisors also worked

18. Elizabeth Ward, *No Dudes, Few Women, Life with a Navajo Range Rider* (Albuquerque, 1951), *passim*.

closely with the Indians on introducing improved rams, bulls, and stallions to the bloodlines. This sometimes involved arranging credit for the Indians and supervising repayment. If he was astute and conscientious, the district supervisor came to know each Navajo family personally, the number of children and wives the husband had, whether he drank, used peyote, or philandered, his financial standing, and, of course, his attitude toward the government.[19]

The shortwave radio network established between the district headquarters and Window Rock in 1938 also brought the Navajos into a closer relationship with the government. District supervisors controlled only land and livestock management and many other questions had to be referred to Window Rock by either radio or telephone. The supervisors reported to the tribal headquarters on a weekly schedule about weather conditions, school attendance, protest meetings, epidemics, and other matters.[20] In addition, the radio network was used to receive programs from Window Rock which usually consisted of speeches or panel discussions by government employees and tribal leaders. Local Navajos were encouraged to meet at district headquarters to listen to such broadcasts to achieve a better understanding of government programs.

Improved communication contributed toward reducing the tribe's loyalty to the old six agencies and to the chapter organizations that had been developed prior to the New Deal. The chapters were often retained, but only as powerless precincts of the land management districts. Several years elapsed before the Navajos accepted the new district plan. Even though their district supervisor could normally obtain a response from Window Rock on questions that the Indians raised, many of the Navajos still wanted to talk to Fryer, "the first boss," in person. Completely oblivious to protocol, they sometimes jumped the chain of command and tried to contact the superintendent (or even Collier or Ickes) with complaints. "They didn't get much sympathy from Window Rock," one former district supervisor recalls, because officials told them to return home and to submit their queries through regular channels.[21] Fryer's policy of visiting troublespots and focusing hostility upon himself helped strengthen the position of the district supervisors. Although the Navajos never fully

19. Mr. Zweifel Interview.
20. Mr. Zweifel Interview.
21. Mr. Zweifel Interview.

accepted the district plan as long as it regulated land use and live-stock numbers, their petitions by the late 1930s indicated that they had become conscious of the units.

Even though Fryer achieved remarkable success in developing the Navajo Service into an effective organization, he was unable to avoid clashing with the Morgan faction. The first controversy arose almost before the new superintendent had settled into office. The issue dealt with the Fruitland irrigation project, located on the San Juan River southwest of Farmington, New Mexico. Discussed long before the New Deal, Fruitland was begun in 1933 with PWA funds. The 5,100-acre plot was by far the largest of the many irrigation efforts undertaken by the Collier administration. A dam built above Farmington diverted water from the San Juan into a main canal which carried it some eighteen miles downstream to the irrigated land. When Fryer took office, the work on the dam and the canal was virtually completed and the preparation of the land—removal of brush, grading, and installation of laterals—had started. A small portion of Fruitland was ready for the Navajos' use by the planting season of 1936.[22]

In early April 1936, Fryer dropped a bombshell when he an-nounced that the previously planned allocation of twenty acres to each family at Fruitland would be reduced to ten acres. The superin-tendent also declared that each allotee must give up all his livestock and support his family solely from irrigated farming.[23] The changes caused strong protests from local Navajos who reportedly threatened a Fryer subordinate with bodily harm when he presented the new plan at a meeting. The objectors complained that they had been promised the larger acreage and, proceeding on that assumption, they had contributed one day of free labor per week while employed

22. Little information exists on New Deal irrigation development on the Navajo reservation. In his first appearances before the tribal council, Collier spoke loosely of providing 25,000 acres of irrigated land, but this amount obviously was never developed. Collier perhaps hoped to undertake the "Turley Project" which involved irrigating a huge tract of highlands south of the San Juan River near Farmington. References in official correspondence indicate that Fryer ordered a survey of existing irrigation projects shortly after he became superintendent and the government subsequently built numerous small irrigation projects at scattered sites. Leaders during the 1930s occasionally spoke of relocating Navajos to an irrigation project on the Colorado River at Parker, Arizona, but I have found no evidence of this being done before 1942. Later some Navajos were moved to Parker.

23. *Farmington Times Hustler*, 10 April 1936, p. 1, and 24 April 1936, p. 1.

on the irrgation project since 1933. Now their holdings would be halved, their livestock lost, and outsiders allowed to share in the benefits. When Fryer visited Shiprock some time in mid-April to face the protestors, the Indians treated the young superintendent rudely and he answered back with equal heat.[24] According to J. C. Morgan, not always the most trustworthy witness, Fryer "pounded his fist on the table and said that the Indians can object or oppose the program from now to doomsday, it is going to be carried out. He meant the sheep reduction will continue along with the balance of his program."[25]

Viewed strictly from the perspective of subsistence needs and reservation resources, Fryer's decision was correct. He realized that most Navajo families farmed an average of only five acres of irrigated land, an amount which provided them with all the corn, beans, squashes, and other produce that they wanted. A large portion of the twenty-acre allotments would likely go unused. Moreover, the original acreage far exceeded the amount of productive farm land available to other members of the tribe. If all the crop land on the reservation were distributed equally among Navajos at the time, each family would have received 2.2 acres of irrigated land, 4.6 acres of flood irrigated land, and 1.0 acre of dry farm land.[26] The most important reason for halving the Fruitland allotments was the growing realization among land management personnel that the livestock industry, regardless of land use improvements, range management, or improved livestock breeding, would never fully meet the subsistence needs of the Navajos.

A study of tribal resources then being completed by McGinnies and the land management division obviously guided Fryer's decision on Fruitland. Land management officials calculated that each Navajo family needed $235 (based on prices charged at trading posts) in annual income to subsist. This figure could be achieved by the ownership of fifty-seven ewes or six acres of irrigated land. The study

24. Roman Hubbell to Collier, 17 May 1936, Collier papers, YU.

25. "New Navajo 'Program'—Much Talk—Little Wisdom," *The American Indian* 5 (April-May 1936): 8.

26. Flood irrigation consisted of soaking the land adjacent to streams or washes during annual floods by constructing a temporary dam or some sort of water-spreading device. Because water was applied only once, the method was not as productive and less certain than the more sophisticated irrigation systems designed by the government. Dry farming, of course, was even more tenuous than flood irrigation.

further estimated that the livestock industry could support 7,193 families, leaving 2,807 families to rely on arts and crafts, farming, or government jobs as a means of livelihood.[27] Based on this information, halving the size of the Fruitland allotments made sense. Fryer's decision eventually enabled many young educated Navajos from other parts of the reservation to take up subsistence farming. To such returned students the only other sources of income were wage work or relief.

Whether the decision was sound statescraft was highly debatable. Fryer and other Window Rock spokesmen tried to explain away the earlier promises of twenty-acre allotments by claiming that they were only tentative and made by unauthorized personnel. Government leaders also stated that the pledges had been caused by pressures from a few wealthy Navajo families who did not really need the irrigated land. The Fruitland Navajos clearly, however, had been promised the larger plots before they agreed to contribute their labor. During the coming years, the controversy continued as more irrigated land became available. Local Indians refused to accept the decreased allotments despite numerous attempts at compromise. The stalemate remained unbroken until 1940 when forty-three Fruitland families moved onto the project.[28] These and other local Navajo families who followed never became fully reconciled to the reduced allotments and as late as the early 1950s the council delegate from Fruitland was a long-time resident who had "been very outspoken in criticism of stock reduction and the land assignment system on the Fruitland Project."[29]

The debate over Fruitland benefited J. C. Morgan. The Fruitland-Shiprock area was the center of his political strength and the locale where most of his missionary work took place. At the time of Fryer's appointment, Morgan and Paul Palmer, a white lawyer from Farmington, were in Washington protesting against Collier's policies.[30]

27. "The Agricultural and Range Resources of the Navajo Reservation in Relationship to the Subsistence Needs of the Navajo Indians," 12 May 1936, Hubbell Trading Post.

28. Tom Sasaki, *Fruitland, New Mexico: A Navajo Community in Transition* (Ithaca, New York, 1960), p. 43. This study contains a very full treatment of the difficulties between local Navajos and the government over the distribution of irrigated land and the frictions between Fruitland Indians and the outsiders that took up allotments.

29. Tom Sasaki and John Adair, "New Land to Farm," *in* Edward H. Spicer, ed., *Human Problems in Technological Change* (New York, 1952), p. 103.

30. *Gallup Independent*, 18 March 1936, p. 1.

Morgan's opposition to the forced sales of livestock in the New Mexico checkerboard indicated that he had now come round to using herd reduction as a direct weapon against the government.[31] Upon his return to Farmington, Morgan quickly denounced Fryer's decision on Fruitland as another example of government duplicity, unfairness, and high handedness. He also reported the incident and his views of it to Bruner's American Indian Federation and the Indian Rights Association. Both organizations soon published critical stories on Fruitland in their propaganda campaign against Collier.[32]

The uproar over Fruitland sparked newspaper reports in early May that the Navajos were poised to revolt against the government and had given Fryer and his staff thirty days to leave Window Rock.[33] The new superintendent denied the stories, saying that he knew of no threats against government officials. He blamed the rumors about violence on the furor at Fruitland and hinted that Morgan and a few whites were behind the false reports. Fryer characterized the entire business as a "studied attempt" to intimidate his administration and to discredit its efforts to keep the reservation from becoming a barren wasteland.[34]

The person responsible for publishing the reports was Columbus Giragi, and the episode was the first of several clashes between Fryer and the outspoken young editor. Giragi and a brother owned small but prosperous papers in Winslow and Holbrook and leased the larger Coconino Sun in Flagstaff.[35] The three locations along the southern edge of the reservation gave Columbus unusual influence as a commentator on Navajo affairs. Perhaps as a carry-over from the pungent style of frontier journalism, Giragi's editorials on any subject served up hyperbole, humor, gossip, fantasy, and occasional truth with exceptional punch. He especially delighted in deflating egos by personal jabs and his editorials broadly classified Collier (nicknamed the "Little Rooster") and Ickes as American counterparts of Hitler and Mussolini for their handling of Navajo affairs. Giragi's running commentary during the New Deal kept Window Rock officials alternating between moods of rage and amusement,

31. Ickes to Trotter, 21 February 1936, Hubbell Trading Post.

32. "New Navajo 'Program,' " p. 8; "Navajo Unrest," Indian Truth 13 (May 1936): 2–3.

33. Coconino Sun, 8 May 1936, p. 1.

34. Gallup Independent, 7 May 1936, p. 1; Santa Fe New Mexican, 8 May 1936, pp. 1, 5.

35. Coconino Sun, 31 October 1941, pp. 1, 3.

but the tongue-in-cheek attacks were probably not taken too seriously by Giragi's readers.

The Fruitland controversy had hardly lost its edge when a new outburst took place with the premature release of future plans to reduce Navajo livestock. The McGinnies report on Navajo resources and subsistence needs fell into the hands of the *Gallup Independent* and the newspaper published two long stories derived from the data on June 5 and 6, 1936. The stories emphasized that the tribe currently owned 1,269,910 sheep units, while the grazing capacity of the reservation was only 560,000 units. In the future, the government would reduce 944,910 head of sheep and goats to 361,000 ewes; 25,000 head of cattle would be cut to 9,000; and 45,000 horses, mules, and burros would be lowered to 30,000.[36] Fryer assumed that the information had been given out by someone who wanted to embarrass the government. When he made inquiries in Gallup, however, he learned that Collier had unwittingly mailed the McGinnies report to the local papers.

Unfortunately, the revelation that Navajos would have to reduce their livestock holdings by fifty-six percent proved a serious mistake. The government was in no way prepared to implement any reduction as the district supervisors had not been trained nor had the grazing capacities of the individual land management districts been established. Fryer had frankly told the Navajos that they would have to sell more livestock eventually, but he explained that he could not establish sales quotas until the surveys of the land management districts were completed.

The untimely disclosure of livestock reduction plans provoked a series of emotional protests similar to those during the closing weeks of the Wheeler-Howard campaign of the previous summer. The seriousness of the discontent was shown by Chee Dodge's personal attack on Collier when he visited Window Rock in mid-June. At a meeting of 200 government workers and Indian leaders, Chee charged that herd reductions had produced hunger and epidemics among Navajos. He also denounced Collier for failing to consult with the tribe on important affairs.[37] An exchange amounting to a debate followed when Collier tried to rebut Dodge's charges.[38]

---

36. *Gallup Independent*, 5 June 1936, p. 1, and 6 June 1936, pp. 1, 4.
37. Ibid., 20 June 1936, p. 1.
38. *Farmington Times Hustler*, 26 June 1936, p. 1.

The reaction of the Morgan faction to reports of new livestock reductions was more extreme. His supporters firmly believed that Collier intended to use livestock sales to punish them for rejecting the Wheeler-Howard Act a year earlier. Protestors from the Manuelito district charged that "Collier got mad at us and now he wants stock reduction again, but we don't want to give him one more head no matter how much he fights against us because he didn't give us one half of what he promised us the first time."[39] Another group of dissidents demanded that the entire Collier program be abandoned so the tribe could return to the old six agencies and their situation before the New Deal.[40] Morgan himself used the new wave of discontent to deride the land management districts. Twisting Collier's 1933 statements to the council on the need to unite the tribe and its administration, Morgan claimed that the new district plans were additional evidence of the commissioner's perfidy. Instead of tribal unity, the government now wanted nineteen Navajo tribes. With more validity, Morgan warned that the districts were a prelude to new livestock removals.[41]

A meeting of prominent Navajos on July 7 at the Ganado chapter house carried several ominous overtones. Called so the leaders could informally register their reactions to recent Collier statements that the tribal council needed to be reorganized, the gathering excluded all government spokesmen and other whites.[42] Morgan and Chee Dodge both appeared and spoke in opposition to the government. Not all councilmen appeared, but many attended from the eastern half of the reservation and the New Mexico checkerboard.

A group of over 300 Navajos listened to speeches devoted to council reorganization and the government's future plans for range and livestock management. According to a local newspaper story, the group "adopted the attitude they would refuse to comply with range control methods until definitely shown that unwatered areas of the reservation will be developed."[43] This view unquestionably reflected the Dodge faction's contention that the reservation was not really overgrazed and the tribe could keep existing levels of livestock if

39. Navajo Indians of the Manuelito district to Jake Morgan, 30 June 1936, St. Michaels Mission.
40. Twin Lakes Chapter to Leonard Haven, ca. 3 July 1936, Chavez papers UA.
41. *Farmington Times Hustler*, 3 July 1936, p. 1.
42. Letter addressed to George, 6 July 1936, Hubbell Trading Post.
43. *Gallup Independent*, 9 July 1936, p. 1.

more wells were drilled. Morgan claimed that the meeting unanimously adopted resolutions against further stock reduction and any
revision of the present tribal council and demanded a return to the
old six agencies.[44]

The appearance of Morgan and Dodge together at Ganado and
the prospective alliance of traditional and educated factions potentially could have been an insurmountable obstacle for Fryer, but the
threat lasted only briefly. Chee issued a statement strongly supporting the government in mid-August. In a spectacular flip-flop, Dodge
blamed recent tribal discontent on a few whites and Navajos who
had misrepresented the Wheeler-Howard Act.[45] The reason for
Chee's startling reversal is not difficult to detect. Earlier in August
Collier had met Dodge in Albuquerque and spent an entire morning
rewinning the old Navajo's support. Chee's intense dislike and
jealousy of Morgan certainly played an important part in his reversal
of attitude toward the government.[46] Navajo politics afterward re-
gained their normal pattern with Morgan as an outspoken critic and
Dodge as the reluctant and intermittent supporter of the Collier
administration.

The controversies on the reservation were matched by criticisms
of Collier from regional and national sources. In May 1936, Mable
Dodge Luhan broke with the commissioner. An avant-garde ex-
patriate from New York, Mrs. Luhan had married a Taos Indian
soon after World War I and first introduced her friend Collier to
native American culture in 1920. A capable propagandist, Mrs.
Luhan now loudly demanded that Collier fire Dr. Sophie Aberle,
the superintendent of the United Pueblo Agency, for a long list of
failures and incompetencies. The charges and countercharges
exchanged in public (and even more so in private) between Collier
and Mrs. Luhan aroused much gossip and speculation.[47] Even worse,
Collier found himself under a growing barrage of criticism in the
Indian Affairs committees of both the House and Senate, particularly
from Senator Dennis Chavez's stubborn fight against the New Mexico boundary bill. Senator Elmer Thomas of Oklahoma, Chairman

44. *Farmington Times Hustler*, 24 July 1936, p. 6.
45. *Gallup Independent*, 15 August 1936, pp. 1, 4.
46. Collier to Ickes, 4 August 1936, Collier papers, YU.
47. The best sources for the Collier-Luhan fight are letters in the commissioner's office
files at the National Archives and correspondence between Mrs. Luhan and Senator
Dennis Chavez in the latter's papers at the University of Albuquerque.

of the Senate Indian Affairs Committee, announced that he would personally lead an investigation of reservation affairs as soon as Congress adjourned that summer.[48]

As a result of disputes on and off the Navajo reservation, plus some wishful thinking among some circles, newspapers in Arizona and New Mexico spread the rumor in early July that Collier was on his way out as commissioner. The only question, according to the reports, was whether he would resign after the Democratic national convention or following the November elections.[49]

Despite these rumors, Fryer continued his efforts to make the Navajo Service an effective organization. He had some difficulties with Calkins and the district SCS office in the summer of 1936, but the problem was settled to both men's satisfaction a short time later.[50] The dismissals and transfers of the old guard continued as Fryer implemented his plans for the Navajo Service.

No doubt the quickest improvements were in CCC operations. By hiring C. H. Powers to head the program, Fryer found an exceptional leader who demanded a rigid discipline of the young enrollees and reformed the program to meet the needs of the land management division. Powers did so under considerable handicaps. The large CCC budgets of the first three years of the New Deal ended just after Powers assumed office and he was forced to reduce personnel by forty percent during the latter half of 1936. Moreover, Powers inherited worn out heavy equipment which needed replacement. Finally, he faced a serious problem in maintaining a well-drilling program started earlier. The new wells contained large quantities of sand which clogged and wore out pumps, requiring substantial maintenance and repair.[51] Nevertheless, Powers was able to keep the CCC operating as one of the most effective programs on any Indian reservation.

The most rewarding of Powers' efforts was the providing of education for Navajo enrollees. Up to this time the Indian CCC had emphasized production achievements far more than any sort of

48. See Chapter 6 for a complete discussion of the hearings and the fate of the legislative struggle.

49. *Farmington Times Hustler*, 10 July 1936, p. 3.

50. Fryer to Calkins, 2 July 1936, LAFRC, Box 72938.

51. "Brief Narrative Report of Emergency Conservation Work," ca. 1 July 1936, File 59055, 36, 344, Navajo—Volume I, NA, RG 75.

rehabilitation. In 1936 national officials, however, urged field leaders to start classes in safety and first aid training and to place more emphasis on education. The Navajo CCC quickly responded to the new policy and the training program which Powers and his associates started for Navajo enrollees in 1936 became a model for other Indian CCC units. This was especially true of classes in literacy and on-the-job training after 1936. Because of Powers' successes, the CCC program remained virtually free from reservation controversies.

In the summer of 1936 drought conditions reappeared on the Navajo reservation and, during the severe winter which followed, the government undertook its initial general relief program. Notice of the drought first appeared in June when a local paper reported that water holes had dried up and the grass had been scorched by a lack of rainfall. A medicine man and several colleagues revived and staged a ceremony reputed to bring rains, but their efforts proved unsuccessful.[52] In August officials learned that midwestern feeders would buy only about one-fourth of the Navajos' fall lambs which meant that the remainder would have to be retained on the reservation during the winter. Knowing that the Navajo range would not support the unsold animals, Fryer asked the federal government to declare the reservation a drought area so Navajos could receive extra feed for their livestock, but his request was unsuccessful.[53]

As seems typical of weather in the Southwest, the dry summer was followed that winter by severe blizzards. A storm in early January 1937 dropped temperatures to ten degrees below zero and deposited large amounts of snow across the reservation. Two Navajo girls froze to death near Keams Canyon when they became lost in the blizzard. The same storm trapped a party of 300 Indians in the remote Zuni Mountains south of Gallup where they had gone to pick piñon nuts. Fryer dispatched trucks and snowplows to reach the stranded group and he helped direct the rescue from an airplane.[54] The relief party finally located the piñon gatherers, who were in amazingly good shape, and carried them back to the reservation. A second blizzard hit Navajo country later the same month and brought two to three feet of new snow. Although less severe than the winter of 1931–32,

52. *Santa Fe New Mexican*, 27 June 1936, p. 2.
53. F. H. Walton to John Herrick, 13 August 1936, File 62306, 1935, 720, NA, RG 75.
54. *Santa Fe New Mexican*, 1 January 1937, p. 1, and 2 January 1937, pp. 1, 4.

the bad weather killed many livestock that could not reach the grass under the thick white coating.[55]

Fortunately Fryer had already made preparations before the winter to meet the tribe's relief needs. Richard Van Valkenburgh, an SCS employee, had conducted a survey of Eastern Navajos in 1936 aimed at determining the extent of destitution.[56] After this study Fryer established relief stations throughout the Navajo country. Although relief was not new to Navajos who lived close to the old six agencies, this network was the first systematic attempt to bring commodities to the reservation as a whole. By November 1936 a total of 829 people were receiving relief supplies valued at ten dollars per family each month. Included were flour, sugar, beans, coffee, salt pork, baking powder, canned tomatoes, canned mutton, and salt. Dried and canned fruit were given to families with small children. There was nothing extravagant about the quantity of relief given to Navajos. The commodities amounted to about one-fourth the value of goods offered by the WPA to recipients elsewhere.[57]

The Navajos' reactions to relief paralleled the humiliation and bewilderment experienced by many non-Indians when first placed on the dole during the New Deal. Many older tribesmen emphatically rejected the free handouts. Their ethical principles simply did not permit them to consider taking anything without working for it. Employment on the emergency relief programs, however, never raised the same stigma among Navajos that it did for the general public. The Indians did not question the source of their wages, but they believed that they must earn whatever anyone gave them.[58] The policy of advancing wool for weaving rugs and then collecting money for the raw materials when the rugs were sold at trading posts, answered the need for a small portion of Navajo relief recipients, but most simply had to adjust to a dole. By April 1937, approximately five percent of the tribe was on relief.[59] Many Window Rock officials feared that the program would destroy the

55. Ibid., 18 January 1937, p. 3. Informal estimates of livestock losses ranged from two to ten percent.

56. Richard Van Valkenburgh, "Report of Survey Made of Destitute Navajo Indians outside Proposed New Mexico Boundary Extension," ca. May 1936, Van Valkenburgh papers, AHS.

57. *Southwest Tourist News*, 25 November 1936.

58. Fryer Interview, 1970.

59. *Farmington Times Hustler*, 30 April 1937, p. 1.

Navajos' strong self-reliance, but the seriousness of malnutrition during the winter overcame such hesitations. The welfare state arrived among the tribe in the winter of 1936–37 and it remains today as one of the strongest, although not the most admired, legacies of the New Deal.

One program dealing with livestock which federal officials undertook that did not raise controversy among Navajos was the establishment of a sheep breeding laboratory at Fort Wingate in 1936. The new venture represented an attempt to develop a strain of sheep which retained the hardiness, strong mothering traits, and long staple wool of the Navajos' own stock, but which would overcome such drawbacks as late maturity, low weight of fall lambs, and unstable color and fiber content of fleeces. The idea for the laboratory started when Robert Youngblood, Principal Agricultural Economist in the USDA's Office of Experimental Stations, made a study in 1934 of Navajo trading and economics.[60] He observed that past crossing of native Navajo sheep with improved breeds produced short staple wool which weavers found too kinky and oily to wash and card by the crude methods available to them. Yarn from such wool was so soft and knotted that rugs woven from it were bulky and uneven compared to those made from the long staple wool of native sheep. Youngblood concluded that the rug industry would decline further unless something was done to preserve the quality of wool.

When he returned to his regular post in Washington, Young-

60. Youngblood's investigation grew out of the tribal council's discontent with trading practices and Interior Secretary Harold Ickes' request that the Department of Agriculture study trading posts. Youngblood and several assistants started their survey of forty-seven trading posts in April 1934. His lengthy report contained a description of trading operations and numerous charts dealing with such matters as operating costs, credit arrangements, assets and liabilities, and profits. Youngblood concluded that the Navajos must farm more to improve their economic situation. He took the moderate position that the traders' profits were somewhat higher than normal, but he attributed this partly to their lower operating expenses. Navajos, according to the study, badly needed to develop storage facilities instead of selling their goods to trading posts and afterward buying back the same goods in piecemeal fashion at much higher prices. Youngblood further recommended the appointment of a fulltime supervisor of trading who was experienced in retailing and accounting. He also advised the formation of a three-man arbitration committee, consisting of a representative of the Indian Service, the United Indian Traders Association, and the tribal council, to oversee trading practices. See Youngblood, "Navajo Trading," U. S., Congress, Senate, Subcommittee of the Committee on Indian Affairs, 74th Cong., 2nd sess., 1936, Pt. 34, pp. 18036–116.

blood learned that Dr. J. I. Hardy of the Bureau of Animal Industry
had just completed experimental work on wool characteristics and
developed new procedures for testing fiber which might be useful in
studying Navajo sheep. After the two men visited the reservation,
Hardy recommended that Collier seek a federal appropriation to
create an experiment station to develop a new strain of sheep. If the
Indian Service would provide the physical facilities, the Bureau of
Animal Industry would agree to supply the personnel needed to
carry out the research program. Collier succeeded in getting a grant
of $75,000 by mid-1935 and he signed a cooperative agreement with
the Bureau and the SCS to set up a sheep breeding station at Fort
Wingate on 19,000 acres of range land.[61] J. M. Cooper, formerly
head of a similar program at Dubois, Idaho, became the first director.

The Southwestern Range and Sheep Breeding Laboratory had
four major objectives: (1) to determine the type of sheep best suited
to the needs of the Navajos and their range conditions, (2) to breed
this sort of sheep, (3) to achieve maximum production by experiments in range and flock management, and (4) to hold field days and
demonstrations among Navajo herders.[62] Most of the work at the
laboratory before 1942 emphasized the first two objectives and after
that time the remaining goals began to receive more attention.

In 1936 Cooper and laboratory personnel started their work by
purchasing 800 native ewes and twenty rams from remote areas of the
reservation such as Navajo Mountain and Black Mesa where cross-
breeding had been least common. The experts started two breeding
programs that winter. The first was repeated "in-line" or reciprocal
matings of the native stock. The offspring of each new generation
after 1936 were carefully examined for traits which the experts
wanted to develop and animals bearing the desired characteristics
were then retained for subsequent breeding. The second breeding
program consisted of crossing native ewes with Corriedale and
Romney rams. The latter two breeds were selected because their
wool was fairly suitable for home rug weaving. In addition, Cor-

61. "Cooperative Project Agreement. . . ," 6 February 1937, File 73062, 1939,
021.5, NA, RG 75.

62. George M. Sidwell, Jack L. Ruttle, and Earl E. Ray, "Improvement of Navajo
Sheep," (Las Cruces, New Mexico State University, Agricultural Experiment Station
Research Report, 172, 1970), p. 1. This summary of the work of the laboratory is the best
single source available. It contains a bibliography of the general and technical publications which resulted from the experiments between 1935 and 1966.

riedales and Romneys offered some improved traits, such as larger body weight and early maturity, which the experts hoped would overcome weaknesses in the Navajo sheep. After 1936 the Navajo-Corriedale and Navajo-Romney crosses were bred together and the strain, which then consisted of one-half Navajo, one-quarter Corriedale, and one-quarter Romney, was reciprocally bred until 1942 to strengthen and "fix" desirable traits.

The laboratory also conducted extensive tests of the wool of the two strains of sheep. Small samples from different parts of the fleeces of animals were clipped and cross sections were examined under microscopes to determine various types and percentages of fiber. Other studies evaluated the amount of grease in the wool and shrinkage characteristics. Cooper hired Navajo women to process the wool by their own methods and to weave small sample rugs to determine the usefulness of various types of wool. A lot was shipped off to a textile plant in a federal prison to study its adaptability for manufacture by commercial machinery. In 1940 workers at the laboratory devised optical equipment which projected a highly magnified image of wool cross sections onto a ground-glass screen which greatly facilitated research.[63]

The experiments and selective breeding conducted at the laboratory before 1942 produced mixed results. The researchers were most successful in developing a strain of native sheep which produced fleeces with a uniform fiber texture and coloration. They also found that selective breeding removed the hair-like outercoat which had previously depressed the price of wool from native sheep on the commercial market because only the carpet industry would buy such low quality fleeces. Unfortunately, the wool from the native sheep crossed with Corriedale and Romney breeds was finer than that needed for home rug weaving. Also the selective breeding techniques employed in producing both strains of sheep did little to increase the weight of fleeces, leading the experts to conclude that this trait was the most difficult to alter. Improvements in weaning weight were apparently somewhat limited as well. After 1942 new crosses were undertaken to see if these problems could not be corrected.[64]

The many federal and private introductions of improved rams

63. Cecil T. Blum, "Improvement of Navajo Sheep," *Journal of Heredity* 31 (March 1940): 111.
64. Sidwell, "Improvement of Navajo Sheep," p. 6.

made before and during the New Deal era have rendered it impossible to assess the impact of the Fort Wingate laboratory on the Navajo sheep industry. The Navajo Service purchased hundreds of registered rams for distribution among Navajo herders. Some traders followed the same practice. Such purchases were at odds with the purposes of the breeding laboratory as most of the rams were meat-type Rambouillets. Their introduction was aimed at providing larger fall lambs for the midwestern feeder market. Some traders, most notably Bill and Sally Lippincott at Wide Ruin, encouraged their Navajo customers to obtain native rams from the herd at Fort Wingate to improve the quality of rug weaving, but this practice was unquestionably dwarfed by the widespread introduction of Rambouillet rams during the late 1930s. Most Navajos seemed disinterested in the Fort Wingate sheep and preferred the Rambouillets.[65] Also the rug weaving industry seems to have declined in the late 1930s and especially during World War II. By 1948 only ten percent of Navajo wool was used for rug weaving. By this same time the Fort Wingate technicians decided to concentrate on developing a fine-wool strain of sheep for the commercial market and they pursued this goal until the laboratory closed in 1966.

The major turning point in Fryer's efforts to end the old animosities between the Indian Service and SCS workers was a five-day conference sponsored by the land management division at Flagstaff in early March 1937. Meetings for various purposes, especially education and health, were commonplace throughout the New Deal, but the gathering of 250 delegates at Flagstaff State College had special importance.[66] It offered an opportunity for land management spokesmen from all levels and many fields to explain their work to other Navajo Service employees. In addition the conference permitted leaders to define their future plans for the reservation.

Recording his impressions of the meeting, Walter Woehlke wrote Collier that the "amalgamation and integration of the two services have made much more progress than I would have thought possible." The commissioner's advisor believed that participants thought and acted as if they belonged to one organization. "Fryer dominates the

65. Wagner Interview; Zweifel to writer, 23 January 1973.

66. *Coconino Sun*, 5 March 1937, pp. 1, 5; "First Navajo Service Land Management Conference," 1937. Flagstaff State College is presently known as Northern Arizona University.

Navajo organization in its totality," Woehlke further reported. "He knows where he wants to go, knows how to delegate authority, yet he has an immense knowledge of detail."[67] The one exception to the general unity was in education.

While the Flagstaff conference symbolized the success of Fryer's intensive efforts to make the Navajo Service effective, the Navajo administration had strayed even further from the policy emphases of Collier in 1933. Self-rule and preservation of Navajo culture, although still important, were now clearly secondary to herd reduction and range management plans.

If the government now had the machinery to effect its program, it had done little to counter the growing resistance which had developed on several fronts during the past four years. The mass of Navajos remained terribly opposed to any further herd reductions even though Fryer had not yet acted on that problem. The most able opponent of the government, J. C. Morgan, had finally come around to using the unlimited tribal hostility against reduction as a major weapon against Collier's philosophy of cultural pluralism. Equally alarming, his influence now covered a much wider geographic area than ever before. Although the northeast section of the reservation remained the strongest center of his support, Morgan by early 1937 had followers throughout Navajo country. His ability to act as a spokesman for the entire tribe perhaps already exceeded that of Chee Dodge. When Fryer reopened the Navajos' past wounds by reviving livestock reduction in 1937, he found Morgan to be an unbeatable foe.

67. Woehlke to Collier, 7 March 1937, Collier papers, YU.

# 6

## Senator Chavez and the New Mexico Boundary Bill

Among the many conflicts between the Collier administration and local whites, none aroused more frustrations for the government than the long struggle over the New Mexico boundary bill. The proposal was significant for Navajo affairs because Collier had promised the additional land during the Tuba City council in 1933 to gain its acceptance of herd reductions and the remainder of his conservation program. His failure to meet the commitment during the coming years was a major hindrance to administering tribal affairs and a personal embarrassment. Also, Collier's attempts to secure passage of the legislation offended some of the most powerful vested interests of New Mexico and their animosity seriously handicapped federal efforts among the Navajos. This was especially true after Senator Dennis Chavez entered the controversy in 1935 and the boundary bill question became enmeshed in the turbulent New Mexican politics. Chavez's opposition, plus some extraordinarily bad luck, eventually forced Collier to concede almost total defeat.

The desire to enlarge the reservation predated the New Deal by several decades. After earlier failures to obtain more land, the Secretary of Interior in 1931 had withdrawn 4,000,000 acres of public domain from sale or entry in Arizona and New Mexico to the east and to the south of the reservation. The freeze had been made to allow the Indian Service a chance to straighten out the crazy-quilt land holdings known locally as the "checkerboard." The name was partly derived from the alternating strips of land owned by the Santa Fe Railroad along its right-of-way. In addition, New Mexico and Arizona owned three sections of school land in each township in portions of the public domain frozen by the 1931 order.[1] Intermixed

1. A township, or more properly a survey township, is thirty-six square miles of land created by the federal system of measuring land which places range and township lines at

were numerous white homesteads and private holdings and a far greater number of Navajo homesteads and allotments. Also included were various plots of land which the Navajo Council had purchased or leased in the past.

The confusing labyrinth of ownership severely hampered effective land use. Leasing was the only method that brought any money to the Santa Fe Railroad and the two states, but the returns were diminished by the scattered nature of the holdings and the inability to collect from all users. The public domain itself was a virtual no man's land where white and Indian owners grazed livestock without any controls or payment. Some of the 10,000 off-reservation Navajos lived on 160-acre allotments, others had been assigned holdings but did not know the locations, and many simply squatted on areas of public domain used by their ancestors. Many Indians leased their land to whites. The hopelessly tangled situation created much bickering between Indians and whites over trespassing stock, water rights, and fencing, and the diffident Navajos were almost always losers. The lack of range and inadequate government protection and services kept such Navajos in chronic poverty.

Theoretically, all parties would benefit from a program of land exchanges and purchases after 1931 which would consolidate the checkerboard lands into large holdings. The railroad and the two states would increase their revenues by leasing bigger tracts and the federal government would eliminate white pressures on Indian allottees. Before the New Deal, the Santa Fe Railroad had agreed to an exchange program which would consolidate its land. The next stage was to secure permissive legislation to complete exchanges and sales for the rest of the checkerboard. Thanks to Senator Carl Hayden's negotiations with ranchers, Congress passed legislation to consolidate the Arizona checkboard in 1934.[2]

Attempts to secure similar legislation for New Mexico encountered strong opposition as early as June 1933. The most vigorous objections developed in the San Juan valley and areas to the southeast. White sheepmen used the latter region to winter their large herds after grazing them in the Colorado mountains during the summers.

six mile intervals. It has nothing to do with local government, although the term is employed in the Northeast and the upper part of the Midwest to designate units under the county level.

2. U. S., *Statutes at Large* 48, pt. 1, p. 960.

Irrigation farmers of the San Juan valley, who sold hay to sheep
ranchers, also supported exempting the winter ranges from the extension. In addition, Farmington and Aztec were major livestock
shipping points and buyers feared losing commissions on thousands
of fall lambs marketed outside the Southwest. These three groups—
ranchers, farmers, and buyers—possessed considerably more influence than the merchants of Farmington who supported an extension because Navajos were more apt to spend their money locally
than whites.[3]

Although it stood to lose far more land, McKinley County offered
little objection to the Navajo extension in 1933. The only resistance
came from people who feared that enclosing more of the county
within the reservation would diminish the tax rolls and place a greater burden on the remaining property owners. Gallup merchants,
however, pointed out at a meeting in July 1933 that the Indian Service had agreed to rebuild and maintain several major roads and the
savings to the county, which currently bore the expense, would
more than offset the meager tax losses. The advocates also maintained that nearly all the county's taxable property lay within Gallup and the nearby coal mines and these would remain outside the
reservation.[4]

With the support of McKinley County seemingly assured, James
M. Stewart, Land Director of the Indian Service, went to San Juan
County in late 1933 to iron out local complaints. Stewart agreed to
omit some land and he promised that ranchers could continue to use
an important stock drive even though it would be inside the reservation.[5] A week after Stewart's arrival, the San Juan County Commissioners dropped their opposition and endorsed the extension.
Their counterparts in McKinley County supported a duplicate
resolution three weeks later.[6] Thus passage of the New Mexico boundary bill appeared certain during 1934.

The legislation drafted by Stewart to consolidate the New Mexico
checkerboard that winter was complex. It required seven pages of

3. O. K. McCarty, "Minutes of Association of San Juan Co. Tax-Payers," 5 August
1933, NMSRCA.

4. *Gallup Independent*, 18 July 1933, p. 1.

5. Stock drives are lanes established on public domain by the federal government to
permit ranchers to move their livestock without encroaching on someone else's grazing
rights. An area designated as a stock drive cannot be sold or homesteaded.

6. Collier to Cutting, 23 May 1934, NMSRCA.

precisely worded text to define the new boundary in terms of the federal survey. The largest area to be enclosed was an irregular strip immediately east and south of the existing reservation. This annexation started in southern San Juan County and ran south to approximately Crownpoint where it turned west to take in the land around Gallup. That town and the adjoining area, consisting of some three townships, were entirely surrounded by the extension.

In addition, the 1934 legislation called for the annexation of four major areas east of the reservation. The largest and most important involved some twenty townships in southeast San Juan County, northwest McKinley County, and western Sandoval County in the heart of the migratory sheep ranchers' winter range. Two remnants of the tribe who had never migrated westward during the Spanish period, the Puertocito Navajos in northwest Socorro County and the Cañoncito Navajos in Valencia and Bernalillo Counties, each received approximately three townships of land. Finally, the extension included a large body of land south of Ramah. All the areas to be added to the reservation amounted to approximately 2,500,000 acres but upward of 1,000,000 acres were either allotments or tribal land.

The procedures for the transfer and consolidation of land in the bill were relatively simple. New Mexico was given the right to select land from the public domain outside the extension of equal value to that relinquished to the Navajos. Private owners would either sell their holdings or exchange them for land from the public domain. They were also to receive full value for any improvements on tracts they had previously leased. The bill authorized $482,136.22 in reimbursible funds to pay for the extension and for a previous boundary settlement in Utah. Once passed, the federal government guaranteed that the Navajos would not take up any additional allotments outside the new reservation boundaries and the remainder of the land withdrawn in New Mexico in 1931, approximately one-half million acres, would be unfrozen.[7]

The introduction of duplicate House and Senate Navajo boundary bills in early 1934 aroused no criticism in New Mexico. Representative Dennis Chavez mentioned the legislation in his weekly column without negative comment. The *Santa Fe New Mexican*, owned by

7. U. S., S. 2531, "To Define the Exterior Boundaries of the Navajo Reservation in New Mexico . . . ," 73d Cong., 2d sess., 1934, pp. 1–9.

Senator Bronson Cutting, gave the measure strong editorial support. The first protests in 1934 arose in May when San Juan valley citizens sent a flurry of telegrams to the governor and the congressional delegation, claiming that local residents "were very much opposed to any further extension of the reservation." Both Collier and Secretary of Interior Ickes responded that the complaints had already been met by Stewart's compromises. The commissioner contended that additional concessions would be unfair to the Navajos.[8]

Potential reductions in local and state tax revenues figured very prominently in the 1934 objections. Based on government figures, however, only 36,160 acres owned by private individuals and 665,353 acres owned by the Santa Fe Railroad were subject to taxes. The 141,080 acres held by New Mexico and the remainder of the land, belonging to the federal government or the Navajos, were not taxable. Even though no one seemed sure of the exact figures, the tax loss was negligible. The real issue in 1934 and afterward was the stockmen's objection to losing free or virtually free grazing rights in the extension area, although they frequently invoked the tax issue as an argument against the boundary legislation.

Congress's failure to enact the boundary bill in 1934 was unrelated to resentments against tax losses. Instead, Collier became so involved in passing the more important Wheeler-Howard bill that he failed to secure a vote upon the Navajo extension. When later asked about the matter, he expressed regret that he had failed, but he predicted that passage was certain during the next session.[9]

The forceful protests of New Mexicans during the next few months showed that the commissioner's confidence was ill-founded. Meeting in December 1934 at Thoreau, ranchers from eastern McKinley County resolved that the Indian Service must assess holdings before enactment of the extension and the federal government must assume part of the county's bonded indebtedness. Kelsey Presley, a local politician-stockman and head of the group, repeated what had become tenets in the ranchers' fight against the boundary bill: the government was guilty of bad faith; the county tax losses endangered public education and roads; and the Navajos already had plenty of

8. *Farmington Times Hustler*, 16 February 1934, p. 2; *Santa Fe New Mexican*, 2 March 1934, pp. 1–2; Colorado and New Mexico Stockmen's Association to Governor Hockenhull, 9 May 1934, Collier to Cutting, 23 May 1934, and Ickes to Hatch, 28 May 1934, NMSRCA.

9. *Gallup Independent*, 16 July 1934, p. 1.

land. The ranchers demanded that Collier either meet their complaints or they would seek a reversal of the 1931 withdrawal order and place the checkerboard under the Taylor Grazing Act of 1934.[10]

Two months later Stewart conferred with McKinley County representatives to answer the objections. Explaining that while no federal support would be available for local schools, he again promised that the Indian Service would build three roads to relieve the county of that burden. The land director also argued that tax losses would be slight because ninety percent of the land to be annexed in the county was already in Indian hands.[11] His explanation apparently satisfied the audience, for Gallup-area residents raised no major complaints in 1935.

The same was hardly true of the San Juan valley where lasting compromises seemed unattainable. During February Stewart and other Indian Service personnel met with various groups of local civic and ranch leaders to explain the slightly revised 1935 boundary bill and to promise that the government would ask for no additional extensions and would revoke the 1931 withdrawal order. In March the *Farmington Times Hustler* announced that local agreements guaranteed passage of the boundary bill.[12]

Despite the successes of the meetings, various stockmen continued to bombard political leaders and newspapers with complaints that the Navajos did not need more land and would only lease it to whites. Such charges, reportedly emanating from the large sheep owners who wintered herds on the checkerboard, reached Senator Carl Hatch in early April. A week later Governor Clyde Tingley of New Mexico visited Washington and he persuaded Hatch to delay the 1935 boundary bill temporarily.[13]

10. See *Gallup Independent*, 22 December 1934, p. 1, and 28 December 1934, p. 1. The Taylor Grazing Act was an important measure passed to correct the previous chaos, interloping, and overgrazing on the public domain. The legislation created the Grazing Service within the Department of Interior to establish and administer grazing districts in western states. Field workers and advisory committees, made up of ranchers, determined who would receive grazing permits, the amount of livestock allowed in each district, and other basic policies. See U. S., *Statutes at Large*, 48, pt. 1, p. 1269.

11. *Gallup Independent*, 1 March 1935, p. 1.

12. *Farmington Times Hustler*, 8 March 1935, p. 6.

13. C. L. Russell to Cutting and Edward T. Taylor, 6 March 1935 in an unidentified clipping, NMSRCA; *Albuquerque Journal*, 22 March 1935, p. 8; *Santa Fe New Mexican*, 23 March 1935, p. 2; Stacker and Radcliffe to Zeh, 8 April 1935, LAFRC, Box 33550; *Santa Fe New Mexican*, 16 April 1935, p. 3.

The local resistance was probably less a factor in Hatch's action than the pressures of Floyd Lee and the powerful state livestock lobby. Although Lee lived at San Mateo, several miles east of the proposed extension and did not run livestock in the checkerboard, his almost fanatic opposition to any federal land acquisitions made him "an articulate and a most compelling speaker in opposition to the boundary bill."[14] Lee possessed great leverage within New Mexico. He was a long-standing member of the state senate and he and his wife were major figures in the Republican party. His chief influence, however, came from his presidency of the New Mexico Wool Growers Association and his prominence in the New Mexico Cattle Growers Association. Despite his reputation as a staunch Republican and bitter foe of the New Deal, Lee's participation in these associations assured him easy access to the Democratic congressmen from New Mexico during frequent visits to Washington.

Whether the opposition of Lee and other stockmen to the boundary bill can be explained purely by their self-interest appears debatable. Indian Service employees believed that part of the stockmen's antagonism sprang from an active prejudice toward the Navajos which created a peculiar sort of paternalism and discrimination. The ranchers, for example, condemned Collier for causing starvation among the Indians by livestock reductions and yet they contradictorily criticized him for pampering the tribe with New Deal work programs. On a more personal level, the white ranchers protested their unlimited affection for neighboring Navajos and their willingness to care for the sick and needy. Government officials, however, contended that these same whites ruthlessly kept the Navajos impoverished by not compromising on the boundary question. Certainly some ranchers did even worse. They grazed on Navajo allotments without paying, enclosed such holdings with illegal fences, and occasionally used violence to put down Indian objections.[15]

14· James M. Stewart to writer, 15 October 1971.

15. Ibid.; Fryer Interview, 1970. Although the Indian Service charges may have been exaggerated, friction between white ranchers and Eastern Navajos was fairly commonplace and violence sometimes resulted. Mr. O. J. Carson, a former checkerboard trader, told the writer that one stockman made a practice of browbeating the Indians who happened to be in his way. In one incident, sometime before 1936, this rancher drove his stock into a Navajo's water hole and ruined it. When the Navajo protested, the rancher's son hit him. The upshot of the dispute was that the Indian protested to the local superintendent and that official settled the dispute by getting the rancher to pay five dollars.

Floyd Lee launched his crusade against the 1935 boundary bill well before Hatch's decision to delay passage in April. Although Governor Tingley earlier endorsed a general program to consolidate scattered state lands in the public domain by exchanges with the federal government, the New Mexico Senate adamantly refused to pass the necessary legislation in January. The defeat came even after an amendment stipulated that none of the exchanged land would be given to Indians. According to the newspapers, Lee led the majority who were determined not "to turn the state back to the government." At the annual convention of the New Mexico Wool Growers Association in March, the San Mateo sheep baron sharply criticized Collier's efforts to expand Indian reservations and his organization passed strong resolutions to this end.[16]

Collier and Stewart moved to meet the now serious objections on both the local front and in Washington. On April 23 about one hundred stockmen from New Mexico and Colorado met Indian Service officials at Farmington to discuss new compromises. The group decided to establish a committee made up of stockmen and county government representatives from seven counties in New Mexico and three in Colorado who, with the land commissioners of the two states, were to meet in Santa Fe within ten days and reach a final settlement on the boundary question.[17]

Earlier, Hatch had held his own "show down" conference on April 29 in Washington. Collier, several staff members, and Representative Edward Taylor of Colorado attended the session. Ed Sargent and Clarence Iden appeared as representatives of New Mexico. Sargent, who lived at Chama, New Mexico, was the largest of the migratory ranchers who wintered sheep in the checkerboard. He was also a major figure in the New Mexico Wool Growers Association. Iden represented the New Mexico Tax Payers Association, a powerful bipartisan lobby with a "semi-official" status in state government. Even though the main goal of Iden's group was to shift the tax

---

Jim and Ann Counselor, in their memoirs of trading on the checkerboard, mention that a minority of stockmen were "range hogs." Such individuals grazed over Indian allotments and deprived the owners of the grass and water needed to feed their own herds. By bullying the Navajos, range hogs evaded paying for the use of allotees' land. Carson Interview; Jim and Ann Counselor, *Wild, Wooly and Wonderful* (New York, 1954), pp. 211–14.

16. *Santa Fe New Mexican*, 8 January 1935, p. 2, 20 February 1935, p. 8; *Albuquerque Journal*, 29 March 1935, p. 8.

17. *Farmington Times Hustler*, 26 April 1935, p. 1.

burden from real estate to a business or sales tax, its resistance to any enlargement of federal land holdings equalled that of the stockmen's associations. The conference in Hatch's office and a second at the Indian Bureau produced several major omissions from the extension, mostly in the area east of Crownpoint where Sargent wintered his sheep.[18]

A few days later Sargent and Iden participated in a conference of local spokesmen at Santa Fe. The meeting was less representative than stipulated at the Farmington gathering but more inclusive than any previous conferences. It included State Land Commissioner Frank Vesely, Stewart and other Indian Service leaders, assistants to the governor and state tax commissioner, and representatives of five counties in New Mexico and one in Colorado. The "Santa Fe Agreement" automatically accepted the revisions recently negotiated in Washington and made several additional inroads into the proposed extension. The most important change negotiated at Santa Fe was the omission of the Bloomfield irrigation project east of Farmington. The total reductions of the conferences at Washington and Santa Fe amounted to about one-eighth of the land asked for in the original 1935 bill, but the compromises seemingly removed all objections to the measure.[19]

Delays in redrafting the bill and winning Ickes' approval unfortunately created far more serious obstacles. On May 20 Hatch from the Senate floor amended the original bill with the new provisions.[20] Eight days later he made additional corrections of a few minor typographical errors and the Senate approved the measure. Before discussion turned to other matters, Hatch suddenly asked that the bill be restored to the calendar as Senator Dennis Chavez, a member of the Indian Affairs Committee, wanted an opportunity to study it further.[21] Chavez had been in office only a few days, having been appointed by Governor Tingley to replace Bronson Cutting who had been killed in an airplane crash earlier in the month.

Chavez's excuse that he needed more time to study the measure appears questionable. He had earlier supported similar legislation as a member of the House Indian Affairs Committee and he had never

18. Ickes to Hatch, 4 May 1935, Legislative Records, NA, RG 46.
19. Frank Vesely to Hatch, 6 May 1935, Chavez papers, UA.
20. *Congressional Record*, 74th Cong., 1st sess., 1935, 79, pt. 7, pp. 7798–99.
21. Ibid., pt. 8, p. 8293.

been identified before as an opponent. Already possessing a general familiarity with the bill, Chavez received a file of correspondence on the 1935 legislation, a copy of the "Santa Fe Agreement," and the most recent amended version of the measure from the Indian Office four days before he asked for a recall. The next day Collier or one of his staff telephoned Chavez evidently to gain his support for the legislation.[22]

The most likely explanation for Chavez's action was his grudge against Ickes and Collier because of their support for Senator Cutting in the election of 1934. That contest personified the always hectic nature of New Mexico politics. For several years prior to 1934, Cutting's Progressive Republican faction had feuded bitterly with the GOP conservatives, especially after he endorsed Franklin Roosevelt in 1932 and supported New Deal legislation. By the summer of 1934 rumors arose that the Democrats might place Cutting on their ticket for the full-term Senate seat and Chavez would run for the two-year seat that Hatch had been filling since Senator Sam Bratton's resignation in 1933. Despite such speculation, the state nominating conventions saw the Republicans unite behind Cutting for the full-term seat, while the Democrats put forward Chavez as his opponent.

Except for their political astuteness, the two candidates shared few similarities. Cutting was a former Long Island aristocrat who grew up knowing and idolizing Theodore Roosevelt. After Groton and Harvard, Cutting became a resident of New Mexico in 1910 because he suffered from tuberculosis which physicians diagnosed as terminal. Not only did the twenty-two-year-old easterner soon recover his health, but he also purchased the *Santa Fe New Mexican* and became intensely involved in newspaper work and politics. Like many Progressive Republicans, Cutting pursued an erratic course in party affairs after 1910, frequently switching factions and causes, crossing party lines, and neatly intermingling personal idealism with practicalities. His rapport with Spanish Americans was always fundamental to his political career. He spoke Spanish fluently, identified with "native" aspirations, and won their votes by awesome margins. His opponents often grumbled that Cutting workers were not above freely dispensing five dollar bills on election days to swell his returns.

22. Collier to Chavez, 24 May 1935, and Chavez to Collier 25 May 1935, Chavez papers, UA.

After serving as an infantry officer in World War I, Cutting's cultivation of veteran votes gave him still another major source of political support. Despite the handicap of a squeaky, high-pitched voice which caused endless gossip about his sexual preferences, Cutting battled his way to an appointment to the Senate in 1927 and election to a full term in 1928.

Chavez's career, by contrast, represented an arduous struggle from a humble Spanish-American background. He received little education before being forced to work as a delivery boy in Albuquerque. Later he joined the city engineering department as a rodman, but he eventually became a self-trained surveyor and supervisor. Befriended by a politician, Chavez in 1917 joined the staff of the Secretary of the U.S. Senate in Washington. Married and father of two children, he somehow worked his way through the Georgetown University Law School by 1922. He returned to Albuquerque and began a highly successful career as a criminal lawyer and state legislator. In 1930 Chavez won the first of his two terms in the House of Representatives.

Even by New Mexico standards, the 1934 senatorial contest between the "native" leader and the former Long Islander was waged with unusual bitterness. With the veteran vote conceded to Cutting, Chavez concentrated on the Spanish-American population, hoping that his ethnic background would break their loyalty to his opponent. As a minor component of the intense campaign, Chavez's supporters charged that Ickes and Collier allowed Indian Service workers to help Cutting. If the Spanish-American leader held any doubts about Ickes' preferences, these were emphatically removed the day after the election when the *Albuquerque Journal* reprinted a telegram from the Interior Secretary warmly congratulating Cutting on his narrow victory.[23]

Chavez's accusations did not cease with his election defeat. He charged that Cutting workers had tampered with the returns in San Miguel County and he tried unsuccessfully to contest the election in New Mexico. Later he brought his case before the U.S. Senate Elections Committee.[24] Although that group had not reached a decision before Cutting's death in May 1935, most observers freely

23. *Albuquerque Journal*, 9 November 1934, p. 1.
24. U. S., Congress, Senate, *Hearings Before the Committee on Privileges and Elections*, 74th Cong., 1st sess., 10 April and 4 June 1935, *in* Legislative Records, NA, RG 46.

predicted that Chavez's plea would be denied. His appointment to the upper house, therefore, averted an otherwise crushing setback to his career and his much-cherished goal of becoming the first Spanish-American to serve in the Senate.

While Ickes and Collier could appeal to Cutting's idealism, Chavez was an entirely different type. To a large degree, the Spanish-American leader saw politics as a means of rewarding supporters and punishing opponents. His correspondence with Governor Tingley and other members of their faction constantly discussed how to tap the cornucopia of New Deal jobs and who should be weeded out of office because of disloyalty. In sum, Chavez was a throwback to the nineteenth century wardheeler, albeit on a much larger scale. With the aid of his bother, David, he soon became a master patronage broker and the dominant figure in New Mexico politics.

Already embittered by the election of 1934 and convinced that Ickes was an untrustworthy maverick, Chavez used his recall of the Navajo boundary bill in 1935 as a means of gaining control over Interior patronage in New Mexico, especially the jobs in the Public Works Administration. The tactic backfired completely. In July Ickes named Edgar F. Puryear, Cutting's former secretary and right-hand man, as national director of employment in the PWA. Led by Chavez, infuriated New Mexico Democrats dispatched a wave of hostile messages to the Roosevelt administration. Chavez commented indignantly in a personal letter to the President that Puryear's appointment was a "blow and slap" at the party faithful in New Mexico and placed many non-civil service posts under a hostile Republican. In discussing the Puryear episode with Tingley, Chavez promised that he would block Ickes' pet proposal to create a "Department of Conservation" if it ever came before the Senate. This same motive led Chavez to take the Navajo boundary bill off the calendar and send it back to committee, insuring that the measure would not be enacted in 1935.[25] Both then and in the future, any compromise on the Navajo extension would demand an agreement between Ickes and Chavez on patronage.

Repeatedly in the future, Chavez would find reasons for blocking the Navajo extension which disguised his partisan motives. He

25. John E. Miles, *et al.*, to Chavez, 22 July 1935, Chavez to Roosevelt, 23 July 1935, and Chavez to Tingley, 17 July 1935, Chavez papers, UA; *Congressional Record*, 74th Cong., 1st sess., 1935, 79, pt. II, p. 11952.

explained to constituents that he had withdrawn the bill because of disagreements over mineral rights in state lands involved, but the Indian Service had already compromised on this point. In truth, there was no definite trend in public opinion either for or against the boundary bill. Ranchers still objected strongly to the measure, but Chavez received some mail in support of the annexation. Most of the advocates, however, were politically weak whites who had home-steaded on the checkerboard during an earlier wet cycle. Now trapped by the dust bowl and depression, these small owners wanted to sell out to the government and to escape a bleak situation. The cagey Chavez responded to both sides by claiming that he supported the Navajo extension in principle, but that he wanted all parties treated fairly before he consented to passage of a bill.[26]

Chavez's obstructive tactics obviously upset Collier. When asked about Chavez's referring the bill back to committee, Collier told a reporter in August 1935 that he did not understand the senator's action. The commissioner testily warned that failure to pass the bill might "stir up a race feud," and he hinted that he might place many more Navajos on allotments in the checkerboard, confusing the tan-gled land situation even more. He hesitated to do this because, in his words, "we want a friendly adjustment."[27]

In November Chavez dropped his ambiguous public stance on the Navajo extension when he announced his candidacy for the 1936 senate race at a rally in Gallup. He told his followers: "I'll let the Indian Bureau know that all the people in New Mexico are not Indians." He promised that no bill would pass without protection of state mineral claims, stockmen's grazing rights, and federal funds to offset tax losses on the 350,000 acres of private land.[28]

Whether Chavez's exaggerated and erroneous statements were mere political talk or genuinely reflected his position perplexed Collier even more. He asked Richard H. Hanna, a mutual friend and prominent Democrat from Albuquerque, to assess the senator's true feelings. After a two-hour conversation, Hanna reported that Chavez remained somewhat indefinite on the boundary bill but admitted that local pressures did not dictate his opposition. He also denied

26. *New Mexican Examiner*, ca. 30 July 1935, and O. H. Ridling to Chavez, 13 August 1935, Chavez papers, UA.

27. *Gallup Independent*, 7 August 1935, p. 1; *Santa Fe New Mexican*, 6 August 1935, pp. 1, 3.

28. *Gallup Independent*, 30 November 1935, p. 1.

*Fig. 1.* Government personnel frequently held demonstration days such as this one at Steamboat to display better land and livestock management techniques to the local Indians.

*Fig. 2.* Chee Dodge, first chairman of the tribal council, who led the traditionalist faction during the New Deal.

*Fig. 3.* Father Berard Haile and the drafting committee at work on the ill-fated tribal constitution.

*Fig. 4.* J. C. Morgan's inauguration as tribal council chairman on November 8, 1938, climaxed his bitter struggle against reservation policies of the New Deal. On the left is Howard Gorman, vice chairman, and on the right is Henry Taliman, retiring chairman and Morgan's foe.

*Fig. 5.* John Collier, E. R. Fryer, and Moris Burge watch a stunt pilot at the first Navajo Tribal Fair in 1938.

*Fig. 6.* "Hogan School" at Navajo Mountain was one of four such installations built during the 1930s. Navajos invariably believed that the architecture was discriminatory and demanded schools similar to those white students attended.

*Fig. 7.* A large crowd milling in front of the tribal council building between sessions of the council.

that Ickes' appointment of Puryear was personally upsetting. Hanna believed that Chavez's renomination and reelection were virtually assured, implying that he would not need to use the Navajo extension as a ploy for the 1936 election. Hanna predicted that Chavez would prove more cooperative in the future.[29]

Collier reintroduced the Navajo boundary bill when Congress reconvened in early 1936. The latest measure followed the same lines set down in the "Santa Fe Agreement," changing only the future status of the land east of Crownpoint where Sargant wintered his herds. That area was still deleted from the extension but was to be placed under the Taylor Grazing Act. Even in compromise form, however, the 1936 bill touched off an uproar among checkerboard ranchers.

Before the annual battle over the Navajo boundary bill started in 1936, J. C. Morgan made his first entry into the controversy. In mid-February the Navajo leader arrived in Washington to protest against herd reduction, the headquarters at Window Rock, and other issues.[30] A week after his arrival, Morgan and Lawrence Lindley of the Indian Rights Association conferred with Collier and complained that herd reductions among eastern Navajos around Torreon, Star Lake, and Pueblo Alto, areas now excluded from the extension by the 1936 boundary bill, had impoverished residents and that the government had failed to provide sufficient relief. Morgan later repeated the same charge to the House Indian Affairs Committee.

Collier reacted quickly by wiring Superintendent Faris for information on the amount of destitution and the adequacy of relief measures. Soon afterward the commissioner became even more concerned about the Navajos left outside the extension. If they had been leasing their land to whites by verbal agreements, instead of written contracts, the Indians could not qualify for grazing rights under the Taylor Grazing Act. In mid-March Collier ordered a family-by-family survey of the Eastern Navajos to obtain information on leasing arrangements and poverty.[31]

Richard Van Valkenburgh, then an SCS employee, conducted an

29. Hanna to Collier, 19 December 1935, Collier papers, YU.

30. Joseph Bruner to Elmer Thomas, 16 February 1936, Chavez papers, UA; "Memorandum," 20 February 1936, St. Michaels Mission.

31. Collier to Faris, 27 February 1936, and Collier to Faris, 17 March 1936, Van Valkenburgh papers, AHS.

investigation which revealed the sickening squalor that existed among the 2,500 Navajos outside the proposed boundary. The SCS worker estimated that at least fifty percent of the people over sixty were blind or partially blind from trachoma, while tuberculosis and other diseases affected a large number of all ages. He calculated that sixty percent of Indian land was rented to whites and suggested that most leases were mere verbal agreements which would not protect the Indians' grazing rights if the Taylor Grazing Act was applied.

Van Valkenburgh emphasized that leasing had become commonplace because many Navajo families owned no livestock and their only income was derived from renting their allotments during the winter months. He disagreed with Morgan's charge that poverty among the Eastern Navajos could be blamed solely on herd reductions. The SCS worker believed that the shocking destitution was the product of several factors that had been operating during the past decade—lack of government services and protection of grazing rights, general decline of the sheep industry because of drought, severe winters, and depression, and the sale of breeding stock to buy liquor from white bootleggers. Many Indian families who once owned sizeable herds had been forced to sell or butcher their stock until an insufficient number remained to support themselves. The forced sales of 1933 and 1934 had not only contributed to this dire result, but "for every head of Navajo stock that left the range, one white man's animal replaced it." Van Valkenburgh bluntly stated that the herd reductions on the checkerboard had been a dreadful mistake. He summarized his report by writing: "The general situation is beyond belief. I have never seen on the reservation proper anything that could compare with the misery of these people. My interpreter, Danny Bia, stated that he had never realized that Navajos lived like that."[32]

Despite Collier's determination to enact the boundary bill in 1936, he still had to deal with Chavez. When the senator returned to Washington early in January, he renewed his fight to remove Puryear as director of employment for the PWA. In an appeal to James Farley, Democratic National Chairman, Chavez complained that Puryear had named numerous Republicans to PWA posts in New Mexico.

32. Richard Van Valkenburgh, "Report of Survey Made of Destitute Navajo Indians outside Proposed New Mexico Boundary Extension," ca. May 1936, Van Valkenburgh papers, AHS.

Even though Farley neatly avoided taking any action, Chavez continued his fight. "I will not discuss anything with the Interior Department," Chavez wrote Tingley, "if Mr. Puryear is going to have any say whatsoever in the matter of employment."[33] In the first of many legislative harassments, the senator successfully amended an appropriations bill for the Interior with a proviso that none of the money spent under the Wheeler-Howard Act could be used in New Mexico to buy land for Indians.

When the Senate Indian Affairs Committee opened hearings on the Navajo extension in late May, Secretary Ickes made a surprise appearance. The "Curmudgeon of the New Deal" charged that "predatory interests that have no scruples . . . have been preying upon the Indians." He claimed that white bootleggers had deliberately used illegal sales of liquor to secure the stock of the Eastern Navajos in order to drive them off their land. Ickes further warned that "we will have serious disorder and bloodshed in that country in the next year or two unless some of these wrongs are redressed."[34] For at least a week afterward, Ickes' bombastic charges resulted in a exchange between New Mexcio and Washington about whether the checkerboard was on the verge of a rebellion.

The Ickes attempt to force the boundary bill past Chavez miscarried badly. In the week of hearings which followed, the New Mexico leader hotly denied that the Navajos needed any land and he stressed that an increase in their livestock and additional irrigation could easily solve their problems. Collier replied that even the fullest utilization of resources would never meet the subsistence requirements of either the reservation or the Eastern Navajos. Although the commissioner more than held his own in committee debate, Hatch and Chavez put off a decision on the bill for 1936 by persuading Chairman Elmer Thomas of Oklahoma to conduct a field investigation of the boundary controversy as soon as Congress adjourned later in the summer.

On June 8 Hatch and Chavez answered Ickes' charges with lengthy speeches on the Senate floor. Never very interested in the issue because he lived in and mainly represented eastern New Mexico,

33. Chavez to Tingley, 3 February 1936, Chavez papers, UA.

34. U. S., Congress, Senate, Subcommittee of the Committee on Indian Affairs, *Hearings, Survey of Conditions of the Indians in the United States*, 74th Cong., 2nd sess., 1936, pt. 34, pp. 17497–99.

Hatch took a moderate position, explaining that the pending investigation would produce a fair settlement. Chavez's address, however, skillfully played up to his constituents' animosities for the Indian Service. He again accused Collier of creating starvation among the Navajos by livestock reductions and other misguided policies and then relieving the distress by feeding the Indians beef from South America. In another clever thrust, Chavez contrasted the impoverished, hard-working stockmen of his state with the overpaid Bureau employees "who are sapping the very lives of the Indians and who are receiving good salaries . . . [from] the money that is appropriated by Congress for the Indians' use."[35] In terms of western biases, the address was splendid propaganda.

Two months later Senator Thomas brought his special subcommittee to Gallup to initiate hearings on the boundary bill. Appearing with the chairman were Senators Lynn Frazier of North Dakota, Hatch, and Chavez. Representative John Dempsey of New Mexico, currently an enemy of Chavez's, also attended but seldom participated. One-day sessions were held at Gallup, Farmington, and Window Rock before the group moved to Santa Fe for two days of hearings which mostly dealt with Pueblo affairs. Characteristically, Collier had ordered that an extraordinary amount of research be done before the hearings and he arrived early to steep himself in the materials and to prepare his testimony.[36]

Appearing as the first witness at Gallup, Collier reiterated the standard arguments of the government. He maintained that a successful administration of the Eastern Navajos and relief of their distress were basically dependent on a consolidation of their land and that this would help whites, too. Collier then announced that he had decided to drop the "Santa Fe Agreement" and would press for the annexation of 2,154,000 acres which would enclose all but 850 Eastern Navajo families. Essentially the new boundary lines paralleled those of the 1934 bill.

Collier also presented data from research that a team of Indian Service workers had completed on county tax payments on real estate and personal property (mostly livestock) in the four counties most affected by the new boundary bill. Their findings on the years 1927 through 1935 showed that local residents inside the proposed annexa-

35. *Congressional Record*, 74th Cong., 2nd sess., 1936, 80, pt. 9, pp. 9205–13.
36. Collier to Ickes, 13 June and 4 August 1936, Collier papers YU.

tion paid taxes of only $4,000 annually. The four counties spent $28,395 on roads and education in fiscal 1935, but this compared to an outlay of $193,325 on the same items by the Indian Service. The evidence not only completely demolished one of the pet arguments against the boundary bill, but it indicated that migratory sheepmen were adept tax dodgers.[37]

Except for some juggled statistics, Floyd Lee and other ranchers who appeared at Gallup were quite candid in their testimony against the boundary bill. They frankly admitted that they were antagonized by what they saw as preferential treatment of the Indians, especially the contrast between the plush new schools Collier had built for Navajo youngsters in the checkerboard and the converted boxcars in which white students attended classes. Ed Sargent demanded that the government relocate the 850 Navajo allottees not affected by the new legislation inside the reservation before he would accept a settlement. The ranchers feared, perhaps justifiably, that leaving these families on public domain would serve as a future excuse for another extension. Although more subtly expressed, the stockmen indicated that a major reason for their increased resistance of late was the upturn in livestock prices.[38] They had lost their eagerness to leave ranching and would compromise only if Collier paid them more.

The hearings did not produce much local support for the extension. Indeed, no Gallup or Farmington merchant appeared before the subcommittee. O. H. Ridling, who lived south of Gallup, spoke

---

37. *Survey of Conditions*, pp. 17620–40, 17548–49, 17972–73. The evasion of taxes was made easy by the vastness of the area east of the reservation and the inability or unwillingness of local assessors to determine how much livestock was grazed on the checkerboard. An additional problem was that sheep herds were grazed across state and county lines. Theoretically, owners were to prorate tax payments to the different units of government according to what fraction of the year the sheep remained in a county or state, but this too posed obvious problems in collection.

Collier admitted that the figures on tax revenues presented to the subcommittee did not cover all county governments' tax losses. Both the state and local governments stood to lose minor gasoline and sales tax revenues. New Mexico also would have been denied some grazing fees collected under the Taylor Grazing Act. This legislation required that one-half of the funds collected from stockmen leasing the public domain be returned to the states. If the area east of Crownpoint has been placed under the act, as promised in the Santa Fe Agreement, New Mexico would have received additional monies. This writer has not found any figures on the possible returns. Even so, the evidence on tax losses submitted to the committee was a serious blow to the local opponents of the Navajo extension.

38. Ibid., pp. 17676–700.

briefly on behalf of other homesteaders who wanted to sell their land to the government. Of the dozen or so traders in the checkerboard, only Jim Counselor dared to incur the hostility of ranchers by pleading for the boundary bill. A legendary figure, Counselor operated a post in the desolate area between Cuba and Farmington. He shared the normal white hatred of the Indian Service, but he also attacked local prejudice against the Navajos with equal ferocity. As a part-time rancher himself, however, Counselor found himself in a dilemma over the extension. He refused to endorse the relocation of the allottees, but he wanted white grazing rights protected, too. He confessed, "I can see the problem, but it would take a smarter man than I am for the solution."[39]

In addition, the varied testimony of Navajos did not lend much aid to the extension. Several Indian witnesses used their appearances to complain about herd reductions and policies on the reservation.[40] Chee Dodge testified in behalf of the boundary bill, but he weakened his presentation by meandering badly in discussing the Navajos' historic claims to the checkerboard.[41] J. C. Morgan was completely erratic in his testimony. Appearing first at Gallup, Morgan argued strongly that Navajos had always lived in the eastern area and the government had promised the tribe the land in the nineteenth century.[42] The next day at Farmington, Morgan opened his testimony by reasserting that his people "could have half of New Mexico," but he abruptly dropped the subject and informed the subcommittee that the tribe's best hope for rehabilitation was the construction of a huge irrigation project south of Farmington.[43] He was referring to the "Turley Project" which had been proposed some thirty years earlier to benefit Navajos and whites. Local residents had perennially agitated

39. Ibid., pp. 17721, 17818–19. I detected a similar ambivalence in interviewing O. J. Carson, another checkerboard trader-rancher. Mr. Carson originally endorsed the boundary bill because he feared that the white stockmen would drive the Navajos out of the area. He implied that he had changed his mind on the question, at least in part, because of his friendship and admiration for Ed Sargent. Carson Interview.

40. For the most effective criticism, see Scott Preston's testimony, *Survey of Conditions*, pp. 17912–19.

41. Ibid., pp. 17902–06.

42. Ibid., p. 17726. Morgan claimed that Navajos were promised the checkerboard in return for the tribe's cooperation with the army's wars against the Apaches. From Dodge's testimony and other evidence, it is clear that several versions of such promises existed in Navajo folklore during the 1930s.

43. Ibid., pp. 17831–32.

for federal funding of the project and probably some Farmingtonite's overnight coaching explains Morgan's sudden change of views.

A handful of Navajo leaders from the checkerboard pleaded for additional land, but they, too, criticized Collier's programs, especially the past livestock reductions. Having read Van Valkenburgh's survey of the Eastern Navajos, Collier reacted to the complaints with unusual candor. He frankly admitted that forced sales had been a serious mistake which harmed the Indians and allowed whites to run more livestock. Although he blamed the arbitrary livestock reductions on S. F. Stacker, the former superintendent of the Eastern Navajos, Collier took responsibility for harm done by a subordinate. He added that he had ordered foundation sheep distributed among residents to correct the error. This was hardly adequate recompense, for Eastern Navajos had to buy the sheep on loan and pay for them with part of the offspring.[44]

At Santa Fe the subcommittee heard various state leaders who opposed the Navajo extension. C. M. Botts, a former state judge and chairman of the New Mexico Land Use Committee, presented his group's resolutions against the measure. Floyd Lee served on the committee and had influenced its previous opposition to the Navajo extension. The only difference in the group's position in 1936 was the argument that the Eastern Navajos should not be segregated from whites. "We think it is better," Botts explained, "instead of enlarging the boundary of the Navajo Reservation, to give the Navajo Indian every opportunity to become one of us, to compete with us, and we with him."[45] His philosophical views were mere window dressing, for the livestock associations completely dominated the Land Use Committee.

On balance, Collier gained an edge over Chavez during the hearings. While the lengthy transcript did not support Ickes' wild allegations about deliberate bootlegging and an impending rebellion, the testimony proved that tribesmen had lived in the checkerboard for generations until white ranchers appeared early in the twentieth century and took over the land, either by legal means or informal pressures. Moreover, the widespread practice of Navajos leasing allotments to whites was invidious because it kept the Indians from developing their own subsistence herds.

44. Ibid., pp. 17786–94, 17801–03.
45. Ibid., pp. 18131.

Even though Chavez was less adept in committee debate than Collier, he won reelection that fall, in part, by exploiting his constituents' biases against the federal government and the Indian Service. In September Chavez's campaign workers mailed 5,000 copies of his June speech in the Senate to voters. Soon afterward, a Spanish translation was printed in large numbers and distributed.[46] The Senator's victory in November was primarily dependent on the Roosevelt landslide over Landon, but opposition to the Navajo extension was also a popular issue.

When the Senate reconvened in early 1937, Collier adopted a conciliatory approach to the extension question. He introduced a "committee print," an informal proposal for legislative study and revision, instead of a regular bill. The measure contained the same provisions as the rough-draft bill discussed before the Thomas subcommittee in 1936, but Collier obviously hoped that Chavez and the ranchers would now compromise.

The New Mexico Senator ignored the Commissioner's peace overtures and, still incensed over his exclusion from PWA patronage, he harassed Collier constantly throughout the 1937 session. In mid-January, he introduced a bill to exempt all the Indians of New Mexico from the Wheeler-Howard Act.[47] Soon afterward, he arranged for the New Mexico House to petition Congress against any further federal land acquisitions in the state.[48] At various points Chavez tried to reduce Indian Service appropriations but with limited success. What most stung Collier and threw him on the defensive, however, was Chavez's cooperation after March with Senators Lynn Frazier's and Burton Wheeler's bill to repeal the Wheeler-Howard Act outright. Collier believed that the Wheeler-Howard Act was basic to Indian self-rule, economic improvement, and protection of land. Without it, no permanent reform of Indian affairs was possible. But in successfully fighting off the repeal, the commissioner failed to get hearings on the Navajo boundary bill in 1937.

Chavez's alliance with Morgan in early 1937 was an important

46. A. C. Holder to Chavez, 28 September 1936, and Ernie and Bob to Chavez, 14 October 1936, Chavez papers, UA.

47. *Santa Fe New Mexican*, 16 January 1937, p. 3; *Albuquerque Journal*, 26 January 1937, p. 3.

48. Chavez to Patsy Vigil, 28 January 1937, Chavez to Hub Kane, 2 January 1937, and Chavez to C. C. Royall, 11 January 1937, Chavez papers, UA; *Congressional Record*, 75th Cong., 1st sess., 1937, 81, pt. 2, p. 2936.

factor in the legislative vendetta against Collier. The association between Morgan, a notorious Catholic baiter, and Chavez, a Catholic politician often accused of anti-Indian bias, was decidedly strange. Although the two men's cooperation had more bearing on tribal politics than it did on Washington, Morgan supplied Chavez with a large quantity of protest letters and petitions during the 1937 fight. Morgan, in June, led a delegation of discontented Navajos to testify against the commissioner before the Senate Indian Affairs Committee. Such activites fortified the senator's allegations about Collier's total mismanagement of the reservation. Morgan and Chavez continued their efforts against Collier for the next two years. Even after the Navajo leader settled his differences with the government in 1939, he sometimes corresponded with Chavez on major issues.[49]

After Congress adjourned in 1937, Collier turned to a new tactic by attempting to organize checkerboard Navajos and whites into a lobby group to secure passage of the boundary bill. By September the Indians had formed the Eastern Navajo Boundary Association with George Castillo as secretary. With funds from Oliver La Farge's American Association on Indian Affairs, Howard Gorman, the former mission worker at Ganado and more recently an interpreter and assistant to Fryer, resigned his government post in November and became the main organizer of the new group. Still later in November, Gorman and Castillo met with a small group of checkerboard Navajos and white homesteaders at Albuquerque and formed an inter-racial organization known as the New Mexico Eastern Boundary Association. The white members included both the homesteaders from the Gallup-Thoreau area who had always supported the Navajo extension and new figures from northwest Sandoval County who lived south of Jim Counselor's trading post.[50]

Among the newcomers, Mrs. Bessie Lee soon became the most

49. For greater details on the alliance, its role in tribal politics, and a discussion of both participants' motives, see Chapter 7.

50. *Albuquerque Journal*, 14 November 1937, p. 1 and 29 November 1937, p. 1; Gorman Interview. La Farge's organization had a local affiliate in Santa Fe, the New Mexico Association on Indian Affairs, led by Mrs. Charles R. Dietrich. Moris Burge and his first wife, Margaret McKittrick Burge, served as field representatives during the early New Deal. Both the national and state organizations took an active role in Navajo affairs throughout the period by field investigations, encouragement of better weaving, and publications. Their efforts in behalf of the Navajo extension, however, yielded little result.

articulate and fiery advocate of the homesteaders' cause. A highly attractive widow, Mrs. Lee claimed that her husband had died from the extreme cold during the winter 1931–32. She complained that the area where she lived was too destitute to provide even the minimum of schools, post offices, and other essential public services. She castigated white stock owners who ran their herds across the land of Navajos and homesteaders and obstructed a settlement of the tangled land question.[51]

Even though Gorman organized several meetings and issued press releases in support of a boundary bill, he was unable to develop an effective lobby against Chavez. A small number of homesteaders lived in the checkerboard and only a handful took part in pressure activities. None possessed the wealth and political influence of the ranchers. Opponents of the Navajo extension answered the publicity of Mrs. Lee with charges that the homesteaders were shiftless vagabonds who never utilized their land and whose only motive was to unload their holdings on the government at exorbitant prices.[52] As an astute politician, Chavez knew automatically that he could safely ignore the new association. Twice in December Mrs. Lee begged him to join her and Indian Service workers in a visit to Sandoval County to see conditions at first hand, but Chavez rejected both invitations. The association continued for a few months but without measureable impact.[53]

After first indicating that he would renew the struggle for the Navajo extension in early 1938, Collier soon abandoned the fight. When advised by La Farge in March that Navajos and white homesteaders wished to visit Washington to testify in behalf of the legislation, Collier replied that the House calendar was clogged and, more importantly, Chavez had shown no signs of allowing the bill to get through the Senate Indian Affairs Committee.[54]

Chavez, in the meantime, continued to harass Collier legislatively. After a visit by Morgan and two other Navajo leaders in February,

51. *Albuquerque Journal*, 20 November 1937, p. 1.

52. See Mary Starr to Chavez and enclosed clipping, 3 January 1938, Chavez papers, UA. Mrs. Starr's attack on the Navajo extension appeared in the *Albuquerque Journal*, 6 December 1937, p. 8.

53. Lee to Chavez, 9 December and 23 December 1937, Chavez papers, UA; Stewart to writer, 15 October 1971.

54. *Farmington Times Hustler*, 28 January 1938, p. 1; Collier to La Farge, 15 March 1938, Collier papers, YU.

Chavez introduced a bill to deny the Interior Department the power to regulate grazing on the Navajo reservation. A second measure sought authorization to investigate the effect of grazing controls among the Navajos. Neither bill passed, but Chavez reported that Senator Thomas had promised to take his subcommittee to investigate grazing controls sometime after August 1.[55] Thomas's strenuous primary campaign that summer forced him to renege on his commitment, although he later dispatched Albert Grorud, an assistant, to the reservation.

Editorial policy changes in the *Santa Fe New Mexican* and the *Albuquerque Journal*, important sources of newspaper support for Collier in New Mexico, very likely influenced his decision to abandon the fight over the Navajo extension. After Cutting's death, the *Santa Fe New Mexican* was sold and its editorial stance became largely neutral. This had not harmed Collier very much, for E. Dana Johnson, the former editor and the state's outstanding journalist, had become a columnist for the *Albuquerque Journal*, continuing his witty commentary on the Collier-Chavez feud. Although Johnson scored both men liberally, he clearly directed most of his fire toward Chavez. In one column, for example, Johnson noted that Chavez's indifference to the Navajo population increase and need for more land might be cured permanently if the Indian Service would periodically ship a railroad carload of Navajo babies to Washington for the senator's edification and care.[56] Johnson's sudden death in late 1937 was a great blow to Collier, both in terms of the loss of a close personal friend and his influence on public opinion.

Equally unfortunate, the *Albuquerque Journal* soon afterward began cooperating with Floyd Lee's campaign against federal land acquisitions. In mid-March 1938, Lee and H. B. Pickerell, editor of the *Journal*, made a swing through western New Mexico to visit the reservation and the checkerboard. Pickerell returned to Albuquerque brimming with the ranchers' well-worn arguments. In a front page story a few days later, the editor depicted the Navajo extension as harmful to tax revenues and the ranching industry and criticized the Indian Service for wasteful spending.[57] In December Lee headed

55. See Ickes to Thomas, 29 March and 14 April 1938, Chavez to Morgan, 21 May 1938, and Thomas to Chavez, 11 August 1938, Chavez papers, UA.

56. *Albuquerque Journal*, 27 November 1937, p. 6.

57. *Farmington Times Hustler*, 18 March 1938, p. 1; *Albuquerque Journal*, 20 March 1938, pp. 1, 4.

several meetings in western New Mexico at which ranchers drafted resolutions opposing the Navajo extension and all federal acquisitions of land. David Chavez, state officials, and civic leaders from Gallup and Farmington, attended Lee's appearances. Clearly by this time, the stockmen had seized the initiative in their long fight. Significantly, Indian Service leaders did not respond to any of Lee's speeches.

The ranchers' meetings resulted in the passage of a joint memorial against the Navajo extension by the New Mexico legislature early in 1939. The memorial stated that the Navajo extension would cause serious tax losses, threatened future reclamation and revenues from gas and oil discoveries, and endangered the ranching industry. The sponsors quickly railroaded the measure through the legislature. Mrs. Charles H. Dietrich, chairman of the New Mexico Association on Indian Affairs, complained that the memorial went through three readings in the lower house in one day without debate. The next morning she asked to testify in senate committee hearings and the chairman promised to notify her when to appear. Mrs. Dietrich later learned that the memorial received its second and third readings in the senate that afternoon without being debated or even printed. She protested to Chavez that the presence of officials from the stockmen's associations in Santa Fe during the two days might have had something to do with the legislators' expeditious behavior.[58]

The prolonged dispute over the Navajo boundary bill finally came to an end on September 1, 1939, when Secretary Ickes placed the checkerboard area under the Taylor Grazing Act. The meager records on Ickes' action do not indicate whether he and Collier had arranged some sort of bargain with the ranchers and Chavez, but this seems unlikely. One factor which motivated the decision to create "Grazing District 7" was the worsening situation in the checkerboard in the past few years. As all the adjoining regions had come under the Taylor Grazing Act, tramp ranchers, unable to qualify for grazing rights, had illegally moved their stock into the unorganized range. One official reported in 1939 that perhaps as much as half of the white-owned stock in the checkerboard belonged to the intruders who should be banished in favor of Indian and legitimate white ranchers.[59]

58. House Memorial No. 1, Fourteenth Legislature, State of New Mexico, 30 January 1939, and Dietrich to Chavez, 25 February 1939, Chavez papers, UA.

59. *Gallup Independent*, 20 September 1939.

Collier's behavior in accepting the defeat of the Navajo boundary bill closely resembles his actions after the tribe rejected the Wheeler-Howard Act in 1935. In other words, he tried to implement his principles, in this instance through shaping the way the grazing district was organized. Since the Interior Department administered the Taylor Grazing Act, Collier had some voice in the selection of a sympathetic regional grazer, the official who administered the day-to-day operations of the grazing district. A representative of the Navajo Service sat on the Range Conservation Committee that passed on applications for grazing permits and was made up of officials from various Interior and Agriculture agencies. The Indian Service official on the group was to "represent individual Navajos or groups of Navajos in all district matters," according to the district charter. Although the regulations did not specify how the Advisory Board actually represented area stockmen, newspaper accounts indicated that the checkerboard was divided into subdistricts which each elected a Navajo and a white member.[60]

The abundant references to frictions between white ranching interests and the Grazing Service after 1939 indicate that controversy did not end with the establishment of the new grazing district. Laissez-faire attitudes ingrained from years of free use of the public domain caused ranchers all over the West to rail against the implementation of the Taylor Grazing Act, but the government's efforts to protect Navajo rights made the situation far worse in the checkerboard. After numerous protests by the ranchers, Kelsey Presley resigned as chairman of the Advisory Board in March 1942, charging that the government had moved Navajo herds from the reservation to the checkerboard and pressured white ranchers from the area.[61]

In reviewing the long fight over the Navajo extension, perhaps the most significant factor in the defeat of the boundary bill was the nature of New Mexico's economic and political structure. Without a sizeable urban population or varied and large industries, the state economy in the 1930s was almost solely dependent on ranching, farming, and mining interests. By antagonizing the powerful stockmen,

60. "Rules for the Administration of New Mexico Grazing District 7 . . . ," 1 September 1939, File 60177, 1939, 013, Navajo, NA, RG 75; *Farmington Times Hustler*, 24 November 1939, p. 1, and 1 December 1939, p. 1.
    61. *Gallup Independent*, 11 March 1942.

Collier created a foe that exerted more influence than he could counter. His basic weapons of maintaining a freeze on the withdrawn lands, threatening to put more Indian allotments on the checker-board, and moral suasion were simply ineffectual.

Collier was also weakened by the anomalous position that the Indian Service has traditionally occupied in trying to protect Indian interests. Neither New Mexico nor Arizona at this time allowed Indians to vote. This thrust the entire burden of their well-being onto the federal government. To compound the problem, J. C. Morgan headed a strong faction of Navajos who opposed the commissioner. Through his alliance with these dissidents, Chavez was able to defeat the boundary bill and, at the same time, to pose as a protector of the Indians.

In somewhat similar fashion, Chavez found that his opposition to Navajo extension offered countless political advantages without any real drawbacks. For all his astuteness and power, he never enjoyed political security in New Mexico, because the state's population was almost equally divided between Spanish-Americans and Anglo-Americans and between the Democrats and Republicans. While Chavez could largely depend upon the ethnic loyalties of "native" voters after Cutting's death, he always needed to identify with issues which would attract some support from the Anglos. By playing upon his constituents' xenophobia and ingrained hostility against the federal government, Indians, and easterners, Chavez won not only the backing of ranchers in the checkerboard but the applause of the general public. His opposition to the Navajo extension was, therefore, an eminently "safe" position, much like denouncing low tariff rates on imported beef or raw wool. It did not endanger Chavez's well-publicized reputation as a defender of Spanish-American con-stituents, guardian of the "little man," and liberal New Dealer.

It should be stressed that Chavez's liberalism, despite his ward heeler tactics and anti-Indian outlook, was something more than a pose to win votes. He joined the crusade of the 1930s to pass an-tilynching legislation when blacks made up only a minute portion of the New Mexico population. His outspoken support of labor prob-ably cost Chavez more votes than it gained from a constituency that was highly rural. He was, in short, a complex man with varied and somewhat contradictory motives.

Finally, the battle over the Navajo boundary bill points up the extraordinary control that western congressmen held, and still hold, over Indian affairs. Senators and representatives from the states with large Indian populations dominated the Indian Affairs Committees of both Houses. Each committee member demanded a veto over any legislative proposal which dealt with his state and the others automatically agreed because they wanted the same power. Senator Thomas's refusal to allow a committee vote on the boundary bill until Chavez consented was standard practice. The attempts by western senators to cripple Indian Service appropriations, to repeal Collier's pet legislation, and to remove him from office were unusual only because he fought back and, with Ickes' support, kept his post. Normally such disputes never reached public notice because the Indian Bureau quietly retracted offensive measures.

In conclusion, the defeat of the boundary bill was the worst blow the Navajo administration suffered in the New Deal. The reservation Indians underwent the trauma of livestock reductions without getting all the additional land that Collier promised at Tuba City in 1933. For the Eastern Navajos, the failure to pass the extension was even worse. They continued as the most impoverished segment of the tribe, with only a semblance of the services and protection provided on the reservation. They remained what they had always been, a foundling group living in a no man's land.

# 7

## The "Headmen's Council" and the New Grazing Program

In 1937 both the Chavez and Collier conflict over the New Mexico boundary bill in Congress and the running feud between the Morgan faction and the Navajo Service came to a climax. Even though Morgan's basic complaints against government policies remained unchanged, his alliance with Chavez and the resentments of Navajos against the new 1937 grazing program made him a far more effective opponent.

After the defeat of the Wheeler-Howard referendum, Collier's decision in 1936 to make the tribal council more representative raised the first outcry among Morgan's supporters. Despite numerous meetings earlier in the New Deal, the tribal legislature had become completely moribund after Thomas Dodge's resignation as chairman in May 1936. Collier told reporters during a visit to Window Rock in June that the council "had largely gone by default" and he announced plans to create a new and more representative body.[1]

Fryer waited until November before he acted on Collier's suggestion. At that time the young superintendent asked Father Berard Haile to assist in reorganizing the council.[2] Haile possessed sound qualifications for the task and equally firm views about its accomplishment. A resident of the reservation since 1901, the priest had developed an exceptional reputation as a student of Navajo language and culture. Later he completed a Ph.D. degree at the University of Chicago under Edward Sapir, a comparative linguist noted for his discovery of the tonal qualities of Athapascan. From early in the New Deal, Haile had been employed as a consultant by the Indian Service to develop a system of written Navajo and to train interpreters.[3]

1. *Gallup Independent*, 16 June 1936, p. 1; *Farmington Times Hustler*, 19 June 1936, p. 1.
2. Haile to Fryer, 6 November 1936, Haile papers, UAL.
3. Sapir had moved to Yale University by the time of the New Deal. For biographic

A long-time opponent of the six agencies because of the jealousies they created among the tribe, the Catholic linguist wanted the Navajos united under a council made up of headmen. Traditional leaders, he strongly believed, held their position because of demonstrated abilities, truly reflected tribal sentiment, and would unselfishly cooperate with the government, if its programs were valid and carefully explained. Haile disliked Morgan and other returned students' efforts to dominate tribal politics. Their education and ability to speak English gave them an exaggerated opinion of their talents and they lacked the wisdom, integrity, and empathy that Haile associated with traditional leaders. Like Collier, Haile felt that adding more headmen to the council was a most desirable reform and he willingly gave up his linguistics work to serve as a consultant.

On November 24 the tribal council met at Window Rock, under Acting Chairman Marcus Kanuho,[4] to take up reorganization and several other matters. Morgan was among four delegates not in attendance, although officials claimed they had telephoned members about the meeting a week earlier and also notified them in person. This may have been the case, nevertheless Morgan did not attend. After some confusion over whether to proceed, the delegates, including Morgan's followers, unanimously adopted a resolution which authorized an executive committee to reorganize the council and draw up a constitution for the tribe.

The issue which evoked far more discussion was a government request that a committee be appointed to adapt Department of Interior grazing regulations to fit the new land management districts. The delegates' sensitivity to any form of livestock control immediately led them to draw back from the subject. James M. Stewart sensed the Navajos' hesitation and reemphasized that the government was not asking for an endorsement of the grazing regulations but merely wanted the committee to share in reshaping them to fit the tribe's situation. Still uncertain, the delegates finally accepted the proposal. Compared to the stormy sessions of 1934, the deliberations went smoothly.[5]

sketches on Haile, see Van Valkenburgh papers, AHS, and Mrs. White Mountain Smith, "Gentle Padre Inventor of Alphabet for Navajo Tribe," *The Desert Magazine* 2 (March 1939): 7–9.

4. Kanuho became acting chairman after Dodge's resignation. He was a boarding school product from the Leupp area who spoke English quite well but did not occupy a very important role in tribal affairs. He dropped out of the picture after 1937.

5. "Meeting of the Navajo Tribal Council at Window Rock" 24 November 1936,

Morgan quickly reacted to a reorganization of the tribal council with hostility. He claimed that he had never been notified of the council meeting and contended that the body had lost its authority when Thomas Dodge resigned as chairman. In addition, he charged that the Navajos would now feel the full effects of their denial of the Wheeler-Howard Act and Collier's efforts to restrict their freedom of grazing. Using phrases he would repeat constantly in the future, Morgan criticized Collier for wanting a "hand-picked" council of "long hairs" subservient to his will.[6]

Ignoring Morgan's charges, Fryer immediately proceeded with plans for reorganizing the council. On December 3 the executive committee met with Haile and the superintendent at Window Rock. The group agreed that they would canvass the Navajo country to identify the grassroots leaders of the tribe. Father Haile would accompany the committee as a consultant and secretary. Later they would return with a master list of headmen and select seventy people who would serve in the constitutional assembly.

On December 5 the committee met with the Two Wells residents in the first of their many forays across the vast Navajo country. There would be something slightly bizarre and yet heroic about the sojourners' efforts. One committeeman was arrested on the eve of their departure and Jim Shirley of Ganado replaced him. Other members included Marcus Kanuho, Nalnishi, George Bancroft, Fred Nelson, Allen Neskahi, Chee Dodge, and Dashne Clah Cheschillege with Henry Taliman as chairman. The harassed little priest tried to keep the group under watchful surveillance, but some members still managed to get tipsy. No teetotaler himself, Haile expressed his disgust at the offenders' efforts to lead discussions and interpret at meetings when plagued by hangovers. The unseasonably cold weather, blizzards, terrible winter roads, and stalled cars delayed the committee's work.[7]

As the canvassing committee toured the reservation, local groups assembled for meetings at trading posts, chapter houses, and ceremonials. After each session, Father Berard summarized the discussion and listed the audiences' nominees in his journal, adding brief notes on the qualifications of prospective assembly men. The committee

---

Department of Interior Library, Washington, pp. 5, 13–15.

6. *Gallup Independent*, 4 December 1936, p. 1.

7. Father Berard Haile's journal, 5 December 1936–19 April 1937, Haile papers, UAL. The rest of the information on the canvass is taken from this journal.

members were divided over whether to name educated or traditional leaders. Chairman Taliman and other returned students preferred younger tribesmen who spoke English, while Dodge invariably supported headmen. Taliman, however, was unwilling to challenge the prestigious Dodge directly.

Even though Morgan failed to appear at any of the meetings, his influence was felt throughout the committee's work. Before they first set out, the canvassers had sent a letter to the protestor, maintaining that they had full authorization to select a constitutional assembly and requesting him not to hold counter-meetings. Morgan retorted that the committee was denying him freedom of speech. His followers visited localities before the committee, warning Navajos against the new council.

The only serious confrontation, however, came on January 13, 1937, at Shiprock. Over 200 Navajos appeared at Morgan's stronghold to hear Taliman explain the purpose of the committee. When he finished, Robert Martin expressed his anti-Catholic views by condemning Father Berard's presence. Morgan's lieutenant then told the audience that the Arizona and New Mexico portions of the reservation would soon be separated, so the group's visit was pointless. He denied that he had known the intent of the council resolution approving reorganization when he voted for it. Allen Neskahi accused the Morgan spokesman of feigning ignorance and told the audience that the council had been thoroughly briefed before their vote. Acrimonious debate followed in which Martin charged that the government programs were communistic. Haile concluded that the failure of the audience to applaud Martin's attacks and its willingness to name candidates showed serious weaknesses in the Morgan faction's appeal.

The outbursts at Shiprock were an updated version of the old rivalry between Morgan's "students" and Dodge's traditionalists. What made the situation more serious now was Morgan's cooperation with Chavez. Morgan and Chavez had previously made an arrangement in early 1937 by which the Navajo leader agreed to drop his support of the eastward extension and to supply the senator with wholesale quantities of protest letters and petitions for his fight against the New Mexico boundary bill. Chavez, in return, introduced a bill exempting the tribe from the Wheeler-Howard Act and tried to force Collier to resign.

Morgan's reasons for making an arrangement with Chavez are

somewhat unclear. On the surface, the exemption legislation made no
sense, for the tribe had already rejected the Wheeler-Howard Act in
1935. Morgan, however, realized that Collier was still applying the
principles of his pet measure and the missionary evidently believed
that a specific repeal of the Wheeler-Howard Act in New Mexico
would permit his people to overturn present policies and restore the
reservation administration of the pre-New Deal. As Martin had
mentioned at the Shiprock confrontation, some of the Morgan faction had a tenuous plan to break away from the Arizona Navajos
and operate as a separate tribe.

Morgan's willingness to abandon 9,000 Eastern Navajos to
continued pressures of white stockmen in the checkerboard may also
be partly explained by the missionary's complete devotion to assimilation. Perhaps Morgan rationalized that the Eastern Navajos should
continue to intermingle with whites and avoid coming under Collier's
hated "monkey show." Thomas Dodge reported in early 1937 that
Morgan soothed his conscience about the extension issue by telling
followers that tribal funds would be used to acquire the checkerboard
gradually and the land shortages would be relieved by approval of
the huge Turley irrigation project south of Farmington.[8]

Morgan's desire to become the chairman of the tribal council
may also explain his obstructionist tactics. A reorganized council
dominated by headmen seriously threatened Morgan's position in
tribal politics. In the back of his mind may have been the idea that
an alliance with Chavez and agitation against the government would
not only defeat Collier's policies but might bring him the chairmanship.[9]

After completing their canvass in late February, the reorganization committee met at Window Rock on March 8 to pare the 250
nominees for the constitutional assembly to seventy actual delegates.[10]

8. These comments on Morgan's "bargain" with Chavez and the rationalizations by
Morgan are derived from Thomas Dodge's belief that Morgan and Chavez had con-
summated an alliance during a recent meeting in Albuquerque. See Fryer to Collier, 10
February 1937, Collier papers, YU.

9. The interpretation that Morgan's prime motivation was his political ambitions
sometimes appears in the confidential Indian Service correspondence. Howard Gorman,
who knew Morgan intimately, has expressed the firm belief that Morgan's opposition to
the government throughout the New Deal was mainly based on his hopes of becoming
chairman. Gorman Interview.

10. Haile journal, Haile papers, UAL. The apportionment was evidently based on 500
adult residents per grazing district.

Because the land management districts varied considerably in population, Haile told the committee to appoint one delegate for approximately every 500 Navajo residents in a given district. This question caused little problem. But committee members refused to accept the proposal that they should select individuals to the assembly who would act as a provisional council with Ickes appointing the chairman. Even though Haile believed that the members had thoroughly understood and accepted these procedures during the canvass, Allen Neskahi and others claimed that they had never agreed to such an arrangement.

Several factors caused the committee's sudden reluctance, loss of memory, and apparent naiveté. The educated members of the group had been strongly schooled in the efficacy of elections and they complained that appointing the delegates was undemocratic. Neskahi could not believe that Ickes could name a chairman he did not know personally. More importantly, both educated and uneducated members of the committee shied away from making any decisions because they feared the criticism of fellow tribesmen. Chee Dodge totally boycotted the Window Rock sessions, probably because he wanted to see how people reacted to a reorganization of the council.

The committee groped as they tried to solve these problems and to satisfy Fryer's and Haile's demands that they act and take responsibility. Neskahi finally suggested that all 250 candidates be brought to Window Rock and allowed to select the seventy members of the constitutional assembly and decide on its procedures and powers. After this was beaten down, he and other members unsuccessfully demanded that the delegates be popularly elected. At one point during the dispute, Neskahi burst into a tirade saying that the appointment of leaders would be communistic. Despite the committee's obvious reluctance to accept the responsibility, the members finally surrendered to Haile's demands that they select seventy assembly delegates from the master list.

Haile's other attempts to mold the reorganization succeeded only in part. Fryer and Thomas Dodge successfully objected to Haile's wish that council members be appointed as a permanent practice, although they accepted the idea of the Secretary of Interior naming the chairman and the constitutional assembly acting as a provisional body. Haile's hopes were further weakened by a number of headmen who refused to be nominated to the assembly during the canvass.

The title "headmen's council," is used in this study to identify the new group, but the seventy-man body also contained a goodly number of educated Navajos. None of Morgan's main associates, however, were appointed.

The question of Morgan's appointment to the constitutional assembly perplexed the committee members. Haile argued that Morgan's inclusion might be regarded as an acceptance of his ideas and would provide him with a new avenue for attacking the government. When Fryer was consulted, he endorsed Morgan's appointment, maintaining that his leadership had to be recognized. Fryer's advice coincided with some committee members' hopes that Morgan would be less dangerous inside the assembly, where he might be curbed, than outside where his agitation would be unrestrained, and they included him in the assembly.

Morgan's actions provided little support for the committee's hopes. In early January 1937, Morgan sent a strong letter to the editor of the *Farmington Times Hustler* repeating earlier charges that he had not been notified about the November council and that reorganization was illegal. The government should "try to stop drunkenness, gambling, sickness and diseases on the reservation which . . . [are] growing," Morgan complained, instead of accusing him of duplicity.[11] He and his followers filled Chavez's office with new protests which the senator used in support of his fight against the New Mexico boundary bill and his exemption legislation. As the time approached for the constitutional assembly to meet in April, Morgan unsuccessfully attempted to have Chavez stop the meeting.[12]

On April 9, 1937, the assembly met at Window Rock for a two-day session.[13] The traditionalists among the delegates came dressed in black hats, jeans, and velveteen shirts, laden with turquoise

11. *Farmington Times Hustler*, 1 January 1937, p. 3.

12. For the most cogent protest letters see Roger Davis to Chavez, 6 February 1937, Chavez papers, UA. Also see, "News Release," 24 February 1937 and Chavez to Morgan, 5 April 1937, Chavez Papers, UA.

13. My discussion of this session is based on "Meeting of the Navajo Tribal Council Held at Window Rock, Arizona on April 9 [–10], 1937," File 30853, 37, 054, NA, RG 75, 17–45, *passim*; "Council Notes, Taliman Succeeds Chairman Kanuho," *The Navajo Service News* 2 (n.d.): 2. Although the election of a chairman of the Headmen's Council was supposedly abolished in favor of his appointment by the Secretary of Interior, Taliman was elected by the delegates. Perhaps the confusion of the session caused the change or Collier had earlier vetoed the idea. The council selected Irwin Morgan as secretary and Fred Nelson as treasurer but neither assumed their duties.

jewelry, with their long hair bound into buns with yarn. Morgan's followers filled the audience seated on the outer edges of the council chamber. The agenda had obviously been arranged to avoid trouble and, if nothing else, to wear down the protestors by sheer boredom. G. A. Trotter introduced the main leaders of the Navajo Service to the colorful delegates and Henry Taliman and Jim Shirley reviewed the reorganization committee's work. During the afternoon, Fryer spoke on the formation of the council in 1923 and how it tended to divide instead of unify the tribe. He emphasized that the present assembly was a petitioning body and that the constitution must be approved by Ickes and Collier. In closing, Fryer declared the old council was dissolved and the constitutional assembly was now a provisional council by order of the Secretary of Interior. Chee Dodge ended the long preliminaries with a speech advising the delegates to cooperate with government.

Any hopes that Morgan would quietly submit to reorganization quickly vanished. In the late afternoon when Taliman introduced a resolution to make the assembly into a provisional council, Morgan seized this opening to attack what he obviously felt was a complete injustice. He insisted that the tribe should have approved dissolving the old council by a popular vote. What Fryer termed "organized heckling" then broke out among the audience and delegates during the following discussion. In the pandemonium, Morgan's followers reportedly shouted epithets such as "long-hairs" and "tools of the government" at the bewildered headmen and interrupted speakers as the chair tried unsuccessfully to quiet the audience.

Fryer and Morgan finally confronted the basic issue in the middle of the turmoil when the missionary asserted: "There is no authority to dissolve this [old] council." Fryer quickly responded by asking: "Mr. Morgan, the Navajo Tribal Council was created by the Secretary of Interior, was it not?" When the Navajo leader answered "yes," the superintendent pushed home the point that Ickes could also dissolve the old council and authorize a new one. Fryer promised that any constitution would be approved by the tribe. This seemed to cow Morgan who dropped out of the discussion the rest of the afternoon.

This exchange did not quiet the hecklers or Roger Davis, a Navajo missionary worker from Indian Wells. Davis rose, angrily shook his finger at Fryer, and charged that the selection of the delegates had not been fair. The superintendent answered that the old council had authorized the reorganization committee to search out the best headmen in hopes of bringing in new leaders. As the heckling continued, Fryer demanded that either the audience quiet down or "it is going to be necessary to clear the hall." The afternoon session closed with Thomas Dodge's reiteration that the delegates were being asked to decide two questions: (1) did they wish to become a provisional council; and (2) did they want to draft a permanent constitution?

When the assembly reconvened that evening, Morgan had "withdrawn" from the delegates and sat in the audience. Without any interruptions, the assembly passed the resolutions and elected Taliman as chairman. The delegates later named Roy Kinsel of Lukachukai as vice chairman.

During the second day, Taliman introduced a resolution directing the appointment of a committee to draft a constitution. The completed document would be forwarded to Ickes for his approval and then sent back to the council and the tribe for ratification. Morgan had returned to the floor and participated amicably in the discussion, but the new resolution somehow rekindled his animosities. In a long tirade against the government, he questioned whether the new council would have any real powers and reasserted that the reorganization was undemocratic. "This is not the way you white people elect your officers," Morgan complained. After claiming that his freedom of speech had been impaired and the Treaty of 1868 violated, Morgan and a half-dozen followers bolted the council.

The assembly then quickly accepted Taliman's resolution and moved to other business. Despite Morgan's bolting the convention, Taliman named him to chair the drafting committee, along with Jim Shirley, Robert Curley of Leupp, Roy Haskan of Tuba City, and Frank Mitchell of Chinle. Taliman next appointed an executive committee of nineteen men, one from each of the eighteen land management districts, along with Jose Apache who represented Puertocito and Cañoncito.

During the next month or so after the first session of the Headmen's Council, Morgan was able to arouse many Navajos against the government. Morgan's personal complaints centered on his somewhat vague but strong belief that the new council violated the Treaty of 1868 and the citizenship rights of Indians. Although most tribesmen did object to the legislative body on these grounds, they were worried about the recent organization of the land management districts and numerous rumors about an impending livestock reduction. Morgan's success in associating his own grievances with those of his followers was graphically demonstrated when two government workers (probably Thomas Dodge and Howard Gorman) walked in and surprised Morgan during a protest meeting at Burnham's Trading Post in late April. An older Navajo lady "explained that her sheep and other property were made possible by the great efforts of the old Navajo leaders who signed the Treaty of 1868. The only protection the Navajos had for their possessions was this old treaty and she wanted to have that document preserved for the Navajo people."[14]

Morgan also refused to serve on the drafting committee, announcing that the constitution had already been written before the assembly met at Window Rock. He drew this conclusion from an ambiguous statement in a telegram he received from the Associated Press asking him to authorize the release of a story on the new constitution.[15] Although Morgan may have misinterpreted the telegram, he was partly correct in his assertion. Thomas Dodge and Howard Gorman had written up a working outline of basic provisions for the drafting committee.[16] Convinced of wrongdoing, Morgan condemned the entire business of reorganization as another "prearranged deal" by the government.

Morgan's opposition to the constitution forced the drafting committee to proceed without him. On April 23, the members started their work under Haile's direction. A week later, Taliman announced that they had adjourned, without taking any final action, to discuss parts of the constitution with constituents before they reconvened.[17]

Taliman a few days later issued a blistering attack on Morgan's recent charges. The chairman claimed that Morgan had assured him that he would gladly serve on the drafting committee on the morning before his walkout on April 10. Taliman additionally lashed

14. Memo to Fryer, 30 April 1937, LAFRC, Box 72938.
15. Morgan to Chavez, 19 April 1936 [sic.], Chavez papers, UA. The contents of the letter definitely indicate that the proper date was 1937.
16. In a letter to Collier, Walter Woehlke mentioned that Thomas Dodge had shown him an outline of the proposed constitution on March 29. See Woehlke to Collier, 29 March 1937, Collier papers, YU.
17. *Santa Fe New Mexican*, 1 May 1937, p. 1.

Morgan for "ducking out of sight whenever something important confronts our tribe." The chairman's sharpest criticism, however, was that Morgan bled Navajos frightened by livestock reductions to raise funds for his "wild goose chases" to Washington.[18]

As the turmoil on the reservation grew, Morgan turned to Chavez for support. He wrote in April that he could have ten or more protestors in Washington whenever Chavez desired.[19] Morgan finally left New Mexico on June 4 at the head of a delegation of fourteen Navajos to testify before the Senate Indian Affairs Committee. He used the trip to Washington not only to protest but to show other members of the delegation the virtues of white life. Although returned students made up a majority of the delegation, three or four others were traditionalists whom Morgan especially wanted to impress.[20] The delegation detrained at Denver and Chicago for interviews and sightseeing and Morgan led the group around Washington to confer with Collier in the Indian Office and to visit historic spots in Virginia.

Paul Palmer, the Farmington lawyer whose presence baffled many observers, joined the Morgan delegation soon after their arrival in Washington. Prominent in the Mormon Church and civic affairs, Palmer acted as Republican county chairman. Representing the San Juan County stockmen in 1935, he had helped negotiate the abortive Santa Fe Agreement which supposedly settled all complaints against the New Mexico boundary bill. These activities should have made him persona non grata to the Navajos and Chavez, but Palmer not only served as the spokesman for Morgan's delegation at the 1937 hearings, but he remained a crucial, although always enigmatic, figure in reservation protests for the next two years.

On June 17, Morgan's delegation finally testified before the Senate Indian Affairs Committee.[21] Palmer appeared as the first witness and

18. Henry Taliman's letter to the editor, *Farmington Times Hustler*, 7 May 1937, p. 7.

19. Morgan to Chavez, 12 April 1937, Chavez papers, UA.

20. Beside Morgan and his son Irwin, the delegation included Begoshe Begay, Indian Wells, Arizona; Charles Damon, Tohatchi, New Mexico; William Goodluck, Houck, Arizona; Adolph Maloney, Tuba City, Arizona; Tall Man, Teec-Nos-Pos, Arizona; Robert Martin, Shiprock, New Mexico; Wallace Peshlakai, Rehoboth, New Mexico; Scott Preston, Tuba City, Arizona; Murphy Spenser, Indian Wells, Arizona; Todechon-Tse, Newcomb, New Mexico; John Watson, Rock Point-Manuelito, New Mexico; and Chis Yazzi, Kimbeto, New Mexico. *Farmington Times Hustler*, 4 June 1937, p. 1.

21. All information on delegates' testimony is from U. S., Senate, Subcommittee of the

he attacked virtually every major policy attempted on the reservation since the start of the New Deal. The lawyer especially criticized the reorganization of the tribal council, insisting that it had no support except among Indians who held government jobs. A tribal council selected by local chapters with a popularly elected chairman and vice chairman was needed. Palmer also recommended that Collier, Fryer, and Thomas Dodge be dismissed.

Navajo witnesses supported Palmer's statement but tended to focus more attention on the livestock regulations and the land management districts. Charles Damon of Tohatchi told the committee that the new districts were illegal because the Treaty of 1868 prohibited any division of the reservation without the popular consent of the tribe. He also claimed that new livestock reductions would create starvation. Throughout the testimony, the Navajo protestors repeatedly charged that the Wheeler-Howard Act was responsible for their problems with the government and Collier was punishing them for rejecting the measure. When Senator Thomas asked Damon if he realized that his people had voted down the legislation, the Navajo replied: "Well, we all think that we are treated under the Wheeler-Howard bill. We think that way. The Indians think that the Wheeler-Howard bill is what is doing all this damage to us."

Because of their current efforts to repeal the Wheeler-Howard Act and oust Collier, Senator Chavez and Senator Wheeler entered their opinions into the hearings record. Chavez tried to create the impression that serious Collier blunders had caused mass suffering among the Navajos. In one humorous bit of testimony, Chavez displayed a photograph of a run-down hogan with a bedraggled Indian man and woman standing in front. The senator then asked Charles Damon to look at the picture and "tell the committee whether or not it is a typical scene of Navajo life on your reservation." Unaware of Chavez's intention, Damon blandly replied, "Not all Navajos have houses like that. Some of them have good houses." Chavez and Wheeler had more success with several white witnesses who criticized the poor quality of building construction and conservation projects.

Neither the delegates' testimony nor the government defense[22]

---

Committee on Indian Affairs, *Hearings, Survey of Conditions of Indians in the United States*, 75th Cong., 1st. sess., 1937, pt. 37, pp. 20909–73.

22. A short time after Morgan's delegation returned to New Mexico, three Navajos

revealed any new information, but Morgan left Washington ebulliently confident that he could destroy Collier's "monkey show." The missionary's return to Farmington was a prelude to the stormiest period of Navajo protest of the entire New Deal.

The dissidents' plans, however, involved more than a mere restoration of past policies. According to Wallace Peshlakai, a member of the delegation and interpreter for the Christian Reformed Church, the antigovernment forces in New Mexico planned to revive the old chapter organizations and possibly even incorporate themselves as a separate tribe operating under New Mexico laws.[23] On July 15 Morgan and Palmer held a meeting at Shiprock and informed their followers of plans for a convention at Farmington "to discuss ways and means to reestablish tribal Govt. thru [a] real Tribal council to be duly elected by the vote of the people." In reporting on the meeting to Chavez, Morgan mentioned nothing about dividing the reservation, so he evidently planned to use the impending convention to supplant the headmen's council rather than as a separatist device.[24]

If Morgan's goals were unclear, there was no mystery why Navajos rallied to his side. During this period, the government had finally completed studies of the grazing capacities of the land management districts and, with the help of the committee of Navajos appointed at the 1936 council, established a new set of grazing regulations for the reservation.[25] Walter Woehlke on June 23, 1937, announced that the grazing code would permit an accurate determination of the ownership of livestock enabling the government to end the past practice of large Navajo owners evading reduction by secretly dividing their stock among relatives. The regulations would also

appeared before the Senate Indian Affairs Committee as representatives of the tribal council. The first witness was Dogol-Chee-Bikis, a sixty-nine year old headman from Tohatchi. Like many traditional leaders, Bikis was completely open and thoroughly independent. He criticized early herd reductions but vaguely realized the need to correct the overgrazing problem. Frank Mitchell, a chapter leader from Chinle and bitter opponent of Morgan, defended the government very strongly, especially Collier's work programs, schools, and hospitals. Henry Taliman's testimony mainly concerned a defense of the Headmen's Council and its validity. Howard Gorman accompanied the delegation as an interpreter and spoke briefly on his decision to break with Morgan and support the government conservation efforts. Fryer closed the testimony by discussing the livestock reduction program.

23. Peshlakai to Chavez, 5 July 1937, Chavez papers, UA.

24. Morgan to Chavez, 16 July 1937, Chavez papers, UA.

25. Grazing Regulations for the Navajo and Hopi Reservation, 2 June 1937, Haile papers, UAL.

achieve a fair distribution of livestock among all Navajos. Woehlke promised that the new program would bring the livestock load of the land management districts into balance with their grazing capacities.[26]

Even though Woehlke exaggerated its merits, the new grazing program was far superior to the ill-conceived reductions of the past. By a semigraduated system of sales, the program would mainly affect large owners and most small owners would be undisturbed. More significantly, the reductions would largely be surplus horses and unproductive livestock and not sheep. The new program also offered a flexible approach, since the grazing load within any district would be adjusted to fit its particular capacity and situation. Two or three districts were already under recommended grazing loads. Another two or three could reach the limits by the sale of surplus horses. If the program had been attempted earlier and explained carefully, it might have been accepted, but Navajos obviously were in no mood to cooperate with any sort of livestock reduction effort in 1937.

Despite its merits, the new program contained serious defects. Several districts were so badly overgrazed that no family could have subsisted on the livestock quotas set by the SCS. Unfortunately, such areas were mostly in the northeast region of the reservation where Morgan's strength was. Moreover, the complicated nature of the program caused frustration in explaining it and winning the tribe's acceptance.

The implementation of the new program involved several distinct phases of future work by land management personnel. The first was to tally the number of sheep and goats that each Navajo family dipped in the summer of 1937. In the second stage the range riders were to conduct large roundups of horses, burros, and cattle. The roundups were not reservation-wide in 1937, but covered such areas as Tohatchi, Lukachukai, Kaibito, and Teec-Nos-Pos where surplus horses were most numerous. The rest of the reservation escaped the roundups until later. Crews of CCC enrollees and range riders drove the stock into corrals and brought in local Navajos to establish ownership. The animals were then branded with their owner's mark and the tribal brand. After finishing with one region, the roundup crews moved to another area and repeated the process.

Once a roundup was completed, the district supervisor tried to

26. *Gallup Independent*, 23 June 1937, pp. 1, 4.

persuade the Navajo owners to sell their unproductive livestock, especially surplus horses. Officials arranged for off-reservation buyers to appear at the corrals to bid on the mustangs. Most of the horses ran semiwild and were so starved that many barely survived the drive to the corrals. The average price for the hoses was only two dollars per head. To the Navajos, however, the ownership of horses was a measure of a family's prestige and only by strong pressuring were any sales made.

The Navajos, however, had a good knowledge of the quality of horses. When their horses were penned in the corrals and the buyers appeared to bid, the Indians invariably found some excuse to delay the sale until the next day. Knowing they must dispose of some stock to pacify the supervisor's demands, the owners engaged in some frantic overnight trading. When the whites returned the next morning, all the good horses had been removed, leaving only the poorest in the corral. This, of course, led to more haggling as the buyers lowered the price for the remaining nags.

During the horse sales, the district supervisors submitted the data on dipping records of sheep and goats and other types of stock to Window Rock. There the land management division assembled the information, compared it with the grazing capacity of that particular district, and determined how many sheep units each owner should be allowed to graze.

The method used to calculate how much livestock each owner could graze was complicated by the translation of the various kinds of livestock into sheep units. Basically, however, the range experts divided the number of owners of a district into its total estimated grazing capacity, expressed in sheep units. The resulting figure was the "base preference" or the average amount of livestock that each owner could graze if all were given an equal number. The experts next determined which Navajos' herds were smaller than the base preference level. By subtracting the total of their holdings from their base preferences and adding this figure to large herders' quotas, the land division established the "maximum limit" that anyone in a district could graze. The maximum limit was the crucial part of the new program. Anyone whose stock exceeded that amount was forced to sell off his livestock until he came under that level. Those already under the maximum limit were to be allowed to keep the same amount of livestock owned in 1937 but not to exceed that number in the future.

District 1 or the Kaibito area seems fairly representative of the way that the new grazing system operated. The land management division determined that Navajo herders of District 1 should be grazing 34,221 sheep units, but 319 owners ran the equivalent of 55,313 sheep. This meant that the Indians must remove 21,092 sheep units. The maximum limit of 261 sheep units per person severely affected two wealthy Navajos. The largest owner, aptly named Many Goats, currently ran 844 sheep, 206 goats, 161 cattle, and 165 horses or approximately 2,500 sheep units, while the second stockman, Crooked Fingers, ran about half that amount. To meet the maximum limit, Many Goats was required to sell almost ninety percent of his stock, while Crooked Fingers had to dispose of approximately seventy-five percent. Their only alternative was to remove the stock to private lands off the reservation. Many Goats and Crooked Fingers, however, were exceptionally rich and their situation did not typify most owners in District 1. Out of the 319 owners, 268 were not forced to sell any animals because they currently held less than 261 sheep units. Most of the fifty-one Navajos with holdings above the maximum limit could reduce their livestock by selling surplus horses.

Both Navajo and white critics raised legitimate complaints against the new grazing program. They especially disliked the fact that it penalized the more energetic Navajos who had carefully built up their herds over many years while less diligent tribesmen were left untouched by the reductions. Critics also objected that the program denied small owners an opportunity to increase their herds. Even worse, the program did not permit parents to set aside livestock as patrimony for their children.

The most telling weakness of the grazing program was that the government could not provide adequate economic alternatives to the Indians. Even government field workers who believed that overgrazing on the reservation justified the new reduction scheme were unable to foresee how wage work, improved breeding, increased irrigation, education, and other avenues could ever meet the basic subsistence needs of the Navajos. Rudolph Zweifel, then supervisor of the badly overgrazed District 9 where the maximum limit was eighty-three sheep units, found it impossible to answer the Navajos' questions about what they were to do for a living after reductions. In retrospect, Zweifel has stated, "Hell! I knew it wouldn't work from the start. No man could raise a family on 83 head of sheep, and we didn't have a good, sound program to offer them."[27]

The Navajos were already apprehensive about livestock reduction well before the limited roundups started in mid-1937. By then a rumor spread that Fryer would lower the livestock load from its present level to 500,000 sheep units. Herd owners knew that any new program would be based on the number of sheep and goats dipped during the summer. Understandably, they hesistated about bringing in their flocks to the government vats and many turned to Morgan for help.

At the Shiprock meeting on July 15, Morgan claimed that Fryer had ordered the sheep and goats brought to the vats earlier than normal, warning that the government would punish violators with a fine of $100 or six months in jail. Morgan and Palmer were vague in advising Navajos about dipping, but certainly their statements encouraged owners not to cooperate. Palmer told the Shiprock audience, "What would I do if a Govt. man came to me and told me what I must do with my seven little sheep; I would kick him off the place so quick that it would make his head swing."[28] From the perspective of Navajo Service workers, such statements encouraged violence even though few Navajos actually failed to obey the dipping regulation.

Palmer's role in the trip to Washington and the subsequent protest meetings especially embittered and frustrated government workers. They understood Morgan's motives perfectly. He simply wanted to return to pre-New Deal policies and aspired to become chairman of the tribal council. Palmer's reasons, however, remained obscure. Zealously committed to the new livestock program, Fryer viewed the Farmington lawyer as an outside troublemaker. The government leaders also knew that Morgan had collected a fairly large sum to finance the protest delegation's trip to Washington, and they believed that Palmer obtained some of the money by promises of legal relief for the Navajos that he could not deliver.[29] Officials suspected that Palmer's ties with Chavez and the stockmen opposing the New

27. Mr. Zweifel Interview.
28. Morgan to Chavez, 16 July 1937, Chavez papers, UA.
29. Fryer Interview, 1970.

Mexico boundary bill meant the lawyer had something more than legal fees in mind.

Such suspicions led to an undercover investigation of Palmer in mid-July. An Indian Service worker named Montie S. Carlisle from the United Pueblo Agency served as agent for the sub rosa operation.[30] Carlisle visited Farmington posing as a wealthy eastern sightseer interested in real estate speculation. He poked around Farmington for several days talking to local businessmen and assessing Palmer's activities. On three different occasions, Carlisle met with Palmer in his office.

Carlisle's report, if accurate, revealed that Palmer's motives were as tangled as Navajo Service officials suspected. During one interview, Carlisle inquired how Farmington, with a population of 1,800, could support three lawyers. Palmer responded that the isolation of the town helped his practice considerably, and since he had been named "Chief Counsel for the Navajo Indians that he had more business than he could handle." Once steered in a discussion of this work, Palmer reveled in defeating the government and obstructing Collier's policies. Playing dumb, Carlisle asked who Collier was. Palmer replied, "Mr. Collier was probably a Russian, at any rate a Communist, and that he did not know a nigger from an Indian." Palmer went on to explain that he and the Morgan group "were opposed to all Indian Bureau policies and that they would soon succeed in getting Collier and Fryer ousted from office." Later the attorney mentioned that Chavez was his close friend and "was assisting him in every possible [way] to remove Mr. Collier from office."

The interviews also indicated that real estate speculation, as well as ego satisfaction, explained the lawyer's interest in Navajo affairs. Palmer at various times spoke rather loosely about his interests in local oil and gas wells and mining operations and his ties with outside investors. More specifically, he bragged that he had kept Collier from passing a bill to buy 5,700 acres of land near Bloomfield, New Mexico, on which the Indian Service wanted to develop an irrigation project for the Navajos.[31] The attorney claimed that an Indian

30. My account of Carlisle's investigation is based on his report. See Carlisle to Brophy, 23 July 1937, LAFRC, Box 72938.

31. The Bloomfield project was located southeast of Farmington. Palmer apparently was referring to his role in the Santa Fe Agreement in 1935. This meeting, which Palmer

Service employee had furnished him with a complete set of maps and geological information from a survey of the project which cost the government $25,000 to complete.[32] Palmer said he could sell the land for $50,000 and he promised that he would "paint any kind of picture" Carlisle wanted reported to prospective eastern buyers.

Carlisle's investigation was cut short by the protest convention at Farmington that Palmer and Morgan had arranged for July 23 and 24. At first, the undercover agent planned to stay for the meeting, but when he learned that Pueblos from Jemez and Taos would attend, Carlisle knew that he would be recognized. Expressing his desire to do some more traveling, he bowed out of Palmer's invitation to stay for the convention. Carlisle promised he would return later and look over the Bloomfield land with Palmer. Despite this beginning, Carlisle apparantly did not renew the investigation, nor did Indian Service officials ever publicize his findings.

The convention at Farmington attracted an estimated 500 delegates and resulted in the formation of the Navajo Progressive League. Both the educated Navajos and the traditionalists poured into the town to support Morgan. "There was a king's ransom in turquoise settings in beads, necklaces, bracelets and earrings at the Navajo pow wow," the local paper noted.[33] Jammed into the Mormon Community Center, the audience heard Morgan, Palmer, and numerous other orators discuss the recent visit to Washington and denounce the "hand-picked" council. Perhaps playing it cagey, Morgan did not accept any office in the League and the convention elected Wallace Peshlakai as president,[34] Charles Damon as vice president, Murphy Spenser as recording secretary, and Irwin Morgan as corresponding secretary.

The resolutions adopted by the convention showed conclusively that Morgan intended to use this organization to supplant the reorganized council. After protesting the undemocratic nature of selecting the new council members, the convention resolved that "if

---

attended, resulted in the Bloomfield project being dropped from the New Mexico boundary bill.

32. Carlisle identified Mark Radcliffe, one of Stewart's assistants in the Land Division, as the person who turned over the survey data to Palmer. Other documents repeat the charge, but the writer has never found any conclusive evidence about Radcliffe's guilt or innocence.

33. *Farmington Times Hustler*, 30 July 1937, p. 1.

34. Peshlakai, while attending a religious conference a few days after the convention, drowned in the Colorado River.

a fair election is not called in a reasonable time and a representative tribal council formed, this group will continue its organization and so form a tribal council to represent the people." Copies of this resolution and others demanding a complete revision of reservation personnel and administration were forwarded to Ickes and the Senate Indian Affairs Committee.[35] The positive definition of goals was uncharacteristic of Morgan, who normally preferred the role of critic over that of advocate.

In the weeks which followed the convention, tensions of the reservation brought the tribe close to rebellion. One incident which nearly sparked an uprising was the arrest of Hosteen Tso, Morgan's brother-in-law, who lived near Tohatchi. The arrest grew out of Tso's earlier refusal to dip his sheep. The district supervisor reported this to Fred Croxen, head of the Navajo police. On August 2, Tso and three other men stopped at a store in Gallup on their way home from a protest meeting. When they came out, three Navajo policemen tried to arrest Tso and he refused to go with them voluntarily. A fight broke out and the police hit Tso and his son several times with blackjacks and a revolver. The local sheriff arrived in the midst of the fracas. After seeing the warrant for Tso's arrest, he allowed the Navajo police to take their prisoners to the reservation.[36] The incident proved enormously embarrassing to the government. The fact that the Navajo police made the arrest outside the reservation, where they had no jurisdiction, and the severity of the beating made the episode newsworthy and the story made both local papers and the national wire services. Senator Chavez seized on the arrest of Tso to censure Collier in a Senate speech on August 20.[37] To quiet criticisms Collier sent Oliver La Farge to the reservation to investigate the arrest. Except to admit the Navajo police made a serious error, the author's report a few days later supported the government's current policies. He tried, not very successfully, to draw attention away from the Tso beating and place the blame for the reservation's unrest on the incendiary statements of Morgan and Palmer and their cooperation with Chavez's efforts to defeat the boundary bill and remove Collier.[38]

35. *Farmington Times Hustler*, 30 July 1937, p. 1.

36. See Statement of Bob Lee, n.d., and Dee Roberts to Chavez, 12 August 1937, Chavez papers, UA.

37. *Congressional Record*, 75th Cong., 1st sess., 1937, 81, pt. 8, pp. 9436–39.

38. *Gallup Independent*, 12 August 1937.

The discomforts of the government over the Tso affair persisted for sometime afterward. The three men arrested in Gallup were released when later tried before a tribal court. Probably no Navajo judge could have withstood the pressures of fellow tribesmen which would have accompanied a conviction. The three policemen, however, were arrested and convicted under state charges and spent a short term in the New Mexico penitentiary. After Chee Dodge, Collier, and Fryer intervened on their behalf, the governor commuted their sentences sometime before February 1938.

Although no aspect of reservation administration is more murky than law enforcement, illegal arrests of government opponents had been commonplace before the Tso episode. Louis C. Mueller, head of all law enforcement for the Indian Service, had previously warned Croxen in March against off-reservation captures. He repeated the same advice during two later visits to the reservation.[39]

Even though the Tso episode ended the off-reservation arrests, Morgan and Palmer continued to issue charges about mass jailings and physical mistreatment of Navajos. Such allegations were no doubt exaggerated, for the limited jail facilities on the reservation could never have held all the people Morgan and Palmer claimed were behind bars. Nevertheless, Morgan's followers had more than their share of troubles with the police and the evidence indicates a measure of truth in the charges.[40]

The type of Navajos who served as police also give some credence to the Morgan-Palmer charges. Only an inordinately strong-willed Navajo could have served as a policeman during the New Deal.

39. Mueller to Collier, 24 August 1937, File 54974, 1937, Navajo, 175, Classified Files, 1907–1939, NA, RG 75.

40. My efforts to gather information on the frequency of arrests of dissidents and the extent to which this technique may have been used to intimidate government opponents have been unavailing. In the 1937 annual report on law and order for the Navajo reservation, the largest category of arrests was liquor violations with 108 cases on the reservation and 76 tried in federal courts. Disorderly conduct ranked second with 101 cases. The remainder of the arrests were widely scattered under such headings as theft, adultery assault, reckless driving, and unauthorized fencing of tribal lands. I did not find any cases under violations of the grazing regulations. Certainly, allegations about mass arrests were exaggerated. When the Tso incident took place, Fryer wired Collier that seventy-six Navajos were in jail on the following charges: drunkenness 45; adultery and prostitution 10; horse theft 4; assault and battery 6; gambling 4; contempt of court 3; and violating grazing regulations 4. See "1938 Annual Statistical Report, Law and Order (Calendar Year 1937)," Statistics Division—Reports and Other Records, NA, RG 75; Fryer to Collier, 8 August 1937, Collier papers, YU.

Those at Fort Defiance under Croxen's personal command were exceptionally tough. Jack Johnson, a half-Navajo and half-Negro, for example, was a mainstay of Navajo police work until he was imprisoned after the Tso arrest. Over six feet in height and fearless, Johnson could whip three or four Navajos in a fight and Croxen constantly sent him to handle dangerous situations.[41]

The extremely informal trial and sentencing procedures employed in the tribal courts also supported the Morgan-Palmer charges of government intimidation. Croxen's association with Navajo judges when they heard cases on circuit aroused criticism that he influenced decisions. The judges' habit of sternly lecturing prisoners and then letting them go on the promise of good behavior led to similar disapprobation. Scoldings were very much a part of headman leadership, but the judges often told opponents of the government that they could go free if they promised not to engage in further agitation.

Amid wild rumors of a march on Window Rock and the intervention of the army, Morgan's career as a protestor climaxed in mid-August at a meeting at Teec-Nos-Pos called to discuss the current roundup of horses in the area. Located in District 9, one of the worst overgrazed parts of the reservation, Teec-Nos-Pos was also the home territory of Tall Man, a huge and much feared medicine man. Government workers believed that the old shaman played upon his reputation as a witch to develop opposition to federal programs. Despite Morgan's aversion to medicine men, Tall Man was an important confederate until his death in May 1938.[42]

The situation in the area and Morgan's invitation to Fryer, Thomas Dodge, and Howard Gorman to appear in behalf of the government made the Teec-Nos-Pos meeting a tense confrontation. Having wind of the dangerous mood of local Navajos and worried about his son's safety, Chee Dodge feared that the audience might physically attack the three government spokesmen. Chee asked

41. During one interview of a Navajo who knew Johnson, I asked if the hatred and fear of him, frequently expressed in letters of Morgan supporters, had anything to do with his being half Negro. The interviewee responded that it was solely Johnson's fighting ability and not racial origins which motivated Navajos' criticism. Anonymous Interview, 16 August 1971. One of the reasons why Croxen and Fryer wanted the sentence of the three imprisoned policemen commuted was so Johnson could return to police work. They learned after his release that a felon could not serve as a policeman, although Johnson reportedly rejoined the force sometime during World War II. See Croxen to Trotter, 2 March 1938, and Croxen to A. G. Myers, 30 April 1939, Law and Order File, LAFRC.

42. Morgan to Chavez, 18 May 1938, Chavez papers, UA.

Gorman a few days beforehand to cancel the meeting.[43] When this failed, the elder Dodge drove to Teec-Nos-Pos with a carload or two of armed supporters. Once they arrived, Dodge and his men did not mingle with the crowd but remained semi-hidden in a cottonwood grove a short distance away.

Morgan clearly staged the Teec-Nos-Pos affair to intimidate Fryer and his two companions. A large throng of Navajos had gathered near the cottonwood grove and Morgan lounged on a wagon seat covered with an abundance of rugs and pillows. His "throne" was attached to the top of a wagon that served as the speaker's stand, so his half-reclining figure was above the crowd. Close by stood the menacing Tall Man. After working their way through the crowd, Fryer and his companions found Morgan in a mood of delirious confidence. If they were not already apprehensive, they should have been by their vulnerable position. Hemmed in by several hundred unfriendly Indians, the three men were in a dangerous situation if any trouble erupted.

As soon as the speeches started, Fryer sensed that Morgan and his men intended to harangue the crowd until they would physically attack the three government leaders. Either because of their refusal to take the bait and lose their tempers or because of Chee's men in the background, the plan failed and the crowd's mood reached a peak of frenzy which gradually wore itself out until no real danger remained.[44] When it came his turn to speak, Fryer plunged to the heart of the controversy. "Your horses have their heads in your flour cans," he admonished the crowd. The plain-spoken superintendent went on to explain that the "crowbait" horses were of no value, they trampled and ate grass that the sheep needed, and they sapped the livelihood of the Navajo families. In their speeches, Thomas Dodge and Gorman denied that the government had any punitive designs in removing the unproductive horses and they tried to convince the crowd that the grazing controls would benefit the tribe.[45]

Conflicting explanations have developed regarding the conclusion of the Teec-Nos-Pos meeting. Navajo accounts of the affair invariably mention that a snake crawled out from under the wagon and

43. Gorman Interview.
44. Fryer Interview, 1970.
45. Gorman Interview.

this bad omen frightened the group, causing it to disband in panic before everyone had spoken. Morgan's supporters afterward charged that someone had deliberately released the snake to break up the meeting.[46] Fryer and other whites in attendance recall nothing about the incident. The superintendent remembered only that the crowd dispersed quietly after the frenzy subsided. He was not fully aware of the danger himself until he saw Dodge's men standing in the grove as he walked to his car.[47]

In the weeks which followed the Teec-Nos-Pos meeting the tensions gradually moderated. The limited campaign to count and brand horses and cattle continued, usually without much organized resistance but with only partial success. In November the roundups planned had been completed everywhere except in the Piñon and Kayenta areas. Several individual owners had rejected branding until Morgan approved, but only one owner had completely refused to cooperate. If Navajos accepted the roundups without major resistance, they still did not cooperate with the sale of horses and other non-productive livestock. Only 18,400 ewes, 8,320 wethers, 4,831 cattle, and 4,979 horses were purchased from August 1937 until late April 1938.[48]

The disappointing sales and the intense hostility of the Navajos forced Fryer to delay the final and most critical stage of the new grazing program, the issuance of grazing permits, in November 1937. The superintendent had hoped to distribute the permits in District 11 by October 15 and then force owners to sell all livestock in excess of their individual maximum limits. The SCS technicians, however, were unable to decipher ownership records and compute grazing quotas quickly enough to take advantage of the fall sheep market. Fryer decided in November to issue the grazing permits in two or three districts as soon as possible, continue horse sales, but not require the disposition of excess sheep until the fall of 1938.[49] Even

46. Gorman Interview.

47. Fryer Interview, 1971; Mr. Zweifel Interview.

48. Carl Beck to George Weber, 26 April 1938, and Fryer to Collier, 29 April 1938, File 59055, 36, 344, Part 3, CCC-ID, NA, RG 75.

49. Fryer to Woehlke, 3 November 1937, LAFRC, Box 72935. Dating the issuance of the grazing permits has been difficult. There is definite evidence that some permits were issued in District 9 and District 3 in early 1938. Whether a distribution was made in other districts is not clear. Perhaps the resistance to the permits was too great, which forced Fryer to delay the program until later. See Morgan to Chavez, 13 January 1938, and

these plans were not achieved and reduction efforts ceased generally from early 1938 to the summer of 1939.

The draftting of the constitution, the issue which most concerned Morgan, had lost much of its previous urgency. Fryer and other officials probably recognized that the tribe would never approve a constitution. The drafting committee, nevertheless, continued to hold sessions periodically during the summer of 1937 and they finished their task by late September and turned to writing a set of bylaws.[50] A month later Fryer submitted the final draft of the constitution and bylaws for Ickes' approval.

The superintendent now took a surprisingly negative attitude about the reorganization of the tribal council. He told Collier that only an enactment of Congress would give the constitution the legal validity and permanence it needed. "Navajos as a whole are not ready to consider this document, and probably will not be ready for a year—perhaps longer," Fryer added. Before the constitution was voted on by the tribe, he warned, it should be explained to the headmen until they completely understood it. Fryer wanted in the meantime to extract the basic provisions of the constitution and bylaws, have Ickes issue them as departmental regulations, and then hold new tribal council elections to replace the provisional council.[51]

The second meeting of the provisional council on January 18, 1938, symbolized the impasse that had developed over herd reduction and reorganization. Even though Morgan's faction boycotted the session, Taliman and Chee Dodge still feared the council would heckle Collier, who was scheduled to appear the next day.[52] The Navajo elder statesman lectured the delegates to respect Collier's position and his efforts to help the tribe even if they disagreed with his policies.

Throughout the three-day meeting the new livestock program dominated the deliberations. Apprehensive progovernment delegates desperately searched for some way to satisfy their constituents' complaints and yet obey government wishes. This impulse no doubt accounted for Chee Dodge's remark that he favored a friendly

Carl Allen, Sam Tozzie, and Johnny Walker to Chavez, 23 April 1938, Chavez papers, UA.

50. Fryer to Collier, 29 September 1937, LAFRC, Box 72925.

51. Fryer to Collier, 25 October 1937, LAFRC, Box 72925.

52. James M. Stewart, "Personal Impressions of the January 18–20 Navajo Tribal Council Meeting," *Indians at Work* 5 (March 1938): 16–19.

test case of the Navajo grazing regulations. Chee asked that reduction be stalled while the council hired a private attorney to prepare the case. He further advised the Navajos to accept the court's decision as final.

The idea of a test case had been suggested at various times since the new livestock program started. Fryer, the main proponent, favored legal action to destroy the Morgan faction's assertions that the Treaty of 1868 prohibited the land management districts and that Navajos could legally ignore the grazing regulations. Fryer had met with Nathan Margold, Solicitor General of the Interior Department, at Albuquerque in July 1937 and worked out preliminary arrangements to charge dissidents with a conspiracy to defraud the government.

Collier apparently vetoed the suit then and he took a similar position when he appeared the second day of the council. He explained to the councilmen that federal courts had already upheld the authority of the Interior Department's grazing controls on other reservations and a test suit would be pointless. If the special grazing code for Navajos were overthrown by the courts, the tribe would have to submit to much more rigorous national regulations. Collier advised the delegates to appoint a committee to review the existing rules and correct any injustices. The Council subsequently passed a resolution establishing the committee.[53]

The reorganization of tribal government received scant attention at the council. Almost as an aside, Collier told the delegates that the present council was legally valid despite Morgan's statements. The commissioner denied that the protest delegation's trip to Washington in 1937 achieved anything except to allow Chavez to confuse the boundary bill issue. Collier promised that he would call elections for a new council sometime in the summer of 1938. The constitution was never mentioned.

If hopes for reorganization had dimmed, Fryer's statements to the council about CCC fund cuts and new regulations indicated that this important program was also in trouble. Appropriations for the CCC were reduced from $1,225,000 in 1937 to approximately

53. "Proceedings of the Meetings of the Navajo Tribal Council and the Executive Committee," Window Rock, Arizona, 17–20 January 1938, File 30853, 37, 054, Navajo, NA, RG 75. See especially pp. 42–43, 70–80, 165; Fryer to Collier, 29 July 1937, Office File of Commissioner John Collier, NA, RG 75.

$600,000 for 1938. Coupled with the decrease was a new policy that the CCC must employ one enrollee for each $930 received from the national organization. The new limitation meant that the cost of feeding, housing, and paying the enrollees would absorb about sixty percent of the CCC funds. The remaining forty percent had to pay for supervisory personnel, machinery, materials, transportation, and all other expenditures.

The severe retrenchment and the $930 limit per enrollee were both inopportune. By this time, the enrollee program, which stressed literacy and job training, had gained a reputation as one of the best educational organizations on any reservation. On the production side, the CCC was in the midst of an extensive program of drilling more wells. The $930 limitation forced the discontinuation or sharp reduction of drilling and other activities which emphasized the use of machinery. The CCC sometimes overcame the new regulations by getting some other federal agency—SCS, Irrigation, or WPA—to assume the costs of machinery and materials, while the CCC provided the labor. In other cases, the local Navajos were asked to donate labor to projects. The flush days of the early New Deal had ended about the time that Fryer became superintendent in 1936. Now two years later he faced far greater cutbacks which forced him to lay off one-half of his CCC work force.[54] From 1938 to World War II, funds for relief work became even scarcer.

Morgan's behavior during early 1938 was surprisingly moderate, even conciliatory. Perhaps he realized that Collier's promise to hold elections for a new tribal council would fulfill his long-standing ambition to become chairman. In late January 1938 Ira A. Watson, a Navajo Service worker, visited Morgan in Farmington to confer about the grazing program and the stalemated Fruitland irrigation project. The official reported he "was able to secure considerable cooperation from Mr. Morgan, and some hope for future good feeling in the area under his control."

When Watson returned to Farmington the following week to put the finishing touches on an agreement, he found Morgan had suddenly left for Washington with two wealthy Navajo stockmen to protest against stock reduction. Watson believed that the missionary's sudden departure was due to Palmer's "emphatic measures" to check

54. Fryer to Collier, 18 January 1938, File 59055, 1936, Navajo, 344, CCC-ID, NA, RG 75.

any compromise. The day after Watson's first talk with Morgan, David Chavez, now a state district judge, had appeared in Aztec to try a few minor cases. Watson was certain that Chavez really came to squelch any compromise. Orval Ricketts, editor of the *Farmington Times Hustler*, told Watson that "Chavez had Palmer under his thumb," because the lawyer tried most of his cases in the district court.

Embittered by his inability to complete a compromise, Watson visited Palmer in his office. The government worker left the unfriendly interview with much the same impressions that Carlisle had reported. Watson believed that Palmer relished his sudden notoriety. At one point, the lawyer told Watson, "I am closer to Washington than these Indians are to Window Rock." No supporter of stock reduction himself, Watson was convinced that Palmer would "keep the pot boiling indefinitely" because "certain political groups wish to keep the northeast [Navajos] in a state of turmoil."[55]

Sometime in mid-February, Palmer joined Morgan in Washington where the two conferred with Fryer and Walter Woehlke about the Fruitland controversy. Morgan and Fryer agreed to drop the dispute over the size of allotments and to allow a local committee to determine the acreages based on the needs of individual families. After his return to New Mexico, Morgan told a meeting of Shiprock Navajos they should settle the Fruitland dispute. More importantly, he advised the audience to abide by the new grazing regulations because they would remain valid until Senator Chavez secured legislation to prohibit their application.[56]

A month later Morgan and a party of Navajo leaders met with Fryer and several Navajo Service personnel at the Fruitland Day School. They agreed to allow a committee of Navajos to collect information on all those Indians who wanted land at Fruitland preliminary to a final distribution. Morgan stayed out of the discussion entirely until near the close of the meeting. In another of his reversals, he then took a position strongly at odds with his Fruitland followers by advocating that returned students should be given first preference for the plots. Young educated Navajos "should live as an example for all the other people," and Fruitland, Morgan argued,

55. Ira A. Watson to Collier, 5 February 1938, LAFRC, Box 72958.

56. E. K. Burlew to Chavez, 17 February 1938, Chavez papers, UA; Fryer to Trotter, 12 March 1938, and Trotter to Fryer, 7 March 1938, LAFRC, Box 72938.

offered a good opportunity to achieve this.[57] Despite Morgan's advice, the Fruitland dispute remained unsettled because local Indians and the district supervisor could not agree on the distributions.

A confrontation between Fryer and Palmer a few days after the Fruitland meeting permanently destroyed any chance that the two whites would ever settle their differences. Angered by something, the young superintendent decided to beard the lawyer in his Farmington office. Fryer emerged completely flabbergasted after what he termed "a most amazing three hours with Palmer." Writing Collier about the meeting the next day, Fryer described the Farmingtonite as "an enigmatic composite of a religious fanatic, a hypocrite, a small-time lawyer, and a political demagogue."

Reared a Mormon himself, Fryer was especially disconcerted by Palmer's religious views, and recounted the following conversation to Collier:

> *Fryer*: What is your game, Palmer? You and Morgan have set the Navajos back fifty years in their relations with and their confidence in the Government.

> *Palmer*: I have a mission to perform. There is a prophecy in the Book of Mormon which states that the Lamanites (Indians) will save the Constitution of the United States. This prophecy must be fulfilled. It may not happen in fifty years, or, for that matter, in a hundred years, but the Indians will never be ready to fulfill this prophecy as long as they are kept under the domination of the Indian Bureau. They must be set free to take their places in the scheme of things.

> *Fryer*: Why make the Indians suffer? Why take your spite out on them? If you have a grudge against the Bureau, why don't you attack its policies, attack me, the Commissioner, whoever you want to attack, but why effect sedition and breed contempt for the Government among the Indians just to accomplish your own end?

> *Palmer*: I can only fight the Bureau through the Indians. If I don't get the Indians stirred up, they will say the Bureau is all right, then where would I be?

57. "Minutes of Meeting at Fruitland Day School," 14 April 1938, Chavez papers, UA.

*Fryer*: If you and Morgan continue your tactics, it is not impossible that some misguided Navajo will take a shot at a Range Rider or District Supervisor. Are you and Morgan prepared to accept the responsibility for such possible happenings?

*Palmer*: American liberty was not won without bloodshed. The Boston Tea Party was worth the lives it cost. These Indians have a right to liberty. If it costs a hundred lives, it will be justified.

*Fryer*: How do you make a statement like that coincide with the principles of your religion?

*Palmer*: I was a little worried about that myself, until I saw Senator King [of Utah] in Washington. He didn't know I was a Mormon when I called on him. I said 'Senator King, I have come to make some complaints against the Indian Bureau.' Almost at once, to my complete surprise, he said: 'Damn the Indian Bureau. Anything you want to do against them is all right with me.'

I then told Senator King that I was a Mormon and we had a long talk. If Senator King, who is a good Mormon and an officer in the Church, as well as being a high official in the Government, thinks that way about the Indian Bureau, then anything I do to get it abolished is justified.[58]

Soon after the Palmer interview, Collier finally consented to new council elections without first holding a referendum on the tribal constitution. In late March 1938, Oliver La Farge had urged Collier to issue a simple code and hold the constitution in abeyance until later.[59] After an exchange of correspondence, Fryer advised Collier that the drafting committee now wanted no part in endorsing a code which would bind future councils and they much preferred that Ickes issue a set of regulations that went "no further than to provide a method for the election of a new Tribal Council." The drafting committee completed their work on the election code in July and Taliman and Ickes approved it soon afterward.[60]

58. Fryer to Collier, 20 April 1938, Office File of Commissioner John Collier, NA, RG 75.

59. La Farge to Collier, 28 March 1938, Collier papers, YU. La Farge noted that the Indian Rights Association also wanted an election.

60. Fryer to Collier, 23 April 1938, and Fryer to Zweifel, 12 July 1938, LAFRC, Box 72925.

Morgan, during the summer months of 1938, continued to alternate between hints of cooperation and moderate agitation. In July the Navajo Progressive League held its second convention at Farmington with far less publicity than a year earlier even though Chavez spoke to the 850 delegates. Morgan's stance remained ambiguous as he again refused to take any official post with the group. The League's resolutions no longer demanded the removal of Collier and Fryer or spoke of a rejection of all New Deal policies but demanded only a free election of a new council and a Senate investigation.[61]

When Fryer received Ickes' approval of the election regulations, the superintendent issued instructions to the district supervisors for conducting the voting. Morgan's reactions indicate that he and Fryer had arrived at no bargain beforehand. Immediately after reading the election rules, the Navajo leader wrote Chavez complaining that the entire business was unjust because government workers were to supervise the polls. He was no doubt far more upset by a rule that candidates for the chairmanship must reside on the reservation or on an Indian allotment. Morgan somewhat evasively asked that Chavez force Collier to change the code or that he at least delay the election until Navajos better understood it.[62]

Despite Morgan's opposition, the elections took place as scheduled. Using the same apportionment system established by Haile's committee, each land management district was broken down into subunits and polling stations were established in each. On August 16, local Navajos met at the polling stations and nominated up to three candidates for the council seat for their particular electoral district. The selection of candidates for the chairmanship of the council took place eight days later at "provincial conventions" held at Tuba City, Klagetoh, Fort Defiance, and Shiprock. Only council members participated in selecting candidates for the chairmanship.[63] Morgan became the candidate of the provincial convention at Shiprock and his residence was not later challenged by the government. Howard Gorman of Ganado, Lee Bradley of Kayenta, and Alfred Hardy of

61. *Farmington Times Hustler*, 29 July 1938, p. 1; 700 Navajos to Chavez, 21 July 1938, and Morgan to Chavez, 27 July 1938, Chavez papers, UA.

62. Morgan to Chavez, 9 August 1938, Chavez papers, UA.

63. Fryer to District Supervisors and Range Riders, 4 August 1938, LAFRC, Box 72938.

Fort Defiance were the other candidates. Gorman, considered progovernment and something of a Chee Dodge protégé, offered the only challenge to Morgan. Hardy and Bradley did not figure as serious contenders. Bradley, in fact, soon withdrew or was ruled ineligible.

The final election on September 24 is well remembered because of the use of colors to designate the candidates. The rules specified that a secret ballot must be used in the final poll and all of the participants were to draw for colors by which they could be identified on the ballots. There was considerable speculation that the Navajos' preference for certain hues might influence their voting. The men running for the council drew immediately after being nominated. The three candidates for the chairmanship visited Window Rock for that purpose soon after their nomination. Morgan drew silver, Gorman brown, and Hardy gold.[64] District supervisors then placed posters with the local and chairman candidates identified by name and color in day schools and trading posts, so the Navajos could make their choices on election day.

The election seemed almost anticlimactic. Neither Morgan nor Gorman held any mass rallies or exchanged charges. Everyone recognized that the antigovernment leader would win easily and electioneering was pointless. Out of approximately 11,000 votes cast, Morgan recieved 7,927 and Gorman became vice chairman by collecting the next highest total. Morgan's supporters also displaced most of the headmen in the council races.

Morgan's victory, even when coupled with the partial defeat of council reorganization, was far less momentous than it appeared. As in the Wheeler-Howard referendum three years earlier, the government salvaged what it could out of the defeat. The principle of a more representative council remained and became fixed in tribal politics. If Navajos lost some guarantees embodied in the constitution, some observers feel that they have since benefited by escaping possible restrictions that the provisions might have imposed. According to this view, the tribe did not need an elaborate constitution that they could not understand nor apply. What they needed was the simple law and order code and election rules that Ickes had proclaimed.

What diminished the importance of Morgan's victory even more

64. *Farmington Times Hustler*, 2 September 1938, p. 1.

was that his election in no way affected the government livestock program or Fryer's determination to complete it. As witnessed repeatedly, Indian self-rule during the New Deal was limited and in reality the movement to balance livestock loads with grazing capacities lay beyond the Navajos' control. Any chance of voiding the livestock program was confined to the test case then pending in the federal court. In sum, Morgan's five years of agitation may have culminated in a personally satisfying victory, but it had no impact on the issues which most worried the new chairman's followers.

# 8

## John Dewey Among the Navajos

Despite the importance of conservation and revisions in the tribal government after 1933, the improvement of Navajo education was one of the main goals that John Collier sought to realize during the New Deal. He had vigorously criticized the previous policy of sending Indian children to boarding schools that, in his opinion, fitted them for life neither in white society nor with their own people. He had applauded the efforts of W. Carson Ryan, director of Indian education during the Hoover administration, to replace boarding schools with day schools that allowed students to be educated while living in their own culture. When appointed commissioner in 1933, Collier made a notable exception from his demotions of top personnel in the Indian Office by leaving Ryan in charge of education. Despite this unity of purpose at Washington, the application of progressive educational policies on the Navajo reservation would create struggles that sometimes resembled the battles over livestock reduction and the reshaping of the tribal council.

In truth, the government had never offered the Navajos much education before the New Deal, nor did the average tribesman really care. With the exception of seven small day schools, Navajo children attended ten boarding schools in or near the reservation. Some advanced students were placed in more distant schools, at Albuquerque, Phoenix, Santa Fe, or even outside the Southwest. An estimated 13,000 Navajo children were of school age in 1933, but fewer than 5,000 were being educated.[1] In part, the low percentage stemmed from their inability to reach schools.

Parents' attitudes toward education, however, constituted a much greater obstacle. Many were suspicious and resentful because officials

1. *Annual Report of the Secretary of the Interior*, 1934 (Washington, 1934), pp. 87–88. This figure apparently included the students in mission schools.

had virtually kidnapped students for schools in the past. More significantly, most Navajos simply could not see any purpose in education. Many deemed schools useful for the handicapped or destitute, but their brighter and stronger offspring should be kept at home to work. Parents also recognized that many students, especially girls, became discontented when they found no opportunities after their schooling.[2]

The ambitious plan which Collier proposed to the tribal council in October 1933 at Tuba City should have overcome at least part of these objections to education. Collier spoke then of providing some twenty-five installations which would not only serve as day schools but also as community centers, subagencies, and medical clinics. Even at this preliminary stage, he associated education with administrative consolidation, the conservation program, and the development of community centers.

Some three months later in an informal memo to Ryan, Collier discussed the integration of Navajo education with the conservation program. He stressed that bilingual training would be required to carry out the "Navajo economic readjustment" and he proposed the construction of eighty day school–community centers by the fall of 1934. The same memo contained other goals which Collier hoped to realize. He wanted progressive educational techniques applied which were related to the remainder of his program and the Navajos' own situation. No one should be forced to attend school, Collier stated, and classes for children would be delayed until parents requested them. Until that time, most of the attention would be given to educating adults and hiring and training teachers.

Collier's memo also revealed his strong disdain for conventional curricula and teaching methods. A devotee of John Dewey, the commissioner characterized traditional education as "superstitious and blighting even to our own white life." He suggested Ryan establish from six to ten experimental schools in those areas now served by boarding institutions which would "rapidly supplant the stereotyped kind of school which we desire to change or be rid of."[3] The commis-

2. See Howard Gorman's comments, "The Community Day School Programs on the Navajo," 21 February 1939 (radio transcript of KTGM), Van Valkenburgh papers, AHS.

3. Collier to Ryan, 31 January 1934, Central Classified Files, File 58349, 137, 800, Navajo, NA, RG 75.

sioner's memo apparently inspired the construction of four "hogan schools" at Mariano Lake, Cove, Navajo Mountain, and Shonto.

Soon after his memo to Ryan, Collier sent R. M. Tisinger and Alan Hulsizer[4] to establish the new program. At a conference with Indian Service and Soil Erosion Service leaders in Gallup on April 16, 1934, the two educators presented a set of proposals aimed at the integration of education into the general conservation program. Like Collier, the conferees stressed the use of schools as community centers where adults could learn about prevention of disease and improvement of their homes and income. "The direct teaching of English and arithmetic," Hulsizer noted, "shall occupy not more than one hour and a half of each day of several aged groups of children, adolescents and adults."[5] All education at the new schools must be coordinated with other government efforts; the Soil Erosion Service had already been given the power to approve or reject the location of the new community schools.

For the next year, the implementation of the educational program suffered from many of the same vicissitudes experienced by William Zeh and C. E. Faris as they tried to reorganize the six agencies into a single headquarters. One major trouble resulted from the large-scale construction program to put up some forty new day schools on and near the reservation. Financed from a Public Works Administration grant of approximately 1.5 million dollars which had to be spent quickly, Tisinger and other administrators hurriedly tried to locate the schools, draw up plans, and complete construction. As a result, day school sites were located at trading posts. No schools were built at posts doing less than $30,000 in annual trade, while those grossing about $30,000 were the sites of one-classroom buildings and those doing $60,000 in business were the sites of two-classroom schools.

Hampered by delays, only three schools were completed by early 1935 and a few did not open until 1936. In the rush to finish the new structures, serious mistakes were perhaps inevitable. Tisinger built a few day schools in areas where Navajos seasonally moved from summer to winter pastures and attendance rose and fell dramatically as a consequence. In other instances, supervisors located schools

4. Hulsizer's correspondence reveals that he had previously worked in Haiti and he obviously was well read in and sympathetic toward rural community education projects.

5. Notes of the Navajo Community Program, April 1934, Central Classified Files, File 30153, 1934, 800, Navajo, NA, RG 75.

without first assuring an adequate quality or quantity of water. The worst mistake was at Aneth where the day school was built on private land belonging to a trader.[6]

Despite all the problems, the new day schools were an impressive achievement. Except for the four hogan schools, the architecture was something of a compromise between a Pueblo style and the typical white school of the period.[7] All were built of native stone that Navajo workers cut, dressed, and laid. Exposed vegas supported the flat roofs. In addition to the classrooms, the new schools provided quarters for the teachers and a kitchen used to prepare the noon meal. The latter facilities were also available for local residents to use for cooking, baking, or canning. The schools likewise afforded other important services to the nearby community, such as free water, showers, laundry, sewing machines, and a small shop. Proponents often argued plausibly that the noneducational services were as useful to the Navajos as the actual classes.

The frustrations involved in the rush to build the new day schools were probably less important than the feud over the educational philosophy which developed simultaneously. Although only random glimpses of the struggle can be seen in the documents, the disagreement over educational policy seriously divided even those field workers who supported Collier. Hulsizer totally accepted the commissioner's ideas on self-rule and progressive education. After negotiating the location of the new schools, Hulsizer tried to hire educated Navajos to take charge of the community-oriented program. Sally Lucas Jean, an expert in health education and close friend of Collier, supported Hulsizer's views after she arrived on the reservation. Described as a person of "integrity and zeal," Jean agreed with Hulsizer that Indian wishes should be paramount.

Tisinger and Zeh were the chief opponents of Hulsizer and Jean.

6. George A. Boyce's autobiography was published when I was working on the final draft of this study. The director of Navajo education from 1941 to 1949, Boyce discusses the start of the day school system. He maintains that serious miscalculations were made in the first budget request for operation of the new day schools. The Indian Service, for example, requested only six dollars per school for educational supplies when the intention was to ask for six dollars per student. The error was not discovered until after Boyce became director. See George A. Boyce, *When Navajos Had Too Many Sheep: the 1940's* (San Francisco, 1974), pp. 39–61, 109–10, 119.

7. Of the more conventional buildings, three were one-room affairs, twenty-three were two rooms, six were three rooms, three were four rooms, and one (at Fruitland) eight rooms. Seven schools were either old day schools or a combination of new and old buildings.

Tisinger felt that the day schools should emphasize schooling for the young rather than adults. According to Jean, he exhibited little sympathy for Indian self-government.[8] Zeh contended that putting untrained Navajos in charge of the new schools would be a disastrous mistake and he wanted only qualified teachers (meaning almost entirely white) employed. Petty jealousies, arguments over authority, and direct appeals to Collier by Hulsizer and Jean enlivened the dispute.

Collier's own inclinations alternated between several possible educational goals. At a closed meeting at Keams Canyon in July 1934, Collier expressed a strong willingness to turn education entirely over to Hugh Calkins and the Soil Erosion Service despite the conservationist's obvious reluctance to accept the task.[9] The commissioner dropped this idea and decided to appoint a director of education with total authority over the community schools and agricultural extension. Such an individual would be empowered to make decisions without reference to the Washington office and would report to the General Superintendent at Window Rock.[10] Collier's subsequent moves are unclear, but he apparently placed Jean in charge of all education with the title of "Coordinator on Community Centers."[11] With this appointment Jean's troubles with Zeh reached a breaking point. She adamantly refused to place herself under his authority and successfully demanded that she have total control of education in current plans to consolidate reservation administration.[12]

Soon afterward, the community day schools undertook a controversial experiment. In October 1934 the government selected fifty young Navajos as community workers and brought them to Red Rock Cove for training before being put in charge of the day schools. The move seemingly was a total victory for Jean's concept that the new educational program should be under native leadership and shun conventional subject matter. The Navajo trainees' classes stressed land use, community relations, health, and tribal culture.[13]

8. Edna A. Gerken to writer, 29 November 1972; Jean to Collier, 23 March 1935, Collier papers, YU.

9. "Minutes of special conference at Keams Canyon," 13 July 1934, Collier papers, YU.

10. Collier to Ickes, 7 August 1934, Central Classified Files, File 58349, 1937, 800, Navajo, NA, RG 75.

11. Collier to Miss McGair and Dr. Ryan, September 1934, Collier papers, YU.

12. W. W. Peter to Jean, 9 October 1934, Collier papers, YU.

13. The only detailed account the writer has located on this subject is in the *Gallup Independent*, 29 October 1934, p. 3.

Few, if any, of the trainees ever headed day schools, but the idea of unqualified youngsters acting as teachers touched off severe criticism among Collier's enemies. Doubtlessly much of their hostility was exaggerated and malicious, but the critics had at least one valid objection. Both they and many of Collier's defenders recognized that the supply of gifted young Navajos capable of teaching, communicating in both languages, and leading fellow tribesmen was woefully short. Most qualified individuals had already taken jobs with other government programs. A superficial training for those selected to head the day schools and a lack of intensive supervision once on the job would only have created confusion. In addition, most Navajos, because of their cultural preference for older leaders, simply would not cooperate with younger tribesmen.

Little is known about how the dispute between progressive education and traditional methods was resolved, but by July 1935 Collier surrendered and allowed only qualified teachers to be hired. During that same period, he reassigned Jean and Hulsizer and appointed C. M. Blair, then superintendent of the Albuquerque Indian School, to act as education director. The day schools opened that fall with mostly white teachers in charge and Navajo school employees resumed their normal roles as assistants, cooks, bus drivers, and janitors. These changes, it must be stressed, did not eradicate progressive education from the day schools. The teachers were still expected to emphasize subject matter related to Navajo problems and government programs. In addition supervisors encouraged teachers to act as extension workers by visiting students' homes and inviting local Indians to use the school facilities. Though the day school program lost much of its emphasis on community action, it retained its adherence to progressive methods of teaching.

The Navajos' reactions to the new day schools and the change of educational policy in 1934–35 varied from a pragmatic "wait and see" to bitter denunciations by antigovernment people. Chairman Thomas Dodge, who took a strong interest in education, early warned Collier that the tribe would not accept hogan schools.[14] Whether educated or not, most Navajos resented sending their children to inferior buildings. If whites met success after attending classes in a modern building and by learning the three R's in a disciplined atmosphere, Navajos reasoned that the same should be true for their

14. Collier to La Farge, 1 February 1934, Collier papers, YU.

children. Utterly pragmatic, the Navajos believed that education should allow their children, especially boys, to escape camp life and secure good jobs.

The same sort of thinking led Navajos to want both existing boarding schools and the new day schools. Numerous areas of the reservation petitioned for one of the new day schools in 1934, but Navajos argued that even if they succeeded, the boarding schools would still be needed for advanced students. With even greater practicality, poorer Navajo parents favored the continuation of boarding schools because they provided clothes, shelter, and food for the students. Many insisted that the day schools should offer more services, including a noon meal, transportation by buses, and free clothes.[15]

An extreme hostility toward the day schools and the new educational program was shown by Morgan and his followers. Collier's attempt to close the boarding schools at Tohatchi and Chinle was the reason for Morgan's first open attack on the commissioner and not until later did the Navajo leader win a much more widespread following by taking up the cause of herd reduction. It was inevitable that Morgan and his colleagues should fight against the day schools. All had attended boarding schools where military discipline, absolute attention, harsh punishments, and repugnance for Indian life prevailed. Learning under such circumstances was not fun and they could not understand nor accept the sight of children "learning by playing" in the day schools. Even more strongly than most Navajos, the Morgan faction saw education as an avenue of advancement and they demanded that the curriculum stress English and other white subject matter.

Morgan's objections also reflected the misgivings that Protestant missionaries and other white critics frequently expressed—that Collier's policies obstructed Indian progress. The only positive result that the missionaries ever admitted that resulted from government education was improved health training and personal hygiene. Invariably, the critics pointed out that government students scored much lower on achievement tests than national averages, while youngsters at the mission schools either equaled or exceeded these standards. Defenders of government schools, however, maintained that the comparison was unfair. The bulk of mission students came

15. Zeh to Collier, 21 June 1934, Central Classified Files, File 30153, 1934, 800, Navajo, NA, RG 75.

from educated parents who spoke English in the home, but nearly all children in government schools lacked bilingual backgrounds and their education was seriously hampered.[16]

The missionaries' objection to government education was not totally concerned with criticism of its quality. Many Protestant church workers resented Collier's ban on Indian students being compelled to attend religion classes taught by missionaries in government schools. Prior to the New Deal, incoming youngsters were forced to declare which denomination they wished to join and attend both religion classes and church services. Collier's reversal of this policy aroused the missionaries, but in reality few students took advantage of their right to reject religious activities. Either because they had nothing else to do or because of teachers' pressures, most received religious instruction. Missionaries also disliked the day schools. Not only did they not rescue students from an environment of paganism that the missionaries were trying to overcome, but the schools were very inconvenient to reach.[17]

By late 1935 the main outlines of the Navajo education program were complete and they would not change basically during the rest of the New Deal. The forty-seven day schools offered four grades of instruction. The boarding school at Tohatchi had been converted to a day school by late 1935 and the one at Chinle received both day and boarding students. Navajo pressures eventually forced the conversion of both back to their original status. The boarding institutions at Crown Point, Fort Defiance, Fort Wingate, Keams Canyon, Leupp, Toadlena, Shiprock, and Tuba City remained unchanged. Although an advanced curriculum was offered at these schools after 1935, few students attended beyond six grades. Only Fort Wingate had anything close to the stature of a secondary school and it clearly was a show piece in its academic standards, arts and crafts program, agricultural training, and the newness of the plant. Around 1940 the

16. Bass Interview; Thompson Interview. A different sort of protest arose among whites who feared that Collier would close all off-reservation boarding schools in his campaign to replace such institutions with day schools. The Arizona House of Representatives, for example, directed a formal resolution to Ickes in February 1935, asking him to restore funds to the Phoenix Indian School. Responding to the same vested interests, Representative Isabella Greenway of Arizona launched her own campaign in Congress against the "Indian Bureau's unannounced, but very definite plans to gradually abandon Indian boarding schools." See "House Resolution No. 5," 19 February 1935, and Greenway to James C. Scrugham, 21 December 1935, Isabella Greenway papers, AHS.

17. Boyce, *When Navajos Had Too Many Sheep*, p. 55.

boarding schools at Tuba City and Shiprock began offering high school courses, but few students enrolled.

At Window Rock the administrative staff in charge of education consisted of the director, assistant director, and a handful of supervisors and assistant supervisors. The supervisory personnel were distributed among several catagories: elementary, health, vocational training, and home economics. Their main tasks were to create and develop teaching programs for the classroom, to visit classes, to check on instruction, and, occasionally, to settle disputes between local Navajos and teachers. Hence, the Window Rock staff spent a good deal of time battling reservation roads. The principals of boarding schools handled administrative matters other than instruction and obtained materials both for their teachers and for the day schools in the general vicinity.

The Indian Service also subsidized the education of some Navajo students in off-reservation public schools. A notable instance of this was an agreement with school officials at Thoreau, New Mexico, which permitted local Navajo elementary students to attend classes with whites after 1935. Under this cooperative arrangement, the federal government provided $40,000 for a new building and paid tuition costs for Navajo students.[18] The limited records on this and similar ventures do not indicate the results of integrating Navajo and white children.

Beside federally financed education, approximately 1,000 Navajo students attended five missionary schools. The largest and most noted school was operated by the Presbyterians at Ganado for both primary and secondary levels. Schools supported by the Catholics at St. Michaels and the Christian Reformed Church at Rehoboth were smaller but quite active. The Methodist school at Farmington originally offered only a primary education but in the mid-1930s it began to expand to the secondary level. The Episcopalians provided a small school in conjunction with an orphanage at Fort Defiance.

In September 1935 the day school program started its first full year even though some facilities were unfinished. Blair noted that many buildings still needed screens, the transportation system was incomplete, several schools did not have teachers, and the water supply was a problem at some locations. Because of fall ceremonials, Navajo

18. The Thoreau experiment and similar cooperative ventures are only mentioned in passing in the documents. See *Albuquerque Journal*, 24 March 1935, p. 6.

children were slow in starting the school year.[19] By mid-November, with attendance more or less stabilized, Blair reported an enrollment of 1,693 in the day schools and 2,698 in boarding schools for a total of 4,391 students. During the same period, well over 2,000 Navajos had visited the day schools to use the facilities for bathing, washing, or repairs.[20]

Although officials hoped to raise enrollments at the day schools, the figures grew with painful slowness after 1935. The fact that day school attendance continually fell far short of capacity perplexed the educational staff, but nothing they attempted seemed to raise enrollments. Even with the rapid surge in school-age population, the Navajos ended the New Deal with only one out of two children attending classes, only slightly better than the ratio in 1933. In addition, Collier's dream of supplanting the boarding schools went unrealized. Enrollments at these installations remained generally high and they continued to attract the majority of Navajo students.

The most obvious factor which thwarted the success of education was the controversies which swept the reservation in the 1930s. Discontent caused by livestock reduction and Morgan's agitation repeatedly led recalcitrant parents to withhold their children from schools. Morgan probably did not directly advise this, but teachers constantly complained that attendance dropped drastically any time a controversy arose in their area. Usually the boycotts developed over herd reduction, but they also occurred over other grievances.

Tribal hostility and indifference, however, were not the only reasons for school enrollment problems. Transporting the students to and from classes over unpaved roads was a major problem in good weather and an impossibility during rains and blizzards. The government purchased a fleet of buses and pickups in 1935, but primitive roads and inexperienced drivers took a fearful toll on the vehicles. During bad weather, the drivers not infrequently ignored the dirt roads and struck off across the desert to avoid getting stuck. Many children had to walk several miles to reach bus stops and often waited long periods because rain or snow delayed the drivers. Sometimes school vehicles never did arrive and the cold and wet youngsters walked home.

19. Blair to Collier, 20 September 1935, Central Classified Files, File 52136, 1935, 803, Navajo, NA, RG 75.

20. *Dine' Dah-Si-Zai-Bi Na'Locos* [Navajo Community Center Paper], 1, n.s., (December 1, 1935): 8–9.

Because of these problems, teachers found very little time for instruction on many days. Students who walked or rode horses drifted in around nine o'clock when classes were supposed to start. Those who were bused arrived as late as eleven o'clock or so. The teacher then had to interrupt lessons to get the newcomers out of their wraps and into seats. If it was time for student's baths, usually given twice per week, classes had to be delayed even more while the teacher and assistants supervised this task.

Afterward the staff treated illnesses and minor cuts and bruises. Trachoma was especially prevalent with 34.5 percent of the boarding school students and 37.8 percent in the day schools afflicted in 1937.[21] The discharge of matter from infected eyes, the pain and irritation, and the gradual loss of sight sickened many teachers. Treatment itself was an ordeal. Sufferers were placed on a table on their backs while the teachers everted the youngsters' eyelids and irrigated the eyes with painful caustics. Revulsion from observing and treating trachoma limited many teachers' careers in the Indian Service to a single year.

After baths and nursing, hot lunch was served, and classroom work itself started in the early afternoon. If the roads were bad, however, the teacher usually relented to the driver's demands that school be dismissed early, so he could get the students home before dark. Part of the youngsters left around two-thirty instead of four o'clock when the school was supposed to close.

The arduous nature of the day school teachers' duties and their isolation caused a high turnover in personnel, but poor job opportunities in the depression undoubtedly kept the rate lower than normal. The typical new teacher was a recent graduate from a college outside the Southwest, often from the South where the pay scale was low, who had been trained in conventional pedagogy. Unable to find a job in her home area, she passed Civil Service exams, and Navajo school administrators selected her name from lists issued by that agency. She arrived in Gallup on the eve of a new school year with virtually no knowledge of Navajos or reservation life, a little fearful of Indians, and with no inkling that she was supposed to act as nurse, counselor, conservation expert, relief agent, community leader, and disciple of John Dewey. Some newcomers openly expressed a desire

21. J. G. Townsend to Polk Richards, 2 August 1937, Central Classified Files, File 63292, 1935, Navajo, NA, RG 75.

to resign upon their arrival and many served only a year or two until they found another teaching post or married.

Although most teachers could not adjust to reservation life, some not only stayed but relished their work. Those who succeeded inevitably had an affection for the Navajos, tremendous devotion to teaching, and a practicality mixed with an appreciation for the Indians' culture. Mary Eubanks is often cited as an example of the type of secular missionary that Collier hoped would become a community leader as well as teacher. Stationed at remote Navajo Mountain and isolated during winter months except for radio contact, Eubanks delivered babies, treated the sick, settled personal disputes, and made herself a fixture in the community until her retirement, years after the end of the New Deal. Florence McClure at Greasewood enjoyed the same sort of rapport with local Indians. Fascinated by Navajo life, McClure spent her free time in visiting students' families and joining them to attend ceremonials and other types of outings. She had enough appreciation of Navajo religion to understand a medicine man's anger when a Navajo school assistant unwittingly hauled away a pick-up load of logs that had been used in a ceremonial and were supposed to be left undisturbed. McClure quickly reprimanded the assistant for his stupidity and ordered him to replace the logs.[22] Unfortunately, only a handful of teachers possessed the qualities that made Eubanks and McClure effective.

The emphasis on progressive education techniques continued after Ryan stepped down as head of Indian schools in late 1935 or early 1936. Ryan and his successor, Willard Beatty,[23] were both active in the Progressive Educational Association and admirers of Dewey's approaches to teaching. To Beatty, progressive education meant simply working on problems facing the Indians and using whatever resources were at hand. He did not accept the more extreme interpretations of Dewey's ideas and eventually dropped out of progressive education circles when "all sorts of people started . . . to call their ideas progressive education and get under the blanket." Beatty favored a truly dualistic approach to Indian education, with

22. Thompson Interview.
23. Beatty was superintendent of public schools at Bronxville, New York, and president of the Progressive Education Association when appointed. See *Albuquerque Journal*, 10 December 1935, p. 2. For additional information on Beatty, see Boyce, *When Navajos Had Too Many Sheep*, pp. 15, 25–26.

special stress on bilingual training. A forceful administrator, he demanded instant change and made his influence felt well down the educational hierarchy.

School officials' efforts to realize Beatty's ideas in Navajo education created something of a split at Window Rock which persisted, more or less undercover, throughout the New Deal. Fryer and other conservationists were somewhat indifferent about progressive techniques or viewed them with disdain and amusement. To the superintendent and his associates, the main purpose of the Navajo program was to utilize and protect the tribe's physical resources. Although admitting the importance of this goal, school officials believed that education should try to develop the tribe's "human resources" by improving Navajo health, sanitation, and literacy. At the Window Rock level the argument remained undercover and the two groups usually cooperated. Teachers and other field workers, however, frequently clashed, especially when the grazing program caused parents to withdraw students from school.[24]

Progressive pedagogy not only puzzled many noneducators, but teachers also had difficulty applying Dewey's principles in the classroom. As a remedy, the Indian Service held a six-week conference in the summer of 1936 at Fort Wingate for teachers from the Southwest and Oklahoma. Out of 200 who attended, 109 taught in Navajo schools. The instructional staff consisted of well-known progressive educators, figures from medicine, nursing, and public health, and Washington leaders, including Collier and Beatty. Some of the staff appeared only briefly, while others remained for the entire conference.

To illustrate progressive education, officials organized two demonstration classes of Navajo children and the conferees spent most of the mornings observing the youngsters' classwork and afterward discussing the day's activities with the teachers in charge. As was typical in the day schools, there was little correlation between the ages and class standing of students in the demonstration classes. A fourteen-year-old might be getting his first exposure to education, while an eight-year-old might be in third grade. The conference provided additional classes on arts and crafts, conservation, health

24. My information on Beatty's ideas and the split between educational officials and other Navajo administrators is derived from the Thompson Interview.

and nursing, anthropology, recreation, and several other subjects. During two weeks in August, ninety-nine Indian assistants came to Fort Wingate to study subjects appropriate for their work.[25]

Conferences similar to the one at Fort Wingate in 1936 became a mainstay of in-service training during the coming years. Held at various major Indian schools in the Southwest, such conferences always provided subject matter relevant to the teachers' own reservations. In addition to the more comprehensive training at the summer institutes, Navajo school administrators sponsored short workshops during the school year. A majority of these were devoted to health and sanitation. Because teachers had close and daily contact with a large segment of Navajos, the cooperation between school and medical personnel was especially close.

By the end of 1936, Collier and Beatty obviously had become dissatisfied with Blair's administration of Navajo schools and had decided to replace him whenever a transfer could be arranged.[26] The reasons for the move are not entirely clear, but Blair was probably another example of an older official who could not adjust to the changes effected after 1933. At heart a traditionalist in education and still committed to boarding schools, Blair was accused of worrying too much about enrollments and too little about installing a progressive curriculum.[27] Sometime in the summer of 1937 Beatty reassigned Blair and named Lucy W. Adams, an SCS employee and an expert in adult education, to head Navajo education.[28]

Adams' appointment resembled the decision in 1936 to replace Faris with Fryer. In both cases Collier expected no major revisions in previous goals but the achievement of those already laid down,

25. Homer C. Howard, "Wingate Summer Demonstration School, 1936," Central Classified Files, File 45855, 1936, 806, Navajo, NA, RG 75.

26. Collier to Woehlke, 5 December 1936, Collier papers, YU.

27. Some insight into Blair's ideas can be gained from an essay he wrote in late 1936 replying to a recent article in *Indian Education* entitled, "Why the Boarding School Failed." While not attacking the day schools, Blair argued that the boarding schools had provided a training for Indian youngsters in the past which reshaped and improved reservation life. The old system, he added, had laid the ground work so that the present day schools could succeed. Regardless of whether he was correct or not, Blair's ideas certainly won no applause from top educators in the Indian Service who viewed the old boarding schools with near horror. See Fryer to Beatty, 24 December 1936, Central Classified Files, File 87508, 1936, 801, Navajo NA, RG 75.

28. For information on Adams' background, see "Lucy W. Adams," *Navajo Medical News* 7 (25 November 1940): 13–14.

particularly the integration of education into other reservation programs. Adams stated her views on Navajo education shortly after assuming her new post. "The Navajo problem is primarily an economic one, the solution of which is to be achieved largely in terms of proper land use, and probably ninety per cent of the school product will live and make its living on the reservation." She believed that most Navajo youngsters would stay in school only a short time and needed a much different training than that presented in white schools. Adams hoped to concentrate instruction on four major areas: "(a) health, (b) training in the use and control of reservation resources by means of technical information covering land and stock use, home building, etc., (c) training for civic participation through a knowledge of the background of Navajo economy and society, of the reservation program, and the opportunities for Navajo participation, (d) development of manual skills appropriate to reservation life." Like Beatty, Adams saw the teaching of English as the key to students' future education and life.[29]

Adams quickly received a rude introduction to reservation controversies. In compliance with Washington orders, she refused to provide free clothes for school children when the fall term of 1937 started. Long accustomed to having their children clothed at federal expense and already in an uproar because of the horse reduction program, disgruntled parents completely boycotted a half-dozen day schools in the Shiprock area. The boarding schools at Tohatchi and Chinle reported only three and sixteen students in attendance respectively when school opened.[30]

Collier refused to rescind the new policy when criticism arose. The commissioner stated that most families could afford the clothing and he would allow parents without funds to work at schools to pay for apparel issued to their children.[31] The school boycott dropped enrollment during 1937–38 about twenty percent. Not until after Morgan became council chairman did the resistance cease.

Adams' attempts to realize her educational goals during the next four years were less dramatic than the conflict over the clothing policy but no less difficult. Even though day school enrollments

29. Adams, "Program for Navajo Schools," 6 December 1937, Central Classified Files, File 58349, 1937, Navajo, NA, RG 75.

30. Adams to Beatty, 11 September 1937, Central Classified Files, File 58349, 1937, Navajo, NA, RG 75.

31. Collier to Chavez, 9 October 1937, Chavez papers, UA.

gradually rose until World War II, the schools were never filled to capacity.[32] As Washington superiors were prone to point out, the low Navajo enrollments constantly embarrassed their efforts to obtain additional funds. Despite strong official pleas that adults' use of school facilities was an important function and should be considered in funding, the Budget Bureau rejected this notion completely and based their recommendations solely upon student attendance. The community program, hence, had to be paid out of education appropriations or, more truthfully, out of the devotion and free time of teachers and their assistants. Moreover, constant overhead expenses such as staff salaries, building maintenance, and transportation allowances gave Adams little flexibility in financial matters.[33] When the school budgets after 1938 sharply reduced funds for transportation, she and other officials increasingly discussed the possibility of converting some of the day schools into boarding schools to save money.

Even though severely hampered by these problems, Adams made the school system operate with some adherence to the goals laid out by Collier and Beatty. Through in-service training and the admonitions of supervisors, most of the teachers made an effort to use progressive techniques in their classrooms. In the hands of an imaginative teacher, Dewey's methodology worked well in reaching the younger students. Absolutely terrified of whites, over ninety percent of the Navajo first graders came from camp life without any knowledge of English. A "game" in which the shy students identified objects with both Navajo and English words not only helped youngsters to become bilingual, but it avoided the harsh personal adjustments and frequent runaways of the old boarding schools. The more adept instructors even combined several types of learning in a single project. A lesson in which students cooked and served a meal could be expanded from home economics to health, language training,

32. Figures on attendance for 1939–40 totalled 2,855 students in boarding schools and 2,558 in day schools. Adults' use of the schools continued high with 6,086 visits to laundry and shop facilities. See Lucy Adams, "What the Government Is Doing on the Navajo; Navajo Schools," *Navajo Medical News* 7 (25 November 1940): 12.

33. The budget for 1939 amounted to $979,300 broken down into the following: regular and irregular salaries, $670,000; heat, light, and power, $134,800; food, $70,700; transportation, $64,000; clothing, $18,500; school room supplies, $11,700; and equipment, $9,600. See Lucy W. Adams' comments, "The Community Day School Program on the Navajo Reservation," 21 February 1939 (radio transcript of KTGM), Van Valkenburgh papers, AHS.

and even geography. Some older teachers simply could not adjust to the progressive teaching methods and preferred rote learning and keeping students in their seats. If the teacher seemed effective, supervisors tended to overlook such methodological lapses, although they still encouraged the instructor to present "practical" subject matter.[34]

Adams also tried diligently to make Navajos more aware of the government's general programs. A high level of imagination and thought went into Navajo paraeducation after 1937. Using techniques devised earlier by the SCS, school officials outfitted a "Show on Wheels," a panel truck equipped with various audiovisual materials, such as charts, pictures, and dioramas especially designed for Navajo audiences. The mobile classroom became a major drawing card at fairs, open-house days at schools, and other gatherings. Although Navajos did not fully accept the government's propaganda, large numbers came to see the movies shown by the "Show on Wheels."

Adams developed numerous other stratagems to bring education to the Navajos. She and other staffers appeared on station KTGM to discuss the school system and its ideals and operations. Through a firm in New York City which specialized in designing audiovisual materials, she developed an extensive series of posters. Each poster, drawn by a Navajo artist and with captions in both Navajo and English, conveyed a simple message attacking a common problem on the reservation. Examples included a poster devoted to the danger of spitting on hogan floors because this practice spread tuberculosis and another which encouraged Navajos to hoe their corn because neglect lowered production.

School officials devoted considerable attention to giving Navajos a sense of pride in their tribal heritage. Richard Van Valkenburgh, earlier an SCS employee but later an anthropologist and general handyman on Adams' staff, completed several well-researched studies of Navajo history, geography, and anthropology which were distributed among the schools. Van Valkenburgh's works informed the teachers about Navajos and, more importantly, provided instructional materials for classrooms. A large historical pageant with 1,500 actors at the Window Rock fair in 1940 doubtlessly was the most impressive single attempt to stimulate an appreciation of their

34. Thompson Interview.

cultural legacy. Van Valkenburgh wrote the script for the historical play, which was then translated into Navajo. The nightly performances unfolded the major periods of Navajo history from their arrival in the Southwest through their contacts with the Spanish and Mexicans, their defeat and assignment to Bosque Redondo, and their reservation life. The authentic dress of the actors, the excellence of lighting and staging, and the ambitious nature of the pageant prompted enthusiastic comments.

Other educational efforts sought both to explain the Navajo heritage and to provide an economic means of adjustment to modern life. Existing programs in arts and crafts were improved by hiring additional skilled weavers and silversmiths for schools. The Fort Wingate school annually staged an exhibition of students' arts and crafts in the late 1930s which attracted numerous Navajo and white visitors. The same school cooperated closely with the nearby sheep breeding station's experiments dealing with livestock management and the weaving of high quality rugs from long-staple wool. Fort Wingate officials in the late 1930s claimed that ninety-eight percent of the jewelry and rugs made by students passed the rigorous standards of quality and authenticity imposed by government inspectors. In 1938 the arts and crafts staff at Fort Wingate formed a guild for students and local craftsmen which offered a sales outlet and higher profits for superior quality jewelry and rugs than those granted by traders. The success of this venture played a major role in the formation of a reservation-wide guild in 1941.

A major breakthrough in educational efforts came in 1940 when the Indian Office announced that a simplified system of written Navajo had been completed by Oliver La Farge and John P. Harrington, the latter a linguist in the Bureau of Ethnology at the Smithsonian Institute.[35] Government publicity optimistically held out several advantages to be derived from the La Farge-Harrington system. In the future, instructional materials could be written in Navajo so as to avoid the "Dick and Jane" readers that had little

---

35. *Kansas City Star*, 27 February 1940, Van Valkenburgh papers, AHS; *Farmington Times Hustler*, 26 April 1940, p. 2. La Farge's main contribution was in convincing Collier and Indian Service educators that written Navajo could and should be simplified. In his appearance before a Senate subcommittee in 1948, La Farge mentioned that he battled behind the scenes for five years before his concept of a simplified orthography was accepted. See U. S., Senate, Subcommittee of the Committee on Interior and Insular Affairs, *Hearings on S. 2363, A Bill to Promote the Rehabilitation of the Navajo and Hopi Tribes . . .* , 80th Cong., 2nd sess., 1948, p. 359.

relevance to the students' everyday life. Teaching beginning students to read Navajo would shorten the time they required to learn English. An even more important possibility was that the new system would reduce the chronic misunderstandings and confusion that always existed because the tribesmen and white officials could not communicate. Government policies, decisions by the tribal council, and other important information could be conveyed by posting announcements in written Navajo at schools and trading posts or circulating them in a tribal newspaper.

The adoption of the new system of written Navajo climaxed nearly seven years of official efforts in linguistics. Since only around five percent of the Navajos were fluent in English, many people recognized that something should be done to reduce the serious communications gap. In early 1934 Collier had hired Father Berard Haile, the Catholic linguist, to serve as a consultant for bilingual training in the new day schools.[36] A few months later Collier commissioned Edward Sapir, a noted Athapascan linguist at Yale, to do an introductory Navajo grammar. The commissioner also appointed Gladys Reichard, an anthropologist at Barnard College, to establish a hogan school during the summer of 1934 to test the feasibility of teaching Navajos to read and write their own language.[37] At least three main purposes were embodied in Collier's actions: (1) to improve Navajo interpreters' skills, (2) to train white officials to have at least a rudimentary knowledge of the language, and (3) to reduce Navajo to a written language which could be taught in the day schools to both adults and children.

The frictions that developed in 1934 presaged future efforts to solve the language problem. Haile had labored on a written system of Navajo for many years and he would not accept interlopers who could not render the difficult language perfectly or who disagreed with his methods of transcribing it. He cooperated well with Sapir, his former mentor in graduate school, but he had little use for Reichard, whom he deemed something of a dilettante with a bad ear for Navajo.[38] Petty personal and pedantic differences kept the three major participants from achieving much progress.

In addition, the general confusion which existed on the reservation

36. Collier to Haile, 18 January 1934, Haile papers, UAL.

37. Reichard to Franc Newcomb, 10 March 1934, Reichard papers, MNA; Sapir to Haile, 6 June 1934, Haile papers, UAL.

38. Haile to Sapir, 4 July 1934, Haile papers, UAL.

in 1934 because of administrative consolidation hampered the work. Both Reichard and Haile complained that Zeh and his staff seemed disinterested in language training. Indeed, the only major achievement in the linguistics program in the early period was an institute for Navajo interpreters that Haile and Albert Sandoval, an interpreter and long-time assistant of the priest, conducted in January 1935. The institute concentrated on sharpening the top interpreters' skills in translating technical terms associated with the medical program, the Wheeler-Howard Act, and other New Deal efforts.[39]

For the next eighteen months after the interpreters institute, nothing of major significance developed in the language program, although Haile continued to serve as a consultant and Sapir worked on the grammar. Some time in mid-1936, the priest visited Washington and learned that Beatty and Collier had decided to reject the alphabet for written Navajo that Haile and Sapir had been using. The Sapir-Haile orthography was complex, but Haile claimed it was capable of rendering the tonal qualities and other intricacies of Navajo sounds perfectly. Through the urging of La Farge and Harrington, Collier and Beatty had decided to endorse a simplified system which used the regular English alphabet that could be written by a standard typewriter. Although the Sapir-Haile alphabet was technically superior for specialists interested in comparative linguistics, it was ill-suited for practical education of the Navajos.

The "battle of the systems" immediately became heated. While visiting Washington, Haile told Collier in Harrington's presence that a simplified alphabet would not work and the Smithsonian linguist insisted that it would. Two weeks after returning to the reservation, Haile again attacked the "monstrous alphabet" in a letter to Collier. Soon afterward, Haile claimed that Beatty had reendorsed the Sapir-Haile alphabet during a visit to the reservation.[40]

Haile's victory over Harrington was short-lived. The priest's participation in organizing the new council and drafting the abortive constitution from late 1936 through the summer of 1937 forced him

39. Haile to Ryan, 26 January 1935, and "Interpreters Institute," 28 January 1935, Haile papers, UAL. There is some indication that Haile conducted other institutes and perhaps even operated a full time interpreters school in this period.

40. Haile to Sapir, 27 June 1936, Haile to Collier, 12 July 1936, and Haile to Sapir, 20 August 1936, Haile papers, UAL.

to abandon linguistics. In the meantime, Harrington had been retained in 1937 to develop a simplified alphabet and write a set of primers for reservation schools.

To assist in developing a simplified orthography, Harrington employed Robert W. Young, a white graduate student, and William Morgan, a young Navajo. Both Young and Morgan subsequently worked on linguistics at the Fort Wingate sheep-breeding station. Although Harrington was an excellent phonetician, he had had little experience with Athapascan languages. This proved advantageous in Young's opinion, for he was freed from having to defend or attack any previous written systems. With the aid of Young and Morgan, Harrington devised an orthography which used entirely English letters and a minimum of supplemental markings to indicate nasal sounds and tonal qualities.[41]

Harrington had less success with subject matter. Somehow he overlooked the fact that bears were among the Navajos' strongest taboos and his devotion of one primer to a story about these animals both horrified and amused those familiar with tribal culture. The primers were supposed to be published in 1938, but they apparently had to be scrapped and Beatty's staffers started on a new set. The first primer was finally published in 1940. Others followed quickly. All were attractively illustrated by Navajo artists. The stories were in both English and Navajo and depicted reservation life.[42]

41. Young and Morgan soon became major figures in research and publications on Navajo linguistics. Young also became involved in the administrative and planning activities on the reservation after World War II. His comments in a letter to me and his willingness to send his manuscript on the history of written Navajo were both useful in filling several gaps in my own research and understanding of the linguists' efforts. Young's manuscript was written for a forthcoming collective volume entitled, *The Creation and Revision of Writing Systems,* edited by Professor Joshua A. Fishman.

42. Unlike most New Deal programs, work on Navajo linguistics increased after 1941. Young and Morgan issued a dictionary in 1941 and several other publications followed. In the same period, the Wycliffe Bible Translators opened an office at Farmington and started translating the Bible into Navajo, using a slightly modified version of the La Farge-Harrington alphabet. The organization shortly afterward established reading classes on the reservation. In 1943 Window Rock began to publish a newspaper in Navajo which continued until 1957. In his letter to the writer, Robert Young expressed the belief that these efforts reduced the language barrier, but they would have been even more successful if they had been supported by traders and missionaries who really wanted to "exterminate the language." Most of those who learned to read Navajo were already fluent in English. The advantage for such Indians was that they could read subject matter in Navajo at a much higher level of difficulty than they could in English. This permitted

The posters, primers, and simplified alphabet marked the apex of Adams' goal to reach the mass of Navajos, but they certainly did not end heated debate over the proper kind of education for the tribe. Despite his increasing cooperation with the government after becoming chairman in 1938, Morgan never altered his position that schools should stress English, the three R's, and other white subject matter. The Navajo leader particularly found fault with the La Farge-Harrington system. He and like-minded critics saw bilingual education as amounting to rank discrimination which would keep Navajos locked in their hogans, perpetuate the tribe's ignorance, and deny their chances of gaining the comforts of white society.[43]

In early 1941, Collier promoted Adams to a post in the Washington office and assigned George Boyce to direct Navajo education. A curriculum specialist, Boyce was already familiar with Navajo conditions through two earlier visits to the reservation.[44] The new director's overall policies supplemented rather than altered those of his predecessors. While Adams had emphasized the dissemination of information to the mass of Navajos, Boyce and his staff attempted additionally to make tribesmen realize the importance of education and to break down their basic indifference toward schools. Some observers felt that the Navajos' appreciation for education after World War II started as early as 1941 when Boyce became director.[45]

Soon after Boyce's appointment, Vice Chairman Howard Gorman introduced a five-point program of educational improvements to the council on April 10, 1941. Included were requests that some day schools be changed into boarding schools, that day schools offer six grades of instruction instead of four, that all the boarding schools

---

them to read translations of grazing regulations, election rules, and legislation with a fuller understanding and to explain the contents to illiterate Navajos. The Navajos' failure to create their own tribal literature was a major shortcoming of the linguistics program, according to Young. The nearest approach to this was the Navajos' willingness to record their thoughts for publication in the tribal newspaper. Until very recently, the Navajos have not created a written literature despite the potentially rich subject matter. Young to writer, 31 July 1973.

43. Morgan's attacks started in the fall of 1940 and continued for the next year or so. See Morgan's letter to the editor in *Farmington Times Hustler*, 29 October 1941, p. 3.

44. During Boyce's second visit, he had written a summary of government programs in the Kiabeto district, as part of a general drive around 1939 to assess the effectiveness of the New Deal policies as an aid in future planning. Fryer authored a more general analysis entitled "The Government and the Navajo" (1941).

45. Thompson Interview.

provide junior and senior high courses, that the curriculum devote more attention to economic problems, and that either Fort Wingate, Shiprock, or Tuba City offer courses in advanced vocational training and college preparatory work. Beatty attended the council and he responded sympathetically to the council's petition. He admitted the necessity of solving the transportation problem of the day schools and expressed the hope that all schools could provide more instruction. Funding would be difficult, especially if Navajos did not send more children to upper grades.[46]

Whatever possibility Boyce might have had to accomplish the council's program was curtailed by World War II. That conflict disrupted many government functions on the reservation, but none suffered greater dislocations than education. Indeed, the severe problems earlier faced by Blair and Adams seemed minor compared to those of the war years. Boyce's main concern after 1941 was to keep even part of the schools open rather than attempting to expand services.[47]

Navajo education in the New Deal presented a mixture of successes and failures which fell far short of initial aspirations. The goal of creating day schools which would become community centers failed because Navajo society lacked the cohesiveness and structure which could permit the attainment of this objective. Except where devoted teachers supplied the impetus, the schools never became the foci of local groups. Similarly, the schools never realized Collier's hope that virtually all children would receive an education. This was not the fault of the schools as much as Navajos' inability to see much purpose in education, their tendency to withhold youngsters from classes because of grievances, and the lack of transportation facilities on the reservation. The schools, however, provided services to adults and students that were very beneficial. The facilities at the schools, water from the wells, and medical treatment of children had an importance to Navajos far greater than would have been true for a more opulent group.

If the central goal of Navajo education was to provide a balanced instruction that would permit Indian youngsters to live either on the reservation or among whites, then the government's efforts were at

46. See "Proceedings of the Navajo Tribal Council," 8–11 April 1941, File 9659, 36, E, 054, Navajo, Part 5, NA, RG 75, pp. 118–45.
47. Thompson Interview.

least a partial failure. Spurred on by their devotion to Dewey's teaching methods and by pressures to integrate education into other government programs, the Navajo school administrators saw little value in emphasizing academic training, particularly when the depression forced nearly all graduates to remain on the reservation. Despite the sizeable amount of publicity about bilingual training, government educators did not fully appreciate the necessity of teaching youngsters to become fluent in English. This became evident during the wholesale exodus from the reservation after 1941, which revealed that most young Navajos were woefully unprepared in language skills needed for jobs in industry and the military. As high as eighty percent of Navajo draftees, for example, were rejected because of illiteracy. Thus it appears clear that Navajo education during the New Deal did not provide the type of training that would allow students to live successfully in either Indian or white society.

# 9

# The Blind and the Sick

Of all the major federal services for the Navajos, none was more inadequate at the start of the New Deal than medical care. In spite of some improvements during the Hoover administration, the government had never made more than a hesitant start in responding to the tribe's serious health problems. No basic data was available on such questions as the birth and death rates, the extent and causes of infant mortality, how many older Navajo children died from communicable diseases, and other important information. An overwhelming majority of births and deaths occurred at home and were unreported. Even though government doctors knew something about the major types of illnesses for those patients who appeared in government hospitals, their data on the whole tribe was speculative. The medical staff, for example, estimated 900 active tuberculosis cases among Navajos, but precise figures on the number of sufferers who went undetected and untreated were unknown.[1] Similarly, the government knew nothing about the incidence of trachoma until surveys of school children in 1937 revealed that a little over one-third were afflicted.

Although tuberculosis and trachoma were the most common diseases, Navajos suffered from a variety of other illnesses. Hundreds of infants died each year, usually from bronchial pneumonia, severe diarrhea, malnutrition, or a combination of the three. Even if children survived past infancy, doctors repeatedly discovered cases of malnourishment so severe that three-year-olds weighed no more than twenty-one or twenty-two pounds.[2] Such emaciated children had

1. *Albuquerque Journal*, 3 May 1935, pp. 2–3.

2. Nathaniel Safran, "Infant Mortality," *Navajo Medical News* 7 (15 January 1940): 13–15. Although this publication apparently started in 1933, the writer has found only a few scattered issues from 1940 and 1941. See Central Classified Files, File 50979, 1938, 760, Navajo, Part 1, "Navajo Medical Center," NA, RG 75.

little resistance to epidemics of measles, whooping cough, diptheria, meningitis, smallpox, influenza, and typhoid which swept across the reservation during the 1930s.

The most obvious factor contributing to Navajo medical problems was their extreme poverty and inadequate supply of food. Poorer Navajos lived on an unvaried diet of potatoes, tortillas, and coffee. Children in such families received no milk after weaning and ate meat infrequently. Navajos enjoying moderate incomes had a better balanced diet. They depended heavily on sheep and goats and their consumption of the entire animals, including the viscera, largely answered their nutritional needs. Wealthy families, on the other hand, often purchased snack-type foods that were too heavy in sugar and starches.[3] As a result, they seldom enjoyed a balanced diet even though they could afford it.

The Navajos' ignorance about sanitation also caused many illnesses. Their lack of outhouses, use of contaminated drinking water, and failure to wash cooking utensils and dishes properly all led to typhoid, diarrhea, and other intestinal disorders. Navajo mothers delivered their babies at home and their unfamiliarity with the proper care for the umbilical cord often resulted in infection of the abdominal lining and death from blood poisoning.[4] The winter cold and drafts and the dirt floors of hogans caused a high incidence of colds, tuberculosis, and other pulmonary and bronchial complaints.

In part the Navajos' severe health problems sprang from their strong cultural attitudes regarding illnesses and cures. Almost invariably Navajo patients turned first to their medicine men for treatment by religious rites and native medicines. While this often effected a cure, especially when the illness was psychosomatic, white doctors frequently complained that the shamans could do little for serious physical injuries or diseases. All too often, a patient's health deteriorated steadily under a medicine man's ministrations until he shrewdly deduced that the case was hopeless and advised taking the ill person to a hospital. Repeated instances of patients with terminal illnesses arriving at hospitals led even the most culturally tolerant physicians to condemn a practice which lessened the chance of successful treatment and allowed the medicine men to escape responsibility for their own failures.

    3. See William J. Darby, et al., "A Study of the Dietary Background and Nutriture of the Navajo Indian," reprinted from The Journal of Nutrition 60 (November 1956).
    4. Safran, "Infant Mortality," p. 13–15.

Other cultural beliefs created equally significant problems. Most Navajos had no concept of the germ theory which underlay white medical treatment. Instead, the Indians attributed illnesses to the patient's spiritual shortcomings or some enemy wishing harm upon him. Navajo thinking on diseases was also largely dominated by patients' symptoms. While the Navajo language contained no word for germ, it reportedly had fourteen words or derivations for describing the characteristics of pneumonia. Despite efforts to express basic white medical terms and concepts in Navajo, the language barrier remained a major difficulty for medical personnel.

The typical Navajo patient also found hospital life disturbing. Deeply fearful of any dwelling where a person had died, the average tribesman cringed at the prospect of even entering a hospital. The daily routine of taking temperatures, receiving shots, eating strange foods, taking baths, and using bedpans further bewildered the camp Navajo. Already upset by the strangeness of the hospital, the patient suffered from the seeming indifference of the hospital personnel who, because of the language barrier and press of duties, could not explain the nature of his illness or its treatment. Doctors often complained that homesick patients fled from hospitals as soon as they had partially recovered from illnesses.

Given the reputation of Indian Service hospitals in 1933, the Navajos' flight was probably wise. Before the New Deal the government operated nine hospitals located at Chinle, Tuba City, Shiprock, Crownpoint, Leupp, Tohatchi, Fort Wingate, Fort Defiance, and Toadlena. Some idea of the hospitals' low quality can be gained from the fact that only three of the institutions, Fort Defiance, Shiprock, and Tuba City, possessed X-ray machines before 1935. The absence of this equipment, of course, seriously hampered diagnosis and treatment of fractures and tuberculosis. None had laboratory facilities and all such work was done by Sage Memorial Hospital at Ganado or the state health departments of Arizona or New Mexico. An Indian Service clinic at Gallup headed by a doctor was supposed to treat day patients, but the position was usually unfilled and only a nurse remained on duty. Three sanitariums located at Fort Defiance, Kayenta, and Winslow treated tuberculosis patients, but Navajo attitudes toward the disease usually meant that the cases went undetected until they were terminal. Dental care was virtually nonexistent. One or two traveling dentists appeared on the reservation periodically, but they were so overburdened that most of their work consisted of extracting students' infected teeth. Similarly medical services were limited to school children, with little attempt at treating the general Navajo population.

A majority of the medical buildings were originally designed for some other purpose and had been converted to hospitals and sanitariums. Doctors frequently commented that the facilities at Shiprock, Leupp, and Kayenta badly needed replacement, but the hospital at Fort Wingate was even more notorious. It occupied a barracks constructed seventy-five years earlier when Fort Wingate was a frontier military post.

The quality of doctors was no better than the state of medical facilities. Except for a few younger men who temporarily took reservation positions to repay medical school debts, the average doctor in the Indian Service in 1933 was unlikely to be very capable, energetic, or well-informed on recent advances. Some were older physicians who lacked formal training in medicine and had learned their profession by the apprentice method. Several could not perform surgery. Others had failed in private practice because of drinking or some incident and turned to employment in the Indian Service as a last resort. Such men gave only indifferent attention to their duties and some callously used the most painful treatments even when more humane methods were readily available.

Navajos received medical care from two nongovernment sources during the New Deal. A hospital endowed by the Christian Reformed Church and headed by Dr. R. H. Pousma at Rehoboth, New Mexico, served patients in the Gallup area. Unfortunately, the small hospital lacked sophisticated equipment because of a low endowment. It was, however, normally full and also served many day patients. The Sage Memorial Hospital at Ganado, in contrast, was the showpiece of the Presbyterian Church's home missionary program. Dr. Clarence G. Salsbury, the superintendent, was a highly successful fund raiser and the Ganado hospital was accredited by the American College of Surgeons. In addition to seventy-five beds, the hospital offered laboratory facilities, ample equipment, and an ambulance. One or two physicians assisted Salsbury at Ganado and also made regular visits to outlying clinics. The hospital even ran a small nursing school for Indian girls. Its first class graduated in 1933 and the school grew steadily in the coming years until it was training a dozen nurses annually.[5]

5. More detailed information on Salsbury's work at Ganado is contained in his recent

Although cooperation between the Ganado staff and the government physicians could only have benefited both and provided better medical care for the Navajos, dissensions seemed to characterize their relationship. Salsbury, like most Protestant missionaries, saw a benevolent type of assimilation as the only solution to the Navajos' problems and he suspected Collier's ideas from the first.[6] At several points the veiled dislike erupted into the open. In 1934, for example, Salsbury staged a "Navajo Chautauqua" at Ganado which offered band concerts, sports contests, religious services, vocational training, and a free medical clinic presided over by specialists in various fields. Intensely hopeful that the first venture would succeed, Salsbury distributed numerous large posters over the reservation which contained a statement that government experts would teach Chautauqua classes on livestock management. This upset Collier who felt that the Indian Service should not be identified with any religious proselytizing and he subsequently ordered reservation officials to discourage or play down any cooperation with the Navajo Chautauqua. When notified of the commissioner's feelings, Salsbury retorted that the government had experienced no qualms about letting him give free physical exams to CCC enrollees in the rush to initiate that program in 1933, nor had Collier objected to allowing a Catholic priest to address a recent conference of the Indian Service workers at Fort Wingate. Displays of pettiness came to characterize subsequent relations between Ganado and Window Rock. When later asked by officials to write an article on Navajo health problems, the Ganado superintendent refused, complaining that he had drafted a similar statement before for someone in the government and never received any ackowledgement.[7] Salsbury believed the government started the tribal fair at Window Rock in 1938 to kill the Navajo Chautauqua. Instead of cooperation, Salsbury tended to look upon the government as a competitor. When medical officials offered a new program or medical facility, the Ganado staff considered the innovation as a slap. Lost in the gossip, jealousies, and recriminations was the realization that Navajo health was the paramount goal of both missionary and government doctors.

Collier's efforts to attack the Navajos' health problems in 1933

memoirs. See Clarence G. Salsbury (with Paul Hughes), *The Salsbury Story, A Medical Missionary's Lifetime of Public Service* (Tucson, 1969).

6. Salsbury Interview.

7. Fryer to Townsend, 30 August 1937, Central Classified Files, File 1937, Navajo, 734, NA, RG 75.

and 1934 adhered closely to his self-help philosophy. He clearly felt that an effort should be made to prevent disease rather than merely bolster the treatment facilities in existing hospitals. Hence, Collier's initial plans were directed toward adult health education. Public health nurses and Navajo aides would be stationed at day schools to teach the local population about nutrition, hygiene, baby care, and proper housing. The work would involve not only training of adults and children, but both nurses and aides would frequently visit the hogans to treat minor illnesses and to demonstrate correct sanitation techniques.

The press of initiating emergency programs in 1933 doubtlessly delayed implementation of the commissioner's goals, but sometime in 1934 or early the following year he hired his close friend, Sally Lucas Jean, to devise a training program for Navajo nurse's aides and help integrate medical work with the day school program. She had a wide range of previous experience in public health education. According to Collier, her major successes had been in using "medical technicians to the limit by correlating the school and community with what the medical technicians are doing or trying to do."[8]

In mid-1934, Jean started training ninety-five Navajo girls from ages eighteen to twenty-four as nurse's aides at the Santa Fe Indian School. The classrooms were two hogans specially built for the four-week course. Doctors, nurses, and home economists taught the trainees sanitation, nutrition, and infant care. The presence of Doctors Francis J. Proctor and Polk Richards on the staff meant that the girls received substantial training in treating trachoma, since both men had studied that disease for many years. Richards had once even transferred *Bacillus granulosis noguihi* from a patient to his own eyes to prove that trachoma was a contact type disease and he was prominent in New Deal efforts to eradicate the disease.[9]

Evidently Navajo nurse's aides were infrequently employed in the new community centers just as young Navajos were seldom allowed to teach in the day schools. Very likely, the use of the medical trainees was negated by the many delays in the general administrative overhaul in 1934 and 1935. A lack of funds possibly acted as a contributing factor. Probably the major reason, however, was the

8. Collier to Ickes, 18 August 1933, Collier papers, YU.

9. Jean to Collier, 12 June 1934, Collier papers, YU; *Santa Fe New Mexican*, 11 June 1934, p. 6, and 12 June 1934, p. 3.

strong reluctance of Dr. W. W. Peter to use poorly trained aides except as direct companions of registered nurses.[10]

Collier's hiring of Peter as medical director of the Navajos in July 1934 was another example of the commissioner's success in tapping people with impressive backgrounds. A specialist in public health, Peter had served as a government advisor and researcher in China during World War I, later had carried out similar assignments in several other countries, and had become a prominent figure in public health circles in the United States. Shortly before his appointment in 1934, he and Collier talked over the Navajo program and Peter consented to become medical director despite another job offer which paid three times more than the Indian Service post.[11]

Peter announced his basic strategy for attacking Navajo health problems in February 1935. To improve the quality of existing personnel, he ordered all physicians to meet monthly for in-service training. Nurses were to attend similar classes but less frequently. Peter also planned to establish a board of health on the reservation, hoping that the organization would act as a liaison between the Navajos, the council, and the medical staff and help break down the tribe's reluctance to seek treatment. To provide a reserve staff for treating epidemics, Peter mentioned that he would ask for additional appropriations to hire more people. Similarly, he promised to request funding for a new base hospital, a fully modern installation with adequate equipment and a complete laboratory.[12]

With the exception of the idea of a board of health, which seems to have been lost in the council's general inactivity in the mid-1930s, Peter's initial goals changed little over the rest of the New Deal. The improvement of health care was more gradual than attempts to push through land management, herd reduction, or even the day school program. These tended to be viewed as needing immediate attention. Despite this, Peter managed to raise the quality and quantity of medical treatment available for the tribe. Some changes were remarkably successful, while other efforts produced little improvement.

10. William Zimmerman, Jr. to Zeh, 8 December 1934, File 59912, 1934, Navajo, 728, NA, RG 75.

11. "Minutes of the Meeting of the Navajo Tribal Council," Keams Canyon, Arizona, 10–12 July 1934, LAFRC, Box 72907, pp. 53–54; *Gallup Independent*, 12 July 1934, p. 1.

12. W. W. Peter, "Plans for Navajo Medical Work," 11 February 1935, Haile papers, UAL.

One of the most productive advances by Peter was his success in attracting better quality doctors to replace the inept physicians typical of the pre-New Deal. The depression played a major role in this improvement. Most medical school graduates could earn incomes well above those paid by the Civil Service during normal times, but the $3,200 annual salary during the 1930s attracted many capable young doctors to the reservation. In contrast to the old-line doctors, the new appointees were products of established medical schools and they brought with them advanced treatment techniques, an enthusiasm for work, and even medical research skills. Unfortunately, retaining the new staff members became an increasingly difficult problem when conditions became more prosperous in the late 1930s. Civil Service regulations made it difficult to offer merit raises, worsening the turnover problem.

Training seminars for doctors and nurses became a fairly regular feature of the Navajo Service staff. Nearly all such sessions concentrated on a specific medical problem such as syphilis, trachoma, or tuberculosis. Lecturers at the seminars were usually staff members who had some special interest, training, or experience with the subject under study, and Peter occasionally brought in an outside specialist to keynote the sessions. Despite the unfriendly relations with Salsbury, Peter and his subordinates attended annual clinics at Sage Memorial Hospital where nationally known medical leaders lectured and demonstrated new techniques.[13]

The improvement and replacement of outmoded hospitals was far less successful than Peter had hoped. Except for some new equipment, limited remodeling, and minor improvements, the condition of most installations remained inadequate. As late as 1939, three hospitals still lacked X-ray machines. Sterilizing equipment was often in disrepair, medical records were missing or incomplete, and staff positions remained vacant for long periods. Although many of the complaints of medical personnel were incredibly petty, some were quite valid. Doctors and nurses worked until they were exhausted during epidemics. Even when the patient load was normal, a vacancy in a small hospital staff caused the loss of weekends and extra shifts for nurses. Probably no group of Navajo Service employees became as bitter at inadequate quarters as the nurses. Several

13. Fryer to Collier, 31 August 1938, File 77390, 1937, Navajo, 721, NA, RG 75.

hospitals housed the nurses in the same building with patients and this aroused endless complaints about noise and interruption of nurses' sleep and opportunity to relax during off-duty hours.

The opening of a new base hospital at Fort Defiance on June 20, 1938, was the most important single contribution to reservation medical facilities. To allay Navajos' strong reluctance to enter hospitals and as a means of publicizing the achievement, Peter invited Pete Price, a noted medicine man, and several associates to participate in the dedication by performing the traditional ceremony used to bless a new dwelling. Constructed with WPA funds at a cost of $450,000, the new hospital was the biggest building on the reservation and the largest and best equipped hospital of the Indian Service at that time. In truth, it was probably the first government hospital on the reservation worthy of the name. The new 140-bed facility contained isolation wards, a laboratory, a dental office, and modern equipment. The base hospital handled all laboratory work for the reservation, received cases which required special treatment, conducted in-service training, and became the administrative center of the medical program. The staff at Fort Defiance included Peter's best doctors. The old hospital at Fort Defiance was converted into a tuberculosis sanitarium.

In February 1940 a second hospital of sixty-five beds opened at Crownpoint. Although smaller and less well-equipped than Fort Defiance, the new hospital partly answered a long-standing need for better medical services among the Eastern Navajos. The old hospital had provided for only a small fraction of prospective patients. Unfortunately, many Navajos north and east of Crownpoint remained too isolated to benefit from the new hospital.[14]

Beside hospital treatment, Peter established a network of twelve dispensaries at various points on the reservation in 1936. The program was a reduction of Jean's ambitious scheme of stationing nurses and Navajo aides at larger day schools. A field nurse presided over each dispensary and treated minor illnesses. The nurses were supposed to visit ailing Navajos too sick to come in for treatment and to take the more seriously ill to hospitals. They provided adult education both by calling on individual families to discuss prenatal care, sanitation, and nutrition with mothers or by conducting meet-

14. *Gallup Independent*, 12 February 1940, p. 2.

ings at community centers. Their major duty, however, was to visit
day schools to treat students suffering from trachoma.[15]

Even though the use of field nurses seemed eminently workable,
the new program suffered problems similar to those experienced by
the day schools. The primitive reservation roads destroyed cars and
bad weather often prevented the field nurses from reaching outlying
day schools. There is evidence that some nurses spent a good part of
their time running errands or giving free rides to wily Navajos who
cleverly feigned illnesses. Peter particularly worried about letting
unqualified teachers and school assistants take over the responsibility
for trachoma treatment when field nurses were unavailable. Even
when diligent, school staffs lacked adequate training to handle
advanced cases which required the attention of physicians. Nevertheless, educational personnel usually treated cases of trachoma.
These problems, along with students' frequent absences from schools
and the lack of treatment during summers, severely handicapped
efforts to end the painful eye disease.

In 1938 Peter devised a new program for treating trachoma and
gradually phased out the field nurses. Under this plan, two doctors
and six nurses with special expertise worked primarily among
students of boarding schools in an intensive campaign to eradicate
trachoma. The more advanced cases were treated in the summers by
keeping youngsters in school the entire year. Except for the possible
transfer of some sufferers to boarding schools, the day school situation remained unchanged. The trachoma doctors and nurses visited
the day schools only infrequently and the care of the students still
remained basically in the hands of teachers and their assistants.

The virtual eradication of trachoma from the reservation after
1938 was due less to Peter's efforts than a major advance in treatment. By this time medical researchers had developed the first of the
sulfa drugs. Indian Service doctors tried one of these, sulfanilamide,
in an experimental treatment of 140 trachomous patients at the
Rosebud Sioux reservation in 1937. The high rate of success among
the experimental group showed that sulfanilamide was much more
effective than irrigating the eyes with caustics.[16] It was also infinitely

15. Most of the information on the field nurse program has to be derived from nurse
supervisors' reports. The only detailed information is an article written by Blanche
Chance, a field nurse, in defense of the work. See "Field Nursing on the Navajo," *Navajo
Medical News* 7 (1 May 1940): 13–18.

16. *Albuquerque Journal*, 10 October 1938, p. 8.

easier to use than the previous treatment. The drug could be taken orally and the disease totally arrested in a short time. To further test sulfanilamide and to perfect its use, Fort Defiance Hospital in 1939 administered the miracle drug to 107 students attending the summer trachoma school. Divided into groups, the subjects were given various dosages at different time intervals to determine the best treatment procedure. Doctors also used the groups to study possible damage to white cells, one of several side effects of the drug.[17] In the summer of 1940 a full campaign against trachoma was launched among school children which was pursued vigorously for the next few years.

The resulting victory over trachoma was a tremendous advance not only for the Navajos but Indians everywhere. Except for small pockets of trachoma in Kentucky and among a few immigrant groups, Indians alone had endured a disease which brought suffering to thousands before the 1940s. No longer would teachers have to question the purpose of teaching students to read when a good percentage would be blind or partly sightless when they reached adulthood. A minor and curable disease today, trachoma still remains fairly common, especially among Navajo school girls who borrow each other's eye makeup, but for most of the tribe it exists only as a dreaded memory.

Tuberculosis, the second great scourge of Navajo health, proved far more resistant to New Deal efforts than trachoma. The facilities at Kayenta and Fort Defiance when Peter became director were highly inadequate. The Kayenta sanitarium took in regular patients and did not isolate them from those suffering tuberculosis. The building at Fort Defiance was kept open only as a temporary expedient until the new base hospital opened and the patients could be shifted to the old hospital. The main value of both sanitariums was to separate active cases from the remainder of the tribe rather than effecting cures. The forty-five-bed sanitarium at Winslow was newer and provided treatment procedures.[18] Even after the old hospital at Fort Defiance became a sanitarium in 1938, the total number of beds for tuberculosis was approximately 200. With an estimated 900 active cases, facilities obviously fell far short of needs.

17. See James G. Townsend, "Is Trachoma Nearing Defeat?" *Navajo Medical News* 7 (15 January 1940): 1–5.

18. Townsend to Peter, May 1937, File 39530, 1937, Navajo, 720, NA, RG 75.

Efforts to fight tuberculosis before 1938 were sporadic. In 1935 Peter announced a limited and voluntary program of preventing the disease by vaccinating newly born children with Bacillus-Calmette-Gruerin (BCG). How many vaccinations actually took place is not known, but certainly the program could not have reached more than a small fraction of the tribe.[19] The same year, the sanitariums began using pneumothorax treatment on some patients. The technique consisted of pumping air around an infected lung to collapse it. With the lung immobilized, recovery was supposed to be much more rapid. Information on the new method is almost as sketchy as on BCG. No data seem available on the extent that this therapy was used or its success compared to the conventional methods of keeping patients inactive and supplying them with rich diets. Peter, however, must have felt the pneumothorax treatment was effective, for the technique was still used in the late 1930s. Both BCG and pneumothorax treatments were less important than the policy followed after 1936 when doctors began giving all school children annual physical examinations and taking chest X-rays of all sports participants.

In 1938 a pilot program to detect and control tuberculosis started in the Leupp and Fort Defiance districts. With Dr. E. R. Long, director of Phipps Institute of Philadelphia, acting as a consultant, Peter detailed two field nurses to do a hogan-to-hogan survey of both areas. The nurses administered tuberculin tests to local residents and those who reacted positively were taken to Winslow, Leupp, or Fort Defiance for chest X-rays. The cases discovered were subsequently divided into two classes. Those considered terminal were sent to the Kayenta sanitarium and the less serious were given pneumothorax treatment. A large percentage of the latter were not placed in the sanitariums at Fort Defiance or Winslow but visited these centers at three or four week intervals to renew their treatment. Although Peter hoped that the program could be enlarged and applied throughout the reservation, a lack of funds limited him to the two field nurses employed in local surveys.

During the rest of the New Deal, several other attempts were made to control tuberculosis but no general solution appeared. The

19. W. W. Peter, "Plans for Navajo Medical Work," 11 February 1935, Haile papers, UAL. The BCG vaccinations had to be given at birth and repeated for several years. This would have been difficult to achieve among Navajos because of their remoteness from hospitals.

facilities at Kayenta were improved and efforts were made to upgrade the staff there. After some unsuccessful starts, Peter finally
hired two or three new doctors who specialized in treating tuberculosis. Chest X-rays became a routine procedure for any patient
entering a government hospital. Cooperation between school
officials and the medical staff grew stronger in the detection of cases.

As part of this later drive, Peter and Lucy Adams decided in 1939
to use the Leupp boarding school for students who were suffering
from primary tuberculosis but not ill enough to be hospitalized.
Through providing extra rest periods, enriched diets, and better
medical care, Peter hoped to arrest the disease and cure the students
before they developed secondary tuberculosis. He estimated that
approximately 150 children in the day and boarding schools had
primary tuberculosis, but Adams' efforts to win permission from
parents for the transfer of their children resulted in only forty attending the Leupp school the first year.[20]

A rather complex set of factors frustrated the government's attempts to eradicate tuberculosis. Malnutrition made Navajos particularly susceptible to the disease and conditions in hogans allowed
the disease to be transmitted from person to person very readily.
Navajos with active tuberculosis expelled their sputum on the dirt
floors. When the sputum dried, the bacilli remained alive and were
transmitted to other family members when the dust was shuffled by
people walking across the hogan or by drafts. Because Navajos
tended to associate the seriousness of disease with the intensity of
pain, tuberculosis patients seldom sought treatment until they were
past recovery. A thorough eradication program demanded the
examination of every member of the tribe, a task beyond the financial
resources of the medical staff. Peter once considered using a mobile
X-ray unit, but the cost of obtaining chest X-rays of approximately
50,000 Navajos was prohibitive and the likelihood of winning
appropriations to treat those detected was even more remote. Peter
was thus forced to restrict the drive against tuberculosis to limited
geographic areas, to Navajos who entered hospitals for any reason,
and to school children. These procedures made some inroads against
tuberculosis, but they certainly did not match the dramatic success
of eradicating trachoma.

20. Adams and Peter to Fryer, 26 August 1939, File 19333, 1938, Navajo, 705, NA,
RG 75; *Gallup Independent*, 9 February 1940, p. 1.

In addition to tuberculosis and trachoma, much of the time and energies of medical personnel was taken up with fighting the epidemics of communicable diseases. Enumerating all the many outbreaks is perhaps pointless. Each epidemic overtaxed the local medical facilities and staff, forcing a series of emergency measures and transfers of medical personnel. The overflow of new patients was placed in hospital halls or in nearby schools under the care of teachers. During the outbreak of diptheria in July 1938 at Kayenta, the medical director used the newly installed radio network to order serum to inoculate those still not stricken.

Some inroads were made into other medical problems. After Peter failed to secure an appropriation for a full-time dentist in 1937, the council agreed to establish a $5,000 revolving fund from tribal monies which was used to hire a dentist and to equip an office at the Fort Defiance hospital. Treatment was open to both Navajos and government employees at reduced fees and the money received was used to maintain the fund. Indians who could not afford dental services, however, were treated free. A good portion of the patients did not pay and the tribal council later approved another appropriation to keep the fund alive.[21]

An early emphasis on attacking venereal disease was sidetracked after 1935 because the problem was less prevalent than expected. Detection and treatment, however, never lapsed entirely as the medical staff often made Wasserman tests of suspected cases. In 1938 a weekly clinic for treating syphilis was established at Houck, Arizona. The next year the clinic was removed to Gallup where incidence was the highest because of local prostitution. The main obstacle for both locations was the Indians' lack of transportation to receive the long series of weekly treatments. Starting in April 1940, the medical staff began operating a bus service from Houck to Gallup which largely answered that problem. In reality, venereal disease was not a general or serious problem among the Navajos until after World War II when a virtual epidemic resulted from the return of males who had served in the military or wartime industry.[22]

21. The revolving fund was widely discussed in both tribal council minutes and official correspondence. For a summary of the program and a discussion of it by the dentist involved, see Harvey S. McDowell, "Dental Revolving Fund," *Navajo Medical News* 7 (15 January 1940): 16–17.

22. Salsbury Interview.

The success of the general medical program during the New Deal fell far short of the optimistic hopes of 1933. The reasons for the failures differ little from the problems encountered by other government efforts. The lack of adequate transportation, the language barrier, and the Navajos' attitudes largely frustrated Collier's goal of creating a medical program oriented around preventive techniques, just as these same factors frustrated the day school program. Because of these obstacles, Peter was forced to follow the main approach of his predecessors by curing existing illnesses as a stopgap measure. He succeeded, however, in broadening treatment beyond just school children. Navajo mothers, in particular, were much more apt to have their babies in hospitals by World War II than in 1933.

Unlike education and most of the other New Deal programs, however, medical care did not involve a direct clash with Navajo dissidents. There is no evidence, for example, of Navajos refusing treatment or withdrawing from hospitals as a means of protest against herd reduction or other causes. Even though many still preferred to use medicine men, this cultural trait offered no direct opposition to the medical program. Medicine men, indeed, saw nothing wrong with being cared for in hospitals themselves, especially if they believed that the quality of treatment had improved.

The most serious barrier to a more complete victory over the Navajos' health conditions was a simple lack of money. As was true of other programs, the medical allotments were largely dictated by tangible performance figures, such as the number of patient admissions, treatments, and hospital days, rather than need. Even though Peter was a capable administrator, skillful at the "bureaucratic game," and successful in gradually raising his budget, he still never won the financial support needed to treat existing illnesses, let alone launch a program of preventive medicine. Public health care for the Navajos was a purchasable commodity just as it was in the rest of American society, but Congress proved unwilling to pay the price.

# 10

# Morgan's Reconciliation with the Government

Morgan's inauguration as chairman of the new council on November 8, 1938, was the apex of his career as a Navajo leader. The installation ceremonies especially fitted Morgan's dedication to the white man's way. After a band concert before the council session, Superintendent Fryer called the body to order and ordered the incoming delegates escorted to their seats. Reverend James R. Helms, a long-time Morgan friend, gave the same invocation used in the U. S. Senate, the band played the "Star Spangled Banner," and Fryer administered the oath of office to the new council. The ceremony closed with Henry Taliman and Roy Kinsel, retiring chairman and vice chairman, presenting Morgan and Howard Gorman a copy of the Treaty of 1868 written on parchment and a gavel as symbols of office.[1]

The new chairman's inaugural address revealed his left-over bitterness against the government. He told the council, "I believe I have been abused in many ways already, not because of my crimes but because I have stood for the rights of my people." Stating that Navajos needed sympathetic treatment rather than "all kinds of threats," Morgan asked that Collier abide by earlier promises to end arbitrary rule, protect constitutional rights, and remove unsatisfactory officials.

Despite his rancor, Morgan showed a surprising willingness to forgive past grievances. He saw the recent election of a new council, "in a civilized way," as opening a new era in the tribe's history. Promising to employ his abilities "under the guidance of the Almighty hand of God," Morgan declared that he would cooperate with "our white neighbors if they are willing and ready to wipe off

1. "Proceedings of the Meeting of the Navajo Tribal Council," 7–8 November 1938, LAFRC, Box 72907, pp. 51–56, 64–75.

their war paint and bury their war hatchets." He warned, however, that "under no circumstances will I be a rubber stamp." In outlining his specific goals, Morgan pledged to protect tribal resources and to restore the Navajos' confidence in health and education programs. In closing he advised the council to "forget and put away all hatred and strive to work together."

The only important proposal brought before the new council concerned an executive committee which, if approved, would have made minor decisions when the council was not in session. The group was to be comprised of one delegate from each grazing district. Council members immediately objected that the executive committee would usurp their powers and become a pawn of the government. During the debate, Morgan suggested that day-to-day problems could best be handled locally by district councils. This proposal was eventually adopted unanimously by the delegates. Morgan remained firmly committed to district councils throughout his chairmanship.

Morgan was actually more antagonistic toward the government than his inaugural address indicated. For several months afterward he refused to spend any more time at Window Rock than was absolutely necessary to conduct business. Even when work remained the next day, he repeatedly spurned Fryer's invitations to spend the night at the tribal headquarters, preferring to drive long miles back to Farmington to stay with his family.[2] The new chairman had tried to insure that he would be free of official blandishments before his inauguration. His followers had pledged to help pay his living expenses, so he would not need any support from the government. The subscribers, however, failed to meet their commitments and Morgan was chronically short of funds while chairman.[3]

Morgan's financial problems were caused by his recent resignation as a missionary worker from the Christian Reformed Church following a long dispute. That act cost Morgan approximately $1,300 in annual salary plus a free house and travel expenses. Although he soon founded his own "native church" at Shiprock, the contributions of his small congregation never matched his former salary.[4]

2. Fryer Interview, 1971.
3. Gorman Interview.
4. For details on Morgan's dispute with the Christian Reformed Church, see the author's article, "J. C. Morgan: Navajo Apostle of Assimilation," *Prologue: The Journal of the National Archives* 4 (Summer 1972): 95.

Morgan's campaign to become chairman caused Chee Dodge to shift roles even before his rival's election. Knowing that Morgan would win, Dodge criticized reservation policies in an open letter to Collier on August 31, 1938. He charged that a continuation of grazing policies would bring "financial ruin for the Indian." Characteristically, however, Dodge qualified his remarks, suggesting that Collier and Ickes surely had solutions for Navajo problems which they should reveal immediately.[5]

More significantly, Dodge announced his withdrawal from personal participation in council proceedings after Morgan's election. Speaking to the final session of the Headmen's Council the day before his rival's inauguration, Dodge said that henceforth he would "just sit on the side and listen to their discussions and pay close attention to their work, but some time an opportunity will present itself, then I will make my position clean [clear?] and until that time I shall continue to sit aside and observe."[6] True to his word, Dodge never participated in council discussions while Morgan served as chairman, but during Morgan's first months in office, Dodge worked behind the scene to unseat the chairman. His actions differed from the total retirement of the headmen turned out of the council in 1938. In the Navajo expression, such leaders "went back to their hogans."

Morgan's first move toward reconciliation with the government grew out of an investigation of the Navajo administration by the Phelps-Stokes Fund in 1939. Founded in 1911, the New York philanthropic organization's main purpose was the study and improvement of race relations. Thomas Jesse Jones, Educational Director of the Fund since 1913, was responsible for initiating the investigation.[7] Increasingly bitter attacks by the Indian Rights Association on the Collier administration had climaxed on August 27, 1938, with a fifteen-page open letter to President Roosevelt.[8]

5. *Gallup Independent*, 31 August 1938, p. 1.

6. "Council Proceedings," 7–8 November 1938, p. 35.

7. A minister turned sociologist, Jones had studied the latter field under Franklin Henry Giddings at Columbia University where he received his Ph. D.in 1904. He first met Morgan at Hampton Institute in 1902. Afterward, Jones occasionally dealt with Indian affairs but in a secondary way. He seems to have occupied a peculiar role in minority reform efforts. While he leaned toward the self-help philosophy of Booker T. Washington, Jones also maintained friendly ties with reformers such as Collier who rejected self-help. See "Plan for the Study of the Navajo Reservation," 1 December 1938, LAFRC, Box 72947; *New York Times*, 5 January 1950, p. 21.

8. *New York Times*, 29 August 1938, p. 2.

Jones, an IRA member himself, believed that an impartial investigation would provide a more realistic appraisal of the Navajo situation and lower tempers on both sides. Willard Beatty, in discussing the impending investigation with Fryer, cautioned that Jones was an astute and fearless observer, but he was also a just person who would make a "frank and generous attempt to understand what we are doing and the conditions with which we have been confronted."[9]

Jones brought three co-workers with him when he arrived at Window Rock in January 1939. The best known was C. T. Loram, chairman of the Department of Race Relations at Yale. Like Jones, Loram had had considerable field experience in Africa and on Indian reservations, and Collier had lectured several times at Loram's seminars.[10] Harold B. Allen, an extension specialist, acted as the group's expert on agriculture and land use. Ella Deloria, a young Sioux who had studied anthropology at Columbia, was the fourth member.

The four investigators started with a general conference at Window Rock and individual interviews of senior Navajo Service personnel. Next Jones led his party into the field to discuss the reservation affairs with government workers, Navajo leaders, missionaries, traders, and off-reservation whites. In this phase they heard the emotional complaints about livestock reductions, the Fruitland controversy, and police intimidation.[11] After approximately one month, Jones, Loram, and Allen returned east, leaving Deloria on the reservation until June. Loram and Jones later revisited the reservation but only briefly.

*The Navajo Indian Problem*, published later in 1939, was a generally favorable assessment of Navajo administration. The 121-page report applauded such practices as instituting changes slowly and using Indian guidance in determining policy. Jones's group, however, criticized the lack of cooperation between the government and missionaries, serious weaknesses in agricultural extension and education, and overforcefulness in previous livestock reductions. Doubtlessly because of their past experience with able British colonial administrators, the authors complained about the quality of some district supervisors, range riders, and extension personnel, but they recognized that low budgets and civil service regulations made it

9. Beatty to Fryer, 15 December 1938, LAFRC, Box 72947.
10. Collier to Loram, 31 January 1936, Collier papers, YU.
11. "Impression of Talks," n.d., LAFRC, Box 72947.

difficult to recruit capable field employees. The investigators advised
that the Indian Service make careers more remunerative to attract
better personnel.[12]

Jones attempted to bring Fryer and Morgan into a better relationship shortly after he left the reservation. In mid-February 1939
Jones wrote Fryer that Morgan was agreeable to a conference and
that C. C. Brooks, superintendent of the Methodist mission at
Farmington, would be glad to arrange a meeting. Morgan's radio
address from KTGM three weeks later reflected a slight but significant shift in his previous attitudes. He now took the position that the
livestock program would have succeeded if Navajos had been given
alternative means of income and not arbitrarily forced to dispose of
livestock.[13] The following month Fryer reported that he and Morgan
had met and agreed on several new rehabilitation projects.[14]

Jones's peacemaking was only one of several factors which made
Morgan more amenable. Both Morgan and Fryer wanted the
Navajos to enjoy a greater prosperity through improved education,
health, and economic development. Although they might disagree on
the best means, the limited range of alternatives fostered compromise. In addition, Morgan's exclusion from the inner-workings of
Navajo administration had contributed to his earlier hostility. According to Fryer, Morgan's thinking at the time he became chairman
was dominated by his missionary goals and these provided a very
restricted perspective for assessing reservation policies. Morgan's
outlook broadened enormously once he took office and saw the full
range of problems and how the government was trying to solve
them. Morgan, in Fryer's words, "became one of the most responsible and intelligent of all the Navajo leaders with whom I . . .
worked."[15]

Morgan's relishment of the symbols of his new power also contributed to his cooperation with the government. He doubtlessly

12. Phelps-Stokes Fund, *The Navajo Indian Problem* (New York, 1939), pp. 32–37, 41–42.
Collier and Fryer often noted the problem, which was literally as old as the Indian
Service itself, but they could do little to correct it. Collier attempted to start a cadet training program in this same period by recruiting able young people and placing them in
field work for a few years until they became experienced enough to assume executive
positions. This policy was completely disrupted by World War II.

13. J. C. Morgan, "The Place of the Tribal Council in the Navajo Program," 7 March
1939 (radio transcript of KTGM), Van Valkenburgh papers, AHS.

14. Fryer to Jones, 12 April 1939, LAFRC, Box 72947.

15. Fryer Interview, 1970.

enjoyed presiding over council deliberations, appearing on KTGM, and conferring with Fryer on tribal questions. Prestige was a blandishment that Morgan could not resist. Certainly his conversion had nothing to do with monetary gain, for he was honest to a fault. Despite his financial problems after leaving the Christian Reformed Church, he never asked Fryer for any sort of undercover aid. Somewhat to the superintendent's surprise, Morgan did not seek patronage for his friends and relatives, although family and clan ties make nepotism even more acceptable to Navajos than whites.

Interestingly, a scandal involving Paul Palmer eliminated the Farmington lawyer as an antigovernment leader shortly after Morgan and Fryer began their meetings. In early May 1939, an audit of Palmer's records as city clerk of Farmington revealed a shortage of slightly over $2,000. The state comptroller suspended Palmer from office and reportedly gave him five days to return the money or face prosecution. Fryer, in a gloating letter to Collier, noted that the incident vindicated their past suspicions of Palmer's shady dealings. A week later the Farmington attorney paid all the shortages and officials dropped plans to press charges, but the incident effectively ended Palmer's career as an off-reservation critic.[16]

On May 13, the government enjoyed another victory when the United States District Court in Phoenix announced its decision on the test case involving the authority of the Indian Service to regulate grazing. On April 14, 1938, Navajos in the Leupp area were ordered to dispose of all surplus horses except ten head per family. A month later charges against twelve non-complying owners were filed, accusing the Indians of trespassing on the reservation because they ran more livestock than the grazing code permitted.

Guy Axeline, an attorney from Holbrook, Arizona, represented the accused Navajos at Phoenix. Palmer had visited Axeline several times before the trial to help prepare the case, but the relationship between the two lawyers and the role that each played in the suit are unclear. Obviously the legal fees came from Morgan's faction and the suit was not the friendly test case that Chee Dodge had wanted. In arguing for the defendants, Axeline admitted that Congress had authorized reservation superintendents to remove surplus livestock. The Holbrook attorney, however, contended that the Leupp Navajos

16. *Farmington Times Hustler*, 5 May 1939, p. 1, 12 May 1939, p. 11, and 2 June 1939, p. 1; Fryer to Collier, 5 May 1939, Office File of Commissioner John Collier, NA, RG 75.

actually used their livestock for a livelihood and the grazing regulations were, therefore, unenforcible. Furthermore Axeline argued that the language of the Treaty of 1868, especially one paragraph which forbade the cession of tribal land without the consent of three-fourths of the adult Navajos, also made the grazing regulations unlawful.[17]

William J. Barker, a Special Assistant to the Attorney General, presented the evidence against the first defendant and District Judge David W. Ling on April 24 then accepted Barker's motion that a summary judgment be made for all of the accused. Three weeks later Ling issued a decision which upheld the validity of the regulations and ordered the defendants to dispose of their surplus horses within thirty days. If the Indians failed to comply, Ling warned that he would order the livestock seized by federal marshals and place the Navajos in contempt of court.[18]

The dramatic second meeting of the tribal council under Morgan's chairmanship took place on May 15, only two days after Ling's decision. Most of Morgan's followers came to Window Rock filled with paranoid fears and suspicions and intent on resisting all government proposals, especially those related to herd reduction. Not only had they been caught off guard by the Phoenix decision, but they had no inkling that Morgan and Fryer had already agreed on most questions on the agenda.

The council quickly manifested its distrust when Fryer presented the first resolution. Previously he and Morgan had agreed to ask the delegates to accept a grant of $32,750 from the Farm Security Administration. Fryer planned to use the funds to purchase materials for seventy-five houses for returned students being located on irrigation projects, to complete additional facilities at the tribal fair grounds, and to provide rehabilitation and relief for the needy.[19] Although the FSA grant had no strings attached, Morgan's followers feared that acceptance of the program was a government trap or scheme. Taking the cavalier view that the FSA grant was too insignificant to worry about, Robert Martin demanded that the government give the tribe at least a half million dollars.

17. "Proceedings of the Meeting of the Navajo Council," 15–19 May 1939, General Correspondence Files, 1907–39, File 9659E, 1, NA, RG 75, pp. 82, 142–43.

18. *United States vs. Sadas Kizzie Bega*, E-202 (1939), LAFRC.

19. "Council Proceedings," 15–19 May 1939. For materials used in my discussion, see especially, pp. 12, 14–15, 23–25, 56–57.

While others emotionally criticized the proposal, Morgan stood quietly on the sidelines without revealing his own stand. Only John Curley of Ganado, a progovernment tribal judge and old nemesis of the Morgan faction, answered the objectors' arguments, but to no avail. Roger Davis, the Navajo missionary from Indian Wells, eventually moved that the resolution be tabled. At this, Morgan pointed out that such action would kill the proposal during the current session, implying that he wanted the resolution accepted. When the council vote on tabling resulted in a tie, Morgan declared that Davis's motion failed. The chairman then forced a council vote on a motion to reject the FSA grant. The defeat of this motion by a vote of 26 to 31 was not a positive endorsement, but Fryer wisely overlooked this discrepancy and spent the FSA money as planned.

The major issue before the council was, of course, the recent decision on the grazing regulations. William Barker appeared on the morning of the third day to explain the case. The government attorney emphasized that the main purpose of the case had been to test the grazing regulations and he stressed that Judge Ling's decision fully supported their legality. Even though the delegates showed considerable insight by their questions about whether the decision applied to Navajos living in New Mexico and if other types of livestock beside horses were affected, they were really more concerned about the "evilness" of the grazing regulations than legal matters. They repeatedly asked Barker who was behind the livestock reduction and why they should have to sell livestock. One delegate suggested that someone must want the Navajos' land for its mineral wealth and this explained the recent decision. Barker patiently responded that he had agreed to discuss just the legal facets of the case and he could not answer their other questions.

The only hope that Barker offered was the possibility of extending the time for removing the surplus horses in the Leupp area. When advised that the defendants could not readily sell their animals in thirty days, Barker suggested that Ling would likely grant additional time and Fryer agreed to forward a petition to the court if the council approved. In reality, the young superintendent was less sympathetic to the extension of time than he appeared.[20]

20. Fryer tried to obtain Collier's consent to make an example of those who were slow in selling their horses. Washington leaders, on the other hand, viewed the recent decision only as a test of the regulations and they were willing to overlook a strict enforcement of the time limits. In September 1939 Woehlke reported that Fryer seemed reconciled to the

Still unconvinced by Barker's explanation, the council invited Guy Axeline to discuss the case. The Holbrook attorney's appearance the next day, however, provided no additional hope for overturning the grazing regulations. Axeline advised the council that the best solution was for the government and tribal leaders to work out an informal compromise and to restore peace. In answering questions, the lawyer agreed that the decision could be appealed, but the legal expenses would be high and he showed little enthusiasm for reopening the case.[21] Most delegates seemed to sense that the grazing regulations were irrevocable.

The outcome of the council's own deliberations on herd reduction was surprisingly different from their initial attitude. On the evening after Barker's discussion, Fryer explained again the general livestock program which had been stalemated for nearly two years. It was not by coincidence that he used District 5, where the recently convicted Navajos lived, as an example of how reduction would work. Using multicolored blocks to represent different types of livestock, he launched into a detailed explanation of grazing capacity, base preferences, and maximum limits. Despite their fatigue from the hard benches, the council followed Fryer's comments very closely, frequently interrupting to ask questions and raise objections. An exchange between Fryer and John Riggs, a councilman from District 5, reemphasized the Navajos' difficulty in grasping the grazing program. Riggs questioned how Fryer could really know the number of livestock in the district. The Navajo explained that he had been at the roundups and dipping vats when government workers counted the stock, but he had never seen Fryer. Not realizing that figures could be transmitted from the field to Window Rock, Riggs

---

more moderate approach and now accepted the idea of no legal action except for those who still refused to comply with Ling's decision.

In 1940 the federal court in Arizona took action against two Navajos who defied the grazing code but were not involved in the first cases. One defendant, Little Hat, complied immediately and was not arrested. Kit Seally, a councilman, was judged guilty of contempt charges on August 29, 1940, and spent approximately a year in jail. A third case developed in 1943 when the court ordered Jake Yellowman arrested on contempt charges, but these were dropped three days later. See Woehlke to Collier, 8 September 1939, Collier papers, YU; *United States vs. Kit Seally*, Civ-35-Prescott (1940), Fryer to Albert Sames, 19 August 1941; *United States vs. Jake Yellowman*, Civ-27-Prescott (1943), LAFRC; Robert D. Jordan to writer, 11 May 1973.

21. My discussion of the rest of the session is based on "Council Proceedings," 15–19 May 1939, pp. 13, 44–45, 93–97, 111–17, 122–123, 131, 134, 162–65.

simply could not comprehend how Fryer could accurately discuss the situation unless he had personally counted the livestock himself.

The next morning Fryer presented a resolution to remove surplus horses. His proposal included a promise that the new reduction would not affect either sheep or cattle in 1939. The reaction of the council was mixed but surprisingly subdued. One delegate objected that the reduction of horses was a prelude to sheep sales. Another leader stated that he wanted the Phoenix decision appealed. Most of the council, however, seemed less adamant after having some time to consider Barker's remarks. Roger Davis, in a pivotal part of the debate, condemned past herd reduction because government workers had browbeat the Navajos, but he expressed his willingness "to back up this thing if the people who started it would say they made a mistake." Fryer evidently missed the import of Davis's statement. But when Davis pressed the demand more emphatically, Fryer dramatically apologized, stating that the government had made "many, many mistakes" and had pushed the Navajos too rapidly. He maintained, however, that his men had always had tribal interest at heart.

The superintendent's willingness to apologize for past mistakes had limits. After learning that some Navajos interpreted his remarks to mean that he regretted the suit against the Leupp area residents, Fryer angrily demanded that those delegates who had advised defiance of the grazing code should also stand up and apologize for getting fellow tribesmen into trouble. "I am freely admitting all our errors and regretting those mistakes," he admonished the council, "but I think there should be a burial of the hatchets on both sides."

Fryer's apology-denunciation and Axeline's pessimistic comments on appealing the Phoenix decision broke the council's resistance to the sale of surplus horses. A new mood dominated the delegates on the final day of the council when they discussed a revised resolution. In accordance with Morgan's preference for local decision making, the measure now stipulated that council members would help district supervisors during the roundups, assist in bringing the horses to corrals for branding and sales, and cooperate in the eventual distribution of grazing permits. In an amazing reversal of attitudes, the council approved the horse sales by a vote of 45 to 6.

Equally surprising, many delegates who started the session opposing the government now advocated reconciliation. Roger Davis and other speakers at the close of the session stated that they had done everything possible to fight off reduction, but they had lost. Now that both sides had admitted their mistakes, Davis advised councilmen to return to their people with no ill feelings toward anyone. He urged government officials not to reprove Navajos for resisting the grazing program or to ridicule them after their defeat.

Almost hidden in the long deliberations over the grazing controversy was the council's action in launching an "Age of Enterprise." The authorization of several tribal enterprises marked an important shift in Navajo affairs and the businesses became the hallmark of Morgan's chairmanship. Fryer spelled out the reasons for this new program of self-help by warning delegates that funds from New Deal emergency programs were drying up and that they must look to other means of rehabilitation. The founding of tribal businesses would provide new jobs and produce many items that Navajos and the government had previously purchased from off-reservation sources.

Morgan and Fryer had already agreed that the proposals for starting new business enterprises should take two forms. The first resolution merely asked for the group's permission to establish portable sawmills, tanneries, canneries, and other small firms and authorization for the superintendent and chairman to negotiate government loans up to $20,000 for each business founded. The delegates approved this measure without any debate. A second resolution requested specific approval of borrowing $50,000 from the government to expand an existing sawmill operated by the Soil Conservation Service. Three percent interest would be charged against the loan and it would be paid back from the sale of lumber during the next five years.

Exploiting the magnificent timber stand on the Fort Defiance Plateau had been a problem for many years. Despite numerous plans and attempts by private firms and the government to set up sawmills, all previous efforts had failed. Not only did the tribe need the revenues from the lumber, but the overly mature trees eventually died, toppled, and rotted without benefiting anyone. Arguments based on these considerations, plus the promise of wages, led the council to approve, after a heated but relatively short debate, the first formal tribal enterprise in its history. The group also authorized a $7,500 loan to build a small flour mill at the Round Rock irrigation project in District 11.

A discussion of the law and order code which Ickes had issued in 1937 as a substitute for the abortive constitution brought on bitter comments from the delegates. Numerous councilmen spoke about the existing regulations and unfair treatment by police and judges from first-hand experience. Fully one-half of the council raised their hands when one speaker asked how many had been jailed in recent years. Stewart read a telegram from Collier which recommended that the council petition Ickes for a revision of the law and order code. Seconding Collier's suggestion, Fryer admitted that the regulations were difficult for the police and judges to interpret and enforce. He advised that Morgan appoint a committee to review the code, simplify its language, and translate it into Navajo. The council finally terminated the long session by resolving to establish such a committee.[22]

After the adjournment, Fryer expressed his delight at winning the council's endorsement of the horse sales and at ending his long feud with his former opponents. The meeting, he wrote Jones soon afterward, "was completely successful and resulted in a reconciliation of all groups." Fryer added that Morgan had pledged his cooperation and made several appeals for unity during the recent session.[23]

Morgan's own reaction was guarded. In a newspaper article discussing the council, he wrote that "more constructive business" resulted than from any previous meetings and he believed that the tribe looked "forward to better things." The chairman, however, expressed dissatisfaction that the defendants in the Phoenix case had not been allowed to testify in their own behalf. He cited land, schools, and oil leases as important matters which needed attention at the next council meeting.[24] Morgan's fitful rapprochement had moved from secret cooperation to limited public cooperation.

Interpreting the abrupt change in the council's attitude is somewhat hazardous. Without question, however, the Phoenix decision was a major blow to council delegates and tribesmen at large. Neither

22. For some reason Morgan never became interested in carrying out the revisions. Despite pressure from the council, he did not appoint a committee until much later and apparently nothing was done about its recommendations.

23. Fryer to Jones, 25 May 1939, LAFRC, Box 72947.

24. *Farmington Times Hustler*, 26 May 1939, p. 1.

cajolery nor threats by officials had earlier stopped the Navajos' fight against the livestock program. Morgan and his lieutenants had always convinced tribesmen that the grazing regulations were illegal. When the prestige of the court was brought to bear, however, Navajos suddenly lost all sense of legal impunity and faced the threat of jail sentences. Navajos would continue to despise the grazing regulations, but most simply gave up the struggle once they learned about the court action.[25] Only the strongest anti-government areas continued to resist subsequent livestock reduction.

Cultural factors also help to explain the changed attitudes of the council. Ironically, missionary Roger Davis best illustrated such forces when he pointedly asked Fryer to apologize for past mistakes midway through the session. Davis's request had more grounding in the Navajo traditions of asking an evil person to recant and the desire for interpersonal harmony than it did in a Christian confessional.

Fryer hastily started the program to remove the surplus horses. Because the district supervisors were meeting at Window Rock during the May council session, Fryer kept them over to plan the operations, which started immediately. Five weeks later, roundups and sales had removed 1,700 head of horses from the Leupp and Tuba City areas. Scott Preston and Julius Begay, councilmen from the latter region, actively cooperated with district personnel.[26]

Despite some resistance and prices of only two dollars per head, the removals met with far more success than those attempted two years earlier. Fryer reported in early August that 6,000 horses had been delivered to buyers from roundups covering only slightly more than one-half of the reservation.[27] By the time the drive ended in late 1939, over 10,000 horses—or approximately one-fourth of the total—had been sold.

The success of the horse sales aroused much criticism of Morgan during the summer of 1939 and caused him to demonstrate a strong ambivalence about his new role of semicooperation. He remained completely devoted to assimilation as a panacea for Indian problems. On July 7 he spoke to a missionary conference at Ganado and denounced government encouragement of Indian dances and re-

25. Mr. Zweifel Interview.
26. *Gallup Independent*, 26 June 1939, p. 1.
27. *Farmington Times Hustler*, 4 August 1939, p. 8.

ligious activities.[28] A month later he wrote a newspaper article in which he came close to totally renouncing the current removal of horses, charging that officials had not allowed council members to participate and had taken away livestock needed for subsistence. Indians themselves should decide how much livestock they should keep. "JUSTICE," he concluded, "is asleep or gone fishing that she does not hear the pleadings of the Navajo people."[29]

Morgan's attempts to evade responsibility for the horse sales during the same period brought a strong reaction from one of the priests at St. Michaels Mission. In a memo assessing tribal affairs, one of the Franciscans complained that Morgan was attempting to blame tribal discontent on others when the real fault was his own. The chairman, the memo continued, had never been concerned about solutions for his people and his "apparent interest in land, stock, and school matters is but a cloak under which he aspires to the friendship and good will of his tribesmen whom he hopes to Christianize according to his own ideas."

The priest's comments on the cooperation between Morgan and Fryer were equally pointed. Many Navajos, according to the memo, suspected that the superintendent had secretly placed Morgan on the government payroll and had stopped contributing funds to Morgan. Fryer had also given Morgan free rein to carry out his bigoted missionary aims. Summarizing his assessment of the situation, the author stated: "Chee Dodge has been the one great leader of the Navajos in the present generation; Fryer knows that; but he won't have Chee, because he is too shrewd for him and not pliable enough. His [Fryer's] speaking of looking for leadership is all BOSH. He is not seeking leaders but men he can lead."[30] Morgan's replacement of Dodge as dominant tribal leader had clearly rekindled the old feud between Protestants and Catholics.

Though Morgan no longer led an anti-government movement, natural forces also contributed to the Navajos' resistance to the horse sales. A severe drought gripped the reservation in the summer of 1939; by August conditions were so bad that newspapers claimed the

28. Ibid., 7 July 1939, p. 4.

29. *Gallup Independent*, 16 August 1939, p. 5 (Section 2).

30. "Memorandum," Fall of 1939, St. Michaels Mission. Father Emanuel Trockur's name appears at the top of the memo, but I suspect that the author was Father Berard Haile, based on the writing style and sentiments expressed.

drought was the worst in fifteen years. Fryer stated at the time that
the reservation ranges and corn crop had dried up, the reservoirs
which stored surface runoff were empty, and the stock were beginning to suffer.[31]

Even though the drought was an ideal time to dispose of surplus
horses to preserve the remaining supply of water and grass for productive livestock, many Navajos took just the opposite view. They
seemed to believe that somehow their horses offered a safeguard
against the weather problem. Not surprisingly, the strongest protests
against the horse sales came from the Shiprock area. When officials
reported major successes in the Tuba City and Leupp areas in June,
only 300 horses had been turned in at Shiprock, and District 12 never
met its quota. With the Phoenix decision, however, only someone of
unusual militancy could lead opposition to the livestock program.
Julius Bainbridge, Jr., a chapter official at Toadlena and ex-convict,
emerged in late September as chairman of a vocal group in District
12 known as the "Grievance Committee."

Mrs. Dan Ward, wife of a range rider, has described the Bainbridge
of 1939 as a person who opposed everything. He criticized white
government workers because they did nothing to help the Navajos,
but he also had little use for other tribesmen who attacked the government. After hearing him at protest meetings, she concluded that
agitation made him feel self-important and nothing else did.[32]

Navajo hostility to the revival of stock reduction also manifested
itself in an increase of witchcraft. A little understood aspect of tribal
religion, witchcraft normally remained hidden from whites. Anthropologist Clyde Kluckhohn has suggested that the Navajo are
susceptible to the dark occult for several reasons. Because they lack
a scientific understanding of illness, death, and crop failures, witchcraft provides answers for these and other natural disasters. Sin-
gling out a powerful medicine man or an eccentric older Navajo and
gossiping about his possible misuse of spiritual powers is also a means
of transferring aggression. Normally Navajos do not translate their
fears into violence, but witchcraft becomes dangerous when the person thought to be a witch is held responsible for someone's death or

31. *Gallup Independent*, 2 August 1939, 1; Fryer to X. Vigeant, 9 August 1939, File 53240,
1939, Navajo, 720, NA, RG 75.

32. Elizabeth Ward, *No Dudes, Few Woman, Life with a Navajo Range Rider* (Albuquerque,
1954), pp. 146–47.

serious misfortune. Not infrequently the terrified survivors will brutally kill the suspected witch. Both before and during the New Deal, the government did not know about or intervene in such incidents until after the murder.[33]

Deeply fearful of losing what little security they had, many Navajos responded to the livestock reduction by increased gossiping about witches. This seems evident in one Navajo's statement that "witches are lots more active, since the stock program."[34] Certainly Navajo Service officials had long believed that powerful medicine men such as Tall Man of Teec-Nos-Pos had used their reputation as witches to intimidate Navajos into opposition to the government.

An extraordinary case of witchcraft in District 4 at Piñon in early 1939 confirmed officials' suspicions. The background of Ben Wetherill, the district supervisor, made him uniquely vulnerable to the medicine of a local shaman named Glo-en-zani. Wetherill was the son of John and Louisa Wetherill, early traders at Kayenta. Like many traders' offspring, Ben spent most of his childhood playing with Navajo youngsters and he learned to speak Navajo with such fluency that he thought and dreamed in the language. Much later as an adult, the Navajo Service appointed Wetherill to head District 4 where his linguistic skills seemingly made him ideal for dealing with Indians in the highly remote Piñon-Black Mesa country.

In August 1938, Glo-en-zani and several other Navajos conducted a chant outside the Piñon day school yard to witch all the district employees, including the local Navajo judge and policeman.[35] Some time in January 1939 Glo-en-zani entered Wetherill's yard at night and drew a "strange kind of cross" in the sand in front of the house. Already informed about the chant, Wetherill recognized the hex symbol when he left his home the next morning and identified Glo-en-zani as the culprit. Had Wetherill not been so completely immersed in Navajo psychology, he could have dismissed the sign from his mind. His reaction, however, was the same as any Navajo who believed himself witched. He agonized over something awful happening to himself and experienced horrible nightmares in Navajo.

33. Clyde Kluckhohn, *Navajo Witchcraft* (Boston, 1962), *passim*.

34. Ward, *No Dudes*, p. 121.

35. Ben Wetherill notes, 18 January 1939, Ben Wetherill papers, MNA. There seems to be confusion about the spelling and pronunciation of Glo-en-zani's name. I found it spelled Goni or Glo-en-zi.

During the coming weeks Glo-en-zani terrified the entire district. A Navajo named Clah reported that the medicine man had visited his hogan and inquired about the children and grandchildren of a progovernment neighbor, evidently to identify them as prospective victims. Two days later Clah's own grandson suddenly took sick and died. Glo-en-zani then became quite open about his power, taking credit for the deaths of several children and claiming that he had caused an accident in which a horse bucked off the local policeman and broke his leg. The shaman bragged that a similar fate awaited any other officer assigned to the district.

Fryer first learned of these events in the spring of 1939 when Wetherill phoned the superintendent's office and urgently requested that he and several medicine men be allowed to bring Glo-en-zani to Window Rock before the Piñon Indians killed him. Fryer consented to meet the district supervisor and his group the next morning.

When the Piñon Navajos trouped into Window Rock early the following day, Fryer took a seat at one end of a conference table, the menancing Glo-en-zani sat at the other end, and Wetherill and the medicine men nervously spread out along the remaining two sides. The accusers "began recounting the things that Glo-en-zani had done which were bad and which made him a witch, and which were of such a character that he had somehow to be destroyed, or he had to recant."[36] The shaman seemed unimpressed by the charges and he showed no inclination to confess anything.

Instead, the confident witch used the meeting to frighten the Piñon group even more. One technique for witching is to collect something from the victim's body such as hair or fingernail clippings or an object that he has touched. It had rained the previous night and Fryer noticed during the discussion that Glo-en-zani periodically reached under the table and picked up mud that had dried and fallen off the medicine men's shoes. A hair dropped on the table and he eagerly grabbed it, too. After a medicine man nervously spilled tobacco rolling a cigarette, Glo-en-zani reached out and carefully swept the flecks into the hand that held the mud and hair. Without ever interrupting their denunciations, the Indians unconsciously edged their chairs away from the table. Finally Wetherill, the medicine men, and the interpreter were backed against the wall, leaving only Fryer and Glo-en-zani still seated at the table.

36. Fryer Interview, 1970.

How to deal with the recalcitrant witch perplexed everyone. Sending him back to Piñon would result in his death and yet he had committed no punishable crime, at least by white standards. Finally Wetherill suggested that Fryer place Glo-en-zani under "protective custody." The superintendent sent him off to the Fort Defiance jail with the firm advice that he decide whether he wanted to be murdered at Piñon or recant. The next morning the shaman sent word that he wanted to see Fryer and the entire group reassembled in the conference room at ten o'oclock. Glo-en-zani confessed to all the charges and asked that he be allowed to undergo a recantation ceremony. The rites, held later at Piñon, required the medicine man to show the sincerity of his recantation by holding a burning knot of pitch in his hands and, without dropping it, putting out the flame by spitting on it. He managed this central part of the ceremony successfully, but he was eventually accused of witchcraft again. Doubtlessly, both the first instance of Glo-en-zani's witchcraft and his subsequent activities were a manifestation of the tensions caused by livestock reduction.

Resistance to the horse sales continued in the Shiprock and Piñon areas and influenced the council meeting of November 20, 1939.[37] The discussions indicated that Navajo leaders' attitudes had shifted significantly since the last council. In his opening address Morgan expressed his disappointment at the failure of most councilmen to assist in the horse sales. He pointed out that the council had originally rejected an executive committee in favor of each district organizing its own council to settle problems and cooperate with field officials and he admonished the delegates who had shirked this duty.

The council members were already in a chastened and vindictive mood because of criticisms they had received from constituents about the horse sales. When asked to approve a resolution authorizing Morgan and Gorman to accept a relief grant of $4,000 and any additional allotments of a similar nature, many delegates stated that past government duplicity warranted a rejection of any delegation of power. William Goodluck, an unusually frank councilman, best revealed the troubled attitude of his colleagues. He maintained that tribesmen would reject giving Morgan more control because they believed "he had been taken over on the other side and does not

37. "Proceedings of the Meeting of the Navajo Tribal Council," 20–21 November 1939, File 9659, E, 1936, Navajo, 54, NA, RG 75. See especially pp. 3, 19, 23, 54, 82, 88.

represent the people." Goodluck also stated that his followers no longer respected his own authority and he was afraid to support the resolution. Despite attempts by Roger Davis and others to pacify the critics, the council voted down the resolution by an overwhelming margin.

The council, however, completely reversed their decision the following day. Albert Grorud, an attorney who worked for the Senate Indian Affairs Committee, attended the session and both he and Fryer pleaded with the delegates to reconsider the matter. The superintendent warned that the Navajos faced a severe winter because of the drought and would need whatever relief funds the government could provide. With little debate, the council then accepted the resolution. A proposal to force livestock owners to remove illegal fences on tribal land provoked a vigorous debate which resulted in the decision to table the resolution.

Soon after the council adjourned, a dispute broke out between Fryer and officers of the New Mexico Association on Indian Affairs.[38] Julius Bainbridge's earlier visit to Santa Fe in September 1939 to protest about reservation policies had prompted Amelia White, an NMAIA leader, to wire Thomas Jesse Jones that the Navajos believed the government had violated the council's resolution on horse sales and she requested that Jones conduct an investigation of the problem.[39] Several members of the NMAIA afterward visited the reservation in October to check on relief measures. Margretta Dietrich, president of the group, interviewed Fryer at Window Rock while White toured outlying areas. After their return to Santa Fe, the NMAIA seemed satisfied with Fryer's drought relief preparations

38. The controversy between the NMAIA and Fryer seems inconsistent with the group's earlier lobbying in behalf of the New Mexico boundary bill and the strong support given the Navajo program by Oliver La Farge, head of the American Association on Indian Affairs of which the NMAIA was a local unit. In reality, NMAIA members held grudges against Collier dating back to 1931 when his attacks on Herbert J. Hagerman forced the latter's removal as commissioner to the Navajos. NMAIA members at that time burned Collier in effigy in the Santa Fe Plaza. They were also strong Republicans and much opposed to the New Deal. According to Moris Burge, these factors, more than any real complaints against the Navajo administration, prompted NMAIA attacks on Fryer. Burge to writer, 25 May 1973.

39. Jones to White, 21 September 1939, and Jones to Collier, 21 September 1939, File 53240, Navajo, 720, NA, RG 75. Amelia White was a wealthy New York heiress who moved to Santa Fe in 1923 and devoted the remainder of her long life to a variety of civic and cultural pursuits, including Indian reform and promotion of native arts and crafts. She died in 1972 at the age of ninety-four. See *Santa Fe New Mexican*, 8 August 1972.

except they advised the creation of "long range means to keep such events from happening again."[40]

Disgruntled by the indecisive action of the council, Bainbridge led a party of twenty-four tribesmen from District 12 to Santa Fe in early December. A second group of seventeen Indians from Mariano Lake, east of Gallup, appeared five days later. The Bainbridge party's complaints centered on herd reduction and not inadequate relief. Indeed, their charges covered the broader and typical issues since 1933—false arrests of dissidents, the need to restore the old six agencies, government duplicity at Fruitland, and a return to unregulated grazing.[41] Bainbridge, in short, had inherited both Morgan's role as the leading agitator and his most productive issues.

However, on January 4, 1940, Dietrich issued a statement to newspapers charging that no relief was being given to the Navajos in many areas and tons of supplies remained undistributed in a Gallup warehouse. The Indians, she further claimed, had been reduced to eating the inner bark of trees and breaking into government warehouses to avoid starvation. She said that her information came from a two-week investigation by an unnamed informant.[42]

Dietrich's indictment of Fryer for callously ignoring Navajo deprivation made front page headlines, but her allegations fell far short of the truth. Fryer had started soliciting extra relief funds the previous August when he realized that the failure of normal late summer rains would continue the drought into the winter. After a survey of local conditions, he flew to Washington to obtain more relief work and surplus commodities. He increased the allotment for wage work in 1940 to $500,000 and he secured $22,000 for direct relief and $10,000 to purchase unmarketable livestock.[43]

Fryer's quest for surplus commodities was delayed because he was told to negotiate with Surplus Commodities Corporation officials at the state level. His subsequent interviews with the state directors of

40. Ibid., 6 October 1939, p. 4.

41. "Notes of Meeting, Dec. 7, and 8, 1939. . . ," File 53240, 1939, Navajo, 720, NA, RG 75.

42. *Albuquerque Journal*, 4 January 1940, p. 2, and 6 January 1940, p. 2.

43. Fryer to X. Vigeant, 9 August 1939, File 53240, 1939, Navajo, 720, NA, RG 75; *Gallup Independent*, 21 August 1939, p. 1; Woehlke to Collier, 29 August 1939, Collier papers, YU; *Gallup Independent*, 18 September 1939, p. 1. Because of recent cuts in funds, the increase to $500,000 for wage work was still only half the amount available the previous year.

New Mexico and Arizona proved disappointing, for various obstacles destroyed any chance of help at the state level. He next applied to the Farm Security Administration for wheat and corn and that agency sent a sizeable amount of grain to the tribe. Soon afterward Collier convinced the Surplus Commodities Corporation that it should bend its regulations to send supplies directly to the reservation instead of through the state directors.[44] Fryer had dispatched large shipments of relief commodities in October, November, and December to distribution points throughout the reservation and New Mexico checkerboard.

The disparity between Dietrich's allegations and Fryer's repeated assurances that Navajos had received tons of commodities and were enjoying an open winter led Collier to send Allen Harper, a trusted field representative, to investigate the relief program. Harper found himself involved in a separate controversy when he arrived in the Southwest. Bainbridge, Nalgot Yazzie, and others in the Grievance Committee had held a new series of meetings in January 1940, which attracted large crowds in District 12, including ten members of the tribal council. The protestors defiantly opposed branding horses, fearing that this was a trick to force them to sell their sheep. During the meetings, police attempted to arrest two Navajos who had ignored orders to brand their horses. Both men resisted arrest and the police made no attempt to bring them in by force. In keeping with their militancy, about forty Navajos appeared on January 23, 1940, at Shiprock to demonstrate against the attempted arrests and the current trial of four Indians accused of violating the branding order.

Despite the coverage the Shiprock confrontation received in the newspapers, it was more a scuffle than a rebellion. The tribal court tried and convicted the four defendants, but the judges gave them suspended sentences on their promise to brand their horses.[45] Two of the four then escaped, probably with the aid of the crowd, and they remained at large several months until rearrested.[46] The dissidents conferred at some length among themselves and with the district

44. Fryer to Collier, 9 October 1939, "Press Release," 18 October 1939, and H. C. Albin and Collier, "Memorandum of Agreement," 27 October 1939, File 53240, 1939, Navajo, 720, NA, RG 75.

45. *Gallup Independent*, 25 January 1940, p. 1, and 27 January 1940, p. 1; *Albuquerque Journal*, 25 January 1940, pp. 1–2.

46. *Gallup Independent*, 13 July 1940, p. 1; Fred W. Croxen to Kitty Black Horse, 15 May 1940, Chavez papers, UA.

supervisor before dispersing. According to ensuing Navajo testimony, the only violence occurred when Fred Croxen and his police became overly excited and had to be restrained.[47] Compared to the dramatic meeting at Teec-Nos-Pos in 1937, the Shiprock episode was not very explosive. Certainly it remains far less vivid in Navajo memory than the earlier meeting.

Despite this, Collier believed that the situation was serious enough to order Harper to abandon his investigation of relief temporarily and look into the Shiprock affair. After conferring with Thomas Dodge and Father Anselm at St. Michaels, the field representative spent two days at Shiprock interviewing Morgan, the protest leaders, and the district supervisor. In reality, Harper could do little but listen, for Fryer was on vacation during the altercation and did not return until Harper had visited District 12.[48]

Caught in a crossfire by the Shiprock troubles, Morgan reacted evasively. When asked to visit Shiprock to help settle the disturbance on January 23, the chairman refused, recommended that the demonstrators obey the law, and then left town "on previously scheduled business." A day or so later, he released a statement blaming the incident on the district supervisor's arbitrary actions and advising the official to "quit and leave the country." Morgan stressed that he had not been secretly behind the protest as rumored.[49]

Morgan's real feelings were revealed in a letter to Chavez a month later. Acrimoniously, the chairman blamed recent unrest on Bainbridge whom he denounced as a "law breaker." The ex-convict, Morgan complained, had falsely told Navajos that their relief supplies were poisoned and that they should fight against the tribal council. Morgan also expressed dissatisfaction with "Chee Dodge and a few others who have been trying to interfer with the machinery [of government]." The chairman obviously suspected that Chee was somehow behind Bainbridge's agitation.[50]

Morgan's subsequent actions caused him to become firmly identified as a progovernment leader. He remained convinced that consultations between councilmen and their constituents could minimize

47. Denetsongbega, "Statement on Events at Shiprock, January 23, 1940," 17 May 1940, Chavez papers, UA.

48. *Gallup Independent*, 2 February 1940, p. 8.

49. *Albuquerque Journal*, 25 January 1940, pp. 1–2; *Gallup Independent*, 27 January 1940, p. 1.

50. Morgan to Chavez, 19 March 1940, Chavez papers, UA.

the Navajos' discontent if the government, police and tribal courts would not intervene. Stubbornly adhering to this belief, he joined with Gorman, Thomas Dodge, and others to conduct several meetings with District 12 residents in February and March, 1940. The leaders tried to allay opposition to horse branding and sales by organizing local committees to determine equitably how many horses each family actually needed for farming and transportation.[51]

The meetings produced only limited cooperation from moderates, but they resulted in a new wave of charges that Morgan had sold out to the government. What stung Morgan even more was Bainbridge's claim that he alone could be recognized as spokesman for District 12, rather than Morgan or the local councilmen. Already convinced that Bainbridge was an utterly disreputable person, the chairman's indignation at this challenge to his authority made him become even more defensive and pushed him further toward the government.

The results of the misunderstandings over the relief program and the Shiprock disturbance were indecisive. District 12 remained steadfastly opposed to the livestock program. To forestall NMAIA complaints in the ensuing months, Fryer carefully publicized the exact quantities of relief supplies distributed each month until midsummer of 1940 when all but permanent recipients were taken off the rolls. Harper's report on the relief scandal almost completely exonerated Fryer. The main suggestion for improvement was that the government should have adopted policies which would overcome the Navajos' reluctance to accept charity by starting work programs and loans of wool to rug weavers instead of an outright dole. Probably the most important occurrence during the winter was the large amount of snow and rain which fell in February and March on parts of the reservation. The moisture partially broke the drought and resulted in a fairly prosperous year in 1940.

Harper's report caused a deepening of the feud between Collier and the NMAIA. The investigator mentioned that he had interviewed Dietrich and asked her to identify specific Navajo families who had not received relief, but she refused to respond or name the source of her information. Harper concluded that Dietrich's real grudge was not against the relief program, but "she was aiming to make capital out of the consequences of the drought by leveling

51. *Farmington Times Hustler*, 29 March 1940, p. 1.

criticism against the Administration."[52] Collier later learned that Dietrich's source was Mrs. Franc Newcomb, a trader's wife and author, who had opposed the government since 1933. The commissioner was certain that Newcomb's "rather hysterical" allegation was another of many critics' attempts to discredit him. In an exchange of letters with Dietrich in early 1940, Collier politely but firmly rejected her complaints as false.

In April 1940, the NMAIA hired Maria Chabot, a student of Indian arts and crafts and colonial administration, to investigate Navajo affairs. In conducting her research, Chabot became involved in a controversy within a controversy. She spent six weeks in May and June, 1940, traveling 2,000 miles while visiting 150 hogans and interviewing traders, missionaries, and government workers. She then appeared at Window Rock and asked Fryer to open his files. He refused to cooperate until he knew how much staff time would be required to answer her questions and what Chabot planned to do with the information.[53] Dietrich contacted Collier, but he did not reverse Fryer's decision.

As might be expected, Chabot's report, published in August 1940, was decidedly hostile toward Navajo administration. Although she claimed impartiality, her information was largely drawn from disaffected interviewees and she made little attempt to balance this with data justifying government programs. The chief contribution of her study was to express the bewilderment and fear that many Navajos still experienced over livestock reduction. Chabot's pamphlet apparently ended the NMAIA's involvement in Navajo affairs during the remainder of the New Deal.[54]

While the NMAIA and the government feuded during mid-1940, significant new developments in the herd reduction program took place. District personnel at that time renewed the long-delayed distribution of grazing permits to livestock owners. The work proceeded in two phases. Field workers first passed out forms to each owner which contained his name, the maximum limit for his particular grazing district, and the number of livestock he was allotted, based

52. Harper to Collier, 14 February 1940, Collier papers, YU.

53. Fryer to Collier, 8 July 1940, File 53240, 1939, Navajo, 720, NA, RG 75.

54. Maria Chabot, *Urgent Navajo Problems, Observations and Recommendations Based on a Recent Study by the New Mexico Association on Indian Affairs* (Santa Fe, 1940).

on his past dipping record and horse tally. The head of the family was supposed to check the figures for accuracy and complain if anything was in error. Workers carried out the second phase by issuing the actual grazing permits which were printed on official-looking safety paper.

The Navajos' response to the grazing permits varied greatly from one district to another. In Districts 9 and 12, which had still not completed their horse sales, only a few Navajos accepted the permits. The Navajo reaction in another ten districts was mixed, but a strong majority opposed the permits. By June 1940, Fryer claimed that six districts (3, 7, 8, 14, 17, 18) had completed the distribution. District 17 had even drawn up a plan for range use that Fryer considered ideal.

The variation in the Navajos' reactions was based on both intangible and practical considerations. In districts where supervisors and range riders had developed rapport with local leaders, the permits caused little dissension. The success in District 17, for example, grew out of several years of harmonious relations between District Supervisor Alvin Jonas and the local residents. Another factor was the size of the maximum limit assigned to a district. The northeast corner of the reservation and District 4 at Piñon were severely overgrazed and low maximum limits frustrated field workers' efforts to win cooperation. Years of antigovernment efforts by Morgan's faction further contributed to the areas' animus.

Because the distribution involved face-to-face confrontations, the issuance of grazing permits was a dangerous time for supervisors and range riders. They were supposed to deliver the permits personally, explain the figures to the owners, and obtain their signatures. Some Navajos bluntly refused to accept the papers or defiantly tore them up in the presence of the field workers. The less courageous managed to be away when field workers visited their hogans and the district personnel usually stuck the permits in the door and left.

Somewhat surprisingly, Navajos seem to have attacked only one government worker during the tense period. A range rider named Charlie Cole, stationed in the northeast corner of the reservation, was on his way back from an unsuccessful foray to hand out permits when four Indians on horseback ambushed him. As seems characteristic of the Navajos, the four men did not kill Cole, but they gave him a severe clubbing, took his horse and the grazing permits, and warned him to leave the reservation. After walking many miles back to his home, the battered Cole decided that a salary of one hundred dollars per month should not stand in the way of following such sagacious advice and he promptly resigned.[55]

Navajos usually confined themselves to threats and impassioned speeches. Todechini Tso, described as a "tall, thin old man with a scraggling mustache," orated against the livestock program at sings and protest meetings around Sheep Springs. After Tso told his followers that Dan Ward, the local range rider, must be killed, Ward swore out a complaint against Tso which resulted in the old man spending several months in the Shiprock jail. Without a leader, overt opposition at Sheep Springs quickly diminished.[56]

The fears engendered by the distribution of grazing permits created a troubled background for the council's four-day session on June 3-6, 1940. Morgan cleverly arranged the agenda to avoid herd reduction and to take up subjects which satisfied his puritanical impulses. Despite strong objections, the chairman forced the delegates to discuss the Navajos' growing use of peyote and the spread of the Native American Church, the national Indian religious organization which mingles Christian and native rites for peyote users.[57] The religious cult started among the Navajos in 1935 or shortly before in the area between Shiprock and Aneth, Utah. The first Navajo priests of the Native American Church received their initiation from the Utes and visiting Oklahoma Indians at Towaoc on the Southern Ute reservation north of Shiprock. Soon several Navajos could conduct peyote ceremonies and by 1940 the movement had spread south to Tohatchi, Crystal, Fort Defiance, Sawmill, and Window Rock, and as far west as Navajo Mountain.[58]

David F. Aberle, who investigated the peyote movement between 1949 and 1953, concluded that the initial use of peyote was chiefly the result of deprivation suffered by owners who lost sheep and goats in the 1933 and 1934 reductions. The sale of horses in 1939 and 1940

55. Ward, No Dudes, pp. 77–78.

56. Ibid., pp. 85–86.

57. The amount of literature on peyote and the Native American Church is much too great to list here. General studies include Weston LaBarre, The Peyote Cult (New Haven, 1938), and James S. Slotkin, The Peyote Religion: A Study in Indian-White Relations (Glencoe, Illinois, 1956). For information dealing with the Navajos, see David B. Aberle, The Peyote Religion among the Navaho (New York, 1966).

58. Aberle, Peyote Religion, p. 109.

played a far less important role in attracting followers to the cult. Aberle also determined that the areas where peyote was first used still tended to be the strongholds of the religion. District 9 or the Aneth area, for example, had approximately eighty percent peyotists in the early 1950s, while four western districts had only negligible membership in the cult.[59]

Morgan seems to have been unaware of the existence of the peyote cult until a few months before the council meeting. In late March 1940, he wrote Chavez that Oklahoma Indians had introduced peyote "within the last year or so." Morgan added that he had learned of this only recently and he waited for confirmation of the rumors before deciding to ask Chavez to investigate the "evil stuff."[60] Perhaps the surreptitious nature of peyote cult operations and the isolation of District 9 explain Morgan's belated awareness. Once he entered the battle against peyote, however, the chairman vigorously sought to outlaw its use among his people.

Probably under pressure from Chavez, the Washington office had detailed Howard Gorman to look into the use of peyote before the council met. Gorman's long report to the council contained a detailed description of the peyote ceremony, a list of Navajo priests, and numerous statements by Indians who claimed knowledge of the new cult.[61] Although some of Gorman's materials were based on witnesses who stated that peyote had cured their alcoholism or illnesses and provided great spiritual benefits, the bulk of his information was highly antagonistic. He read statements that the substance caused male users' prostate glands to swell which, in turn, provoked sexual orgies at the ceremonies. Other hostile interviewees charged that priests of the Native American Church were disreputable people, interested only in seducing young women and taking participants' money. Users invariably neglected their livestock and crops, squabbled with their families, and underwent a general physical, mental, and moral decline. To a remarkable degree, the views in Gorman's report have characterized the opponents' arguments against peyote ever since 1940.[62]

59. Ibid., pp. 252–81.

60. Morgan to Chavez 25 March 1940, Chavez papers, UA.

61. Woehlke to Chavez, 30 March 1940, Chavez papers, UA; "Proceedings of the Navajo Tribal Council," 3–6 June 1940, File 9659, E, 1936, Navajo, 054, NA, RG 75. See pp. 11–42 for Gorman's report and the council discussion of the peyote question.

62. In my interview with Scott Preston, the former councilman and vice chairman, I

After listening to Gorman's report, both Christian and traditional Navajos roundly condemned the new religion. To Morgan and Roger Davis, peyote was not only a dangerous drug, but the Native American Church was a total desecration of Christianity. The traditionalists denounced the new cult as an alien threat to Navajo religion.

As the council debated, Morgan drafted a resolution which stated that "any person who shall introduce into the Navajo country, sell, use, or have in possession . . . the bean known as peyote shall be deemed guilty of an offense against the Navajo tribe."[63] Morgan originally wanted to punish violators with nine months in jail, a fine of $100, or both. Judge John Curley, however, pointed out that the maximum sentence that tribal courts could impose was six months and the council amended the resolution to lessen the penalty.

Hola Tso, a delegate from Sawmill and later head of the Native American Church in Arizona, was the only council member who defended the peyotists. He asked that a scientific analysis be made of the "herb" to determine if it was harmful. Readily admitting that he had participated in peyote ceremonies, Tso told the council that he had seen none of the "disgraceful things" which opponents claimed. The councilman maintained that peyote had solved his drinking problem and he advised that the same was true of other Navajos mentioned in Gorman's report.[64] He then sarcastically remarked that "since Howard has gone into it so thoroughly, I suppose he is the main priest in it." Tso's relatively brief but strong defense did not sway the council which voted fifty-two to one in favor of Morgan's resolution.

---

found little doubt about his obsessive hatred for peyote. Even though I tried to keep the interview focused on Morgan, Chee Dodge, and the clash over livestock reduction, Scott kept launching into tirades against peyote. In detailing all the evils of the substance, he pointed to his chest and warned that use of the stuff could create "bad things and big growths in there." Preston Interview.

63. "Council Proceedings," pp. 31–42. Morgan's reference to peyote as a bean meant that he, like many whites, was confused concerning the nature of the substance. Peyote buttons are obtained from a small cactus commonly found in the Rio Grande valley in Texas and Mexico. The top portion of the cactus plant is cut off and dried and either chewed or brewed as a tea. According to Prof. J. L. McLaughlin of the School of Pharmacy at Purdue University, researchers have identified some fifty compounds in peyote, forty of which are alkaloids. The most active ingredient is mescaline although other compounds have some effect on consumers.

64. Tso died on 22 October 1973, at the age of eighty-three. See *Navajo Times*, 1 November 1973, p. A-14.

The Indian Service enforcement of the ban in the ensuing period was highly erratic. Certain that peyote was not physically harmful or addictive, Collier had protected the cult on other reservations before 1940. He also believed that the Native American Church was entitled to protection under the Bill of Rights. There are strong indications that he tried to pressure Morgan into ignoring the peyote question before the council met, but obviously without any success. Fryer, by contrast, opposed the new cult but never very strongly.[65] After the council outlawed peyote, Collier reluctantly approved its action because of his belief in self-government. However, he refused to co-operate when antipeyotists demanded that Fryer arrest cult members in 1941. The commissioner reasoned that federal funds should not be used to enforce the tribal ban on peyote. Since Navajo police were financed from that source, he prohibited the wholesale arrests that opponents demanded. For several years afterward, the resolution received what Aberle describes as "a sort of intermittent and haphazard enforcement" which dissatisfied both peyotists and the opposition.[66]

Once the council acted on the peyote question, it drifted over a variety of issues—marriage and divorce laws, dental care, support for national defense, transfer of a Christian Reformed Church missionary that Morgan disliked, employment preferences for Navajos, and exclusion of whites from tribal membership.[67] Finally on the third day, the council took up the question of grazing districts. The subject was close enough to livestock reduction that nothing short of a forced adjournment could have kept the delegates from castigating the administration with an anger reminiscent of earlier sessions when Morgan had led the dissidents. Their complaints differed little from those voiced when the districts were established in 1936. When the discussion became too heated, Morgan called a recess and asked Fryer to answer the criticisms.

The superintendent's response was diplomatic but firm. He complimented the honesty and sincerity of the delegates' statements, but he stressed that overgrazing had been studied since 1931 and the

65. As Aberle notes, Fryer stayed out of the council discussion of the issue, but he later informed the anthropologist that he disapproved of peyote because of the many reports that it was harmful. Aberle, *Peyote Religion*, p. 111.

66. Ibid., p. 114.

67. For other matters discussed by the council, see "Council Proceedings," 3–6 June 1940, 42–193, *passim*.

government had not laid out the districts with a capricious intent. Despite his conciliatory tone, Fryer warned that any recommendations by the council to replace the districts must provide an alternative plan which would meet the conservation needs of the reservation.

The council's attempts to answer Fryer's challenge brought them even closer to the current controversy over livestock reduction and the distribution of grazing permits. Morgan, finally interrupting his silence, opposed destroying the grazing districts, maintaining that such action would only renew the large stockmen's domination of the range. Few of the speakers accepted the chairman's argument and most turned to such solutions as delaying the grazing permits, restoring the old six agencies and open grazing, conducting reductions over a five-year period, or relying solely on improved breeding. After listening to their suggestions, Fryer told the council that all ignored the fact that Navajos possessed a limited amount of grass and their livestock must be brought into balance with range capacity.

Nevertheless, Fryer offered some relief for the immediate future. He informed the council that the recent sale of horses had brought many small owners under their grazing quotas. He proposed a moratorium of eighteen months in sales of productive livestock, so that small herders could bring their number of sheep up to the figures authorized by their grazing permits. Such an arrangement, he warned, was dependent on the council's carrying out its pledge to help in the distribution of grazing permits. Fryer said he was unsure that the delegates would shoulder this responsibility.

Fryer's frank statements, especially his reading the council's resolution of April promising to aid in the distribution of grazing permits, stunned the lawmakers. Some did not believe that they had ever authorized the issuance of grazing permits. One newly appointed delegate, who had not been present at the 1939 session, innocently inquired if there was not "some crooked work" connected with the resolution since only a few councilmen admitted knowing about it. The comment infuriated Morgan who heatedly denied that he had ever misrepresented anything to the council. He insisted that he had supported the sale of horses only to save his people from being jailed by federal courts. In a lightly disguised thrust at Bainbridge's faction, Morgan condemned "some of the people who have been misrepresenting the Council or trying to overrun the Council by going back

and forth to Santa Fe and Albuquerque." In his tirade, the chairman
even came close to a total endorsement of the grazing program when
he advised Navajos to accept the grazing permits. Repeating Fryer's
key argument, Morgan stated that the permits conveyed a right to
graze, they should be accepted, and any objections or inequities could
be answered later. Those who refused to take out the permits would
have no reason to complain, Morgan added.

The council's mood had changed greatly when it reconvened the
next day. With relatively little debate, the delegates approved a
resolution which left the grazing districts intact and established
procedures by which minor boundary adjustments could be made by
the mutual consent of district councils, supervisors, and the superintendent. With even less discussion, the lawmakers reaffirmed their
earlier pledge to aid in the distribution of grazing permits. The same
resolution noted Fryer's promise to stop all sales of productive livestock until the end of 1941. An amendment requested the superintendent to aid large livestock owners in leasing land off the reservation for their herds.

While disposing of various minor issues near the close of the session,
delegates discussed a proposal that they receive a larger stipend for
their mileage and living expenses while attending future councils,
and—for the first time—that they be reimbursed for conducting
monthly district council meetings. Frank Bradley suggested that
Morgan be granted a salary and mileage for his frequent conferences
with Fryer and meetings with district organizations. Despite his
financial woes, Morgan expressed reluctance about the matter. He
vetoed the suggestion that he be given a government car, predicting
that he would be accused of using it for his missionary work. Fryer
strongly endorsed a salary and maintained that the growing complexity of tribal affairs, especially the new enterprises, necessitated increased consultations between himself and Morgan. Even with this
support, Morgan refused to present the proposed resolution to the
council and handed it to Roger Davis to introduce. The council
voted a salary of $200 per month for Morgan, while the delegates
were to receive five cents per mile and five dollars per diem for coun
cil attendance, and three dollars per diem for handling district
business.

The council adjourned on its customary note of harmony and
good wishes. This time the delegates' felicitious expressions came

close to the truth, at least for the council and the government. The session also symbolized Morgan's complete transition from anti-government critic to defender. Perhaps Morgan should have used the chairmanship after 1938 to thwart official policies he had so effectively opposed before. For a variety of reasons, mostly centering around his pride and fear of competitors, Morgan gradually accommodated himself to most Navajo Service programs by mid-1940.

Morgan's cooperation, though often erratic, allowed Fryer to continue the government program with little impairment. At this time there was also a lack of any other Navajo leader to assume Morgan's previous role as chief agitator. Chee Dodge undoubtedly possessed sufficient power to obstruct the government, but he preferred to retire from active politics and operate from behind the scenes. Bainbridge's questionable reputation and possible lack of ability seems to have restricted his influence to the northeastern portion of the reservation. Threatened by court action, most Navajos were on the threshold of submitting to Fryer's renewed efforts to carry out the grazing program.

Perhaps without realizing it, Morgan and Fryer had reached a compromise of sorts. The chairman was free to shape council proceedings to realize his middle class and puritanical values by outlawing peyote and common law marriages and by endorsing national defense and patriotism. The superintendent, on the other hand, could now count on Morgan's support in the final stages of the grazing program. Both were completely agreed that tribal enterprises offered a means of offsetting federal fund reductions. Collier, as evidenced in the peyote issue, did not always approve the "gentlemen's agreement" between Morgan and Fryer, but his commitment to self-determination kept him from intervening in Navajo affairs.

# 11

## The Navajo New Deal Becomes a Casualty of War

The closing years of the New Deal witnessed both remarkable successes and failures in the government's efforts to realize its policy goals. Morgan's support cleared the way for the achievement of the grazing program even though most livestock owners never fully understood or accepted its rationale. The tribal enterprises previously approved were established and some promising additions were made in trading cooperatives, arts and crafts, and livestock marketing. Although Navajo administration seemed on the verge of accomplishing most of its aims in 1941, the advent of war created problems that negated the hard-earned advances.

On July 22, 1940, Morgan presided over the dedication of the tribal sawmill. The new enterprise quickly became the showpiece of the drive by the chairman and Fryer to create tribal businesses. The mill employed about one hundred men which helped offset sharp reductions in emergency work programs. Perhaps most important, it created a sense of pride among the Navajos, for the sawmill succeeded where others had failed, and the Indians were not dependent upon an outside group to develop a natural resource.[1]

Even though the sawmill produced three times the output of the older Soil Conservation Service plant, it provided only rough lumber for the government and reservation with limited commercial sales. In April 1941, the tribal council appropriated $165,000 for a second major expansion, so finished lumber could be produced for off-reservation buyers.[2] The men in charge of both programs purchased used machinery, according to Fryer, at about half the normal cost. Not even the strongest defenders of the sawmill, however, claimed

1. *Gallup Independent*, 22 July 1940, p. 1.
2. "Proceedings of the Meeting of the Navajo Tribal Council," 8–11 April 1941, File 9659, 36, E, 054, Navajo, Part 5, NA, RG 75, p. 81.

that the production of finished lumber brought large profits during its earliest years. The first commercial sale was only a dollar per thousand board feet above the cost of production. This low profit margin, however, did not bother Fryer, who believed that the main function of the mill was to create jobs for Navajos.[3]

The dedication of the sawmill was actually preceded by the start of several other tribal enterprises. In a somewhat limited sense, the Navajo Tribal Fair of 1938 might be considered the first tribal business. Local and agency fairs had been common on the reservation since early in the century. The oldest and most successful was the Shiprock Fair which remained very active during the New Deal. Window Rock officials in early 1938 decided to start a reservation-wide fair at the tribal headquarters. One very obvious purpose was to familiarize Navajos with government programs by the use of graphic displays. The sponsors saw an added educational function in soliciting Navajo exhibits of rugs, silversmithing, farm products, and livestock. The various classes of entries were to be judged and cash prizes awarded to the first and second place exhibitors. Officials asked district supervisors to select the best Navajo products from their area and to see that these were entered in the competition at Window Rock. The rugs and jewelry were made available for sale to fair-goers. A final goal of the fair was to involve Navajo students; both mission and government schools were encouraged to send youngsters to participate in fair activities. The fairground facilities were built two miles south of Window Rock in early 1938. During the summer, CCC enrollees completed a stadium to seat 3,500 spectators, stock barns, rodeo pens, camp grounds, race track, and several buildings to house exhibits and concessions.[4]

The first fair opened on September 16 and lasted three days. The event proved successful from the first, approximately 10,000 Indians and whites attended in 1938. Beside the government and Navajo exhibits, visitors witnessed a rodeo during the afternoons with both Indians and range riders serving as performers. Collier made a special visit to open the fair, spoke to the rodeo crowd, and watched a spectacular demonstration of stunt flying by a government pilot. The three evenings of the first fair were devoted to a rendition of the

3. Fryer Interview, 1971.
4. Trotter to Holman, ca. 18 February 1938, Carl Beck to John McPhee, 18 February 1938, and Fryer to All Personnel, 12 May 1938, LAFRC, Box 72940.

Mountain Chant, a traditional ceremonial which government publicity claimed had not been performed in its entirety for forty years. Although few Navajos participated in the planning and operation of the first fair, a larger number served on the fair committee during Morgan's chairmanship.[5]

Another, though less important, tribal business was a small flourmill at Round Rock which opened sometime during the winter of 1939–40. It was first used to mill corn and wheat received from the government relief agencies, but its long-term purpose was to process grain raised by Navajo farmers of the area. A short time afterward Navajo officials completed a cannery at Many Farms. Fryer had learned about a complete set of canning equipment stored in a government warehouse in Texas that was free except for transportation costs. He managed to secure some rehabilitation funds to put up a building and install the equipment.

The cannery became part of both the relief and livestock reduction programs. Using a special grant of $300,000 from the Department of Agriculture, Fryer purchased sheep and goats that traders would not buy or animals taken as payment for dipping fees. A majority of the sheep were "pee wees" or lambs stunted by drought conditions and they and the goats were fattened before being slaughtered. The canned meat was either distributed to relief recipients or to schools.

Fryer used the cannery as a device for managing the prices traders paid for fall lambs and to break the natural monopolies that isolated posts enjoyed. By "pegging" the price of the pee-wees slightly under the level paid for saleable lambs, the superintendent forced traders to offer a fair price or else the Navajos could simply sell to the cannery. The post operators obviously did not like Fryer's policy, but only once did a trader openly rebel. This occurred at Piñon where the Hubbells owned the only trading post. When Lorenzo Hubbell, Jr., offered the local stockmen only a dollar and a half per head for their fall lambs, Fryer arranged to sell them to a trader in another area at twice Hubbell's bid.

The use of guidelines and pressures, rather than rigorous regulations, typified Window Rock's policy toward traders during this period. Sometime around 1938, Horace Boardman was hired as a supervisor of trading. A former co-owner of a trading post himself, Boardman carried out a variety of duties, but most of his initial work

5. *Gallup Independent*, 17 September 1938, p. 1.

dealt with installing a simple bookkeeping system so traders could report on sales and purchases. Data on such subjects as livestock purchases and amounts of goods retailed to the Indians were fed into Window Rock for the human dependency surveys. Boardman did nothing to aid in the collection of debts, always the greatest source of complaint for the traders during the New Deal. His most decisive action, indeed, was to test the accuracy of scales periodically and to adjust or order the replacement of those which were faulty. Boardman also generally checked on the fairness of transactions and in 1941 traders were required to mark prices on all goods. No attempt, however, was ever made to set the value of merchandise.

The most significant change in trading policy was the establishment of several cooperative posts just prior to World War II. Potentially these ventures might have provided Navajos sizeable savings, but the meager records on the cooperatives do not provide much information about their formation or the reason why all eventually failed. But certainly the experience at Mexican Springs indicates that cooperatives should have succeeded.

In mid-1939 chapter officers and government officials at Mexican Springs formed an advisory committee which purchased an existing trading post and hired Ernest Garcia, a capable young Spanish-American, to manage a cooperative at a salary of twenty-five dollars per week. The arrangements were decidedly informal. Garcia merely signed a statement of his duties and the previous owner's building and inventory were purchased on an installment contract for $8,000. A year later the principal had been reduced to $5,800 and the original owner sold his equity to a wholesale house in Gallup for $5,000. Sometime during the next year, the cooperative obtained an interest-free loan from the tribe and paid off the wholesaler. In September 1940, the Mexican Springs chapter formalized the cooperative by drawing up by-laws which provided for an all-Indian board of directors and requirements for membership, distribution of profits, and related matters.[6]

Garcia's business methods stressed a quick retirement of the debt, but otherwise he ran the cooperative as a regular trading post. He charged full prices on goods, purchased livestock and other products from the Indians, and made a considerable portion of his sales by

6. "Memorandum of Agreement," 5 June 1940, and "Articles of Association of Co-operative Association," 10 September 1940, LAFRC, Box 72907.

accepting pawn and unsecured credit. By carrying profitable merchandise which moved quickly, Garcia used his earnings to repay the
debt rather than to increase inventory, expand facilities, or distribute dividends to members of the cooperative. His gross sales in 1941
amounted to $27,175 with a net profit of $1,553. By the end of that
year the cooperative owed only $2,500 on its debt to the tribe.[7]
Based on these figures, the trading post should have been free of
encumbrance sometime in 1943.

Inspired by the success of Mexican Springs, Navajo administrators
encouraged several other communities to form cooperatives. By the
end of 1942 such ventures were established at Many Farms, Red
Lake (or Tolani Lake), and Pine Springs. The cooperative movement
continued until after World War II. White observers have uniformly
attributed the failure of such trading posts to the Navajo managers'
unwillingness to refuse credit to customers, especially those of their
own clan, and their general lack of business acumen.

While the cooperatives eventually failed, the Navajo Arts and
Crafts Guild has persisted as a viable tribal enterprise since 1941.
The encouragement of Indian handicrafts had always been a central
aim of Collier's administration; indeed, perhaps no single subject
fulfilled his aspirations quite so directly. Not only would the manufacture of traditional products help preserve the Indian heritage, but
the sale of goods was a potential source of income. To facilitate both
goals, Collier founded the Arts and Crafts Board in 1936 under the
direction of Rene d'Harnoncourt. The board subsequently attempted
to revive traditional designs, improve the quality of products, and
widen markets by displaying and selling Indian crafts at exhibits and
major department stores.

Although Navajo products were included in the exhibits and Arts
and Crafts representatives sometimes met with the United Indian
Traders Association, reservation craftsmen made only modest in-
creases in profits. The traders' main interest in the first years of the
New Deal was to stop the manufacture of Indian-type jewelry by
several firms in the Southwest which used mass production techniques and undersold native craftsmen. Because Indians operated the
machines, the manufacturers marketed the jewelry as Indian-made.
Secretary Ickes in 1933 banned the sale of such products in National

7. Ernest Garcia to Fryer, 24 December 1941, and "Mexican Springs Community
Trading Center, Balance Sheet as of December 31, 1941," LAFRC, Box 72907.

Park curio shops and then instituted a legal suit against a manu-
facturer in Albuquerque to keep him from selling jewelry under
false pretenses. In a compromise decision, the court allowed the
company to continue making jewelry but prohibited it from claiming
that the items were authentic.

After this limited victory, the Arts and Crafts Board attempted to
win the cooperation of Navajo traders for a system of inspection and
certification to improve the quality of rugs and jewelry, but this
program also fell far short of the government's hopes. Rugs and
jewelry which met high standards of quality, design, and materials
were to be tagged or stamped to certify their excellence. The scattered nature and complexity of the handicraft industry and the
limited cooperation of traders made enforcement of these policies
virtually impossible. After the success of a local crafts guild at the
Fort Wingate school, the Arts and Crafts Board decided to study this
approach, hoping to segregate the more skilled craftsmen's products
and provide a higher return than traders usually paid.[8]

In mid-1940 the Arts and Crafts Board dispatched John Adair
to the reservation to survey the jewelry and rug industries.[9] The
young anthropologist had already researched silversmithing among
the Southwestern Indians and he was particularly interested in
reviving earlier jewelry styles which predated the use of turquoise
settings. After six months of research, Adair filed a report with the
Arts and Crafts Board. He estimated that about 600 Navajos worked
as silversmiths, with around fourteen percent employed full time and
earning $400 to $800 per year. The rest worked intermittently and
made from $100 to $400 annually.[10] Soon after Adair's report,
D'Harnoncourt named him the first director of the Arts and Crafts
Guild.

The techniques which Adair employed in starting the guild were
drawn from similar enterprises established on other reservations.
The new venture commenced in a government warehouse in Gallup
with an initial subsidy of approximately $20,000 from the Interior
Department. Adair's first work consisted of putting out raw materials

8. Nearly all the jewelry produced for traders was light and inexpensive items for sale
to tourists. A truly skilled artisan who possessed the talent to make fine quality products
was paid little more than someone of mediocre ability who worked very rapidly.

9. The following account of the founding of the guild is drawn mostly from Adair to
writer, 31 January 1972.

10. John Adair, *The Navajo and Pueblo Silversmiths* (Norman, Oklahoma, 1944), p. 202.

—silver, turquoise, and wool—to a few master artisans and then buying back the finished products at premium prices. In 1942, Adair moved the guild into a building at Window Rock which provided office space, a showroom, and storage for raw materials. By this time the business had grown enough to employ Ambrose Roanhorse, a noted silversmith instructor. Roanhorse traveled about the reservation distributing raw materials and picking up completed items. Robert Pino, another Navajo, joined the guild a short time later.

Adair's promotional activities also increased in 1942. He displayed superior rugs, particularly those made of long staple wool which had been vegetable dyed, at the Museum of Northern Arizona in Flagstaff and at the Intertribal Ceremonial in Gallup during the summer. At first he marketed all rugs and jewelry through the National Park Service, but by the fall of 1942, an increased inventory permitted him to visit New York City and take orders from several major department stores.

Without question the Navajo Arts and Crafts Guild has become one of the strongest and most positive legacies of the New Deal. After a succession of white managers, Ned Hatahtli, a graduate of Northern Arizona University, became the first Navajo to head the guild several years after World War II.[11] The guild still remains a strong instrument in preserving skills and providing a livelihood for many Navajo craftsmen.

The promising successes of the tribal enterprises were realized just as the rickety structure of New Deal programs was falling into complete disarray. The once abundant supply of funds continued to disappear as war approached. The most serious casualty was the Soil Conservation Service. Some indication of the decline in spending may be seen by comparing fiscal 1937, when the SCS still contributed $830,000 to the Navajo program, to 1940 when the amount dropped to $300,000. In a final blow, Roosevelt's reorganization of government in 1940 saw the SCS turn over conservation work on Indian reservations to the Department of Interior. Although this was a "paper transaction" with funds and personnel transferred from the SCS to the Interior, Ickes complained that he was given far less money to conduct programs than the powerful SCS had received. In planning for the reorganization, Fryer pleaded that Navajo conservation work should become a part of the regular Indian Service

11. Marion Gridley, ed., *Indians of Today* (n.p., 1971), pp. 218–19.

budget, especially the salaries of district personnel, but Collier was only partially successful in meeting this request.[12]

When World War II began, the only major emergency program which still survived with some of its original vitality was the CCC. Despite severely restricted budgets, the organization continued field operations, and the enrollee program regularly received compliments for excellent educational classes and on-the-job training. Unfortunately, the CCC was disbanded soon after Pearl Harbor.[13]

The decline in federal spending was only one of several factors which caused observers to despair about solving the Navajos' problems. Moris Burge, the knowledgeable field representative of the American Association on Indian Affairs, returned from a visit to the reservation in the summer of 1940 in a most gloomy mood. Soon afterward Burge wrote: "I am horribly depressed about the Navajo, not because of any maladministration but because I cannot see any way out of the hopeless situation, and . . . I dont think anyone else can either." While visiting District 3 (Tuba City) Burge was impressed with the cooperation between local councilmen and the district supervisor in the sale of surplus horses and the distribution of grazing permits. But the 1939 drought in the district and an untimely freeze which ruined the corn crop had forced 175 families on relief during the past winter. In other districts where leaders were less capable, Burge believed that the prospects were even bleaker.[14]

The findings of the 1940 census caused more concern about the tribe's future welfare. Sample studies made in Districts 4, 5, and 7 revealed that Navajos had a birth rate of 37.6 per thousand and a death rate of 13.6 per thousand. The increase of twenty-four births over deaths per thousand was three times higher than other Indians and four times greater than the general public. The surveyors warned that their statistics needed to be confirmed by studies over a longer period, but their assessment of rapid population growth was generally accurate.[15] The vital tribe has almost tripled in number since the late 1930s.

12. Ickes to Roosevelt, 6 June 1940, Fryer to Collier, 26 May 1940, and "Memorandum for the Files," 13 September 1940, LAFRC, Box 72942.

13. D. E. Murphy to Fryer, 20 June 1940, CCC-ID, File 4285, 37, 346, Navajo, NA, RG 75.

14. Burge to Allan Harper, 5 August 1940, Office File of Commissioner John Collier, NA, RG 75.

15. Solon T. Kimball, "Navajo Population Analysis," *Navajo Medical News* 7 (28 September 1940): 3.

Those worried about the future of the Navajos received little encouragement from the northeast section of the reservation where obstruction of the grazing program continued in 1940. Despite the council's endorsement in June, Morgan's attempt to win a ratification of reduction from the district councils received little support. In mid-July 1940, Navajo police arrested fourteen Navajos involved in the Shiprock uprising in January, including the two who escaped, and the tribal court sentenced ten of them to jail sentences from one to six months. Inevitably the crackdown led Navajos to issue new protests and petitions to Chavez and Ickes, charging that the police had conducted the arrests at dawn and roughed up several of the prisoners and their wives. There were also fierce new accusations that Morgan was a turncoat who had betrayed his own people for the salary recently voted by the council.[16]

Newspaper reports indicate that part of the complaints originated east of the reservation. Probably these outcries resulted from the government's current efforts to regulate the Eastern Navajos' livestock under the Taylor Grazing Act. The procedures of the Grazing Service so closely resembled livestock programs on the reservation that Navajos—and local newspapers—simply lumped the two together.

Apparently the joining of the two types of protest led to the organization of the Navajo Rights Association and the appearance of new leadership among Shiprock dissidents and Eastern Navajos. Julius Bainbridge had disappeared, reportedly because he had been arrested in Colorado and reimprisoned. Dashne Clah Cheschillege, former chairman of the tribal council, became the major antigovernment leader by the fall of 1940. Dashne's reemergence as a tribal spokesman at this time was doubtlessly based on his fluency in English and his oratorical skills. Moreover, his earlier education at Shiprock at a time when the superintendent placed great emphasis on instruction about irrigated farming provided Dashne with a rationale to criticize herd reduction.[17] As Morgan's problems increased during his final two years as chairman, Dashne became a fairly strong rival for power.

16. *Gallup Independent*, 13 July 1940, p. 1; *Santa Fe New Mexican*, 14 July 1940, p. 1; *Albuquerque Journal*, 14 July 1940, p. 3; Mrs. Julia Denetclaw, letter to editor, *Farmington Times Hustler*, 19 July 1940, p. 6; Mason to Chavez, 17 July 1940, Chavez papers, UA.
17. *Farmington Times Hustler*, 28 February 1941, p. 6.

Dashne's methods of protesting closely resembled Morgan's techniques before 1938. On October 9, 1940, Dashne became chairman of the Navajo Rights Association at an organizational meeting in Cortez, Colorado. The group named Allen George and Peter Begay, both educated Navajos, as vice chairman and secretary-treasurer.[18] Dashne also turned to an off-reservation white for assistance. George Bowra, a frequent critic of Collier and editor of the *Aztec Independent Review*, often met with Dashne and his followers after mid-1940, forwarded protest petitions to Senator Chavez, corresponded with Collier and other figures, and publicized Navajo complaints. Dashne soon tried to extend the NRA beyond the Shiprock area to the rest of the reservation. He and others traveled widely during the winter of 1940 and 1941 organizing local chapters and selling memberships at one dollar per person. By the spring of 1941, he claimed that the association had 5,000 members. If true, the former chairman enjoyed remarkable success, for bad roads during the unusually severe winter must have handicapped the recruitment drive. Nevertheless, Dashne's organization attracted many Navajos, both leaders and rank-and-file, who had formerly supported Morgan. Significantly, Robert Martin joined the NRA and helped enroll new members.[19]

The positions taken by the NRA were surprisingly moderate. The demands stressed the need for government consultation with the tribe well in advance of any major policy changes because the Navajos' lack of education and fluency in English made it difficult for them to understand many technical and legal matters. The NRA also pointed out that the tribe had its own rules and punishments, but it would welcome the assistance of the government in law enforcement, "so long as the administering hand is in compliance with the Constitution . . . , the Bill of Rights, and . . . the treaty of June 1, 1868."

On the crucial subjects of herd reduction and rehabilitation, the NRA took an "irrigationist" line which reflected Dashne's education. Admitting the seriousness of the overgrazing problem, the NRA protested against any new livestock sales, claiming that "range

18. *Montezuma Valley Journal* quoted in *Farmington Times Hustler*, 25 October 1940, p. 10.

19. F. A. Polleck to Richard Van Valkenburgh, 11 November 1940, Van Valkenburgh papers, AHS.

correction can best be made by the application of water to our lands and that this would make it possible for us to raise feeds to feed livestock and thus cut down on the heavy use of the range." The NRA endorsed the current development of tribal industries, but advocated and only Navajos be hired so more of the tribe could learn new skills.[20] Taken as a whole, the platform of the NRA was both mild and responsible.

Incensed by criticisms of fellow tribesmen and defensive about the NRA's challenge to his authority, Morgan hit back at NRA leaders and their ideas with countercharges that were antithetical to views he had espoused as an agitator. If Morgan failed to perceive the irony of his position, he nevertheless demonstrated a stubborn desire to carry out his belief in local decision making. In December 1940, he attended long and bitter meetings of Navajos near Fruitland in another vain attempt to win their cooperation for horse sales. Bravely enduring the audience's violent accusations that tribal leaders had failed to protect Navajos' welfare, Morgan listened to council delegates denounce livestock reduction even though they had voted for it.[21]

Fryer's patience with Districts 9 and 12 had ended several months before Morgan's last ditch meetings. Both the continuation of horse sales and the distribution of grazing permits had succeeded fairly well in other sections of the reservation. The oft-delayed program was still partly stalemated by the moratorium on forced sales of productive stock and the only reduction, except for horses, in recent months had been in lower quality sheep and goats sold to the cannery or pee-wees shipped to Sacaton, Arizona, to be wintered on alfalfa until they became saleable. Scattered owners may have refused to comply with horse removals and to accept grazing permits, and cooperation was given in a begrudging fashion by most Navajos. Only one of the large commercial owners had made arrangements for leasing land off the reservation, although the moratorium would soon expire. Despite this, Fryer had gained sufficient compliance so that he decided to attack the last dissident areas.

On March 24, 1940, federal marshals served notices of trespass against four families in District 9 and ordered them to appear in Federal District Court in Salt Lake City. As happened in the Leupp area in 1938, Fryer selected the defendants to gain maximum impact

20. *Farmington Times Hustler*, 21 March 1941, pp. 1–2.
21. Ibid., 6 December 1940, pp. 1, 6, and 13 December 1940, p. 3.

on other Navajos. All four were from Aneth and Boundary Butte, a remote region of southern Utah with a record of hostility for the government dating back to the turn of the century. Although the opponents to herd reduction around Shiprock always received the most headlines, this grew out of their accessibility to reporters and educated leaders' flair for publicity. The Utah Navajos not only would not submit to livestock regulations, but they would not consider the possibility. If their adamant stand could be broken, the rest of the northeast region would cave in, too.

Nearly a year later on February 11, 1941, the four accused men, James Nakai, Beletso, Nuttley, and Ben Todechennie, stood trial before Judge Tillman D. Johnson. Twice the defendants had failed to appear because they stayed in hiding after being cited. Johnson had refused to render a decision by default, insisting that the four appear in person.[22] Dashne located the fugitives and convinced them that they should stand trial. Johnson, who had once taught school on the reservation and understood Indian psychology, made a drastic departure from normal trial procedures. With Thomas Dodge acting as lawyer-interpreter, Johnson held a private parley with the defendants and allowed them to present their side personally. Despite his sympathy, the judge declared the Navajos guilty of trespass, but unlike the Phoenix decision, they did not have to pay court costs. The case broke the last major stronghold of opposition to livestock reduction, while Johnson's conduct of the trial reduced some of the Navajo resentment.[23]

Only days after the court ruling, Morgan, Gorman, and Fryer visited Washington with a new plan to modify the livestock program.[24] Essentially, their proposal consisted of issuing special grazing permits allowing a maximum of 350 sheep units for the reservation up to December 1, 1941. After operating under that ceiling for a year, the limit would drop to 300. Without the plan, Fryer's moratorium on sales of productive livestock would have expired on December 1 and all owners would have been forced to bring their holdings under the number specified by the grazing permits of their particular district.

22. *Deseret News*, 11 February 1941, St. Michaels Mission.

23. *Farmington Times Hustler*, 7 March 1941, p. 1; *United States vs. Beletso* (No. 140-Civil), *James Nakai* (No. 141-Civil), *Nuttley* (No. 142-Civil), and *Ben Todechennie* (No. 155-Civil), Van Valkenburgh papers, AHS; *Albuquerque Journal*, 27 February 1941, p. 1.

24. *Farmington Times Hustler*, 21 February 1941, p. 1.

In practical terms, the new arrangement did not benefit the small owner who still could not increase his herd above his regular grazing permit. It provided little aid to large stockmen who must either sell or remove from the reservation all but 350 sheep units before the deadline. The group who received the greatest benefit were Navajos with medium-sized herds, especially if they lived in a grazing district with a low maximum limit. The main reasoning behind the plan was obvious. It revived reduction for the large commercial herders, favored by both Morgan and Fryer, and gave a temporary respite to the more numerous subsistence owners. Statistically, the modification meant a reduction of 60,000 sheep units as compared to 148,000 if all Navajos adopted the regular grazing permit limits.[25]

The two Navajo leaders and Fryer faced little difficulty in winning acceptance after arriving in Washington. They easily persuaded Collier that delaying reduction would not seriously harm reservation ranges after the heavy moisture of recent months. The commissioner expressed pleasure that the plan represented the leaders' own planning. With a strong endorsement, he sent the three men to Ickes who also gave them his blessing. Morgan returned to the reservation and on March 8 he enthusiastically announced the modified livestock program on KTGM.[26] Doubtlessly, Morgan exaggerated the importance of government concessions, ignoring that their effect was only short term.

The meeting of the tribal council on April 8–11, 1941, represented the ultimate success of self-government during the New Deal and yet betrayed the fact that the Navajos still misunderstood and distrusted the grazing program. In his first appearance in three years, Collier walked into the council meeting shortly after the group convened. He was deeply touched when the delegates rose in respect and applauded.[27]

Council deliberations on the new grazing concessions, however, quickly revealed the delegates' continued fear of reduction. Indeed, the trip to Washington had provoked additional opposition to the chairman and vice chairman. Their enemies charged that Morgan and Gorman were trying to make themselves famous and that they

25. "Council Proceedings," 8–11 April 1941, p. 16.
26. *Gallup Independent*, 8 March 1941, p. 1.
27. "Council Proceedings," 8–11 April 1941. See especially pp. 13, 15–16, 30–34, 41, 55–57, 61–68 for materials on this council session.

had sneaked off to see Collier and concluded a shady bargain without the council's permission.

As usual, the task of explaining the grazing proposal fell to Fryer. He stated that the revisions were justified by less government wage work, the abundance of grass, improved livestock prices, and national defense. The superintendent outlined a series of conditions he wanted Navajos to meet before they qualified for special grazing permits. Included were provisions that an owner must have branded his horses, sold the surplus, and accepted a regular grazing permit.

Despite Morgan's admonitions that the grazing concessions required little debate and repeated assertions by others that the Navajos could only gain, not lose, by approving the measure, the council discussed the matter for nearly two days. Some delegates wanted not only to reject the special permits but to abolish the entire grazing program. Morgan's best efforts to keep the traditionalists from straying into these troubled waters were unsuccessful. Bazhaloni Bikis, a headman from Black Mountain in District 4, at one point addressed Collier directly and eloquently attacked herd reduction. After describing himself as the provider for a family of ten and a person who spoke no English, Bikis asked how he could earn a living without his sheep. Responding to Bikis' statement that reduction "would mean the ruination of me and my family," Collier replied that 2,500 Navajos had no livestock or land and continued overgrazing would soon destroy Navajo ranges. Collier's answer failed to satisfy Bikis who retorted that he saw nothing wrong in fighting the government over reduction and he would oppose the resolution even if threatened by jail.

Despite Bikis' courageous stand, educated council members eventually wore down the traditionalists during the long debate. Advocates of the special grazing permits repeatedly reminded the council that it must think of the welfare of all Navajos, not just the wealthy who would be forced to sell more stock. Roger Davis, always a barometer of council sentiment and instrument of compromise, endorsed the new concessions midway in the discussion. Scott Preston soon afterward stated that if the council did not approve the revisions, he still wanted them implemented in District 3. Finally, the prolonged arguments ended in a unanimous approval of the special grazing permits and Collier signed the agreement before the council.

Once the modified grazing program was settled, Morgan seemed

content to let council deliberations drift without control. The desultory proceedings centered on informing the delegates about current
reservation policies, especially tribal enterprises, livestock improvements, and education. In addition to approving the expansion of the
tribal sawmill, the council voted in favor of local communities pooling their fall lambs and wool and asking outside buyers to make
competitive bids. This proposal alarmed traders and some attended
the council discussion. There seems to be no evidence that pooling
ever started, probably because of World War II.

In the midst of their deliberations, the council went to the tribal
fairgrounds to select young stallions that Fryer had purchased for
distribution to the tribe. In explaining that the stallions would be
kept at district headquarters to service local owners' mares, the
superintendent mentioned that he had deliberately avoided buying
thoroughbreds. The tribe, he explained in some amusement, already
had enough racing stock and he had decided to secure registered
quarterhorses suitable for either farm work or riding. The distribution of the stallions was part of a reintensified effort to upgrade
Navajo livestock. Fryer had recently established a tribal sheep herd
at Sacaton, Arizona, to raise registered rams, and Navajos at Mexican
Springs had started herds of registered sheep and cattle.

The council's approval of the maximum limit of 350 sheep units
produced one of the most interesting episodes of the many New Deal
protests. A month after the council adjourned, a delegation of six
Navajos led by Shine Smith, an itinerant white missionary, visited
Washington and announced a determination to air their grievances
to President Roosevelt. None of the Indians had been major protest
leaders and all were camp Navajos from Monument Valley and
Kayenta. Smith, however, was hardly the normal Christian prosely-
tizer. He had once served as an ordained Presbyterian missionary at
Kayenta, but he and the church parted ways after some disagreement.
He then drifted about the reservation working at short-term jobs
while he continued his preaching at open air meetings. His chief
fame, however, rested on large Christmas celebrations he staged at
various trading posts. Financed by outside contributions, these affairs
attracted huge crowds of Indians who came to receive candy and
small gifts. A chatty, personable character, Smith exhibited little
piety. Indeed, he used profanity freely and his relationships with
young Navajo girls reputedly exceeded the spiritual realm.[28]

28. For additional information on Smith, see R. Brownell McGrew, "Excerpts from

Smith's group continued to demand a meeting with President Roosevelt about reductions despite Collier's efforts to dissuade them. Rebuffed the first time they tried to enter the White House, Smith led the Indians to interviews with Ickes, Chavez, and other figures. Some three weeks after their arrival, Smith's group was joined by five Navajos from Shiprock. Included was Sam Ahkeah, a rising Navajo leader who eventually became council chairman.[29] A short time later the combined delegations decided to accept Collier's offer to arrange a meeting with Mrs. Roosevelt. Their pleas about the new livestock limits and vivid descriptions of Navajo poverty aroused the First Lady's sympathies to the point that she promised to speak to Collier. The next day, after he had met with Mrs. Roosevelt, Collier called Fryer and ordered him to fly to Washington immediately with a rehabilitation project.

Fortunately, Fryer had a complete set of plans for an irrigation development at Many Farms. The superintendent had earlier tried to win funding for the eight-hundred-acre project, but his budget request had been turned down within the Department of Interior. Taking maps and information on Many Farms, Fryer flew to Washington and, with Collier, proceeded to the White House to speak to Mrs. Roosevelt. During their long conversation about the tribe, Eleanor inquired about the peculiar odor she noticed during the Navajos' visit, and Fryer laughingly explained that the smell represented a compound of piñon smoke, working with sheep, and a lack of water for bathing and washing. Finally Mrs. Roosevelt asked what she could do for the tribe "that's immediate and urgent and will be helpful." Fryer then described the Many Farms project. The First Lady's promise to speak to her husband resulted in a last minute

an Artist, R. Brownell McGrew, in the Lands of the Navajos and the Hopis," *Arizona Highways* 45 (July 1969): 4–39; Franks Waters, *Masked Gods, Navaho and Pueblo Ceremonialism* (Denver, 1950), pp. 126–28.

29. In an interview with Frank McNitt in 1958, Ahkeah (sometimes spelled Akeah) stated that he owned forty-five goats and 550 sheep in 1933. Four years later, his family had eaten most of the goats and sold all the sheep at three dollars per head. His disenchantment with livestock reduction doubtlessly motivated him to enter tribal politics in 1941. There are a few scattered references to Ahkeah before 1942. The most notable is his letter to Senator Chavez in June 1941 assessing tribal affairs and the livestock program. Like NRA statements of the same period, Ahkeah generally accepted the need for reduction, but he criticized the manner in which the program operated, especially the distress faced by the very poor owners. Ahkeah was elected council chairman in 1946 and served until 1952. See Frank McNitt, *The Indian Traders* (Norman, Oklahoma, 1962), pp. 359–60; Ahkeah to Chavez, 18 June 1941, Chavez papers, UA.

inclusion of the proposal in the administration's budget requests.[30] The subsequent approval of the irrigation project represented perhaps the only positive result of numerous Navajo delegations who had visited Washington during the previous eight years.

Reservation turbulence in the summer of 1941 was still evident but less intense than ever before. Even the Shiprock Navajos began to sell their horses and take out grazing permits. The only three pockets of strong resistance that remained were Navajo Mountain, Aneth, and part of Monument Valley, according to field workers. In midsummer a group of fifteen Indians at Navajo Mountain forced the release of a herd of horses that had been corralled for identification and branding. The dissidents, however, did not attack two government employees at the corral. Newspapers reported in July that 300 Navajos at Teec-Nos-Pos had declared war on the government, but officials seemed unconcerned and no serious incident occurred. Soon afterward Dashne, complaining that plenty of grass was now available, announced that the NRA would hold a reservation-wide meeting at Kayenta on August 10.[31] The former chairman invited Morgan, council members, and Fryer to attend. Morgan refused the invitation and advised delegates to do the same. After he received reports the first day that dissensions had arisen and personal factions of NRA "were pointing their fingers at each other," Fryer flew to Kayenta to plead for compliance with grazing regulations and defuse any antigovernment action. When he arrived, the Indians were still divided into separate groups. He picked out the largest body which was meeting in front of Frank Bradley's house, was allowed to speak, and Navajos from the other factions crowded around to listen. Fryer later suggested that his speech of two and one-half hours may not have had as much impact as the fact that four or five Navajos had recently been arrested for refusing to sell their horses.[32]

Even though the last overt resistance to herd reduction dissipated in 1941, Morgan totally lost patience with Dashne and the NRA. In rejecting the invitation to attend the Kayenta meeting, for example, the chairman stated that it was below his or the council's dignity "to

30. Fryer Interview, 1970.

31. *Albuquerque Journal*, 13 July 1941, pp. 1–2; *Farmington Times Hustler*, 1 August 1941, pp. 1, 7.

32. Fryer to Collier, 12 August 1941, Office File of Commissioner John Collier, NA, RG 75.

go out into the sticks . . . at the bidding of the unrecognized group of dissatisfied Indians who are defying the laws of the country and . . . the tribal council they elected." He angrily maintained that the NRA's real motive was to force the council to bow to its will. Morgan questioned the patriotism of his opponents and compared their activities to subversive elements trying to undermine the national government's defense programs.[33]

The growing emphasis on preparation for war after 1938 affected the Navajos much in the same way that retrenchment decimated other New Deal programs. While military spending drained off huge sums of federal funds and forced serious cuts in many programs, by 1940 the Navajos were beginning to offset some of their losses by increased prosperity and employment opportunities. Navajos, for example, received as high as thirty-five cents per pound for their wool in 1941, the highest price they had enjoyed for many years. They benefited also from greater revenues from lambs, rugs, jewelry, piñon nuts, and other products. The Santa Fe Railroad had always hired some Navajos from the southern edge of the reservation for section work, but around 1940 tribesmen from other areas, especially Shonto, were employed in these jobs. By mid-1941, 200 Navajos worked for the Santa Fe. During World War II, other railroads began hiring Navajos and section work remains today an important source of income for many of the tribe. Doubtlessly, Navajos enjoyed some increase in local employment opportunities in 1940. Officials estimated that the tribe earned $125,000 from off-reservation jobs that year, but this was far surpassed in 1941 and during World War II.[34]

The registration for the draft in October 1940 confused many young Navajos who did not understand what was involved. Fryer tried to avoid this by establishing 125 registration points on the reservation and allowing three days instead of one to complete the task. Eastern Navajos received no special arrangements and a group at Crownpoint balked when they heard that they would be hauled away in "big trucks." A talk to the reluctant young men by Morgan won their cooperation. At Wupatki National Monument, northeast of Flagstaff, none of the Indians registered. A local headman had

33. *Farmington Times Hustler*, 8 August 1941, pp. 1, 7.

34. Ickes to Mrs. Roosevelt, 13 August 1941, Office File of Commissioner John Collier, NA, RG 75.

previously told his followers that Navajos should not fight unless Hitler invaded the United States. Something of a guardhouse lawyer, the headman advised a local Selective Service official that "Navajos do not have to go to war if drafted because it is written down in Washington that in 1868 the Navajos agreed with the big ones that the Navajos would never fight anybody again."[35]

Failures to register or to report when drafted were more widespread than Indian Service officials liked to admit, but the Navajos' reasons were quite different from white shirkers' motives. Isolation, general distrust of the government, fears that registration was somehow associated with livestock reduction, and garbled impressions of international affairs made young Navajos hesitant about the draft. Some responded belatedly and only after being threatened with arrest.

In November 1940 the War Department announced the construction of a multimillion dollar ordnance depot at Fort Wingate which provided many jobs for Navajos. By mid-1941 when construction was in full swing, 800 Navajos were working on the project. Commenting on the Indians' performance, one foreman declared that "they are punctual and they tackle the hardest jobs without a word of protest, their only complaint being that they can't smoke." The Navajos quickly demonstrated their skills as truck and tractor operators, masons, carpenters, and cement workers. Army officers and supervisors were baffled by how the Indians had learned such jobs. "The answer," a local reporter wrote, "is that the Civilian Conservation Corps program on the Reservation for the past eight years has enabled many Navajos so inclined to learn these occupations."[36]

American entry into World War II profoundly reshaped Navajo administration and made even more drastic inroads in the New Deal programs. A special meeting of the tribal council convened on January 12–13, 1942. Even herd reduction was overshadowed in the council's discussions. Morgan called on the tribe to support the war effort and reminded delegates that many Navajos, including his youngest son Buddy, were currently fighting in the Philippines. Deeply impressed by defense needs, the chairman asked Navajos to consume less food and clothing and to cooperate with additional

35. *Albuquerque Journal*, 19 October 1940, p. 9; *The Coconino Sun*, 18 October 1940, p. 1.
36. *Santa Fe New Mexican*, 13 November 1940, p. 2; *Gallup Independent National Defense Issue*, June 1941, CCC-ID, File 4285, 37, 346, Navajo, NA, RG 75.

registrations. Fryer's speech cautioned that Navajos must assume a greater responsibility for their own administration in the future. His remarks indicated that each grazing district already had a national defense committee which encouraged more farming, raised contributions for the Red Cross, and sold war bonds.

Wartime changes were even more apparent when Morgan convened his last meeting of the tribal council on June 22, 1942. Fryer had already left the reservation to work on Japanese relocation and James M. Stewart, the former land director, had been superintendent for nearly two months.[37] The war was on everyone's mind. Collier spoke to the council and warned that the CCC was doomed and that the Indian Service would suffer a one-third reduction in funds during the coming year. The commissioner asked that the tribe accept these changes and make other necessary sacrifices.[38]

The council discussions seemed to drift even more aimlessly than usual. After the delegates reacted indifferently to Stewart's plan to spend up to $20,000 for Rambouillet rams, Morgan laid the proposal aside to take up a resolution by Henry Taliman. The former chairman asked for a relaxation of grazing quotas so Navajos could better support the war. Although debated at length, no one seemed sure what Taliman's plan involved and the council finally tabled it.

The desultory session was enlivened when Scott Preston introduced

37. An extremely bitter dispute developed over the circumstances under which Fryer left the reservation. During our interview and untaped conversations in 1970, he maintained that he left the reservation on a leave of absence with a claim to the same post after the war. Stewart's appointment, according to Fryer, was originally as acting superintendent. When Fryer attempted to regain the superintendency in late 1947, both Navajo leaders and Stewart strenuously objected. The Navajos obviously feared that Fryer would revive rigorous livestock regulations and they somewhat unfairly associated him with the wanton slaughter of goats in the early New Deal reductions. George Boyce's autobiography contains what appear to be Stewart's reasons for resisting Fryer's appointment. Boyce's book argues that Collier and Fryer differed for some reason in the spring of 1942 and the commissioner transferred Fryer to Japanese relocation work "without post-war rights to return to the Indian Bureau." Under strong pressures by Norman Littell (tribal attorney in 1947), Navajo leaders, and others, the Bureau withdrew Fryer's appointment and tried unsuccessfully to name him first as director of the district office in Phoenix and then director of resources in Washington. Fryer eventually became a superintendent in Nevada but soon resigned after disagreeing with Senator Pat McCarran over Indian water rights. See George A. Boyce, *When Navajos Had Too Many Sheep: the 1940's* (San Francisco, 1974), pp. 116, 224–27; Fryer Interview, 1970.

38. "Minutes of the Navajo Tribal Council in Session at Window Rock, Arizona," 22–24, June 1942, File 9659, 36, E, 054, Navajo, Part 5, NA, RG 75. See especially pp. 4–6, 17, 35, 44, 52, 94, 120, 131 for materials on this council session.

a resolution the second day condemning the Navajo Rights Association, "who are constantly collecting money, Navajo jewelry and livestock from the Navajo people on the basis of many false promises, [and] sowing seeds of discontent and confusion in the minds of the Navajo people." Such activities, the resolution continued, were "unpatriotic at this time" and should be banned.

The resolution was almost certainly Morgan's and he used Preston to introduce it to the council. Stung by continued criticism from the NRA, worried because his son was missing in action, and intensely patriotic, the chairman was even more willing to associate Dashne's group with disloyalty. In any case, the debate over the resolution became, in Morgan's words, "pretty hot," before the council disapproved it.

Morgan quickly accepted another Preston resolution which demanded that Navajos reduce the number of ceremonials by twenty-five percent to conserve food, tires, and gasoline for the war effort. Many immediately criticized the measure as an infringement on religious freedom. Even Roger Davis complained that the proposal was unconstitutional, while the traditionalists deemed it an insult to their religion. In taking the question, Morgan angered many delegates by first asking for votes in favor and then stating in Navajo, "all those who want to lose the war, vote." Despite his high-handed tactics, the delegates rejected the second resolution. Even after Gorman and Taliman protested about his conduct, Morgan refused to admit any unfairness or to apologize for his handling of the matter.

Evidently behind-the-scenes compromises permitted the council to resolve its differences. On the final day, the delegates approved a Morgan resolution to allow small owners to increase their herds providing their district did not exceed its grazing limit. The group also voted for Stewart's plan to buy more rams with tribal funds. Finally, the council even approved a recommendation for fewer religious gatherings, but the measure specified that both Navajo and Christian services were to be affected.

In his valedictory address, Morgan seemed in a very pensive mood. He recalled that the past four years had brought difficult problems to the council and that Navajos had shown great patience with its actions. The chairman maintained that he had tried "to meet with my people and give them my best thoughts." Not all had accepted his leadership and he admitted that "during the last year or so some of those who have been my very best friends have drifted away and did not want to talk to me." Morgan denied that such reactions bothered him. "Nothing they have said about me, nothing they have tried to do to me, could bother me," he declared, "because I am free and I have been doing my very best."

Morgan subsequently needed all the comfort that a free conscience could provide. After waiting months to hear of his son's fate in the Philippines, the War Department announced that Buddy was alive in a Japanese prison camp. Soon afterward the Morgans learned that their son had died. In the same period, Morgan's political career suffered a final blow. Sam Ahkeah defeated him in the Shiprock primary election for the chairmanship in the summer of 1942. This removed Morgan as a candidate from the runoff election which Chee Dodge easily swept that fall. Chee's tactic of staying in the background and letting Morgan incur the tribe's hostility over herd reduction eventually gave the old patriarch revenge over the hated "bow-legged chairman." Morgan retired to missionary work and never reentered politics.

Inevitably, the spirit and substance of the already battered New Deal programs felt the full thrust of wartime dislocations. More key figures of the Navajo Service left for the military or other positions. Fryer's absence to work on Japanese relocation became more or less permanent when he transferred to North Africa to work on Jewish refugee problems for the Lehman Committee and stayed on as an administrator to help establish civil authority in the wake of Eisenhower's African and European campaigns. Stewart then became the permanent superintendent. Dr. Peter was dismissed as medical director in 1942 because of fund reductions. Several young doctors left the reservation to join the military, five hospitals were closed, and remaining installations operated with restricted staffs during the war.

The education program suffered far greater blows. The always troublesome transportation system broke down completely in 1942 when money was lacking to maintain roads and buses. Many teachers left the reservation and qualified replacements could not be hired. Harried officials asked parents to build hogans at some day schools or converted idle buildings and classrooms into quarters so students could stay overnight. Eighteen day schools were boarded up during the war years. About two dozen of the most able Navajo assistants took over classes. Some became highly effective classroom performers and approximately one-half were retained after the war as fulltime teachers by getting special certification to bypass civil service requirements.[39]

The grazing program faced new difficulties during the war years. Retrenchment caused the dismissal of most range riders soon after Pearl Harbor, throwing more of the burden of maintaining the program onto the district supervisors. These officials faced an increasing problem of probating grazing permits when a family head died and left several heirs. The supervisors began helping Navajos draw up informal wills which were kept on file at the headquarters. This procedure, although upheld by the courts, did not solve the dilemma of how an inadequate grazing permit could be divided among several heirs and still provide anything like subsistence.

The intense pressure which Fryer and his field workers used to gain general compliance with reduction by 1941 began to relax after Stewart became superintendent. Often described by associates as a diplomatic though somewhat lukewarm leader, Stewart lacked Fryer's forcefulness and devotion to the livestock program. He retained the special grazing permits after 1941 and ordered periodic reductions in owners' quotas. Supervisors, however, were supposed to encourage compliance rather than demand it. Calculated to achieve reduction without arousing serious problems, the moderate tactics annoyed the supervisors, kept many Navajos on edge, and perhaps encouraged evasion. When the final cut from the special permits was being carried out in 1945, a very serious incident occurred when a group of enraged Navajos in District 9 attacked Rudi Zweifel, the supervisor, and his Navajo assistant. The Indians gave both men a fearful beating with clubs before kidnapping them and Zweifel's wife. The three managed to escape the next day and their attackers were arrested and imprisoned.[40]

The war created even more off-reservation employment for the Navajos. After the completion of the ordnance depot at Fort Wingate, tribesmen in 1942 helped on the construction of a similar facility at Bellemont, Arizona, west of Flagstaff.[41] Hundreds of Navajos

39. Thompson Interview.
40. Mr. Zweifel Interview.
41. *Coconino Sun*, 6 March 1942, p. 1.

became migratory farm workers and scattered all over the West during summers to harvest fruit and vegetables. Navajo girls for the first time secured jobs as waitresses in Fred Harvey Restaurants, an event hailed by local newspapers as a major social breakthrough. Far more important, however, was the massive movement of Navajos to industrial centers on the West Coast. In 1945 the Indian Service estimated that 10,000 Navajos were engaged in war work of various types.[42] World War II brought about a seasonal and permanent exodus from the reservation which has continued unabated until the present.

The entry of young Navajos into the military also rose sharply after 1941. The most publicized aspect of their participation was the Marine Corps' use of bilingual Navajos as "code talkers" in the Pacific Theater. Sending radio messages in Navajo was one code which even the most skilled Japanese experts could not break. Sergeant Philip Johnston, who had grown up on the reservation, originated the idea and convinced his superiors that pairs of Navajos could be effectively used in communicating messages. Johnston made at least two recruiting trips to the reservation and enlisted approximately 350 men.[43] The Navajo marines participated in almost every invasion of MacArthur's Pacific campaign.

During the landing on Okinawa, the code talkers with the First Division seemed unconcerned despite military planners' worries that the Japanese would repel the invasion from their well-defended positions. Eight Navajos in the division had taken special precautions to insure that the landing went well. The Indians had held a ceremony at the island staging area where they trained for Okinawa. Improvising costumes and ritual paraphernalia from red cloth, chicken feathers, coconuts, sea shells, ammo cans, and rifle cartridges, the code talkers repeated chants which "put the finger of weakness" on their enemies. Three thousand marines watched the dance with solemn fascination. Already confident, one Navajo became even more assured when he saw a rainbow over the convoy en route to Okinawa. A huge naval diversion off the south coast of the island drew the Japanese army away from the actual landing site, permitting the

42. *Phoenix Gazette*, 19 March 1945.
43. *Gallup Independent*, November 1942, p. 1; *Farmington Times Hustler*, 19 March 1943, p. 5.

First Division to come ashore with few losses. To the Navajos, how-
ever, the success was assured by proper spiritual preparation.[44]
Except for the code talkers, the 3,000 Navajo servicemen in World
War II served in regular units.

Regardless of whether Navajos served in the military or civilian
capacities, their off-reservation experiences during the war significantly altered the tribal outlook. As Evon Vogt's study of Navajo
veterans suggests, the impact of life away from the reservation varied
greatly depending on each tribesman's previous acculturation,
education, and fluency in English, along with the type of relationships he had with whites during the war. Uneducated migratory
workers returned from short off-reservation visits little changed.
For other Navajos with different perceptions, exposure to outside
life unavoidably altered their lives.[45] In particular, Navajo servicemen dropped their indifference toward education after they realized
that lack of fluency in English and inadequate job skills badly handicapped them in the armed forces. This change of attitude was almost
universal. One uneducated Navajo interviewed by Vogt spent nearly
three years in the army working in mess halls without learning to
speak English. He did not receive leave before going overseas because
his commanding officer feared that he would get lost. Although he
slipped comfortably back into Navajo life after the war, the veteran
expressed definite regret that he lacked an education. The postwar
era was a time of high optimism because many observers believed
that education and the leadership of returned veterans would solve
the tribe's problems.[46]

Despite their confidence, Navajo veterans and war workers returned to a reservation which offered few opportunities to realize
their aspirations. The New Deal had withered away during the
short budgets and dislocations. The day schools remained and Navajo
children soon filled them beyond capacity, creating a totally different
type of educational crisis than ever witnessed before. The council
survived and, if anything, became rigidly fixed in tribal affairs
during the war. It would soon become even more viable after 1945

44. Ernie Pyle, "Navajo Indians Excellent for Communications Job," in *Phoenix Gazette*,
27 April 1945.
45. Evon Vogt, *Navaho Veterans, A Study of Changing Values* (Cambridge, 1951), pp.
94–99.
46. Ibid., pp. 99, 156–61.

as it faced far more complex problems than during the 1930s. The grazing program had declined from the relentless hostility of the tribe and became virtually extinct after enforcement of the regulations was turned over to the tribe in 1946. There was no CCC, no WPA, and no PWA to respond to postwar needs. What was most apparent, however, was the lack of the ebullient confidence and energy of the New Deal. Collier was ousted from office in 1945 by an Oklahoma congressman who refused to approve the Indian Service budget unless the commissioner "resigned." Ickes left office soon afterward because of disagreements with the Truman administration. The Navajo New Deal had become a casualty of war and it returned crippled in body and spirit at the end of the conflict. Two years passed before the plight of the Navajos reawakened national concern and another three years lapsed before the Truman administration passed new legislation in 1950 to alleviate the tribe's poverty, disease, and educational needs.

# 12

## An Assessment of New Deal Policies

In assessing the Navajo New Deal, no single pattern emerges which shows that the policies of the era were either complete successes or failures. Some programs brought improvements and became fixtures in subsequent administrations. Other policies offered little benefit or were so resisted by the tribe that they have since been discarded. Collier does not appear as the tyrant or as the totally misguided idealist bent on returning Indians to the stone age that his enemies often depicted him. Neither does he emerge as a uniform benefactor whose ideas would have solved all Indian problems except for the machinations of vested white interests, uncooperative Indian Service workers, and western politicians.

One of Collier's most serious miscalculations was his belief that major improvements would result from reviving tribal governments. In his early statements as commissioner, he created the impression that self-rule by councils would practically put the Indian Service out of business. Indian leaders would soon start establishing policy and even administering reservation affairs, leaving regular employees only the task of advising on technical matters and defending the Indians' interests. Obviously, the Navajo experience with self-government never came close to achieving these goals.

In truth, self-rule among the Navajos was always a bit ironic. Ideally, the tribe should have wanted to take charge of reservation affairs, but there was little in its tradition for the type of political unity and decision making demanded for effective government. The Navajos certainly did not ask for self-rule and the government was able to impose it only by administrative fiat. The problem arose because the Navajos lacked the necessary leaders to carry out Collier's programs. Those who had the education to understand government aims, such as J. C. Morgan, Howard Gorman, and Dashne Clah

Cheschillege, spent a good portion of the New Deal era opposing Collier. In a very real sense, self-government was frustrated by the success of the old boarding schools in indoctrinating students in assimilationist ideals. Morgan particularly exemplifies this result, for he never abandoned his white, middle-class values even after assuming the chairmanship.

Such tribal unity as developed in the 1930s largely grew out of the Navajos' opposition to the government. Navajo antagonisms against herd reduction, plus the resistance of traders and missionaries, played a fundamental role in the defeat of the Wheeler-Howard referendum in 1935. Similar circumstances developed two years later when the government attempted to enlist the support of the headmen in the provisional council. Not until Collier decided to surrender to Morgan and agreed to tribal elections in 1938 did the council begin to show any viability. Morgan's conferences with Fryer, the chairman's many travels to district councils, the tribal council's balkiness on some questions, and the limited cooperation between some tribal leaders and district field workers indicate that self-rule had taken on a limited meaning by 1942. Decisions on herd reduction, grazing regulations, and other facets of the conservation program, however, were never really made by the council and Fryer was able to maintain control over these matters by cajoling and pressuring the council delegates, prosecuting selected dissidents, offering the compromise of special grazing permits in 1941, and allowing Morgan to legislate his puritanical ideals.

Although self-rule had only limited success before 1942, tribal elections since World War II have been marked by highly active politicking. The council is no longer considered a strange and remote group of rich and educated Navajos as in the 1920s and 1930s. Candidates for the council, chairman, and vice chairman campaign by speaking at chapter meetings and having their followers display bumper stickers on their cars. Indeed, Navajo campaigns show more activity than is true of white ones. First granted the right to vote in 1948, the Navajos in New Mexico and Arizona have become involved in regular party affairs and have recently elected several tribesmen to county offices and the state legislatures.

Today the Navajos display a very strong sense of tribal unity. Instead of government vehicles adorned with "Navajo Service" in large letters, cars and pickups owned by the tribe now carry large decals with "Navajo Nation" emblazoned on them. The latter phrase symbolizes the widely accepted idea that Navajos should not consider themselves as a tribe but as a "nation within a nation," an example of political pluralism that Collier would have relished.

It is difficult to gauge the success of New Deal efforts to preserve Navajo culture and religion. Unquestionably, maintenance of the tribal heritage received strong encouragement from Collier, Fryer, and other top officials. While educational leaders may not have fully recognized the difficulty of preparing students for life in both cultures, schools no longer deliberately obliterated Navajo customs. Numerous observers point out that religious ceremonials, the chief source of the Navajo heritage, were more frequent in the 1930s than previously. In part this reflects the greater toleration of native religion under Collier's regime, but it is also possible that the Navajos simply had more money from government wages to pay medicine men and the costs of feeding crowds at ceremonials. The use of wages to buy automobiles probably made it easier for medicine men to acquire esoteric ceremonial paraphernalia and herbs that could be found only at special locations by traveling long distances.

The New Deal did cause significant economic changes. The federal money that poured into the reservation during the first years of the era relieved the serious distress of Navajos whose normal means of livelihood was disrupted by the depression. A more lasting effect was the introduction of a wage economy which replaced the barter system of the trading posts. Cash derived from wages afforded Indians greater opportunity to do business at other trading posts or at off-reservation stores and Navajos were able to determine prices more precisely than under the old system. Unfortunately, the wage economy carried several negative effects. The Navajos' access to Gallup and other border towns increased alcoholism, vice activities, and venereal diseases. Although Ickes protested endlessly about scand alous conditions in Gallup, local officials responded with only a few sporadic raids, and the bootleggers, gamblers, and prostitutes were soon as active as ever. Navajos were sometimes victimized by used car dealers who overcharged their gullible customers or sold them wrecks that functioned for only a brief time.

The most striking economic change was, of course, the impact of herd reduction. Probably federal expenditures on the Navajos during the 1930s more than offset losses of income caused by decreased livestock sales, but the government was never able to insure that employment benefits were distributed fairly. Those families who most needed jobs to compensate for their loss of stock might or might not receive work. In limited and ideal situations, such as the demonstration areas and lightly grazed districts, improved livestock breeding and range conditions allowed the Navajos to maintain a normal standard of living. For much of the reservation, particularly Piñon and the northeast corner, the government did not provide the resources necessary to offset the effects of herd reduction.

The need for reduction and the conservation program seems undisputable, especially during the dramatic ravages of the dust bowl. Studies of the reservation grazing capacity made after World War II indicate that New Deal estimates were accurate and if anything too liberal. There is some evidence that grazing capacity declined even with the controls imposed in the 1930s. However, the "psychological costs" of reduction, expressed in the Navajos' anguish and hostility, were excessive. It seems clear that Collier, a latter-day convert to the cause of conservation, seriously erred in undertaking the early livestock sales without well-developed plans and adequate field workers to avoid the tragic mistakes of the non-graduated reductions of 1933 and 1934. Possibly different approaches could have been utilized to soften the blow or to convince the tribe of the necessity of herd reduction, but Collier was only dimly aware of the Navajos' attachment to their sheep and goats. These early blunders served to handicap later attempts to prevent overgrazing by a semigraduated reduction program which concentrated on horses and nonproductive livestock.

An important question is why officials did not provide adequate alternatives once they realized that grazing would only support a portion of the Navajo population. In truth, administrators had few options available. Training Navajos for industrial work was hardly feasible when the general labor market was already glutted with experienced people. In addition, the relocation of a sizeable portion of Navajos off the reservation would have, at this time, raised a greater outcry among the tribe than even the furor over herd reduction. Navajos were simply too tied to their land, their kinsmen, and their way of life to permit many to take up careers elsewhere. Unless one accepts the dubious proposition that officials should have predicted future employment opportunities, failure to prepare Navajos for work outside the reservation was not a major flaw in New Deal administration. Until 1940 reservation officials were unable to foresee job openings and they acted on the theory that tribal problems had to be solved within the reservation.

Other possible alternatives would have been to develop the huge irrigation area south of Farmington known as the Turley Project or to relocate Navajos to the irrigation works at Parker, Arizona. Both solutions had several defects. Based on the indifferent attitude that Navajos displayed toward smaller irrigation projects, most still strongly preferred herding to farming. Moreover, Collier had little chance of funding the Turley Project. Money generally abundant in the early New Deal because of emergency funds became fairly scarce in the middle years and a severe problem in the immediate prewar period. The experience of placing Navajos at Parker, Arizona, after 1942 seemed to have fared badly because they disliked the climate and wanted to be with their own tribe.

Such New Deal innovations as tribal enterprises, the Window Rock Fair, and the Arts and Crafts Guild have remained a part of Navajo administration, but one has to search diligently to find any vestiges of the livestock and land improvement programs. Navajos still maintain a system of district grazing committees and grazing permits, but these procedures, according to observers, are largely a facade and enforcement is rare. Grazing permits are presently bought and sold privately. In essence, all attempts at improved breeding and restraints on grazing are voluntary. The need for horses for transportation has virtually ended with the introduction of pickups since World War II, but some Navajos believe that their ranges contain even more equestrian stock than in the 1930s. Such demonstration areas as Mexican Springs, Ganado, and Steamboat Springs, which grew lush vegetation in the 1930s, are now desolate scenes of grass eaten into the ground, broken check dams, fresh erosion, and complete neglect.

Both progovernment Navajos and whites who underwent the hellish tensions and agonizing self-guilt of putting through the New Deal conservation program now feel a sense of betrayal that their efforts have been abandoned. One of the central arguments of the 1930s was that the reservation must be conserved as a haven for traditionalists even if this meant that the land would not support all the Navajos. In today's situation, the ranges account for only a small portion of tribal income, but they are still not being protected properly and no tribal leader would dare propose, let alone carry out, effective regulation of grazing. The only interest in conservation are recent statements by young Navajo militants who speak of Indian attachment for the "Mother Earth" in their protests against coal strip mining operations on the reservation, but there is no sign that the tribe, in general, sees any pressing need for balancing the livestock load with grazing capacity.

The New Deal deserves credit for improving and modernizing services to the Navajos. Medical care is perhaps the most tangible example of this. While the availability of adequately trained doctors and the discovery of sulfanilamide to cure trachoma were fortuitous products of the time, the new hospitals and better quality of treatment were direct results of official efforts. Despite the Window Rock officials' low estimate of some field workers, the average government employee of the 1930s was apt to be better educated and more dedicated and sensitive to Navajos' needs than the old time workers.

More importantly, the general types of services afforded by the government were better suited to answering the Navajos' real problems. The New Deal ended the past pattern of officials remaining tied to their offices, enforcing rules against polygamous marriages, capturing lawbreakers, obtaining a quota of children for boarding schools, and recapturing runaways. As much as Navajos despised the tribal headquarters and the grazing districts, the new organization brought them into closer contact with the government workers. The more able district staffers were interested in working with the Navajos in achieving better livestock breeding, arranging credit, encouraging Indians to use their irrigation plots, and trying to find alternatives to offset the loss of livestock.

The New Deal also brought about an important redirection in the role that the Indian Service traditionally played in looking after Indian interests. As Collier often complained, Indian affairs before 1933 were really operated to benefit whites more than Indians. Whether New Deal programs were misguided or not, there was little question that figures in the Washington office and Window Rock tried to defend the well-being of Navajos. Acts of petty graft such as Indian Service stockmen secretly acting as buyers for livestock commission firms and superintendents covertly shaping local policies in response to the wishes of missionaries or traders were more apt to be detected and punished in the 1930s than previously. It seems safe to conclude that Collier's refusal to turn the Navajo workers' checks over to trading posts, his ban on involuntary religious instruction in government schools, his failure to cooperate fully on patronage, and his long fight against white ranchers to pass the New Mexico boundary bill were important factors in his political difficulties. Whites, it would appear, experienced their own special problems in adjusting to Collier's policies.

Despite the considerable advances that the New Deal brought to the Navajos, the era did not produce the result that Collier most sought. He hoped fervently that his administration would end the demoralization of Indians, root out the sense that their race was vanishing, and reawaken their energies and purposes. Because of their loss of livestock, Navajos were more disspirited in the 1930s than at any time since Bosque Redondo. How Collier could have conserved the Navajos' land and avoided their alienation posed a question that neither he or anyone else could answer.

# Sources

## I. Manuscripts

J. H. Bosscher papers, Heritage Hall, Calvin College, Grand Rapids, Michigan.

L. P. Brink papers and diaries, Heritage Hall, Calvin College, Grand Rapids, Michigan.

Bureau of Indian Affairs Records, National Archives, Record Group 75, Washington, D. C., cited as NA, RG 75.

Dennis Chavez papers, University of Albuquerque Library, Albuquerque, New Mexico, cited as Chavez papers, UA.

John Collier papers, Yale University Library, New Haven, Connecticut, cited as Collier papers, YU.

Sam Day papers, Northern Arizona University Library, Flagstaff, Arizona.

C. E. Faris papers, Special Collections Department, University of New Mexico Library, Albuquerque, New Mexico.

Isabella Greenway papers, Arizona Historical Society, Tucson, Arizona, cited as Isabella Greenway papers, AHS.

Berard Haile papers, Special Collections Department, University of Arizona Library, Tucson, Arizona, cited as Haile papers, UAL.

Hubbell family papers, Hubbell Trading Post, National Historical Site, Ganado, Arizona, cited as Hubbell Trading Post. (Later turned over to the Special Collections Department, University of Arizona Library, Tucson, Arizona.)

Legislative Records, National Archives, Record Group 46, Washington, D. C., cited as NA, RG 46.

Navajo Tribal Council Minutes (partial file), Department of Interior Library, Washington, D. C.

New Mexico Governors' papers and miscellaneous records, New Mexico State Records Center and Archives, Santa Fe, New Mexico, cited as NMSRCA.

Gladys Reichard papers, Museum of Northern Arizona, Flagstaff, Arizona, cited as Reichard papers, MNA.

St. Michaels Mission, St. Michaels, Arizona. (The mission has considerable correspondence, mimeographed materials on the Navajos, and a clipping file.)

Soil Conservation Service Records, Special Collections Department,

University of New Mexico Library, Albuquerque, New Mexico, cited as SCS Records, UNML.

Richard Van Valkenburgh papers, Arizona Historical Society, Tucson, cited as Van Valkenburgh papers, AHS.

Window Rock Tribal Headquarters records (including some materials from previous superintendencies), Los Angeles Federal Records Center, Bell, California, cited as LAFRC.

Window Rock Area Headquarters, Window Rock, Arizona.

Ben Wetherill papers, Museum of Northern Arizona, Flagstaff, Arizona, cited as Wetherill papers, MNA.

## II. ARTICLES

Adams, Lucy Wilcox. "What the Government Is Doing on the Navajo; Navajo Schools," *Navajo Medical News* 7 (25 November 1940): 12–13.

Blum, Cecil T. "Improvement of Navajo Sheep," *Journal of Heredity* 31 (March 1940): 99–111.

Brink, L. P. "By Way of Introduction," *The Banner* 69 (21 December 1934): 1116.

Brugge, David. "Early Navajo Political Structure," *Navajo Tourist Guide* (1966): 22–23.

Chance, Blanche. "Field Nursing on the Navajo," *Navajo Medical News* 7 (1 May 1940): 13–18.

Collier, John. "Editorial," *Indians at Work* 2 (1 May 1935): 2.

Cooley, A. C. "The Navajo Sheep and Goat Purchases," *Indians at Work* 2 (1 October 1934): 13.

Council Notes, "Taliman Succeeds Chairman Kanuho," *The Navajo Service News* 2 (n.d.): 2.

Darby, William J., *et al.* "A Study of the Dietary Background and Nutriture of the Navajo Indian," reprinted from *The Journal of Nutrition* 9 (November 1956).

*Dine'Dah-Si-Zai-Bi Na'Locos* [Navajo Community Center Paper] 1 (1 December 1935): 8–9.

"District Supervisors School," *The Navajo Service News* 1 (1 July 1936): 10.

Goudberg, William. "Alarm Felt about a Bill now before Congress," *The Banner* 69 (11 May 1934): 429.

Kimball, Solon T. "Navajo Population Analysis," *Navajo Medical News* 7 (28 September 1940): 3.

Kunitz, Stephen J. "The Social Philosophy of John Collier," *Ethnohistory* 18 (Summer 1971): 213–19.

"Lucy W. Adams," *Navajo Medical News* 7 (25 November 1940): 13–14.

McDowell, Harvey S. "Dental Revolving Fund," *Navajo Medical News* 7 (15 January 1940): 16–17.

McGrew, R. Brownell. "Excerpts from an Artist, R. Brownell McGrew, in the Lands of the Navajos and Hopis," *Arizona Highways* 45 (July 1969): 4–39.

Morgan, J. C. "A Voice from an Indian," *The Banner* 69 (December 21, 1934): 1117.

"Navajos on the Map," *Indian Truth* 11 (April 1934): 4.

"Navajo Program," *Indian Truth* 11 (June 1935): 3.

"Navajo Unrest," *Indian Truth* 13 (May 1936): 2–3.

"New Navajo 'Program'—Much Big Talk—Little Wisdom," *The American Indian* 5 (April-May 1936): 8.

Parman, Donald L. "J. C. Morgan: Navajo Apostle of Assimilation," *Prologue: Journal of the National Archives* 4 (Summer 1972): 83–98.

Pousma, R. H. "Rehoboth Jottings," *The Banner* 69 (27 April 1934): 380.

Safran, Nathaniel. "Infant Mortality," *Navajo Medical News* 7 (15 January 1940): 13–15.

Smith, Mrs. White Mountain. "Henry Chee Dodge, Navajo," *The Desert Magazine* 1 (July 1938): 18–20.

———. "Gentle Padre Inventor of Alphabet for Navajo Tribe," *The Desert Magazine* 2 (March 1939): 7–9.

Stewart, James M. "Personal Impressions of the January 18–20 Navajo Tribal Council Meeting," *Indians at Work* 5 (March 1938): 16–19.

Townsend, James G. "Is Trachoma Nearing Defeat?" *Navajo Medical News* 7 (15 January 1940): 1–5.

Van Valkenburgh, Richard, "The Government of the Navajos," *Arizona Quarterly* 1 (Winter 1945): 63–73.

Weber, Anselm. "Chee Dodge," *The Indian Sentinel* (April 1918): 33–36.

Zimmerman, William, Jr. "The Role of the Bureau of Indian Affairs since 1933," *Annals of the American Academy of Political and Social Science* 311 (May 1957): 31–40.

### III.  Books, Pamphlets, and Dissertations

Aberle, David F. *The Peyote Religion among the Navaho* (Chicago, 1966).

Adair, John. *The Navajo and Pueblo Silversmiths* (Norman, Oklahoma, 1944).

Adams, William Y. *Shonto: A Study of the Role of the Trader in a Modern Navaho Community* (Washington, 1963).

Bailey, Lynn R. *The Long Walk, A History of the Navajo Wars, 1846–1868* (Pasadena, 1970).

Boyce, George A. *When Navajos Had Too Many Sheep: the 1940's* (San Francisco, 1974).

Burge, Moris. *The Navajo and the Land.* Bulletin 26, National Association on Indian Affairs, Inc., and American Indian Defense Association, Inc., 1937.

Chabot, Maria. *Urgent Navajo Problems, Observations and Recommendations Based on a Recent Study by the New Mexico Association on Indian Affairs* (Santa Fe, 1940).

Collier, John. *From Every Zenith* (Denver, 1963).

Correll, J. Lee, Editha L. Watson, and David M. Brugge, eds. *Navajo Bibliography with Subject Index* (Window Rock, Arizona, 1969).

Counselor, Jim and Ann. *Wild, Wooly and Wonderful* (New York, 1954).

Downs, James F. *Animal Husbandry in Navajo Society and Culture* (Berkeley, 1964).

Freeman, John Leiper, Jr. "The New Deal for the Indians: A Study in Bureau-Committee Relations in American Government." Ph.D. dissertation, Department of Political Science, Princeton University, 1952.

Fryer, E. R. *The Government and the Navajo* (Window Rock, Arizona, 1941). (Mimeographed).

Gridley, Marion, ed. *Indians of Today* (n.p., 1971).

Hertzberg, Hazel W. *The Search for an American Indian Identity, Modern Pan-Indian Movements* (Syracuse, 1971).

Ickes, Harold L. *Autobiography of a Curmudgeon* (New York, 1943).

———. *The Secret Diary of Harold Ickes*, vol. 1: *The First Thousand Days, 1933–1936* (New York, 1953).

Kappler, Charles J., ed. *Indian Affairs, Laws and Treaties*, vol. II (Washington, 1904).

Kelly, Lawrence C. *The Navajo Indians and Federal Indian Policy, 1900–1935* (Tucson, 1968).

———, ed. *Navajo Roundup* (Boulder, Colorado, 1970).

Kluckhohn, Clyde. *Navajo Witchcraft* (Boston, 1962).

———, and Dorothea Leighton, *The Navajo* (Garden City, New York, 1962).

Kneale, Albert H. *Indian Agent* (Caldwell, Idaho, 1950).

La Barre, Weston. *The Peyote Cult* (New Haven, 1938).

La Farge, Oliver, ed. *The Changing Indian* (Norman, Oklahoma, 1942).

McNitt, Frank. *The Indian Traders* (Norman, Oklahoma, 1962).

Parman, Donald L. "The Indian Civilian Conservation Corps," Ph.D. dissertation, Department of History, University of Oklahoma, 1967.

Phelps-Stokes Fund. *The Navajo Indian Problem* (New York, 1939).

Salsbury, Clarence G. (with Paul Hughes). *The Salsbury Story, A Medical Missionary's Lifetime of Public Service* (Tucson, 1969).

Sasaki, Tom. *Fruitland, New Mexico: A Navajo Community in Transition* (Ithaca, New York, 1960).

———, and John Adair. "New Land to Farm, Agricultural Practices Among the Navaho," *in* Spicer, Edward, ed. *Human Problems in Technological Change, A Casebook* (New York, 1952).

Sidwell, George M., Jack L. Ruttle, and Earl E. Ray. "Improvement of Navajo Sheep," New Mexico State University, Agricultural Experiment Station Research Report 172, Las Cruces, 1970.

Slotkin, James S. *The Peyote Religion: A Study in Indian-White Relations* (Glencoe, Illinois, 1956).

Spicer, Edward H. *Cycles of Conquest, The Impact of Spain, Mexico, and the United States on the Indians of the Southwest, 1533–1960* (Tucson, 1962).

Underhill, Ruth. *Here Come the Navaho* (Lawrence, Kansas, 1953).

———. *The Navajos* (Norman, Oklahoma, 1956).

Vogt, Evon. *Navajo Veterans: A Study of Changing Values* (Cambridge, 1951).

Ward, Elizabeth. *No Dudes, Few Women, Life with a Navajo Range Rider* (Albuquerque, 1951).

Waters, Frank. *Masked Gods, Navaho and Pueblo Ceremonialism* (Denver, 1950).

Wilken, Robert L. *Anselm Weber, O.F.M., Missionary to the Navaho* (Milwaukee, 1955).

Williams, Aubrey W., Jr. *Navajo Political Process* (Washington, 1970).

## IV.  GOVERNMENT PUBLICATIONS

*Annual Reports of the Secretary of the Interior, 1933–1942* (Washington, D. C., 1933–1942).

U. S., *Congressional Record*, vols. 79–87.

U. S., Senate, Committee on Privileges and Elections, *Hearings Before the Committee on Privileges and Elections*, 74th Cong., 1st sess., 10 April and 4 June 1935, *in* Legislative Records, National Archives, Record Group 46.

———. Subcommittee of the Committee on Indian Affairs, *Hearings, Survey of Conditions of the United States*, 74th Cong., 2nd sess., 1936, Part 34.

———. 75th Cong., 1st sess., 1937, Part 37.

———. Subcommittee of the Committee on Interior, *Hearings on S. 2363, A Bill to Promote the Rehabilitation of the Navajo and Hopi Tribes of Indians and the Better Utilization of the Resources of the Navajo and Hopi Indian Reservations, and for Other Purposes*, 80th Cong., 2nd sess., 1948.

U. S., *Statutes at Large*, vols. 47–56.

## V.  NEWSPAPERS

*Albuquerque Journal*, 1933–1941.
*Coconino Sun*, 1933–1942.
*Farmington Times Hustler*, 1934–1943.
*Gallup Independent*, 1933–1942.
*New Mexican Examiner*, 1935.

*New York Times*, 1933–1942.
*Phoenix Gazette*, 1943–1945.
*Santa Fe New Mexican*, 1933–1941.
*Southwest Tourist News*, 1936–1940.

## VI. INTERVIEWS

Bass, Willard P. (former teacher, principal, and superintendent of the Navajo Mission School, Farmington, New Mexico), 31 August 1971, Albuquerque, New Mexico, cited as Bass Interview.

Bosscher, Jacob H. (former superintendent of the Rehoboth Mission), 29 October 1971, Grand Rapids, Michigan.

Burge, Moris (former field representative of the National Association on Indian Affairs and American Association on Indian Affairs), 21 July 1970, Santa Fe, New Mexico.

Carson, O. J. (former owner of a trading post at Carson, New Mexico), 16 August 1971, Inscription House Trading Post, Arizona, cited as Carson Interview.

Fryer, E. R. (former General Superintendent of the Navajo Reservation, 1936–1942), 21 July 1970, and 19 August 1971, Santa Fe, New Mexico, cited as Fryer Interview, 1970 or 1971.

Gorman, Howard (former Vice Chairman of the Navajo Council and present Council member), 10 August 1971, Window Rock, Arizona, cited as Gorman Interview.

Navajo Indian (former translator and government employee who wished to remain anonymous), 16 August 1971, Navajo Reservation, cited as Anonymous Interview.

Preston, Scott (former member of the Navajo Council and Vice Chairman of Navajo Council), 11 August 1971, Ganado, Arizona, cited as Preston Interview.

Salsbury, Clarence G. (former Superintendent of the Ganado Mission), 5 August 1971, Phoenix, Arizona, cited as Salsbury Interview.

Smith, E. R. (former employee of the Soil Erosion Service and the Soil Conservation Service), 24 June 1970, Santa Fe, New Mexico, cited as Smith Interview.

Thompson, Hildegard (former Supervisor and Director of Navajo Education), 9 October 1972, Louisville, Kentucky, cited as Thompson Interview.

Trockur, Father Emanuel (Franciscan priest stationed at St. Michaels Mission), 26 July 1971, St. Michaels, Arizona, cited as Trockur Interview.

Vander Stoep, Floris (former Christian Reformed Church missionary at Shiprock, New Mexico), 29 October 1971, Grand Rapids, Michigan.

Wagner, Sally (former co-owner of the Wide Ruin trading post), 21 July 1970, Santa Fe, New Mexico, cited as Wagner Interview.

Young, William (former owner of the Red Lake or Tolani Lake trading post), 25 July 1971, Ganado, Arizona, cited as Young Interview.

Zimmerman, William, Jr. (former Assistant Commissioner of Indian Affairs), 29 August 1965, Washington, D. C., cited as Zimmerman Interview.

Zweifel, Mr. and Mrs. Rudolph (Mr. Zweifel was former Supervisor of District 9, Teec-Nos-Pos), 13–14 August 1971, Albuquerque, New Mexico, cited as Mr. Zweifel Interview and Mrs. Zweifel Interview.

# Index